Critical Essays on
Thomas Mann

Critical Essays on
World Literature

Robert Lecker, General Editor
McGill University

Critical Essays on Thomas Mann

Inta M. Ezergailis

G. K. Hall & Co. • Boston, Massachusetts

Library of Congress Cataloging-in-Publication Data

Critical essays on Thomas Mann.

(Critical essays on world literature)
Bibliography: p.
Includes index.
1. Mann, Thomas, 1875–1955 — Criticism
and interpretation. I. Ezergailis, Inta, 1932–   II. Series.
PT2625.A44Z5442 1988   833'.912   87-25137
ISBN 0-8161-8837-8

This publication is printed on permanent/durable acid-free paper
MANUFACTURED IN THE UNITED STATES OF AMERICA

CONTENTS

INTRODUCTION   1
    Inta M. Ezergailis

Articles and Essays

Thoughts on the Passing of Thomas Mann   11
    Hermann J. Weigand

In Search of Bourgeois Man   24
    Georg Lukács

Aesthetic Excursus on Thomas Mann's *Akribie*   47
    Elizabeth M. Wilkinson

The Structure of Humor   58
    Käte Hamburger

The Lord of Small Counterpositions:
    Mann's *The Magic Mountain*   78
    R. P. Blackmur

Aspects of Parody in the Works of Thomas Mann   93
    Hans Eichner

Myth Versus Secularism: Religion in Thomas Mann's *Joseph*   115
    Henry Hatfield

The Second Author of *Der Tod in Venedig*   124
    Dorrit Cohn

Thomas Mann's Conception of the Creative Writer   143
    Peter Heller

Much Is Comic in Thomas Mann   175
    Ronald Peacock

On the Political Development of an Unpolitical Man   191
    Hans Mayer

Living in the Metaphor of Fiction   206
    J. P. Stern

Thomas Mann and Tradition: Some Clarifications   219
    T. J. Reed

The Decline of the West and the Ascent of the East:
Thomas Mann, the Joseph Novels, and Spengler   238
Helmut Koopmann

INDEX   267

INTRODUCTION

From the earliest discussions of Thomas Mann's work that accompanied its appearance, ranging from reviews in newspapers to more serious treatments in literary and cultural periodicals, Mann criticism has, in spite of its notorious mass, contained some constants. Even in the less scholarly approaches, questions emerged early that have remained more or less open and interesting. Thus, the theme of "art and life," one that appears most notably with the publication of *Buddenbrooks*, has not disappeared, though it has shed the naiveté of treatments that centered on Mann's "brazen" modeling of actual people and places in the fiction. Political questions, in one form or another, also come soon and are argued with some vehemence. Nor does it take too long for other prominent themes to be defined and analyzed in much the same form in which they will be clothed for decades to come. The exploration of influence—of figures such as Nietzsche, Wagner, Schopenhauer, and Spengler—also enter the scholarly literature rather promptly. Most of these problems and topics are still with us, though not in the same kinds of conceptualization, approaches, or implications. In some ways, then, the criticism appears to pose the same question of "continuity or change" that confronts the Mann scholar trying to assess the opus itself. As change in the latter must be conceded by the most ardent advocate of constancy, so the criticism too, even within similar categories, has undergone considerable development.

It appears, however, that even though Mann criticism does change along with trends in general critical approaches, it does so in a somewhat lagging and gentle way. Thus, one can see a clear line leading from the strictly substantive and thematic approaches of the earlier commentary (not to dwell on the more impressionistic, often ad hominem one with its tendency to approach the ideas in the fiction as a coherent philosophy and judge it as such, without considering the fictional context), to more integrative procedures. It would be possible to trace a line from a philological and positivistic approach through the New Criticism, to structuralist, poststructuralist, and other recent methods, though so far deconstruction or newer varieties of psychoanalytical, Marxist, or feminist criticism have not been represented to a significant degree. There has been

1

some good recent work emphasizing reception and historical context, however, work that has also informed the quality of the commentary in various thematic, philosophical, and structural categories that will be partially enumerated here.

As archival materials, diaries, and letters become increasingly accessible, scholars presented these on various levels—as collections of documents, commented minimally or at great length, or as a springboard for reinterpretations of the work. Hans Wysling, director of the great Thomas Mann archive in Zurich, has made significant contributions in this area. Among other scholars who have continually and conscientiously used insights gained from the archival material to throw new light upon the texts, one must mention Herbert Lehnert. A good example of this work is Lehnert's *Thomas Mann: Fiktion. Mythos. Religion,*[1] along with many other contributions, including biographical researches and ongoing inventories of scholarship, a type of aid that is becoming indispensable for orientation in the massive secondary literature. From such overviews, his and others', it appears that the secondary literature still lends itself to division along traditional lines, such as the discussion of Mann's proverbial irony; philosophical themes seen under the aspect of metaphysics, ethics, or aesthetics; art and disease; politics; the question of influences and literary relationships, with Goethe, Nietzsche, Schopenhauer, Wagner, and Freud still most often mentioned. It should be stressed here, however, that such categorization tends to give an unwarranted impression of sameness and constancy that understates the considerable amount of revision of earlier thought about such hotly debated issues as Mann's political development (or lack of it), his relationship with his brother— which is intimately connected with that development—and his use of tradition. The latter is a complex issue, as Mann's own statements about influence by various figures of the German literary and philosophical tradition cannot be taken uncritically.

In spite of the evidence of "theme-blindness" that Lehnert feared in 1968,[2] there are also interpretations of individual texts as well as a large volume of studies examining elements of structure, genre, and other formal aspects of the work, including an ongoing discussion of Mann's "montage" technique (a term that has increasingly been questioned as a fruitful way of dealing with the author's incorporation of material from others, but whose viability is still—or again—upheld by such serious critics as Hans Vaget), his pseudoerudition, the extent to which the work is or is not "realistic," and some continuing investigation of the function of time in the fiction. Apart from separating East German scholarship for its allegedly conservative Marxist approach, most of the overviews do not give the reader any immediate sense of fundamental ideological differences. Still, as pointed out above, on closer examination one can see real changes in the scholarship. The more traditional Marxist approach of the East German critics does not appear to be matched by critics guided by the several neo-Marxist schools of Western Europe that are quite noticeable in other areas of literary scholarship. The historical interpretations have been dramatically refined by new methodologies and enriched by the available documents, and they are bolstered by the ongoing positive assessment of the historical approach in literary studies. The line of scholarship that traces influence and Mann's relationship to tradition has been similarly enhanced, and changes in emphasis have come about along with the uncovering of lesser known but important sources of influence. Perhaps even more importantly, the meaning of influence itself, and the uses to which it can be put, has been increasingly questioned. Other important and abiding critical methodologies, such as hermeneutics, have made an occasional appearance, but do not seem to have produced a sizable volume of secondary literature, apart from the extent to which they constitute the unnamed assumptions of various commentators. Feminist critics' avoidance of this arena perhaps indicates that they share with others whose assessment of Thomas Mann is basically negative the dismissive attitude toward his portrayal of women and femininity. Typically, in an article in *Der Spiegel* during the centennial of Mann's birth in 1975, Hanjo Kesting reduces it to the proposition that "Thomas Mann's work is a masculine work. His female figures are pure constructs or mere objects of demonstration."[3] However, the final assessment is not quite that simple, and there is work to be done here. In another line, as stated earlier, a promising start has been made by critics using the approaches of reception aesthetics, as demonstrated by Hans Vaget and Dagmar Barnouw, for example.

Academic writing is not the only aid to thinking about Thomas Mann. Clearly, he is not being read exclusively by college professors. The normative question of how one evaluates the work for the contemporary reader is very much alive. One can get some sense of this in various roundups of the commentary clustering around the centennial. Here, there are important differences between East Germany, where Thomas Mann has never been completely out of vogue since he was redeemed for socialist use by Georg Lukács (whose argument is represented in this volume at some length), and West Germany, where a press overview during the hundreth birthday yielded, along with praise, some strongly negative comment,[4] especially by working authors. It may be worthwhile to attend to Hans H. Schulte's summary of the points of attack, since they outline several areas of persistent criticism and controversy. In addition to the press summaries, Schulte's categories also include criticism advanced by Dagmar Barnouw in the work mentioned above.

(1) The failure of Thomas Mann to meet the demands of his time, a charge that has to do with the author's political responses to various current events, the credibility, durability, and tangible results of his conversion from a romantic conservatism to democracy, perhaps democratic socialism, and his tendency to aestheticize political concerns; (2) the lack of realism in his narratives, an objection that centers on his imposition

of patterns, mainly mythical, on experienced reality, as well as his concentration on the bourgeois world that he knew instead of the proletariat, which receives short shrift and is often reduced to a standard-bearer or leitmotiv rather than a class. The question of realism has always been a thorny one and cannot be resolved easily at a time when even historians see their accounts as differing literary plottings of events. (3) A third criticism concerns the eccentricity and preciosity in his narrative manner, especially in the language. Barnouw sees this language as "the complicated ceremonial attitude of the outsider."[5] Hans Erich Nossack distinguishes between two kinds of German usage that have existed for a long time: "the pretentious humanistic written language that uses Latin syntax, and the other one, used for instance by the Storm-and-Stress. . . . On the street today, you can still talk like Büchner and everyone will understand you, but just try to talk like Thomas Mann in the subway or in a shop. . . ."[6] To this, Schulte rejoins that this "precious" language, in all its refinement, can be more daring in exploring the limits of communication than the other. (4) Another criticism involves the "egocentrism" or egomania of Thomas Mann, an author whose work not only aggrandizes itself in its imitation of Goethe but is always self-exploration and self-commentary in the guise of interpretation. Wolfgang Koeppen remarks: "Suffering and greatness of the masters, that means Theodor Storm and Thomas Mann, that means August von Platen and Thomas Mann, Thomas Mann plus Goethe, finally Thomas Don Quijote."[7] This is a working out of the equation "I = German culture" that may or may not have been made by Thomas Mann. The argument against this accusation is contained in Schulte's quotation from Schiller: "The poet can only give us his own individuality."[8] (5) A fifth criticism concerns Mann's nihilistic irony. At this nodal point, the critics converge in force. Schulte summarizes the recent attacks: "for Barnouw, Thomas Mann's irony is an art of avoidance, based on the fear of thinking things to the end. Walser finds the intellectual irony of *The Magic Mountain* questionable when the narrator exposes the reader to debates of 10, 50, 150 pages and then undermines what he himself has set up. Kesting questions the pathos of the middle ground: this middle position, he claims, is merely asserted and finally usurped by an ironic universality. . . ."[9] There may be potential answers to the existence and tenability of the middle ground in the essays in this volume.

In one of the few reviews of scholarship that go beyond a mere overview divided into traditional categories, Hans Vaget, a scholar who has done important work on Mann by using new insights in investigating, for instance, the latter's appropriation of Goethe, looks at the more academic side of the centennial harvest — the collection of presentations given for the occasion in Munich, Zurich, and Lübeck.[10] He sees this collection as representing the state of the art as well as an indication of focal points that characterize the scholarship around 1975. The thematic clusters he finds are much like those noted by earlier reviewers, and crowd around seven issues: (1) Mann's concept of "Bürgerlichkeit," one that cannot be fully described by the ideal of "bourgeois man," as Mann uses it as a cultural, ethical, aesthetic, and not rarely even as a metaphysical category; (2) the political development — represented by five of the contributions — showing the increasing emphasis on clarifying the influences and stations in Thomas Mann's political thinking; (3) "literary orientations" or influences — an area that accounted for the largest representation, though, as Vaget points out, such investigations too often restrict themselves to the general traditional interpretation of literary "relationships" and "influences" without considering the intratextual dimension or the way in which the recognition of such influences directly helps in the understanding of particular texts; (4) language, style, and narrative technique; (5) interpretations of individual texts, an enterprise that, as Vaget puts it, is rendered problematical by the developments in the theoretical debate in the field of literary scholarship and thus takes up relatively little space in the collection (seven out of forty contributions); (6) discussions of Mann's work in the light of the theory of the novel; and (7) accounts and analyses of the reception of Thomas Mann in Germany and abroad, an area that continues to be actively and well represented, and one that can, as Vaget stresses, throw light on "the varying influence range of distinct aspects of Thomas Mann's oeuvre."[11]

Vaget's most pointed critique of the "middle ground" of contemporary Mann scholarship, as represented in this collection (which he feels is, on the whole and granted the celebratory nature of the occasion, a reasonably good representation), is its "liberal tendency to defuse the controversial" and thus to disappoint those who "like their Mann less accommodating, more offensive and uncanny."[12] The existence of extreme views is, as he reminds us, testimony to the continued vitality of the work.

The essays included in this volume cover the spectrum of approaches that is laid out by Vaget, one that is fairly similar in the number and kind of categories to previous accounts, though the relative emphasis varies considerably over time. Any claim of full representation would be false, though there are articles that show the approach to Mann's work through the ideas in his fiction (along with a theoretical appraisal of such a procedure) as well as a "close reading" of a text and recent reevaluations of the work in its relationship to contemporary writing and thinking. Though there is some formalist commentary, and some Marxist, the ideological coverage is by no means complete, as it is in any case disingenuous to pretend to balance opposing viewpoints and methodologies to give the reader a "neutral" crystallization of criticism. Not only is that kind of weighing not very useful, but Roland Barthes is probably right about the hidden biases of this kind of "neither-nor" procedure.[13] To put it plainly, the essays cover some of the persistent problems of Mann criticism to show some of the approaches that have been, and with some modifications continue to be taken to enable a fuller understanding of the opus; they display the writing of some (though by no means most) of the known critics and commentators of Mann's work; and they are presented with the hope that they will stimulate and deepen interest in the texts themselves.

This volume differs from some of the earlier anthologies of criticism (a prominent one being Henry Hatfield's collection of 1964) that were intended primarily as introductions and commentaries on specific works. Now we can assume that the student and the interested general reader are ready for a sampling of some of the important debates that have been going on for a long time about context and ideology and that can enrich a first reading as well as a rereading. Not only are there reevaluations of Mann's relationship to Nietzsche or Spengler, but there is also an examination of how influence is assimilated. There is some emphasis on works that, at least in English, have not been read or discussed nearly as much as the better known major novels and novellas (*Death in Venice, Tonio Kröger, The Magic Mountain*). Not that these are neglected. With some exception, however, they are considered in the context either of historical development, of the debate about the author's political stance, of development in the use of themes or structures, or of intellectual history. At times, we show various strands of criticism as they converge upon a single work. For instance, the Joseph novels are discussed by several of the authors here — in an analysis of humor, from the point of view of Mann's reaction to Spengler, and as repositories of his attitude to religion.

Another way of seeing the interrelationship between the essays is in terms of problems or themes: thus Ronald Peacock's essay (his inaugural lecture of 1963) is an early focusing of attention on the persistence and central position of humor in Mann's work. He sees the latter as a "texture" rather than a theme, a matter of imagination rather than one of ideas. In her important work on the Joseph novels,[14] Käte Hamburger anchors these manifestations in the structure of particular texts and, beyond that, in the structure of the whole opus. In her phenomenologically oriented investigation, she finds a "structure of humor" whose presence or absence can be used to resolve such long debated issues as the distinction between humor and irony. Even though she sees this structure most fully realized in the Joseph tetralogy, we are not able to present or satisfactorily condense her book-length argument of that novel and chose instead to include the introduction to the work. While losing the depth and intensity of her argument, we gain an overview of the effect of the structure of humor in a whole array of Mann's fiction. To represent the important and productive vein of scholarship that concentrates on examining individual texts, there are essays such as that by Dorrit Cohn dealing with the "second author," a narrative consciousness that Mann himself had seen in those terms and that is difficult to see in a work such as *Death in Venice*, where that "interpolated" presence is not attached to a clear and definite personality as it is in works such as *Felix Krull* or *Doctor Faustus*. R. P. Blackmur's essay on *The Magic Mountain* sees the latter as an expression of the tension between the individual and the communal, the burden of culture and its encompassing in the appropriate aesthetic form. The essays by Heller, Lukács, and Hatfield could be seen as outstanding demonstrations of thematic investigation. Lukács's work is a classic of Thomas Mann literature and belongs in any good historical anthology of criticism. His positive view of Mann's search for the true bourgeois presents the process as open-ended, ongoing, and progressive. Hatfield examines various facets of the Joseph novel, stressing Mann's reasons for writing a novel dealing with religion and myth at that time, the sociopolitical implications, and Mann's general attitude toward religion. He finds Thomas Mann's God to be "a beneficent fiction." One might say that this is Mann's "search for humanist man." For Heller, it is the creative writer as portrayed by Mann who stands for the quintessence of the best of humanity as the anticipated bourgeois or "citoyen" does for Lukács and as the humanist Joseph does for Hatfield. In this invocation of "the pictorial and the impressionistic," Heller feels we can get beyond the schematic duality of Spirit/Nature with Art as the mediator and gain a more concrete insight into Mann's world of ideas than those terms suggest. Elizabeth Wilkinson's article takes a different but similarly motivated approach to clarifying and mediating the often negatively seen or at least confusing effect of Mann's extensive use of philosophical, specialized, or technical material. Instead of dismissing it as "pseudo-learning" and encyclopedism, she sees it as a welcome and necessary integration of the life of intellect and feeling, as these bits and pieces become part of the "pure semblance" of the work. Eichner's contribution represents a comparatively early (1952) example of the ongoing concern with parody in Mann's work, as he traces references to parody and the parodistic through the whole opus, correctly stressing the position of *Doctor Faustus* as the work where the parodistic is explicitly discussed and thematized. An investigation of parody is closely connected to the author's relation to tradition, and there are three essays in this volume that take up that problem in varying ways. An interesting view of the Nietzsche connection is presented by J. P. Stern. He sees Mann's escape in *Felix Krull* — at the end of his life — from the "ideology of strenuousness" that he shared with Nietzsche as anything but an escape from Nietzsche himself, but rather as a parallel to the latter's own development toward a view of the world as an aesthetic phenomenon. As Krull realizes that to live metaphorically is to live in freedom, he is partaking of a Nietzschean insight. Koopmann traces Mann's reception of Spengler, in its typical ambivalence and personal engagement (and disengagement), whereas Reed's article addresses itself to the wider question of how we are to approach and evaluate the question of "influence" in Mann's work. He believes that attributing to Mann a depth and atemporal grounding in the philosophical and literary tradition that is not supported by historical, biographical, or literary evidence is to make of him "a mere pawn in the

'Geistesgeschichte' game." In the essay included here (which was later followed by an important book on the subject), Reed demonstrates some of the confusions generated by commentators indulging in the game and proposes a more differentiated approach to defining influence, illustrating this with a proposed qualitative difference in Mann's reception of Nietzsche and Goethe. Hans Mayer's essay sorts the evidence for and against the political evolution of Mann from the conservatism of *Reflections of a Nonpolitical Man* to the strongly democratic ring of his later pronouncements. Though not distrusting Mann's intentions, Mayer finds more continuity than change in the fundamental stance. Hermann Weigand's contribution is a tribute after Mann's death in the form of a personal appreciation. It deals with many of the important works and starts with a consideration of the self-assurance and "pleasurable intimacy with one's own person" that informs Mann's work, in his identification with the heroes of the fiction as well as with those of the essays. The inclusion of this appreciation can perhaps be seen as a tribute in its own right to this scholar whose abiding merit in Mann scholarship can be seen in the still living usefulness of his 1933 book about *The Magic Mountain*.

There are important pronouncements on the work of Thomas Mann that the reader will not find here—some of them because they have been included in previous anthologies, others because they have become a reassuring substructure of criticism. Among those are the work of Weigand that was just mentioned, Erich Heller's lively examinations of Mann's Schopenhauer and Nietzsche borrowings, the work of Bernhard Blume on Thomas Mann and Goethe, the excellent source researches of Gunilla Bergsten and many other scholars, the structural investigations of Herman Meyer, and the biographical labor of love of Peter de Mendelssohn. There is of course much ongoing and productive work on Thomas Mann in languages other than English and German, prominently in Japanese and French.

Inta M. Ezergailis
Cornell University

Notes

1. Stuttgart: Kohlhammer, 1965.

2. "Thomas-Mann-Forschung," part 2, *Deutsche Vierteljahrsschrift für Literaturwissenschaft und Geistesgeschichte*, 42 (1968):132.

3. Gerald Chapple and Hans H. Schulte, eds., "Thomas Mann: Ein Kolloquium," in *Modern German Studies 1*, p. 137.

4. Ibid.

5. Hans Rudolf Vaget and Dagmar Barnouw, *Thomas Mann: Studien zu Fragen der Rezeption* (Bern: Herbert Lang, 1975), p. 95.

6. Chapple and Schulte, "Thomas Mann," p. 142.

7. Ibid.

8. Ibid., p. 119.

9. Ibid., p. 121.

10. Hans Rudolf Vaget, "Thomas Mann und kein Ende: 1. Thomas-Mann-Literature zur Zentenarfeier," *Zeitschrift für deutsche Philologie* 99 (1980):276–88. Much of the following summarizes or paraphrases Vaget's discussion.

11. Ibid., p. 287.

12. Ibid., p. 277.

13. Roland Barthes, *Mythologies* (London: J. Cape, 1972).

14. Käte Hamburger, *Der Humor bei Thomas Mann: Zum Joseph-Roman* (Munich: Nymphenburg, 1965). This is a revised and enlarged edition of Hamburger's 1945 introductory work.

Articles and Essays

Thoughts on the Passing of Thomas Mann

Hermann J. Weigand*

Among the innumerable pictures of Thomas Mann none is so arresting as the well-known photo-portrait that shows the young author at the age of twenty-five, in 1900. Visible to the knee, against a light background, the figure, slightly turned to the right, eyes the beholder with an attitude of grave nonchalance: both hands, thrust into the dark trouser pockets holding back the tails of the buttoned cutaway to reveal a polka-dotted padded cummerbund; the broad black silk tie completely filling the space between the lapels and framing a white stand-up collar that along with the sliver of gleaming cuffs reinforces the note of sober elegance; the face, like the figure, immaculately groomed as to its broad moustache, slightly raised eyebrows and heavy dark hair, parted at the left and brushed back from a broad forehead that is modeled but not yet furrowed; the eyes with a look both dreamy and searching. The portrait seems to say what Thomas Mann wrote three years earlier in *Der Bajazzo*: ["Let's be honest: the point at issue is what you take yourself for, what image you project, and with what assurance you project it"] (*Novellen* I, 77).

This is a young man's philosophy. Taken out of its context, it is the attitude of a man who feels himself poised on the threshold of an extraordinary career but as yet has no tangible achievements to back up his self-appraisal. It is underscored at the end of the story by the reflection that everybody is far too sedulously concerned with himself to find time seriously to have an opinion of anyone else: ["People accept with passive acquiescence the degree of self-respect that you have the assurance of displaying"] (*Ibid.*, 95). What counts is "Sicherheit," self-assurance. But self-assurance is only the visible correlate of an inner pleasurable intimacy with one's own person, "Selbstgefälligkeit" (*Ibid.*, 90), and both the outer and inner aspect of personality, self-assurance and self-love, are contingent

*From *Surveys and Soundings in European Literature*, ed. A. Leslie Willson (Princeton: Princeton University Press, 1966), 290–307, This originally appeared in the *Germanic Review* 31 (October 1956):163–75, a publication of the Helen Dwight Reid Educational Foundation. Reprinted by permission. Quotations from Mann in German have been omitted.

11

upon a regulated give-and-take relation between the individual and society. *Der Bajazzo*, the sketchy analytical autobiography of a man of diversified talent not channeled by any inner drive, a man who finds his life's sum amounting to abject failure, — this early tentative projection of the Christian Buddenbrook type bristles with psychological formulations of ethical problems after the manner of Ibsen and Nietzsche, such as: Is a bad conscience then nothing but festering vanity? ("eiternde Eitelkeit," *Ibid.*, 93). But the central proposition, the only one to engage us at the moment, is: ["There is only one misfortune: to have to suffer the loss of pleasure with oneself. No longer to be pleased with oneself, that is the misfortune"] (*Ibid.*). Here we have a theme destined to find richest development in young Joseph, who mirrors himself in the well by the light of the moon, in the Goethe figure of *Lotte in Weimar*, and in the all-pervasive narcissism of the fabulous Felix Krull. We have a theme intimately lodged, as no one more clearly recognized than Mann himself, in the autobiographical core of Thomas Mann's own unfolding literary personality.

Perhaps all these trenchantly formulated *Erkenntnisse* sound a bit unconvincing as the self-searchings of so anaemic and futile a personality as the "Bajazzo," a decadent — twin brother of his creator only in the ambivalent prognosis ["hero or fool"] (*Ibid.*, 53). In the choice of such a hero the literary climate of decadence was doubtless a determining factor, no less than it was, a few years later, in the tracing of the theme of decline in the sequence of generations of the Buddenbrook family. But it is worth noting that, for all the fashionable pessimism of the age, the front that young Thomas Mann presents to the world, both when he poses for his picture and when he speaks in his own person, does not suggest resignation and decadence. We must not forget that terza rima *Monolog* of thirteen lines, one of his very rare poems, published in *Die Gesellschaft* in 1899 when he was engaged in the writing of *Buddenbrooks*. These lines, opening with a *topos* of modesty and self-depreciation, go on to breathe hope, ambition, self-assurance reflected in the judgment of others and envisage future fame in the dream of the slim laurel wreath that haunts his troubled nights, dispelling sleep.

> ["I am a childish and a feeble fop.
> and erring my spirit sweeps all around,
> and staggering I grab at any sturdy hand.
>
> And still a hope bestirs itself at ground,
> that something, that I thought and felt,
> one day with fame from mouth to mouth will sound.
>
> My name rings softly now throughout the land,
> many mention me with tones of approbation:
> people who have judgment and who understand.

A dream of a slender laurel crown
often at night scares off my restless sleep,
a crown which will one day adorn my brow in reward

For this and that which I accomplished nicely."]

The response to the idea of fame is a touchstone for distinguishing personality types. How apparently healthy and uncomplicated this, Thomas Mann's, frank admission of aspiration to fame. How different, as a literary posture, from the shrug with which fame is dismissed by young Rilke in the opening paragraph of his *Rodin* (1903): ["For fame is, in the end, only the essence of all misunderstandings which gather about a new name"] — a formulation to be repeated in *Malte*. Straightforward, secular aspiration versus saintly self-effacement! Or we may contrast Mann with the paradoxical extreme of the decadent's credo illustrated by the sculptor mentioned in Gerhart Hauptmann's *Vor Sonnenaufgang*: he believed in his art as long as the public ignored it; but when a jury awarded him the commission for a monument on the basis of a model he had submitted, he put a bullet through his brain.

It might have been mere cockiness, this self-assurance (Arno Holz comes to mind by way of example). The record rules this out. Sixty years after the writing of that poem, the "hübsch" of its concluding line — "Für dies und jenes, was ich hübsch gemacht" — has rather the ring of modesty. Or was it conscious understatement? We have our choice of interpretations, as we have it in the case of Mann's prediction, in the *Lebensabriss* of 1930, that, having equaled his mother's age, he would die in 1945 at seventy. Was this a settled conviction? Was it an apotropaeic projection, an oblique prayer to the Powers to grant him that extra measure needed fully to round out his life's cycle?

This is not the place for a glancing survey of Thomas Mann's large-scale achievements — that long series of works of the imagination, in the sustained density of their texture with scarcely a parallel in literary history, flanked as they are by smaller novelistic productions and a steady essayistic output, not to mention the flood of by-products that catered to the tastes and needs of the day. Let us limit ourselves, rather, to exploring in brief some aspects of his work as a continuous process of self-revelation.

It strikes one that in evoking literary or historical personages, whether in narrative or in essay, Thomas Mann has a way of identifying with his subject so as to give the impression of a double tracery: the structural outlines of the personality portrayed are somehow felt to correspond to the alignment of the author's own basic drives and responses. This, the reader's experiencing of a double tracery, holds true for a surprising number of sharply divergent types of personality. In *Schwere Stunde* (1905) the sketch of Friedrich Schiller suggests the delineating hand of a close twentieth-century kinsman, who creates with the same feverish glow in reckless disregard of his pitifully slim physical resources. In *Friedrich und die Grosse Koalition* (1915) it is the defiant amoralism of Nietzsche which seems to fuse author and subject into one personality. The centenary essay on *Lessing* (1929) sparkles with the vibrant clarity of the fearless destroyer of time-honored prejudice, come to life anew. In the many discussions on Wagner only an inner bond of deepest consanguinity can account, it seems, for the uncanny exhibition of the intricate fusion of an imperiously creative drive with the ruthlessly egoistic scheming of a master-seducer. But as time goes on, the identification with Goethe first begins to loom and then, gradually, to supplant all other personality types. The first, tentative indication of this came in the *Goethe und Tolstoi* essay of 1923, where the contrapuntal play with the paired figures of Goethe and Tolstoi, on the one hand, and Schiller and Dostoyevsky on the other, still tended to stress Thomas Mann's affinity with the "spirit" of the second pair as contrasted with the demonic life force, the nature-divinity of the first. But the dynamic equilibrium of the playful arrangement was in a state of flux; every contrast had an inherent tendency to turn into its opposite. Thus the surprise brought by *Lotte in Weimar*, in 1939, where the identification of the Mann personality-type with that of Goethe first fully asserts itself, to retain its dominance to the end, was somewhat tempered by benefit of hindsight. The identification with Goethe involved a gradual readjustment of focus as regards the features of Thomas Mann's mentality. His public had to submit to a course of reeducation.

The education of his public, in a more general way, is a sociological process of momentous significance as regards the age of Thomas Mann. A representative author and his public live in a state of symbiosis. We are on safe ground, I think, when we say: Supposing Thomas Mann had made his literary debut with a work written in the manner of the *Zauberberg*, he would have found only a small coterie of readers interested in esoteric literature. In view of the difficulties he experienced in getting *Buddenbrooks* accepted for publication without a drastic paring-down, it may well be doubted whether a book like the *Zauberberg* would have found a publisher at all at the turn of the century. The taste for Thomas Mann's involved manner had to be gradually inoculated into the public before Thomas Mann could hazard giving full rein to his imagination in the weaving of his intricate novelistic tapestries. Perhaps the matter can be most effectively stated in commercial terms: Before Thomas Mann could foist works like *Lotte in Weimar* and the *Joseph* series on an eager public, tremendous assets of goodwill had to be gradually accumulated. A long series of prior productions of ever increasing difficulty had first to be assimilated in order to pave the way for a willing reception of whatever he had to offer. Since we are concerned with the growing dominance of the Goethe *imago*, let us briefly recall some pertinent features of the *Lotte* novel.

Lotte was and remains an extraordinary performance, even for Thomas Mann. Its achievement as an intermezzo during the twelve years of patient work at the loom of his *Joseph* tapestry stamps it as such. As a novel it is structurally unique. There is no action, no complication, no development, no events to fill those 450 pages—just an inconsequential dinner party at Goethe's house on a September day of the year 1816 during which Goethe exchanged a few polite words with the woman after whom he had modeled the heroine of his *Werther* and whom he had not seen in the forty-four years intervening. This dinner party accounts for the greater part of the last fifth of the story. The preceding four-fifths are devoted entirely to exposition of the subject, Goethe—the first three-fifths to Goethe as seen through the eyes of others; the fourth to Goethe as seen from within.

The narrative, founded on fact, begins with the scene of Lotte Kestner's arrival, early one morning, at the leading Weimar hotel. As soon as the head waiter, an individual who prides himself on his "Bildung," learns the identity of the frail old widowed lady, he is thunderstruck. He showers the incredulous object of his fantastic veneration with a torrent of questions and perorations that turn his conducting her to her room into an exhausting, time-consuming ordeal for Lotte, who has to resort to strong measures in order finally to be left at peace for the two-hour nap she is badly in need of after a night in a coach. From then on she is besieged by a succession of interviewers and callers, for the news of her arrival has spread like wildfire through the little town. First the irrepressible Miss Cuzzle with her sketchbook takes three-quarters of an hour of Lotte's time with her chatter. Then, as she is on the point of going out, Goethe's secretary Riemer comes to make a ceremonial call. She is persuaded with difficulty to accord him two minutes, which turn into hours of densest exploratory psychological dialogue revolving about Goethe. As he leaves, Adele Schopenhauer, who has been patiently waiting in the anteroom, is ushered in, and again Lotte spends hours and hours in talking to this insider and in listening to her account of Goethe and his family problems. Finally Goethe's son August, who had been the central topic of Adele's narrative, appears in person, and again Lotte spends hours in exploring the personality of the young man whose features and manner move her as a powerfully evocative variant of her one-time adorer. Dialogue, dialogue, dialogue without end, interspersed with bits of author's narrative and comment! How many hours have ticked away in this fashion? Eight? Ten? Twelve? Has ever a person of robust constitution, let alone an infirm old lady, withstood so prolonged an ordeal of so packed a dialogue? The marvel of it, she remains alert all the time. To our amazement we notice that Lotte is as keen a listener and as ready a learner as Hans Castorp. How many memorable turns of speech dropped by her interlocutors turn up in her own mouth at unexpected points, in these conversations—and later! It is all a game, of course, this compression of the bewilderingly manifold aspects of Goethe and his milieu into one continuous flow of dialogue. The time here employed is of the quality of rubber: it will stretch indefinitely to suit the author's pleasure. And there is a point where Thomas Mann drops the pretense of the game (by mutual consent, shall we say, of author and reader?): After Adele Schopenhauer has already spent hours in give-and-take with Lotte, we are allowed to take in that part of her story which centers on August, not in its oral, interrupted rendition, but in the form of a well-composed, fluent narrative.

All this is a tour de force, a prodigious strain on the reader's capacity to play the game according to the time rules set by the author. Supposing we have succeeded in playing the game on the author's terms, we are now due for an intermission; we may settle down, after a day that allowed no room for food or drink, to a night's rest. But at seven the next morning— no, not the next but that very same morning, as we find out before the chapter is over—the piper again calls the tune. And what a tune it is!

With no warning whatever we find ourselves participants in a stream-of-consciousness monologue. There is no mistaking the identity of that inner voice: it is that of Goethe awakening from a deep dream vision to the life of the day. To try to intimate this monologue's contents would be sheer folly. What Thomas Mann attempted and accomplished with unparalleled success was to present in an extended moment the totality of Goethe's existence at the time of Lotte's visit—physiological, administrative, scientific, economic, poetic—the flow of multiple energies pulsing simultaneously in that dynamo of organic life. The movement of interests and ideas, creative sallies and musings on high moments of a living past, is as involved and apparently capricious as the planets' tracery of their epicycles in the heavens. The extended moment includes two substantial pieces of dictation (which are merely indicated) to two secretaries and a conversation with August, who has come to report to his father. Thus there are breaks in the interior monologue, but these are merely superficial. All the time we are held in the spell of that personality, which is never at rest for a moment. The duration of the extended moment amounts to three hours, we are told. But here again all ordinary measurement of time turns out to be a delusion.

Here we find ourselves at a point where we cannot avoid becoming personal. Is there any reader, be he ever so steeped in Goethe's productions and personality, who can take in at one stretch all the ultra-dense web of this chapter of eighty-eight pages? Personally I find this quite impossible. The spell of the experience holds one in a vise. The tension rises and rises. But at some point or other it snaps. Stimulation turns into protest: This overwhelms me. I cannot take it! There is a turn of the screw where the magic spell of empathy others itself and becomes sheer torture. The experiencing of this revulsion, this *Umschlag*, applies not to this chapter of Mann alone, but to much of Joyce, to Hermann Broch's *Tod des Vergil* and, doubtless, to others. It applies also, I confess, to Goethe's own "Klassische Walpurgisnacht" when I attempt to take it in in one sweep. As an objective criterion of literary art this purely subjective reaction probably deserves to be shrugged away as unworthy of objective criticism. I think nevertheless it is worth recording as a fairly recent development in the sphere of literary creation.

The dinner party given by Goethe in honor of Lotte, taking up most of the final fifth, makes no such demands. It is a straightforward account of a formal gathering where no one is at his ease. As to the host, the guest of honor carries away a sense of his chilling aloofness. The perfunctoriness of his hospitality is not intentional but due to preoccupation. There is no inner contact. What Lotte means to Goethe now, forty-four years after his infatuation was crystallized in *Werther* — "abreagiert" in the language of Freud — brings to mind Tonio Kröger's classic dictum: ["What has been expressed is disposed of"]. The inherent cruelty of the transitoriness of life's high moments is soberly registered.

We rebound from this to the unbelievable surprise of the final meeting of the principals in the carriage which Goethe had put at Lotte's disposal after her visit to the theater. What are we to make of this meeting, so out of keeping with what has gone before? Is it just a conventional happy ending, a sop for sentimental souls, in outrageous defiance of all probabilities? Is its palpable unreality a humorous author's trick for the benefit and at the expense of a gullible public? — You would not have us believe in this meeting as the organic conclusion of the story's cycle, I remember once saying to Thomas Mann. And I remember his concurring in what I urged, but in a curiously noncommittal way. What I now think was in his mind — he did not elaborate — is something like this:

Yes, such a meeting is a fantastic invention (and there are hints of this both in the playful interchange of the ["thou"] and the ["you"] — reminiscent of the ["carnival freedom"] of the *Zauberberg* — and in the iambic lyricism of some of the dialogue). It is contrary to all the laws of probability. Goethe, aloof and withdrawn in the padded cell of his inner consciousness in order to channel all of his stupendous vitality into tangible work — it is most unlikely that a vibration coming from the real Lotte should strike his inner ear. But dare we rule out the very possibility? Would he be the incommensurable figure that he is if he were calculable? Would you not do well to reread, in the inner monologue, the two pages of Goethe's musings on ["the real"] versus ["the possible"] (252–253)? Do you not recall teasing echoes of these (unheard) musings in the code language of Lotte's words addressed to Goethe in the carriage (447)? In other words: Given the total setting, this scene as a might-have-been is not to be dismissed as impossible.

We have dwelt on *Lotte in Weimar* as the first major work to suggest in a systematic way the idea of an archetypal likeness between Goethe and Thomas Mann amounting to inner identity. How could Thomas Mann have projected from within that welter of vital contradictions, if his own inner world had not also been of the stuff of the incommensurable? The spell of this suggestion pervades the *Lotte* so insistently that for moments we are apt to forget how unlike these two great representatives of the German spirit really were in ever so many respects. How different the controlled self-assurance of the young Thomas Mann from the effervescent emotionalism of the young Goethe! How different the pattern of their family life, how different their lives as a whole: Thomas Mann exclusively the man of letters; Goethe scattering, dissipating his energies in a thousand extra-literary activities. Whereas Thomas Mann's work *is* his life, Goethe's works *can* be viewed as the by-products of an enormously rich, diversified existence. Or think of Goethe's pioneering efforts in so many branches of natural science. In Thomas Mann's case we have nothing of this, we have instead the assimilation of vast amounts of ready-made scientific and scholarly learning and their transformation into thematic material for dialectical play in the tissue of his novels. Goethe's passionate curiosity centered on things, concrete phenomena, while Thomas Mann's curiosity, no less passionate, was concerned with the alchemy of turning things into words — images, sounds, rhythms. Goethe's works spring from the confessional urge, whereas in the case of Thomas Mann the core of personal, private experience is sublimated in a highly intellectualistic way. And let us not forget the prodigal wealth of unfinished fragments that mark every phase of Goethe's career as contrasted with the disciplined economy of Thomas Mann's production. Here the ["unity of life"], underscored as regards Goethe, is exhibited as the unity of an all-absorbing literary drive. In both men this unity is nourished by an unwavering, mystical love of self.

The *Lotte* puts into Goethe's mouth a number of pages eminently worth recalling, but unfortunately too long to quote, that muse with approval on the many varieties of love of self, including autobiography and egocentrism, as higher forms of life-sustaining personal vanity (323–325). Here the trio, Goethe, Nietzsche, Mann, see eye to eye.

If we look closely enough in the *Lotte*, however, we come upon spots where even the inner identification of the author with his subject will not stand the scrutiny of the critical eye. I have in mind one of the many passages of the inner monologue where Goethe comes back to the *Divan*. His musings dwell on the peculiar zest afforded by this engrossing task: there is an invigorating discipline about working one's way into a culture so foreign to that of the West as the Persian, but it is quite another thing for him, the Westerner, to be creative *as* a Persian. He muses on this two-fold challenge as ["this burial of oneself and burrowing of frenzied sympathy, which makes you an initiate of the world gripped by love, so that you speak her language with a free ease and no one shall be able to distinguish the studied detail from the one characteristically invented"]. (335). No question, this passage makes its appeal on three levels. There is, first, Goethe speaking about his *Divan*. There is, next, Thomas Mann characterizing his venture into the culture of ancient Egypt. There is, finally, an unmistakable allusion to the task in hand, Thomas Mann's recreation of the living Goethe. So far, so good. But the concluding turn of the sentence quoted makes Goethe's mind revert to the *Werther* — a shift which we readily follow, having heard so much from Lotte and Riemer on the tantalizing relation of fact to fiction in this novel. And the thought of Werther brings the name of a disparaging early critic to Goethe's lips, pursed in scorn. ["In my youth — Werther was just causing a furor — there was one man, Bretschneider, a boor, concerned about my humility"] (*Ibid.*). A bit of authentic detail, this, for Goethe knew Bretschneider since his foppish days at Leipzig. But now we must listen to the gathering impetus of the tirade that follows:

[He tells me the ultimate truths about myself, or what he thinks them to be. — Don't start getting ideas, brother. There's not as much to you as all that noise your little novel is causing might make you think! What kind of a fellow are you? I know you! Mostly you judge badly, and you know basically that your discernment is not dependable without long reflection. Also you're smart enough to admit right off that those people whom you think prudent are right, rather than to discuss a matter through with them and maybe stick your neck out and show your weakness. That's you! Also you're an unstable nature that sticks to no doctrine but jumps from one to the other extreme. You could be persuaded to become a pietist or a free-thinker, because you're so susceptible it's a fright. Besides, you have a dose of pride, in itself not allowed, to the point that you consider almost anybody besides yourself a weak creature, when you're the weakest of all; namely, to the effect that, in the case of those few whom you think of as clever, you're not at all in a position to judge yourself but rather you follow the general opinion of everybody. Today I'm going to lay it out for you. You do have a grain of ability, a poetic genius that goes to work when you have carried an idea about with you for a very long time, and when you have worked everything over and collected in your mind whatever can serve your cause — anyway, then it's all right, then something may come of it. Whenever you notice something, it sticks to your nature, or in your head, and everything that you pile up, you try to knead into that lump of clay you're working on. You think and reflect on nothing else but that object. That's the way you do it, and there's nothing else to you. Don't get any wild ideas about your popularity! — I can still hear him, that nut, he was such a nut for truth and a crank for knowledge, not at all malicious, probably even suffered himself under the sharpness of his critical insight, the fool — the clever fool, the melancholy, ingenious fool, wasn't he right? Wasn't he threefold right, or all in all at least two-and-a-half-fold, when he rubbed my nose in instability, unself-sufficiency, and determinacy, and in regard to the genius who is able only to conceive and gestate a long time, and to pick out and use subsidia?]

I have quoted the passage in full. To those who know Goethe and Thomas Mann it speaks an unmistakable language. As the passage starts out, this might be some Bretschneider giving a dressing-down to a cocky young Goethe whose inflated sense of self-importance rubbed him against the grain. But as it continues, the literary personality he so trenchantly defines with a malevolent animus is not that of young Goethe at all. At the time of his writing the *Werther* no one in his circle would have interpreted Goethe's literary physiognomy in terms of single-minded tenacity and slow, patient gestation. Herder, who knew him best, derided him as sparrow-brained. No, this is not Bretschneider depreciating young Goethe, this is some rival trying to take the wind out of Thomas Mann's sails, some "brother," who thinks he knows him inside out and airs his own superiority. Since Thomas Mann never had any intimates, there is only one person who could have attacked him in this way. Not quite in this way, to be sure: his rival's insight would necessarily have fallen far short of this retrospective self-revelation. Unquestionably the scene contains echoes of a jealous reaction to the great popular success of his *Buddenbrooks*. Now, nearly forty years later, the latent *élan* of the young man's emergent literary personality is dwelt upon with a sense of triumph.[1]

The page that follows contains a bitter prediction about the Germans that Goethe did not make but might have made — an agonizing echo of the Hitler madness. But the passage we have been analyzing cannot be read in terms of an upthrust of pent-up forces from the depths of Goethe's self.

Seen as a whole, the last phase of Thomas Mann, which dates from the completion of the sinister *Doktor Faustus*, is marked by an easing of tension, a relaxing of that turn of the screw with its often next to impossible demands on the sustaining powers of the reader's empathic response. *Der Erwählte* is light in a heady way, a sparkling draught of champagne that leaves no hang-over. *Felix Krull*, of which more in a moment, is playful throughout. As for the lightness of *Die Betrogene*, it was felt even as a letdown by many reviewers who did not know what to make of the master's new manner.

I have been quoted[2] as saying that *Die Betrogene* was written by Felix Krull with Thomas Mann looking over his shoulder. This statement warrants a little elaboration. There were readers, of course, who sought to probe into what they called the guilt of the heroine in order to see her organic dissolution in terms of a sternly moralistic retribution! But more commonly the old-fashioned technique gave rise to bewilderment. In the main, the story, except for its unmistakable twentieth-century ending that bristles with clinical vocabulary, was felt as a relapse into the carefree manner of the eighteenth century in its simple narrative style, its stiltedly artificial dialogues, and its extended use of such outworn conventions as the long, impeccably phrased soliloquies of the heroine. How was it possible for that most conscious craftsman, Thomas Mann, to revert to so timeworn a manner? Is this encroaching senility? The story itself supplies a different answer. We find it in a transparent dialogue between the emotive, blissfully effusive mother and her sophisticated, clubfooted, and inhibited daughter, the artist, who paints in the intellectual abstract manner. Why don't you for once, the mother pleads, paint something nice that will appeal to the heart—a fresh bouquet of flowers, compellingly fragrant, flanked by figurines, a gentleman blowing a kiss to a lady, and the whole mirrored in a lacquered tabletop? To which the daughter replies: Your imaginings, mother, run quite out of bounds. One cannot paint that way any more. The mother does not understand; so the daughter, in a vain attempt to make her understand, becomes very explicit: ["You just can't. The condition of time and art no longer permits it"] (11). This is Anna speaking to Rosalie. But we must be deaf in one ear if we do not also hear the voice of Thomas Mann raised in amused protest against the insouciant manner of the very story in which this dialogue is imbedded. "You just can't." This sort of thing is altogether passé! You are taking me for a ride! To whom is Thomas Mann protesting? To whom can he be protesting if not to the incredibly talented imp of his creation? This facile elegance is not Thomas Mann's. The roles are reversed, the creature is in the saddle! This is Felix Krull as *spiritus rector*, guiding the redoubtable pen that gave him life in a piece of quasi-automatic writing with his matter in the smilingly acquiescent role of the medium—up to a certain point!

Felix Krull, the confessions of a confidence-man, begun before *Tod in Venedig*, carried as a growing theme for more than four decades, was early referred to by its author as a parody on the German "Bildungsroman." The central idea—the artist and the criminal as twin brothers, both feeding on an excessive diet of the imagination—is already pointed up, as everyone knows, in *Tonio Kröger* and has its roots, no doubt, in a very deep stratum of Thomas Mann's psyche. When the first slim installment appeared (in 1923) the uncanny literary talent of that smooth scapegrace lent an extraordinary charm to his youthful escapades. The blending of vibrant vitality in his style with the fluent use of slick cliché added up to a self-portrait of compelling authenticity. Witness his posture in the scene after his father's suicide: There I stood, he reports, ["covering my eyes with my hand, beside the cooling shell of my sire, and paid abundantly a tribute of tears"]. Does not this language glitter like the lacquered tabletop of Rosalie's imagination?

If Thomas Mann's stylistic identification with his hero's uninhibited ["self-satisfaction"] was a feat to be applauded, the spirit of parody takes an unexpectedly subtle turn in the ensuing course of the story. We note an ever-increasing tendency on the young man's part to become expansive in his descriptions, even to the point of tediousness, although he could not possibly ever be bored with himself. But a feature related to this, yet startlingly different, is the exhibition to which he treats us in the reproduction of his oral discourse. What reader does not remember the creeping sense of dazzled stupefaction at the elaborate, interminable periods in which Krull delivers himself on occasion to an unsuspecting stranger, as when, in Lisbon, he inquires for the location of a street, taking half a page to do it? Have we ever known any one to spin out the web of ingratiating oratory in that peculiar hypnotizing fashion? For all its strangeness it has a familiar ring. As we search in our memory we find the image of Thomas Mann's Joseph stealthily superimposing itself on that of our adventurer. Yes, this is the voice of Joseph echoing from its Egyptian spaces and their disregard of time into the milieu of prewar Europe. What has happened? The creature, so light and full of verve at the outset, has drunk of his author's blood for so many years that a subtle transformation has been effected: First Thomas Mann writes like the budding confidence-man; now Felix Krull, for long stretches at a time, writes like Thomas Mann. First Thomas Mann creates Felix in a spirit of parody; now the creature parodies its author. Did Krull do this, by any chance, with an eye on secretary Riemer? This long-term member of Goethe's household tells in *Lotte in Weimar* that he became so adept in imitating Goethe's style that the recipients of letters from Goethe could not tell those dictated by the master from those of his own composition; he boasts, in fact, that the ceremonial turns of his style were more Goethean than Goethe's own.

Is it possible to speak of Felix Krull without recalling his greatest real-life prototype, Giacomo Casanova? Remember how Casanova fascinated the generation of Thomas Mann, becoming a major theme for Schnitzler and Hofmannsthal in plays and stories and leaving his imprint on Rilke's poems. To what extent Felix Krull's career is an "imitatio" of the adventurer *par excellence* would be an intriguing topic to dwell upon. Without doubt they have some striking fundamental features in common. Theirs is the same narcissistic "Selbstgefälligkeit" that irresistibly infects an overwhelming proportion of their acquaintances, men and women alike, and brings them under a kind of hypnotic spell. This same narcissism supplies the drive behind their incredible exploits and the element of hyperbole in their literary self-exhibition, making them both rank, untutored as they are, among the world's great storytellers. This narcissism allows both, with a degree of good faith, to profess a personal, a kind of custom-made morality: both can perpetrate the most unscrupulous acts on occasion without this engendering any deeper scruples within them as to their being essentially pleasing to God and man. Their sex life shows a similarity and a difference. In their relations with women both derive their greatest delight from giving pleasure to a partner stimulated to dizzying raptures of cooperation; neither would resort to fraud or force for the gratification of sexual desire. Both speak of the culminating act as the sacrifice *(das Opfer)*.[3] But while Casanova makes a cult of his self-immolation and abandons himself to each successive love with the ecstasy of a new experience in which notes of tenderest sentiment mingle with the exhibition of incredible feats of potency, Felix Krull lacks this robust constitution and tempers his comparatively rare sexual orgies with self-preserving caution.

But the most fundamental difference between the two adventurers is to be found in the fact that Casanova's is an active, aggressive temperament that plunges headlong into the turmoil of life without any squeamishness regarding its gross and sordid aspects, whereas Krull is essentially a passive figure so far as real life is concerned. He finds his most exquisite gratification in the realm of the imagination. He did not cooperate actively during his birth, he tells us, and throughout his story, as far as we are able to follow its unfinished course, he is a ["Sunday's child," i.e., favored by fortune] on whom, for the most part, life bestows its gifts without his having to exert himself actively toward their attainment. Casanova experiences ups and downs of the most prodigious range; a grimy beggar today, ravaged by disease and hunger, he will turn up tomorrow a nobleman moving with the ease of one to the manner born in the sphere of aristocracy and royalty, secular and ecclesiastic, in Turkey as well as in Europe. Whatever happens to him, he always has a way of landing on his feet by virtue of an incredible robustness of constitution. Could we imagine Felix Krull surviving fifteen months of torture under the lead roofs of Venice and engineering his eventual escape with a tenacity of will that triumphs over stupendous obstacles? Comparing Felix Krull and Casanova as real characters — an unfair approach, to be sure — the eighteenth-century confidence-man dwarfs the nineteenth-century prodigy. The mere fact that Casanova writes his memoirs at seventy while Krull is through with life at forty points up the difference. If we evaluate the two as literary autobiographies, on the other hand, the scale tips decidedly in Krull's favor; Casanova's extremely uneven account cannot measure up to the stylistic mastery that Felix Krull acquired through the long years of mystical intimacy with his creator.

To our regret *Felix Krull* was left unfinished. What was committed to paper beyond the published first volume we shall doubtless see in due time. But our regrets are tempered by the consideration that Thomas Mann always had a major project in the works. Something was bound to be left unfinished even though in a sense it was there long ago. The themes were all there from way back, the variations, always startlingly novel, could go on *ad infinitum*. There are some lines in Goethe's *Divan* which for many years have haunted me as applying singularly, uniquely to Thomas Mann. They read as though written to hail his coming, to summarize his literary essence. To me they are the most fitting epitaph for a writer who, more than any other, rounded out his life's full cycle, transmuting the raw material of his earthly existence into works that live:

> [That thou canst not end, that makes thee great,
> that thou never beginst, that is thy fate.
> Thy song is whirling like the starry vault,
> beginning and end the same for evermore,
> and what the middle brings is manifestly
> that which at the end remains and was originally.][4]

Notes

1. In the above exposition there is an exemplary error in critical judgment on my part. Immediately after the publication of this essay Mr. Erich Neumann of the Thomas Mann Archive in Berlin very amicably called my attention to the fact that the whole Bretschneider passage is an almost verbatim reproduction of a letter from H. G. von Bretschneider to Friedrich Nicolai, dated October 16, 1775. The letter can be found in Heinz Amelung, *Goethe als Persönlichkeit* (Munich, 1914-Propyläen edition, supplementary Vol. I), pp. 128–130. See also *The Germanic Review* XXXII (1957), 75–76.

2. By Erich Heller (unsigned) in the *Times Literary Supplement* (London), Nov. 11, 1955.

3. The term occurs frequently in the new German translation of Casanova's memoirs that began to appear in thirteen volumes under the imprint of Georg Müller, München, in 1907.

4. An expanded German version of this essay was delivered under the auspices of the Allard Pierson Foundation in Amsterdam on March 21, 1956, and subsequently published in *Neophilologus*.

In Search of Bourgeois Man   Georg Lukács*

Living means fighting within you
The ghosts of dark powers.
Writing is putting on trial
Your inmost self.

Ibsen

I

In search of bourgeois man? Is he not to be found everywhere? Is not the culture of the present (at least in the West), from economics right through to literature and music bourgeois? And is not such a question particularly unjustified in the case of Thomas Mann, a writer who from the beginning committed himself to the bourgeoisie and has continued to do so with greater insistence than is customary among writers today.

The question, however, is made more complex by the complete absence of Utopianism in Mann's work (which is not always true of his thought). We intend this descriptively, not as an evaluation. Thomas Mann is a realist whose respect, indeed reverence, for reality is of rare distinction. His detail, still more his plots, his intellectual designs may not stay on the surface of everyday life; his form is quite unnaturalistic. Yet the content of his work never finally leaves the real world. What we are offered in Thomas Mann's work is bourgeois Germany (together with

*Reprinted from *Essays on Thomas Mann* (London: Merlin Press Ltd., 1965), 13–46, by permission of the Merlin Press.

genesis and antecedent paths). And of this we are offered the inner problems, deeply seized, so that while they point dialectically ahead, they do not conjure a Utopian future perspective into a present-day reality. There are not a few great realist works which are shaped in this way. I would mention only Goethe's *Wilhelm Meister* novels. However kindred Mann is to Goethe, here he is his polar opposite.

This re-emphasizes the bourgeois ideal as the guiding principle in Mann's life and work. He is rightly considered the most representative German writer in the first half of our century. A people can, however, be "represented" by different types of writer. There are "representative" writers who are prophets of the future, and others whose genius and mission it is to be "mirrors of the world." Schiller's urgency and restlessness was just as "representative" as Goethe's embrace of the moment. But likening Mann to Goethe (or to Balzac or Tolstoy), calling him a "mirror," still does not tell us what is specific to him.

Goethe's *Meister* novels contain Utopian elements; there are similar features in Balzac, Keller and Tolstoy. We do not find them in Thomas Mann. We are faced then with a special type of "representative" writer. Thomas Mann presents a complete picture of bourgeois life and its predicaments. But it is a picture of a precise moment, a precise stage of development. (True, this portrait of the German bourgeois of the present only goes up to the period before fascism. So far Mann has not given us a picture of the German as fascist or opponent of fascism). This is why many Germans rediscover themselves so much more deeply, at once more directly and intimately, in Mann's work than in that of other writers. And since the problems are left unanswered, or answered in the most round-about way, since they are communicated at many levels which are in turn ironically dissolved, the impact of Mann's novels has been much greater than that of his contemporaries. Whatever claims his writing makes on the reader's artistic judgment, whatever the intellectual requirements of his delicately spun web of questions and reservations, his plots and characters are simply and straightforwardly drawn and accessible to the simplest person. And since it is a moral world order that he rejects, the impact is a lasting one. The moments he chooses always mark a particular stage in the development of the German middle class, one to which all who have consciously lived through their own and their country's past will feel themselves perpetually drawn.

This very individual kind of "representation" deepens with Thomas Mann's slow organic development. Here, too, he is in harmony with the march of reality. Reality, of course, particularly during the second half of Mann's life, was stormy enough, and it was inevitable that this tempo should be reflected in Mann's writing. But this could not affect the epic character of his work as a whole which was rooted in the sensibility of a very leisurely storyteller. The works which reflect these violent upheavals not only remain unflurried, epic and ironical in character — they ripen slowly so that the problems they deal with have already acquired an ideological maturity. These problems are the spiritual and moral pros and cons preceding a particular step forward which history has taken or is about to take. The actual changes are, therefore, omitted. Mann shows only their reflexes in everyday life. But again there must be no confusion between this slow tempo of development and whatever variety of naturalism. Mann's stories never reflect the day-to-day moods of the German middle class. Rather the reverse: as he matured, the more firmly did he oppose the prevailing reactionary trends. But the way in which he countered them, his choice of intellectual weapons once again marks the summit of bourgeois consciousness at the time. Even in opposition Thomas Mann, the creator, never parts company with the bourgeoisie. The extent of his influence reposes on this firm social basis. He is representative in the sense that he symbolizes all that is best in the German bourgeoisie.

This, of course, only refers to the completed work. But this easy, at times almost easy-going, perfection was the outcome of a long and painful struggle with the manifold, above all inner moral problems of a world from which such a work of art could emerge in clear and organic shape. But if Thomas Mann as an artist is the very opposite of the philosopher Schelling who, as Hegel put it, "undertook his philosophical education in public," if rather his works are rounded summaries of historical stages which have run their course, nevertheless his actual spiritual development necessarily takes place in public.

I believe it wrong to interpret the works of a major writer on the basis of their own theories. If these works are important it is almost always because they achieve a form which can render the conflicts of their times at their fullest range within the given historical reality. Yet these same conflicts pursued in terms of ideas, however fearlessly, can get no further than an honestly stated antithesis which often simply juxtaposes the "yes" and the "no" without connection. Sometimes indeed the conflicts may harden into quite false and reactionary positions. But in the best cases this is more than an artistic rounding-off of what the intellect cannot fully seize. It is the corrective which the process of reproducing reality, the passionate pursuit of this process to its very end, *in fine* which reality itself applies to the false thinking of the writer. Nowhere is Balzac's utopian legitimism or Tolstoy's Christian plebeian dream of brotherhood with the peasants more powerfully refuted than in *Le Cabinet des Antiquités* or *Resurrection*.

Thomas Mann is an extreme type of the writer whose greatness lies in being a "mirror of the world." Not that he is a philosophical dilettante or an inconsistent thinker. On the contrary he possesses the highest intellectual culture of the bourgeois Germany of his time. Few contemporaries have worked their way so thoroughly through the leading reactionary thinkers of this period, Schopenhauer and Nietzsche. Few have lived out so deeply the relationship between their systems and methods and the crucial problems of the contemporary bourgeoisie. There are few contemporaries where so arduously achieved a philosophical outlook has been made so closely a part of artistic creation.

And this is why the refutation of the wrong-headed, the retrogressive by the very logic of the characters, plots and situations is seldom so manifest as in Thomas Mann. Let me take just one small example: *Buddenbrooks* was written at a time when Thomas Mann, and with him a large section of the German bourgeois intelligentsia, looked to Schopenhauer as the leading spokesman of a German philosophy. For Mann the high road of Germany's intellectual development, and this view persisted a good while after *Buddenbrooks*, led from Goethe via Schopenhauer and Wagner to Nietzsche, and from Nietzsche on to a truly German intellectual culture of the present and future. It is not surprising that Schopenhauer's influence made itself felt in *Buddenbrooks*, that Mann portrayed a Schopenhauerian attitude to life. But how does this appear in the actual work? Thomas Buddenbrook is a broken man, his efforts to revive his firm having long since failed. He has lost hope of his son succeeding him and accomplishing what he has failed to do. His relationship with his wife becomes more and more difficult, intellectually and emotionally. It is at this point that he comes across *The World as Will and Representation*. And what is its effect upon him?

> He was filled with a great surpassing satisfaction. It soothed him to see how a master-mind could lay hold on this strong, cruel, mocking life and enforce and condemn it. His was the gratification of the sufferer who has always had a bad conscience about his sufferings and concealed them from the gaze of a harsh, unsympathetic world, until suddenly, from the hand of an authority, he receives, as it were, justification and license for his suffering—justification before the world, this best of all possible worlds which the master-mind scornfully demonstrates to be the worst of all possible ones! . . . He felt that his whole being had unaccountably expanded, and at the same time there clung about his senses a profound intoxication, a strange, sweet, vague allurement which somehow resembled the feelings of early love and longing.

The bitterest opponent of Schopenhauer could not paint a better picture of the philosopher as the apostle of decadence.

We are not concerned at present to examine the way Mann as a thinker looked upon and judged the general problem of decadence at that stage. I gave this example merely to indicate how the intellectual and imaginative questions and answers are separated out in Mann, to justify the methodology of the reflections which follow, that is primarily to concentrate on the works and to interpret Mann the thinker and political man starting from his writing and not, as is customary, the other way round.

II

It is only from this starting-point that the apparent paradox of my first question, the search for bourgeois man as the central problem in Mann and the basis for his popularity and representative position can be meaningfully answered. This question leads us to a fundamental contradiction in the writer's situation in the bourgeois epoch. Friedrich Schiller was the first to define this fundamental tendency of the new bourgeois world by creating the category of "the sentimental" (the elegiac, satirical and idyllic). Schiller's opposing principles have all the captivating simplicity of a great discovery: "The writer . . . either *is* nature or he will *seek* her," he says. It is immediately clear that true realism is the special property of the "naïve" writer. Schiller illustrates this antithesis very well by contrasting the treatment of a similar episode in Homer and Ariosto.

But complication sets in with a further problem. Schiller himself poses it: is Goethe a "naïve" writer and, we would add, is not Tolstoy or Mann also one? If the answer is yes, what is Goethe's attitude to modern reality? How does he view the quest for nature, the "sentimental"? Of small literary figures Schiller was confidently able to say "that they run wild in their age and are protected by good fortune from its crippling influence." But it was obvious to him that simple contrasts of this kind were inadequate to define Goethe's position in world literature. It was a little one-sided of him to ask how a "naïve" writer handles a "sentimental" theme and then to answer his question with a brilliant exegesis of *Werther*, *Tasso*, *Wilhelm Meister* and *Faust*. Of course Goethe is "naïve," but for social reasons he is no longer as obviously and uncomplicatedly "naïve" as Homer. His "naïveté" is both inborn and with difficulty achieved. It determines his initial approach to, and final shaping of, a theme. But in between the "sentimental" has run its turbulent course. Hence one may let Schiller's antithesis stand: "Nature favoured the *naïve* writer with the faculty of acting always as an undivided unity, of being at every moment an independent and complete whole, and of representing humanity in its full extent, as it really was. To the *sentimental* writer she gave the power, or rather instilled the urge, to restore that unity within himself which abstract thought had destroyed, to make humanity complete within himself and to pass from a limited condition to an infinite one." But in the major realists of the bourgeois epoch, Goethe, Keller, Balzac, Tolstoy, this antithesis appears as a dialectical process, in which the "sentimental" becomes by realistic handling simply a stage on the way from the original "naïveté" to the mature.

What, then, is Thomas Mann's position among the great "naïve" novelists of the nineteenth and twentieth centuries? Our detour was intended to explain the apparent contradiction in our earlier description of him. We called his realism a "mirror of the world," but also said that he was representative as a conscience of the German middle class. The contradiction is patent, for where a writer embodies conscience, his native "naïveté" must disappear. The fact of conscience as a force in life gives both expression and acknowledgment to the discrepancy between things as they are and things as they ought to be, between appearance and essence. Have we not got back to Schiller's "sentimental" writer, to the gulf between ideal and reality? And does this not dispose of the "naïve" realism of the epic tradition? We think not. What should be, need not, as in Kant and, for the most part, in Schiller, oppose itself to a differently ordered real world, but can in a Hegelian way emerge from the contradictory identity of appearance and essence. Conscience then is simply the injunction: "Become what you are; be your essence, develop the essential, living core within you, whatever the disruptive influences of the inner and outer world."

It is in this sense that the deeply and consciously bourgeois Thomas Mann is conscience for the German middle class. One could put it that the sociological core of Schiller's discovery of the essence of modern art becomes conscious in Mann. His overriding conviction is that to enquire into the essence of bourgeois man today is to ask what it is to be a bourgeois. The search for bourgeois man threw open to him all the questions concerning the present and future and the culture of our time.

One of Goethe's great successors, Gottfried Keller, wrote an impressive *oeuvre* round this question. But this was in the conditions of mid-nineteenth-century Switzerland. Thomas Mann saw the deep difference (though not at the beginning of his career). In the twenties he said about Switzerland: "We have before us an offshoot of the German people, which, at an early stage, broke away from the main body and shared its intellectual and moral experiences only to a limited degree. But it never lost contact with Western European thought and did not undergo the Romantic degeneration which turned us into solitaries and outlaws. . . . But one thing the Swiss phenomenon can teach us is not to confuse a stage in Germany's history, which though mistaken was inevitable, with the essence of Germany itself. . . ."

Inevitably Mann did not start out from such insights which only the First World War and Germany's defeat vouchsafed him. But then they are not quite so simple and unsociological as Mann himself sometimes imagined them. During the War he wrote about his early work: "It is true that I rather slept through the transformation of the German burgher into a bourgeois. . . ." He underestimates here his own achievement. One need only take the contrast between the development of the Hagenström and Buddenbrook families: the Hagenströms are a perfect illustration of that development of burgher into bourgeois which Mann says he "slept through." So little did he "sleep through" this development that the second half of his first novel, from a sociocultural and moral point of view, turns on the question: who really represent the middle class, the Hagenströms or the Buddenbrooks?

Superficially the answer is simple. The patrician culture of the Buddenbrooks is doomed and the Hagenströms rule the new Germany. So much is clear; and Mann did not "sleep through" it. Nor did he resign himself to it. Had he done so, he would have had to renounce the idea of a contemporary German culture and literature. He would have become a *laudator temporis acti*, a new Raabe.[1]

Instead the question faces him: who is the bourgeois? What does his type look like, what is its pattern and culture if he does not belong with the victorious Hagenströms? In this light the Buddenbrooks appear not simply as a family on the downgrade but, despite their decadent tinges, as upholders of a bourgeois culture which was once Germany's pride and could still be the source of its resurgence, could provide an organic continuation of the glorious past. In this sense the Buddenbrooks saga is the story of what happens to Germany's cultural traditions in the nineteenth century.

Mann's first novel rests on a double contrast. Beside the opposition between the Hagenströms and Buddenbrooks there is the internal opposition between Thomas and Christian Buddenbrook. Between Thomas and Christian the question is whether to surrender to decadence or fight it. The character of Christian (like that of the hero of the story *The Bajazzo*) shows how the modern world, with its break-up of the old patrician bourgeoisie, has thoroughly destroyed the old morality. The type of the turn of the century, the *fin-de-siècle* has its ancestor here: the personality which destroys itself by undermining these bourgeois principles of life which have shaped it — fulfilment of duty, choosing a career.

The same corrosive forces are also at work in Thomas but he keeps them in check through stern self-discipline. Where Christian goes to pieces as a person Thomas forms for himself a bourgeois personality. Yet the source of this form, outer and inner, is despair; he recoils from emotional anarchy and disintegration. "At last he (Thomas, G. L.) said, and his voice had a ring of feeling, 'I have become what I am because I did not want to become what you are. If I have inwardly shrunk from you, it has been because I needed to guard myself — your being, and your existence, are a danger to me — that is the truth.' "

This is the "composure" of Thomas Buddenbrook which becomes the aesthetic and ethic of a new bourgeois culture. Does this mean that Mann has found his bourgeois? No, alas! Thomas is brother to Christian in spirit, too. He has become the good bourgeois by doing violence to his own nature. When he fails with his first and only attempt to participate in the new economic development of the bourgeoisie, the Hagenström path, he becomes more and more a figurehead, acting out his life — and Thomas Mann underscores this with irony.

Is this bourgeois man? The question stays in the balance. In a conversation with his sister, Thomas quotes a remark of his wife's about Christian: "There's nothing of the burgher about Christian. Thomas — he's even less of a burgher than you yourself." His sister is shocked and answers: "Burgher, Tom? What did she mean? Why, it seems to me there is no better burgher on top of the earth than you are!" Thomas demurs: "Oh, well — she didn't mean it just in that sense. . . ."

But this does not resolve Mann's dilemma of "composure" or emotional anarchy. In fact only now does the question take a central place in his pre–First World War writings; especially in *Tonio Kröger* and *Death in Venice*, stories about artists, where the problem is the life of the artist himself. That is, can one by restraining the emotions, by a policy of "composure" turn artistic activity into a career? Mann here takes artistic activity as a symbol for any kind of genuine culture, for any profession or career that comes from within. Of the import of his hero he says in *Death in Venice*: "Gustav Aschenbach was the poet spokesman of all those who labour at the edge of exhaustion; of the overburdened, of those who are already worn out but still hold themselves upright; of all our modern moralizers of accomplishment, with stunted growth and scanty resources, who yet contrive by skilful husbanding and prodigious spasms of will to produce, at least for a while, the effect of greatness. There are many such, they are the heroes of the age." In these words Mann reveals his own impact at the time.

So far so good. Did this mean he had found his bourgeois? The Russian painter, Lisaveta Ivanovna, calls her friend Tonio Kröger a "bourgeois run astray." And Tonio himself sees clearly on the one hand that a real art (a real culture and morality) could only be achieved in his day by taking the path he had chosen. On the other hand he loves life and rates it higher than an art forced to stand aside from life. His description of life is very bourgeois:

> Don't think of Caesar Borgia or any drunken philosophy that has him for a standard bearer. He is nothing to me, your Caesar Borgia. I have no opinion of him, and I shall never comprehend how one can honour the extraordinary and daemonic as an ideal. No, life as the eternal antimony of mind and art does not represent itself to us as a vision of savage greatness and ruthless beauty; we who are set apart and different do not conceive it as, like us, unusual; it is the normal, respectable, and admirable that is the kingdom of our longing; life, in all its seductive banality!

We seem once more to have reached our goal. It is ordinary people like Hans Hansen and Ingeborg Holm who constitute bourgeois life. They do — in the dreams of Tonio and his kind. But if this discovery was anything more than a lyrical irony, Thomas Mann would have had to give up all idea of a bourgeois culture. For the Hans Hansens and Ingeborg Holms have no more relevance to the cultural development of the German middle class from Goethe to Thomas Mann than the Hagenströms or the Klöterjahns, though they are considerably more attractive to look at, which fits them better as the objects of a dream. But even the most sincere of dreams is deceptive. In Mann's *Fiorenza* the dying Lorenzo di Medici says to Savonarola. "Whither the longing urges, there one is not, that one is not—you know? And yet man likes to confuse himself with his longing."

So it would seem after all that "the bourgeois run astray," Tonio Kröger, Thomas Buddenbrook's soul-mate become writer, and the genuine bourgeois with his code of "composure," embody the true ethic of the new bourgeoisie. But Mann again passes ruthless judgment on himself. *Death in Venice* shows this. For what was but dream and tendency in *Tonio Kröger* Gustav Aschenbach brings to full flower. He creates a perfectly formed life and an impressive body of work on the basis of a "composure" ethic. Both life and work rise above the vulgar everyday with a stern pride, above both its small-minded philistinism and its equally small-minded anarchist bohemianism. But it takes only a little conflict, provoked by scarcely anything tangible, and a dream within this conflict, for the "composure" to break hopelessly, irresistibly down, as if it had never been the product of a sincere, self-denying, hard-won life. "That night he had a fearful dream—if dream be the right word for a mental and physical experience which did indeed befall him in deep sleep, a thing quite apart and real to his senses, yet without seeing himself as present in it. Rather its theatre seemed to be his own soul, and the events burst in from outside, violently overcoming the proud resistance of his spirit; passed through him and left him, left the whole cultural structure of a lifetime trampled on, ravaged and destroyed."

This self-judgment forms the balance-sheet of Mann's pre-war work. One should not be led by the happy, comedy ending of *Royal Highness* to underestimate this deeply pessimistic irony. The fate of the hero here is in any case bathed in an atmosphere of fairytale improbability and quite pronouncedly presented as an unparadigmatic exception. On the other hand this second novel is as much a postscript to *Buddenbrooks* as a prologue to *Death in Venice*. In Prince Albrecht the formalism of "composure" dissolves into the self-awareness of its emptiness and triviality. He compares himself and his royal "composure" with the behaviour of a halfwit who thinks he is signalling departing trains to depart: "But 'the Hatter' deludes himself into thinking that his waving sends the train off. That's like me. I wave, and the train starts. But it would start without me, and my waving makes no difference, it's merely silly show. I'm sick of it. . . ." And Dr. Unterbein, tutor to the main character, an enthusiastic advocate of "composure" and the excellent qualities which should spring from it, collapses like Aschenbach—as the result of a tiny unimportant happening. "The quarrelsome and uncongenial man . . . who had haughtily resisted familiarity, and had ordered his life cold-bloodedly with a view to results alone . . . there he lay now: the first hitch, the first obstacle in the field of accomplishment, had brought him to a miserable end."

One should not take this just as a secondary or indeed peripheral question of bourgeois culture in pre–First World War Germany. It touches the very centre: the ethic of "composure" is most intimately connected with the spiritual lives of the finest figures, the most sincere intellectuals in the cultural world of Wilhelmine (imperialistically Prussianized) Germany. For intellectuals — notably for those who were not out to seek their fortunes in the Hagenström fashion — the choice between Christian and Thomas Buddenbrook, between emotional anarchy and "composure," was extremely typical. (Let me note in passing that some of the leading sociologists amongst Mann's contemporaries did their best to Buddenbrookize and Aschenbachize the Hagenström path in a moral and socio-cultural manner. This applies especially to Rathenau, Max Weber and Troeltsch.) The fact that a philosophy of "composure" led logically to Prussianism emerges very clearly from Mann's own development. It was no accident that the writer-hero of *Death in Venice* had earned fame by writing an epic on Frederick the Great; he was foreshadowing his creator's work in the First World War. But Mann the artist occupies a peculiar and paradoxical position here. On the one hand he showed that the way out of the Christian–Thomas Buddenbrook dilemma led to accepting Germany's Prussianization; yet artistically he subjected the whole ethic of "composure" to a withering critique, exposing its worthlessness and unreality.

In this he was continuing the work of Fontane's old age. Fontane, too, even more positively than the maturing Mann, admired and praised Prussian behaviour codes, Prussian military heroes, the Prussian "conquest" of the wretchedness of bourgeois life. But artistically, in *Schach von Wuthenow, Irrungen Wirrungen* and *Effi Briest*, the same Fontane castigates this type without mercy. Yet more than personal sympathies bound Fontane to him. In life, beset by all manner of doubt, he often saw in him a moral way out of the inhuman human predicaments of his time. Fontane and Mann were the first and only German writers to unmask the inner weakness of the Prussian behaviour ethic (in which connection I would draw attention to that little grotesque *The Railway Accident*).

III

Such was Mann's deep ideological predicament as he, reflecting the development of his country, entered the First World War. His situation, looking back on it from the vantage-point of today, was paradoxical to an extreme. The outbreak of this national crisis found both Mann's artistic critique of the Prussian ethic as well as his personal and political attachment to it at their height. And for the historian looking back with prophetic hindsight it is extremely surprising to see how little Mann understood the real achievements of his development and how passionately he drew the wrong conclusions from his work.

But platonic wonder at such a contradiction in a thinking man must give place to a problem, to a task of understanding. This is not, of course, to defend Mann's war writings. If, as still happens in England and America, later works like *The Magic Mountain* are interpreted in the light of the *Reflections of an Unpolitical Man*, the result will inevitably be a reactionary distortion. The problem is rather to realize that Mann's political aberration in the First World War was no accidental stage in his "search for bourgeois man," but a necessary phase in the disastrous development of German ideology as a whole.

Up to now we have examined the problems in Mann's work as they were actually portrayed. What, however, was their social basis? (Not that Mann was aware of this at the time.) Some ten years after the First World War Mann excellently described the attitude of most of the best German intellectuals towards the political and social condition of their country. He was writing of Richard Wagner: "His participation in the '48 cost him twelve years of torment and exile; later, repenting of his 'abandoned' optimism, in face of the *fait accompli* of Bismarck's empire, he minimized his share in it as best he could with the realization of his dream. He went the way of the German bourgeoisie: from the revolution to disillusionment, to pessimism and a resigned, power-protected inwardness."

This attitude of "power-protected inwardness" has a long history behind it, with deep roots in the poverty of Germany's political development. I must briefly touch on it here since it throws a special light, not only on the path of Mann himself, but also on his relationship to the German middle class.

To summarize: apart from exceptional figures like Lessing, the whole of German classical literature and philosophy operated in an atmosphere of "power-protected inwardness." True, German writers and thinkers found this power — the semi-feudal absolutism of the petty principalities — deeply problematic and often downright alien. But when Napoleon's wars of conquest thrust a real power onto the scene which threatened political and social reform, the best Germans fiercely divided. Goethe and Hegel opted for Napoleon and wished to see the whole of Germany turned into a Confederation of the Rhine. The *Phenomenology of Mind*, completed at the time of the Battle of Jena, makes the French Revolution and the new bourgeois society it had created the climax of modern history and allots to the Germans the task of constructing an ideology appropriate to the new conditions — i.e., "power-protected inwardness" plus the guarantee of those political and social reforms which Napoleon, the "great constitutional lawyer," as Hegel later called him, was to introduce, against the wishes of the princes of the Rhine Confederation.

There is no need to waste time today pointing out the Utopianism of this conception. Goethe's views were very similar. The idea that Napoleonic France could permanently stabilize its hegemony over Europe without awakening a desire for freedom among the peoples whom it had purged of their feudal dross was pure Utopianism. The very purging would arouse their national awareness. It was equally Utopian to imagine that Germany could assume ideological leadership of this new world without even trying to become politically independent.

However, it was no more unrealistic than the dreams of the honest Prussian reformers who for their part hoped to implement the achievements of the French Revolution (at least partially) simply by liberating Prussia from Napoleon's yoke and leaving Germany itself undisturbed. They imagined they could abolish the social foundations and political consequences of Prussian feudal absolutism without getting rid of the Junkers and the Hohenzollerns. And the "power-protected inwardness" of Romanticism which sprang from Napoleon's defeat showed only too clearly what a wretched thing this broken Utopia had been. Here then Utopia was ranged against Utopia, mirroring the inability of Germany's ideologists to be anything more than spectators (or pretty ineffective actors) in the drama of their country's destiny. This "artistic period"[2] continued up to the 1830 July Revolution in France. A more realistic course of development set in from this date but was cut short by the tragedy of 1848 and then the tragi-comedy of 1870. In 1848 the Germans really did have the choice of freeing themselves democratically or of retaining their political poverty. In 1870 the intellectuals capitulated once more to the power of the Prussianized German Reich, inevitably a reactionary creation.

Thus the German intellectuals, as Mann rightly wrote of Wagner, continued to live in a state of "power-protected inwardness." But history never repeats itself; similarities are more often formal than real. Hence we must distinguish between the "power-protected inwardness" of Goethe under Napoleon's Confederation of the Rhine and of Thomas Mann during Wilhelmine imperialism. In all essential respects Goethe's outlook was progressive; but it was Mann's fate to be born into the age of decadence, with its peculiar ambience in which one could transcend the decadence only by imaginatively realizing its extreme moral consequences. Further, Goethe's attitude to Napoleon's power involved no obligation to defend reactionary tendencies, no objective conflict of loyalties. But the outbreak of the First World War turned the situation of Mann and the German middle class inside out: "inwardness" had now to become the ideological shield of "power," in other words reactionary Prussian-German imperialism.

Hence, Mann's paradoxical and near-tragic situation in the First World War. But as an artist he could not cease looking for bourgeois man. He wished to seize the predicament of the German bourgeois at its core, to listen for the contradictions between being and consciousness and chart their future course. This alone, to quote Schiller on Goethe, was "a great and truly heroic idea"; and even the greatest of men need not feel ashamed at having made mistakes in such a venture, especially as in this case they were not subjective and personal, but arose out of Mann's deep involvement with Germany which included the many centuries of political poverty.

Thomas Mann was, therefore, quite right, a few years later, to describe his wartime book in this way:

> It was bent on being a monument; if I mistake not it has become one. It was a rear-guard action, in the grand style—the latest and last of German middle class romanticism; fought in the full consciousness that it was a lost cause and thus not without greatness of soul; fought indeed, with insight into the mental unhealthiness and viciousness of all sympathy with the *fey;* yet also, it is true, with aesthetic, too aesthetic contempt of health and virtue, which were felt—and scorned—as the sum and essence of that before which one retreated fighting: politics, democracy.

The passage is an accurate autobiographical commentary. To place it correctly in the wider framework of German history, it must, however, be studied as it was meant to be—from the standpoint of Mann's further development. It was *only* because his rearguard action was followed by an advance towards democracy that it was "not without greatness of soul." If someone today were desperately to defend a hopelessly (and rightly) lost cause, to cling to a doomed past without believing in its right to prevail, then he would not only condemn himself to a comic, unintentional quixotry, an empty stance of "composure." His sad chivalry would turn into nihilist hypocrisy; his retreat be but a preliminary to the assault of a revived reactionary barbarism, a wanton attempt to burn down the new and restore the buried past to a brief vampire-like existence upon a Golgotha of civilization. Mann's noble farewell to the more than problematic past of his country was, in contrast to such tendencies, a real farewell. It opened up a new path, the path to democracy.

IV

Mann's conversion to democracy during the post-war years was the outcome of a great national crisis. Yet though it came as a turning-point, a decisive change in his personal development, it was by no means unprepared, surprising as this may seem to the superficial observer. It emerged from the inner dialectic of the path he had been following. He now takes a new attitude to his sought-for bourgeois. The difference between the pre-war and wartime Thomas Mann and the best of his fellow-Germans is "simply" that he experienced more deeply and followed through more radically the problems which affected them all. Nevertheless, his intellectual and spiritual origins are the same, which is why even the most outlandish of his works has a familiar quality which his fellow-Germans could recognize. When Mann placed his early work by citing the names of Platen, Storm and Nietzsche, he characterized this peculiar situation in a very precise manner. In the rigour of its content and form a solitary *oeuvre*, his work rose from the very midst of the plain it dominated; it incorporated heights and lowlands.

This relationship altered radically with Mann's ideological and political change of heart after the war. The German bourgeois now pursues quite a different path from the questing writer. The ideological baggage salvaged by the Germans from the collapse of their first attempt at world conquest was the "front-line experience" and the hope that they might try once again, with improved methods, to bring off what had eluded them. One method was a more thorough clearing-out of democracy. Thomas Mann, however, not only broke completely and wholeheartedly with German imperialism; he not only grasped the importance of democracy for the rebirth of a truly German culture (during the War he still spurned democracy as un-German). He also saw the connection between ideology and sensibility of decadence and the previous development of Germany. From now on he regards the struggle for democracy as a struggle against decadence. This view takes his war book forward in a fruitfully paradoxical way. In the latter he had bundled together decadence, a sympathy for disease and decay, night and death with his defense of the German war-effort. But this defence became so deeply enmeshed in the bewildering tangle of pros and cons, that at the end of his frenzied attempt to justify German decadence he saw himself convinced of the sole rightness of the contrary principle. The events of 1918 assisted him.

It is education which now moves into the forefront of Mann's writing. But we must ask again whether this did not mean the end of his *faculté maîtresse*, his peculiar genius: the anti-Utopian nature of his talent? Yes and no. And rather more no than yes. For the mature Thomas Mann is an educator *sui generis*. And what makes him this is not only the ironic reservations with which he tells a story or the good-humoured balance he maintains in composition. These give expression to a deeper connection, a more important meaning. He is not the kind of educator who wants to impart to his pupils a lesson from the outside, however well thought-out, however right. He is an educator in the Platonic sense of anamnesis: the pupil himself should discover the new idea within him, and bring it to life.

As the educator of his people, Mann now looks for his bourgeois in a more exploratory way. His search has found a concrete content. He seeks the spirit of democracy in the mind of the German bourgeois, tracking down the newest hints and signs in order to awaken and foster them in fictional form. He tries to implant them not as an alien idea, but as something which the reader discovers in himself, something sought for and at last found.

This is more or less the reason why Mann stood so alone in the Weimar Republic. Just as the reforms of Stein and Scharnhorst were inspired not by a popular movement in Prussia but by Prussia's defeat at the Battle of Jena, so German democracy after 1918 was not something

that had been striven and fought for, but the—unwelcome as it appeared—gift of an adverse destiny. Thus the newborn democracy, which
never really took root, had bitter enemies, opportunistic time-servers, and
few real friends and supporters. And these mostly accepted it as an
offering from Heaven, making not the slightest attempt to link it up with
German history which they had in any case revised. In a word, Thomas
Mann's isolated position during the Weimar democracy was the result of
his search for such connections. As an educator he was looking for a sense
of democracy sprung from a German ethos. This is why he was the only
bourgeois writer of this period for whom democracy became a matter of
Weltanschauung, and a problem of German *Weltanschauung* in particular.

Hence the struggle for German democracy is put into a wide
philosophical frame. It is the struggle of light and darkness, day and night,
health and sickness, life and death. And Thomas Mann, so intimately tied
to Germany's past, sees clearly as an artist that he was resuming an age-old
battle of German ideology. We need only go back to Goethe's attitude to
the Romantics: "Classical I call what is healthy, Romantic what is sick," he
said, rejecting Kleist as a "body with which Nature intended well but
which has been struck by an incurable disease." Now when in *The Magic
Mountain* the spokesman of the reactionary, Fascist, anti-democratic
Weltanschauung, the Jesuit Naphta, sets out his ideas, he does so almost in
the words of Novalis:

> On the contrary, Naphta hastened to say. Disease was very human
> indeed. For to be man was to be ailing. Man was essentially ailing, his
> state of unhealthiness was what made him man. There were those who
> wanted to make him "healthy," to make him "go back to nature," when
> the truth was, he had never been "natural" . . . the whole Rousseauian
> paraphernalia had as its goal nothing but the dehumanization, the
> animalization of man. . . . In man's spirit, then, resided his true
> nobility and his merit—in his state of disease, as it were, in a word, the
> more ailing he was, by so much was he the more man. The genius of
> disease was more human than the genius of health.

We see that a decisive change has occurred in Mann's outlook. Yet
however firmly he takes the side of democracy against the specifically
German decadence which sprang from a reactionary social backwardness;
and however impressive, well-modulated, deeply thought-out the literary
forms he finds for his new outlook, he fails as a thinker to realize that,
objectively, his new stage of development marks a break with the teachers
of youth, Schopenhauer and Nietzsche. He does, of course, see connections
of this kind. What he writes about Hamsun could not be bettered:

> My great colleague, Knut Hamsun, for example, in Norway, although
> an old man now, is an ardent Fascist. He makes propaganda for this
> party in his own country and has not been ashamed publicly to jeer at a

world-famous victim of German Fascism, the pacifist Ossietzky. This is, of course, not the behaviour of an old man who has stayed young in heart. It is the behaviour of a writer of the 1870 generation whose formative literary influences were Dostoyevsky and Nietzsche and who has not moved from the anti-liberal apostasy fashionable at the time. He does not understand what is really happening today and does not realize that he is compromising his talent irretrievably by his political – or I should say his human – behaviour.

But such insights did not stop Mann from wanting to preserve Nietzsche for the world of democratic ideas.

Yet in his creative work Mann was much more definite. The important novel *The Magic Mountain* is devoted to the ideological struggle between life and death, health and sickness, reaction and democracy. With his usual symbolic flair Mann sets these struggles in a Swiss luxury sanatorium. Here then sickness and health, their psychological and moral consequences are not abstract theorems, they are not "symbolic" in a narrow sense, but grow organically and directly out of the physical, mental and emotional lives of the people living there. Only someone who read the book superficially at the time of its publication could have missed the political and philosophical problems which underlay the rich and fascinating picture of physical illness. A closer look shows that it is just such a *milieu* which can bring out all the dialectical aspects of the problem. But the seclusion of life in the sanatorium has yet a more important artistic function. Mann, like most really good novelists, worries little about details of characterization. He rarely "invents" them. But he had an infallible instinct for the right kind of story and surroundings, that which would most clearly bring out his particular problem, which would give most scope for pathos and irony. There is always a delightful mingling in his work of a phantastic or semi-phantastic whole and very down-to-earth detail. Thomas Mann was following on here from Chamisso (*Peter Schlemihl*), E. T. A. Hoffmann and Gottfried Keller, but in an altogether original way. Neither in technique nor in use of detail did he resemble them. "We describe the everyday," he once said, "but the everyday becomes strange if it is cultivated on strange foundations." The small princely court of *Royal Highness* produced just such a semi-phantastic background to the problem of "composure." The sanatorium in *The Magic Mountain* does the same.

The characters are "on holiday," removed from everyday cares and the struggle for existence. The whole mental, emotional, moral world which they bring with them has a chance to express itself more freely, uninhibitedly, more concentratedly, to open out to the ultimate questions of life. What emerges is a deeply realistic portrayal of the contemporary bourgeois which has its tragi-comic distortions and its moments of phantasy. The inner emptiness, the moral instability knows no bounds and often explodes in the most grotesque forms. On the other hand, the better exemplars become aware of a meaning to life of which they have had no time to think in the everyday world of capitalism.

These are the conditions for the "educational novel" which deals with an average pre-war German, Hans Castorp. Its main intellectual theme is the symbolical duel between the representatives of light and darkness, the Italian humanist democrat Settembrini and the Jesuit-educated Jew, Naphta, spokesman of a Catholicising, pre-Fascist ideology. These two wage war over the soul of an average German bourgeois.

It is alas impossible in the small compass of these remarks to give any real indication of the richness of these duels, which are intellectual, human, emotional, political, moral and philosophical. We must limit ourselves to the fact that they end in a draw. Hans Castorp, exhausted by his efforts to reach clarity in his political and philosophical thinking, sinks into the mean, mindless, repellent everyday life of the Magic Mountain. For the "holiday" from material cares has two sides. It may raise one intellectually, but it may also push one down further into the morass of the instincts than would normally have been possible in everyday life "down below." People do not gain any new and better faculties in this rarified, half-phantastic milieu. But the faculties they do have acquire much greater definition. Objectively their inner potentialities are not increased. But we see them unartificially through a magnifying glass, in slow motion. It is true that in the end Castorp "saves" himself from complete submergence by joining the German army in August, 1914. But from the standpoint of German intelligentsia and bourgeoisie, of all those who stood at a crossroads, yet could come to no decision in their "power-protected inwardness," participation in the war, in word or deed, was, as Ernst Bloch once wittily put it, just "one more long holiday."

Thomas Mann's account, then, of the effort of his own new outlook on the mind of the German bourgeois is as sceptical, and justifiably so, as his critique of the anti-democratic ideology is firm. Both themes are developed in the Novelle Mario and the Magician. In between, in Disorder and Early Sorrow, Mann gives a nuanced ironical picture of the melancholy preoccupation with death of a typical bourgeois of the pre-war period, who feels intellectually, emotionally and morally forsaken in the Weimar republic, although he is vaguely aware that his attitude is deeply problematic. "He knows," Mann wrote of Cornelius, "that professors of history do not like history for what it is but for what it has been. They hate upheavals in the present because they feel them to be lawless, incoherent and impudent—in a word 'unhistorical.' Their heart belongs with the coherent, pious and historical past. . . . What has passed is eternal, that is, it is dead. And death is the source of all piety and all traditional values."

The later Novelle is Mario, written in the Weimar years. The story takes place in Italy, which is no accident since what we are concerned with here is the mass tactics of fascism, the use of suggestion and hypnosis. The assault on the intellect and the will—this is what the philosophy of militant reaction comes to once it leaves the study and the literary cafés for the streets, when the Schopenhauers and Nietzches are succeeded by the Hitlers and Rosenbergs. Thomas Mann gives this new phase once more a tangible presence. Again he presents a subtle spectrum of all the different kinds of helplessness with which the German bourgeois faces the hypnotic power of fascism. And again we must content ourselves with one significant example.

A "gentleman from Rome" refuses to submit to the magician's hypnotic command to dance, only to succumb after a short but tough resistance. Thomas Mann adds a penetrating account of this defeat: "If I understand what was going on, it was the negative character of the young man's fighting position which was his undoing. It is likely that *not* willing is not a practical state of mind; *not* to want to do something may be in the long run a mental content impossible to subsist on. Between not willing a certain thing and not willing at all, in other words yielding to another person's will, there may lie too small a space for the idea of freedom to squeeze into." The defencelessness of those German bourgeois who did not want Hitler but who obeyed him for over a decade without demur has never been better described. But what is the reason for this defencelessness?

V

On one occasion Hans Castorp says of Settembrini, the democrat, "You are a windbag and a hand-organ man to be sure. But you mean well, you mean much better, and more to my mind than that knife-edged little Jesuit and terrorist, apologist of the Inquisition and the knout, with his round eye-glasses—though he is nearly always right when you and he come to grips over my paltry soul, like God and the Devil in the medieval legends. . . ." Why can Naphta conquer Settembrini in argument? The question receives a clear answer in the novel. At one point, when Castorp is ill, he has a conversation with his tutor in democracy about the capitalist world "down below." Castorp sums up his own gloomy moral experience in these words:

> One must be rich down there . . . if you aren't rich, or if you leave off being, then woe be unto you . . . it often struck me that it was pretty strong, as I can see now, though I am a native of the place and for myself have never had to suffer from it. . . . What were the words you used—phlegmatic and energetic. That's very good. But what does it mean? It means hard, cold. And what do hard and cold mean? They mean cruel. It is a cruel atmosphere down there, cruel and ruthless. When you lie here and look at it, from a distance, it makes you shudder.

But Settembrini calls all this sentimentality best left to the "drones." He is a harbinger of progress *sans phrase*. He makes no self-criticism, has neither doubts nor reservations, which is why—although he has no personal stake in it—he is such an uncritical standard-bearer of the capitalist system. And that is why he has no really effective intellectual weapons with which to fight Naphta's anti-capitalist demagogy. This brings out perfectly the basic weakness of the average modern bourgeois democratic attitude when faced with a reactionary anti-capitalist demagogy. At the same time it reveals Castorp's own indecision and unwillingness to act, the same pure negativity that we saw in the unavailing resistance of the "gentleman from Rome."

Thomas Mann also shows us in his hero the inner social mechanism of the modern German bourgeois psyche. He says of Hans Castorp:

> A man lives not only his personal life, as an individual, but also, consciously or unconsciously, the life of his epoch and his contemporaries. He may regard the general, impersonal foundations of his existence as definitely settled and taken for granted, and be as far from assuming a critical attitude toward them as our good Hans Castorp really was; yet it is quite conceivable that he may none the less be vaguely conscious of the deficiencies of his epoch and find them prejudicial to his own moral well-being. All sorts of personal aims, ends, hopes, prospects, hover before the eyes of the individual, and out of these he derives the impulse to ambition and achievement. How, if the life about him, if his own time seem, however outwardly stimulating, to be at bottom empty of such food for his aspiration; if he privately recognize it to be hopeless, viewless, helpless, opposing only a hollow silence to all the questions man puts, consciously or unconsciously, yet somehow puts, as to the final, absolute, and abstract meaning in all his efforts and activities; then, in such a case, a certain laming of the personality is bound to occur, the more inevitably the more upright the character in question; a sort of palsy, as it were, which may even extend from his spiritual and moral over into his physical and organic part. In an age that affords no satisfying answer to the eternal question of "Why?" "To what end?" a man who is capable of achievement over and above the average and expected modicum must be equipped either with a moral remoteness and single-mindedness which is rare indeed and of heroic mould, or else with an exceptionally robust vitality. Hans Castorp had neither the one nor the other of these; and thus he must be considered mediocre, though in an entirely honourable sense.

In the novel—the quotation occurs near the beginning and traces the previous development of the engineer, who has just graduated—this mediocrity born of the lack of worthwhile aims may indeed be most honourable, even if with a little irony. But when the Castorp type is confronted by the life-and-death questions of his country, he must be judged differently, just as his situation is different. His honourable mediocrity, his apathy, indecision, his powerlessness before Naphta's demagogy, despite his sympathy with Settembrini, are all transformed into historical guilt. The "gentleman from Rome" was also honourable in his desire to "fight for the dignity of the human race," but this did not save him. He joined in with the rest of the bacchantes who had yielded up their wills to the fascist hypnosis. And this wild dance was within an ace of becoming the death dance of civilization.

If, therefore, Thomas Mann had really found his German bourgeois in Professor Cornelius, Hans Castorp or the "gentleman from Rome"; or, rather, if his search had stopped with his masterly portrait of the German bourgeois who tolerated Hitlerism and even took part in its unscrupulous wars and plundering expeditions "as a good honest soldier,"[3] then his works would have ended on a note of pessimism, deeper than that of any other German writer.

It is, therefore, no accident that during the fearful years of Hitler's rule, while the German people degenerated under fascism, Mann wrote his one great historical work, *Lotte in Weimar* (1939). In the giant figure of Goethe he brought together all the best forces in the German bourgeoisie. Goethe is the Gulliver of Lilliputian Weimar, always in doubt but always rescuing himself and perfecting his intellectual, artistic and moral development. For decades Goethe had been the philistine companion of writers and scholars who used him for their fashionable obscurantism. Mann now cleansed his portrait of reactionary filth. While the German bourgeoisie was degrading itself to the utmost, wading in the bloodstained swamp of a drunken barbarism, here was the image of its highest potentialities, of its, doubtless, problematic but also truthful and forward-pointing humanism.

It is only with the deepest reverence and love that one can treat this book. It saved Germany's honour in the hour of its most dreadful degradation. But this novel of Goethe is more than a monumental song of consolation for a drunken people hurling itself nihilistically into the abyss of fascism. It returns to the past in order to give promise for the future. By re-creating the best that German bourgeois culture had achieved, Mann seeks to awaken its buried, aberrant and brutalized potentialities. Mann's appeal rang with a primal moral optimism; what was possible once could always be realized again.

This is not a forced interpretation. At the end of his important essay *Goethe as Representative of the Bourgeois Age* Mann says:

> The burgher is lost, and loses track with the new or coming world, if he cannot bring himself to part from the life-destroying, easy-going ideologies that still condition him, and address himself stoutly to the future. The new, the social world, the organized, planned and unified world in which humanity will be freed from such human unnecessary burdens, injurious to self-respect and common sense; this world will come, and it will be the world of that great practical sense to which effective minds, all those opposed to a decadent and provincial soulfulness, must today subscribe. It will come, for an outward and rational order of things, adequate to the stage which human intelligence has now reached, must be created, or — in the worst case — be established by violent revolution,

in order that the things of the soul may once more be justified. The great
sons of the bourgeoisie, who grew out of that stage into the intellectual
and super-bourgeois, are witnesses that boundless possibilities lie in the
bourgeois stage, possibilities of unlimited self-release and self-conquest.
The times challenge the middle class to remind itself of its native
potentialities and to become equal to them both mentally and morally.
The right to power is dependent upon the historic task to which one feels
and may feel oneself called. If we deny it or are not adequate to it, we
shall disappear; we shall simply yield the stage in favour of a human
type free from the assumptions, the commitments and the outworn
prejudice which — one sometimes fears — may prevent the bourgeoisie of
Europe from being adequate to the task of guiding state and economy
into a new world.

The figure of Goethe then points out a new path for the German
bourgeoisie, a path into the future. Even today Thomas Mann is still
seeking the German bourgeois who has the will and the ability to take this
path boldly. But Goethe is too distant a spiritual microcosm, separated
from us by far too many crises, and on the other hand (especially in
Mann's realization of him) far too remote a future ideal for the Professor
Corneliuses or Hans Castorps of today to follow as their necessary next
step forward, the step which will take the German bourgeois out of his
abyss of humiliation, and relieve him of his deservedly tormented conscience and self-inflicted despair. There is an important connection
missing here, although Mann is such a great artist of connections. It is
missing because it is absent from the life of the German bourgeois, too.
And Mann's artistic truthfulness never allows him to depict something
which is not present in German bourgeois reality.

Typically, the German languge, otherwise so rich, has not a word to
express what we are speaking of now. The French speak of "citoyen" as
against "bourgeois," the Russians of "grazhdanin." There is no word for it
because German history has never produced the thing itself. Even in
Mann's fine essay on Platen, the militant *citoyen* makes only a sporadic
and peripheral appearance. In comparing Goethe and Schiller Mann says
of Schiller that he "manifests the French side of his nature." Yet to say this
of Schiller is another example of Mann's uncompromising veracity and his
firm roots in the German national character. For probably no one had ever
shown such genuine sympathy with, or described so delicately, Schiller's
heroic and self-consuming struggle for his art as Mann in his *Novelle A
Weary Hour.* If, then, there is a blank here its cause is to be sought not in
the limitations of Mann himself, but in the world whose mirror he was
fated to be. Germany had suffered disastrously for it in the past and no
doubt will do so again in the future, should it remain.

It would be quite unjust to suggest that Thomas Mann did not see this
problem. Indeed, the whole point of his tireless and unavailing search was
that (though for a long time unconsciously) he was really seeking a

German citoyen, the German word, concept and essence of the *citoyen* who was also the true bourgeois. Hence his Faustian impatience with his every conclusion.

Settembrini is powerless before Naphta's social demagogy because he is only the epigone of a real *citoyen*. Robespierre and St. Just, Büchner and Heine never connected a genuinely free, fully consistent bourgeois democracy with the defence of the capitalist upper stratum and its often reactionary and antinational, selfish interests. Nor does Thomas Mann. His work, which began by condemning the Hagenströms, broadened out into Castorp's unease at the cruelty and inhumanity of life under capitalism. Both as creator and as critic, Mann saw to the heart of Settembrini's intellectual and political limitations. Indeed, as we have seen, he goes much further. He prescribed socialism as the future task of the bourgeois for whom he has been looking. If he has been unable, therefore, to create a *citoyen* spirit in his work which could stand against the fascist reaction, the fault was not his but lay in the post-1848 development of the German middle class. It is for this reason that, ever since his conversion to democracy, Thomas Mann has sought to link arms with the workers. This was not merely a tactical coalition; it was an alliance for the regeneration of German life and culture. This is what he writes: "What would be needed, what would after all be typically German, would be an alliance, a compact between the conservative culture-idea and revolutionary social thought: to put it pointedly, as I have elsewhere done once before, an understanding between Greece and Moscow. It would be well with Germany, I repeat. She would have found herself, as soon as Karl Marx shall have read Friedrich Hölderlin. Such a contact, moreover, is about to be established. But I must add that if it is onesided it will bear no fruit."

This is indeed an impressive cultural programme for the German bourgeois. We do not consider it an accident that Hölderlin is chosen to represent German literature, for the point would be lost if one substituted the name of any other German poet, say Mörike, even though, in introducing his idea Mann links Hölderlin and Greece with the notion of a conservative culture. He overlooked the fact that the citizen of the Greek polis was the archetype of the *citoyen* and that Hölderlin was Germany's greatest *citoyen*-poet. Neither was remotely connected with any kind of German "conservative culture-idea." Nor is it important to know whether or not the real Marx in fact read Hölderlin (as far as I know he did). The important thing is how far the heroic, though sparse, traditions of real democracy in Germany were still alive and above all could come to life again in the German working class. Since Marx and Engels they had been buried under reactionary falsification. One mark of the poverty of German history common to both bourgeoisie and working class is the fact that Marx and Engels have so far not entered into the national cultural heritage as Lenin and Stalin have in Russia. The further development, the future, the rebirth of Germany depends to a great extent on how far

German workers and bourgeois will succeed in mobilizing the reserves of freedom and progress in their history for their future national life. How far will this be able to replace the tradition which runs Goethe— Schopenhauer—Wagner—Nietzsche (which Mann himself used to accept and the last three members of which the Fascists have rightly claimed as their own) with a Lessing—Goethe—Hölderlin—Büchner—Heine—Marx tradition? Mann's portrait of Goethe gives a promising start to such a change.

And that is no accident. I have been able to say precious little about the specifically artistic sides of Mann's work. His rank I have taken for granted and have simply picked out one or two important incidents to illustrate certain critical stages in Germany's development. Let me take just one more such example. Thomas Mann's intimate relationship with all that is best in German literature should have emerged even from my very brief remarks. Yet even in the pure literary sense his role goes beyond this. It is Mann who first made Russian literature an essential part of German culture in the same way as Goethe gave us Shakespeare. In both cases it was a more than literary annexation, as is suggested by Thomas Mann in the important conversation on literature and life in *Tonio Kröger*. He points out that in Russia's "holy literature" there is none of the hostile opposition between art and life which filled his own early work. Why not? The answer is clear. It is because Russian literature really has been the conscience of the Russian people and the voice of the *grazhdanin* spirit, from the Decembrist rising to the October revolution and from then on to the present day. The history of the great Russian realist literature from Pushkin to Gorki is interwoven—though never in a simple way—with the freedom struggles of the Russian people. And it is an instructive, though shameful, fact about Germany's ideological development that while its own classical philosophy ran to seed in its bourgeois homeland and turned to reaction, in Russia (and only in Russia) Hegel and Feuerbach found progressive thinkers to carry on their work.

Thomas Mann's aesthetic and ethical horizon took in both Goethe and Tolstoy. As a writer and a realist he has never been modern in the decadent sense. Hence he has been able to continue the best traditions of German literature. His form has never submitted to the disintegrating tendencies of decadence—rhetoric, declamation, decoration, brilliance, pseudo-scientific erudition, but has retained a genuine poetic totality.

Right through, from *Weltanschauung* to form, Mann's work is deeply progressive. His present achievement, and what we hope is to come, will contribute to the regeneration of the German spirit in a way which cannot be overestimated. Mann is still in search of his bourgeois today. For the German bourgeois has yet to be found. And he will not be found until he discovers within himself the *citoyen*, the *grazhdanin*. In this search Thomas Mann's role is crucial. His admirers are certain that his Faustian search for bourgeois man will never cease and that, like Faust, he will always give his answer to the devil of reaction:

> Should ever a bed of ease content me,
> Then let me perish instantly!
> If you by flattery can bemuse me
> Into a self-complacency,
> Or with the sweets of life delude me:
> Let that day be the last for me!

Notes

1. Wilhelm Raabe (1831–1910), a provincial German novelist.

2. *Kunstperiode:* "period of art" — Heine's term for the contemplative ethos of the Goethe period.

3. *als Soldat und brav:* "as a soldier and brave." The quotation is from Goethe's *Faust*, part one. The words belong to the dying Valentin, Gretchen's brother, who perishes at Faust's hand in a duel to defend his sister's honour. The quotation is used as a chapter heading in *The Magic Mountain* where it ironically applies to the death of Castorp's military cousin, Joachim, whom illness has prevented from dying for his country.

Aesthetic Excursus on Thomas Mann's *Akribie*

Elizabeth M. Wilkinson*

To offer aesthetic abstractions as a tribute to Thomas Mann really calls for neither apology nor explanation. Who more than he has made such abstractions the vehicle for symbolizing experience which is by no means peculiar to the artist, experience which is the fate of all civilised men? In this, of course, he was not alone. As Ernst Cassirer pointed out in an article in this journal some ten years ago,[1] ["it is part of the essence of artistic presentation that it does not derive its material solely from the reality of external events, but that the reality of art itself again and again becomes a theme and a problem for it"]. This holds even when art is not made the ostensible theme at all. And it holds in a surprisingly large number of cases. It is the topic under the surface in *Lycidas* and *In Memoriam*, in *Troilus and Cressida* and *Emilia Galotti* and the Marienbad *Elegie*. One could sometimes wonder whether poets are ever really writing about anything else at all but the making, effect, and function of the insubstantial realities they are driven to create.

As to my end of the affair, the abstractions of aesthetics have never

*From the *Germanic Review*, 31 (1956):225–35, a publication of the Helen Dwight Reid Educational Foundation. Reprinted by permission.

seemed to me remote from the intimacies of personal experience. From the time I first began learning them, they have had their effect, perceptible and imperceptible, on the business of everyday living and especially on the practice of relationships. Altogether I am suspicious of the postulated dichotomy between abstractions and concretions, between theory and practice. The bearing they have on each other is incredibly close and fascinatingly complex. How strikingly has recent work in physiology demonstrated the truth of Goethe's statement ["that we are theorizing even with each attentive glance into the world"]! How much of abstracting and interpreting goes to the performance of even the simplest act of visual perception! And if such unconscious theorizing lies at the base of what we like to call our physical seeing, how much do our consciously held theories affect our mental sight. A theory does not just give an account of a state of affairs already in existence. Even as it is made it effects an alteration in the state of affairs it purports to explain. And as it is held its affects behavior at every level. Often alarmingly, savagely — which is what Orwell tried to bring home to us by savage means for the sake of language and for the sake of ourselves. For the views we hold, whether about language or art or anything else, affect our use of them and affect us. Linguistics and aesthetics will have as much practical bearing on what becomes of all of us as ever physics or chemistry.

This is something Thomas Mann understood. None better. It is something he rendered in his work — none more poignantly. He would, I think, have realised that the following aesthetic disquisition is as much a felt expression of gratitude for many things — for his work, his encouragement, for the person he was — as any tribute of a more obviously personal kind.

Ever since the *Zauberberg* Thomas Mann has been exposing himself to attack left, right, and center. Not by experimentation with the form of the novel. His artistic devices are many, but by contrast with a Joyce or a Virginia Woolf he makes an almost deliberately old-fashioned impression, telling his tale in the broad, leisurely, epic manner, adopting either the familiar method of the omniscient author or, as in *Doktor Faustus*, the equally well-worn one of seeming to lend authenticity to past happenings by having his story retailed at second hand. But into this traditional epic framework he introduced a vast amount of startlingly up-to-date intellectual material on all manner of subjects ranging from disease to music, his two ancient preoccupations, and covering almost every aspect of our civilization, past and present: the most recent discoveries of archeology, mythology, and biology, the latest scientific theories about the nature of mind and matter. This is his real innovation: the piling up of technicalities with what seems like a veritable mania for exact detail, a passionately pedantic predilection for specialized knowledge. It is this *akribie*, to borrow a term from himself, which provokes the frontal attack. "He seems to be writing with an encyclopaedia at his elbow" is a typical comment from this quarter. To the right are those who take him to be asserting something about our culture and its origins and, since they disagree with what they take him to be asserting, would convict him either of inaccuracy in the particulars or of falsehood in the whole. To the left the attack looks more like support. For it comes from those who endorse what they take to be diagnosis or evaluation. Yet their very acclamation of the diagnostician, of the thinker, constitutes a menace to the novelist, to the poet. For no less than his attackers these supporters have forgotten that "the poet nothing affirmeth, and therefore never lieth."

In saying "they have forgotten" we imply that knowledge of what poetry is and what the poet does has bearing on our appraisal of particular poems and particular poets. And in implying this we go deliberately counter to the critics who say: "Let the aestheticians keep their hands off poetry!" Not because we think that the bearing of aesthetic principles on critical practice is a direct one: they constitute neither rules to be followed nor a measure to be applied. Nor do we imagine that even the best principles could ever take the place of long commerce with works of art themselves. Nothing but experience of many and varied particulars can give us, here or elsewhere, that prompt sureness of discrimination which we call "Fingerspitzengefühl." But we do hold that it is self-delusion to imagine that we ever perform our particular acts of criticism, or even of appreciation, out of experience alone. Experience in this sense, as Goethe was fond of pointing out, is anyway only the half of experience; the other half, implicitly subsumed, is "Idee." Those who most vigorously disavow theory and principles, who protest, with a curious mixture of pride and humility, that they wouldn't know how to begin to say what poetry is, with their very next breath will hazard an opinion which betrays deep-rooted, if unconscious, convictions, beliefs, not to say prejudices, on the subject. There is indeed no getting away from it: to our every act of interpretation, in this as in any other area of experience, we bring assumptions and expectations which affect what we see and determine how we judge. The more unconscious they are, the more we are their victim. The function of reflection is to bring them out into the open and examine them. The way aesthetic principles affect, or should affect, the criticism of any particular work is by ensuring that the assumptions we are making about it are valid and the expectations we bring to it appropriate. Obviously the process is not one of deliberate reflection each time. If properly assimilated good principles operate with a promptitude rivaling that of the confused unconscious assumptions in those who repudiate principles altogether.

Thomas Mann himself gave us a broad hint of the kind of aesthetic which might best help us to understand what he was up to with all his *akribie*. ["The learned speech,"] he wrote in a lecture on *Josef und seine Brüder*, "is part of the game here, it is, in an indirect way, a comment on style and a joke, a contribution to mock exactitude, very close to persiflage, at least to irony: for the application of science to that which is wholly unscientific and resembles a fairy tale is pure irony."][2] ["Mock-exactitude"]! So that's what it's meant to be! Not exactitude itself, but the mere appearance of exactitude. In taking this hint we are not just committing ourselves to a theory which he himself invented to justify his own *oeuvre*. The term *Schein* leads us straight back to the aesthetics of Weimar classicism. And Thomas Mann was perfectly well aware that it did. As he was well aware of its remoter ancestry too. For the aesthetic of Goethe and Schiller, great achievement though it was, was no invention of theirs. It was part of what we may call the perennial aesthetic; perennial because, however long forgotten or "conclusively" refuted, it has kept on cropping up with a persistence which is testimony to its truth.[3] It rests on the ancient conviction that the poet, like any other artist, is a maker, a feigner, and that what he makes is a fiction, an illusion.

It would of course be pleasant if we could dispense with technical terms and rest content with the sleek elegance of Sir Philip Sydney's language. But the development of human thought is inseparable from the invention of new terms. We might almost say that a history of terms, the analysis of old ones and the coining of new, would itself be a history of thought. "The poet nothing affirmeth" inevitably provoked, and still provokes, the question "What doth he then?" And the reply "He maketh, maketh a fiction" calls forth the further question "To what end?" The great achievement of Goethe and Schiller is that they were able to answer this, and related questions, without too frequent recourse to paradox. And they were able to do it partly by the replacement of the offending word *Täuschung*, with its unfortunate connotations of counterfeit and deception, by the technical term *Schein*; partly by their insistence on the use of three terms instead of two for the elucidation of the form-content problem: *Stoff, Gestalt, Gehalt*. In this way they were able to arrive at a truer understanding of the relation between seriousness and playfulness— *Ernst* and *Spiel* — in the making and appreciation of art. The terms themselves are not important. It is the concepts they denote that matter. And these themselves, of course, require, and have lately received,[4] a more rigorous analysis than Goethe and Schiller ever accorded, or could at that time have accorded, them. But I can think of no wholly satisfactory account of art and literature which has ignored or tried to dispense with any one of them.

The advantages of a clear distinction between *Stoff* and *Gehalt* are at once apparent when we consider the prevailing ambiguity of the word *content* in current critical writing or the frequency with which the ubiquitous preposition *about* has to be hedged in with inverted commas— a sure sign of confusion of some sort. It may be only logical or even purely terminological. But it may also betray a basic misconception about the nature of art. Those commonplaces of modern criticism—"form and content are one," "form is content"—have rightly provoked the censure of our language-conscious philosophers;[5] either a form *has* content or it is an empty form; it cannot itself *be* content. Yet such statements, logically offensive though they be, do reflect an attempt to do justice to a genuinely aesthetic experience: our awareness, when faced with a work of art, that the two are so inextricably united, that no amount of analysis could ever separate them. And if somebody says: "I like pictures to be about something," this, too, may be evidence of a genuine understanding of art. For he may mean: "I like pictures to be expressive of something and not a mere playing with techniques"—not a mere "tickle to the eye," as Rudolf Arnheim puts it in his recent book.[6] And that's clearly what Mr. Geoffrey Grigson did mean when he used *about* in his review of Arnheim's book:[7] "the something which every work of art must be 'about,' the something it expresses, not by likeness, necessarily. . . ." But out of context, or in another context, the same statement of preference is quite likely to provoke disapproving murmurings about "deplorable anecdotal taste." Or at least it was likely to until fairly recently. For in the present, fundamentally healthy, reaction against what Grigson calls "the form snobbery . . . which insists that all a well-bred picture needs is Form" there is often an alarming tendency to confuse the issue in the opposite direction: to welcome a picture just because it tells a story or praise a poem just because it has a paraphrasable significance. Now it doesn't matter at all if Sir Alfred Munnings' amusing picture in this year's Royal Academy Exhibition is ambiguous on the point. It is the prerogative of art to be ambiguous. Entitled "Does the Subject Matter?," it depicts a group of flummoxed viewers before an inchoate piece of sculpture. Are they lost in thought, consternation, or idolatry? We do not know. Is it an ironic comment on the anecdotal taste of the great British Public, or a dig at the aesthetics of pure form? Maybe both. But in the ordinary forms of discourse ambiguity does matter. And it matters, too, to the artist if we demand, or seem to demand, that his work be expressive by likeness only, that it must look familiar and say what it means! What we want to be able to say, with Goethe and Schiller, is that though the *Stoff* is always in some sense indifferent, since everything depends on the *Gestalt* the artist makes of it, the *Gehalt*, the content, the import, is always supremely important.[8]

The concept of *Stoff* presents no difficulty—though we tend to forget just how much it includes. Goethe once put it very neatly by saying that it is what the world offers the poet in plenty. It is what comes from outside of him, in the sense that it belongs to the world that is shared and communicable, the world that is common property. It includes not only objects, natural and man-made, events of the present or of history, people, known or invented (all that makes the latter "recognizable," as we say, is drawn from that shareable world)—but also whatever has been said or written, painted or composed, ideas, ideologies, beliefs and heresies, works of art, his own or anyone else's. And not least the materials of his medium; in the case of the poet, language; "den schlechtesten Stoff" ["the worst material"], Goethe called it, when it happened to be the German language!

Out of any or all of this the artist makes his image, his fiction, a thing of pure semblance, of "aufrichtigem Schein," ["honest illusion"], as Schiller put it. For any sense but the aesthetic sense it simply isn't there — except as so much material,[9] a daub of paint, a hunk of stone, a fury of sound signifying nothing. We cannot set foot in the street on the canvas or hear its sounds; we can only see it. We cannot argue with the actor who treats Desdemona as a whore — or we make fools of ourselves if we do. The making of this illusion is the artist's act of creation. He doesn't just rearrange his materials; he completely transforms them, brings into being something wholly and entirely new. And when they are thus transformed, they are part of the *Gestalt*, the form. All of them — not only the recognizable objects, persons and events, but the thoughts and ideas too. We do wrong if we call these *content* and reserve the word *form* for the palpable proportions and divisions, the rhymes, the metre, and the rhythms. These Goethe and Schiller called "external form," sometimes contrasting it with "inner form," but more often using the word *Gestalt* to connote the whole complex of all possible relations between all the elements.

When they spoke of the artist's "playfulness," they referred to his sovereign attitude towards his materials, his imperious, almost ruthless, deployment of them in the interests of creating his illusion. Whatever their importance to him in other contexts of his life, in this one context they are entirely subjected to considerations of form. Hence he may "play," and in this sense, does "play," with his most cherished convictions and solemn beliefs,[10] with his private griefs and sincerest passions. This is true whether he produces work redolent with irony, such as Thomas Mann's, or of sheer sublimity such as Milton's or Dante's, whether he writes comedy or whether he writes tragedy. And he plays with everything not because he suddenly becomes cynical, but because his seriousness on these creative occasions lies elsewhere: with "the something" (to fall back on Mr. Grigson's phrase) he is trying to symbolize by means of his illusion. That "something" is the content of his form. The paradox of art is that if we won't take art as "Spiel" we never get at its true "Ernst." The virtue of "Schein," of semblance, is that it liberates things from all other purposes — practical, intellectual, moral — and presents their sheer appearance to our contemplation. Thus released, they are free to take on the single, unambiguous, function of symbolizing. Quite ordinary things in the course of our life can and do take on symbolic significance. But most of the time they have other occupations. Just because it is sheer illusion, a work of art has no other occupation at all. If we insist on treating the elements of the form as if they were still mere *Stoff*, according them the kind of attention we should accord them if we met them in other contexts of life, we run the risk of missing the true content, which is implicit in the total form.

The concept of *Gehalt*, by contrast with that of *Stoff*, is difficult. I think we can agree that it is "unaussprechlich,"[11] unspeakable in any other terms than the work of art itself, without being committed to the view held by some aestheticians that art is expressive of "ultimate reality," or even, as Goethe and Schiller sometimes said, of "a higher reality." Elsewhere they gave more helpful indications. It springs from the artist's inner life, "aus der Fülle seines Innern."[12] And the cycle is completed when the form in which he embodies it *speaks to* (not, be it noted, *arouses*) feeling within us.[13] For *Gehalt*, as Goethe said in a famous poem, resides in the human breast. We should beware of taking feeling here in the modern sense of emotion. Accustomed to operating with the antithesis thought-feeling, we have lost the sense of what the eighteenth century and the Romantics meant by it. We should do well to follow Coleridge and replace that opposition by a quite different one: that between thought and Thoughts, feeling and Feelings, sensation and Sensations. Thoughts, feelings, sensations appear as separate entities only when they have been abstracted by means of language into concepts and propositions. But in the experience of our inner life we are aware of no such plurality. "The mind passes on, and in vain would it be to distinguish thought from thought till we had reduced it to words. . . ."[14] Inside of us thought is still part of feeling, felt along the blood, intimate with our flesh and with our pulse. It is part of the life which goes on in all of us uninterruptedly all the time, of which we are always aware, most of the time dimly, occasionally with intense clarity, but which we are never able to communicate, however hard we try. In vain do we struggle, by look and by gesture, and by all the resources of language we have at our command, to convey to those near and dear to us the felt particulars of this inner life. They elude all language save the language of art.

That this is what art expresses receives unexpected confirmation from a source far removed from either Weimar or from classicism. I shall not easily forget the stab of delighted recognition when I was reading along in Faulkner's story *The Bear* and came upon the bit where McCaslin is trying to get at what the boy had really felt when, after four years of hunting the almost legendary animal, he at last came face to face with it — and didn't shoot.

"But you didn't shoot when you had the gun," McCaslin said. "Why?"

But then McCaslin didn't wait for an answer. He went to the bookcase, took down the *Ode to a Grecian Urn* and read it to the boy, repeating the one stanza before he laid the book on the table:

> She cannot fade, though thou has not thy bliss,
> Forever wilt thou love, and she be fair.

"He's talking about a girl," the boy said.
"*He had to talk about something*," McCaslin said.

That, I said to myself, is what Goethe meant by *Gehalt*! Exactly the same awareness of the indifference of the material! Not that it is indifferent in the sense a reviewer recently implied when he said that the novel he was reviewing made it unnecessary ever to read *Bouvard et Pécuchet*. Just as each piece of our experience is never quite like any other, so no work of art is ever quite replaceable by any other. Yet it is evident that in all the variety of our experience similar structures of feeling recur, and this no doubt explains how a poem can be expressive of feeling occasioned by events very different from those the poet used to create his illusion. If this morphology of feeling was what De Quincy had in mind when he said that we shall never have soundly based criticism until we have a good psychology, he was undoubtedly right.

Literature, it is true, presents peculiar difficulties, because the literary artist uses as his medium the ordinary forms of discourse. He seems to be making assertions, often in the first person. But they are not really assertions, for they cannot be verified by reference either to fact or to logic. And the "I" he employs is not really himself, not even in lyric poetry. It is, like every other part of his make-believe discourse, an element of his fiction, of his illusion. Hence it will not do to speak, as Mr. Sell did in this Journal some years ago, of Thomas Mann's "tendency to philosophize *while* entertaining."[15] Either the philosophizing in the novels is *part* of the entertainment or it is wholly and entirely redundant. And it is not *he* who is philosophizing there in the sense that it is he who is philosophizing in his essays and speeches, even if the ideas expressed are identical. When we meet these ideas in their extra-fictional contexts, we may legitimately endorse or refute them. But the organs with which to approach them when they appear in his novels are neither agreement nor disagreement, neither belief nor unbelief. The only criterion of their value there is how they function in the fictional world.

And it will not do either to say, as Mr. Kenneth Wilson did, that the literal meaning of *Tonio Kröger* is stated in the conversation with Lisaweta.[16] If the meaning could be stated literally, there would be no point in creating the story. The meaning of the story, its content, inheres in the total form, not in any one part of it, and is as inexpressible in any other terms as the content of a cathedral or a sonata. It is no more to be equated with what Tonio says to Lisaweta than the meaning of the *Zauberberg* is to be found in Hans Castorp's soliloquy in the snow. All these conversation pieces are just as much part of the semblance as the characters and events, the landscapes and the emotions. And they are tied to these by a thousand strings. Mr. Wilson says that the scene with Lisaweta, unlike the other scenes in the story, is devoid of reference to the "dance." And indeed it is. But do not the ideas here lead a veritable dance? Do not their intricate measures symbolize the complexity of our feeling about the profoundly questionable, highly ambiguous thing we call art?

What Thomas Mann is doing with all his *akribie* is at bottom no different from what every artist is trying to do. Let us put it in the recent words of a writer who uses very different kind of material. In one of those extended stage directions of *Cat on a Hot Tin Roof*, which are as explanatory of his own intentions as of those of his characters, Tennessee Williams writes: "The bird that I hope to catch in the net of this play is not the solution of one man's psychological problem. I am trying to catch the true quality of experience in a group of people, that cloudy, flickering, evanescent—fiercely charged!—interplay of live human beings in the thundercloud of a common crisis." What Thomas Mann is trying to do is just that: "to catch the true quality of experience." No more, no less. Not indeed in a group of people, but in a whole cultural epoch. No more than Williams is he, in his novels, offering solutions or diagnoses, disapproval or appraisal. These things can be done far more efficiently by sociologists and psychologists, historians and philosophers of culture. What he is after is something that eludes even the most adequate account they can offer, something every bit as "cloudy, flickering, evanescent—fiercely charged!" as the interplay of feeling in personal relationships. It is the *felt life* of our culture. And what he hopes to do by making a symbol of it, and thus presenting it for our envisagement, is to give us insight into our feeling of it.

That is what all the intellectual material in his novels is there for—the interminable arguments between Naphta and Settembrini, Krokowski's lectures on psychoanalysis, the disquisitions on theology by Messrs. Kumpf and Schleppfuß, the questionable discourses on philosophy by Nonnenmacher or any other of those symbolically named personages, to say nothing of the narrator's own excursions on musicology and demonology, on the nature of myth and of time. It is not there for its own sake, to shew off Mann's learning, or because he is trying to compete with specialists in those fields. It is there to give the illusion of the European culture of which, for good or ill, we are all heirs. And if it involves the inclusion of a good deal of abstractions, technicalities, specialized knowledge, has not life today become very much an affair of abstractions, technicalities and specialized knowledge? To demand that literature, in order to be about life, should confine itself to the portrayal of persons and events and the feelings connected with these, is to make a very drastic abstraction indeed from the real life of the world we live in today.

What Mann is doing in a bulky tome such as *Faustus* is not in principle very different from what he was doing fifty years before in the slender volume *Tonio Kröger*. If that story is loved by so many who are neither artists themselves nor specially interested in the problems of artists, if it will live long after the dilemma of the bourgeois writer has ceased to matter, it is because the portrayal of that dilemma is not its final aim. It is only part of the material used to symbolize much more: the moment in the games of make-believe when one is suddenly outside the game as well as in, while the other children are still entirely in it; and that other moment, much later, when there comes a sharp pang of conscience because one realizes that one is not wholly identified with what one says and does but is a spectator of it too, the guilty fear that this spells insincerity — until we learn from others that they share the awareness; in more general terms, the whole ambivalent relation between contemplation and action, to which man by his nature is heir, ambivalent because from one side it looks as though only contemplation has a conscience, and that all action involves stupid blindness to some aspect of the whole, whereas seen from the other side it is contemplation that seems inhuman in its aloofness, and only committed action a real test of the workings of conscience. Similarly, in *Faustus* the end is not the portrayal of a German musician and the events of the last war. These are part of the means. The end is the symbolization of the profoundly disturbing connections between ultimate, rarefied, abstractions and bestiality. In field after field of human thought and activity the veil is drawn back on man's striving for absolute purity — for pure form, pure intelligence, pure motherhood — and the felt relations between all these different strivings, even the seemingly most remote, are established by such a closely woven net of formal relations in the language that at whatever point one touches it all the threads seem to move. On the occasion of Mann's death the *Times Literary Supplement* produced the following judgment of this novel: "*Faustus*," it said, "is a wild and undisciplined book in harmony with its subject. . . ." Here we have another confusion, not this time between *Stoff* and *Gehalt* but between *Stoff* and form. I would say that *Faustus* is a severely disciplined, highly articulated book, created to give the illusion of chaos.

In the light of what has been said, some of the criticisms of Mann are clearly based on false expectations of what a novel can ever be or do. But one of those mentioned earlier possibly contains a quite proper, and important, critical question. "He always seems to be writing with an encyclopedia at his elbow" may conceal a wish to exclude from literature supposedly offending materials. If so, the answer is that anything whatsoever is subject-matter for art. There are no offending materials. But it may also express a doubt as to whether all the encyclopedia materials are really necessary to the work, whether they have all been used in the service of the symbol he is creating. This implies a genuine critical question, in fact *the* critical question, the one we have to ask in face of any work of art.

And in the case of Mann's later novels it is not an easy question to answer. Some may be inclined to say that though they fulfil the first of the Aristotelian requirements, that of magnitude, they fall far short of the second, that of order — the due subordination of all parts so that the eye, or the memory, can comprehend the whole in one view "without the least detainment in any of the particular parts." I do not myself share this opinion. Even where the technicalities are quite beyond my grasp, as in parts of the discourses on music, I find the formal relations with other parts of the material so firmly and consistently sustained that I am carried along by the general significance of a passage, and not delayed or irritated by its detail. In any case it is salutory to remind ourselves just how radically judgment — and appreciation — in such matters can change. To the early eighteenth century not only Shakespeare and Gothic architecture, but Michael Angelo, too, seemed sadly deficient in the Ordering of their Designs. It is the occupational hazard of the critic that posterity may well reverse his judgment. How much of Mann's intellectual materials posterity will be able to apprehend as *form* we cannot guess. It will depend not on his achievement alone, but on how knowledge develops, how art develops, how men develop. For there are always two parties involved in the fate of a work of art — its author and its public. ["Every creative writer builds his work out of various elements which, to be sure, one can interweave more organically than the other, but it also depends very much on the beholder and his intellectual presuppositions. If he tends to see things in terms of distinction, then he more or less destroys the unity which the artist is striving to achieve; if he prefers to connect, then he assists the artist and as it were completes the latter's intention. . . ."][17] Thomas Mann's "Absicht" is, I think, the preservation of the vital and essential contact between poetry and the thought of an age. In an age where thought has reached the degree of complexity that it has in ours, this is a grandiose, an heroic, undertaking. Whether he achieves his aim or not, we should, I think, be in no two minds about its legitimacy. When the world that is presented to our intellect is out of touch with the life of our feeling, we are assailed by chaos within and without. Mann, by taking so much of our intellectual heritage as material for his fictional illusions, was a pioneer in forging this vital link between our feeling and much that at present seems esoteric in our intellectual culture. But in so doing he is also in the great tradition of poets. In presenting us sometimes with chaos, and giving us an insight into our feeling of chaos, he may yet prove to be one of our great bulwarks against chaos.

Notes

1. "Thomas Manns Goethe-Bild. Eine Studie über *Lotte in Weimar*," *Germanic Review*, xx (1945), pp. 166 ff.

2. In *Neue Studien* (Stockholm, 1948), pp. 165 f.

3. Surprisingly at the end of the nineteenth century: witness Konrad Lange's full-scale resuscitation of the illusion theory (*Das Wesen der Kunst* [Berlin, 1901]); and again today in Susanne Langer's *Feeling and Form* (New York, 1953). And it haunts, so he recently told us in a paper read at the annual Symposium of the Catholic Renascence Society in Milwaukee (published in *Essays in Criticism* [January, 1956]), Mr. Wimsatt's Catholic mind.

4. From Susanne Langer, op. cit. The linguistic philosophers who quarrel with the details of her analysis may well be right; I am not competent to judge. But it is up to them to give a more satisfactory account of the complexities which practitioners and appreciators of art know to exist, not to oversimplify the state of affairs in order to satisfy the requirements of logic.

5. E.g. Morris Weitz, *Philosophy of the Arts* (Cambridge, Mass., 1950), pp. 35–41.

6. *Art and Visual Perception* (London, 1956).

7. *The Observer*, April 15, 1956.

8. Critics who have taken Goethe to task for insisting on the importance of *Gehalt*, imagining that he thereby detracts somehow from the importance of form, have either imperfectly understood how *Gehalt* differs from *Stoff*, or failed to realise that the expression of content *implies* the successful creation of a form.

9. For a philosophical discussion of aesthetic illusion, starting from Schiller's concept of *Schein*, see S. K. Langer, op. cit., Part 2.

10. ["Religion has the same relationship to art as any other higher interest in life. It is to be considered as material only, one that has the same claims as all other materials from life"] (Goethe to Eckermann, 2 May 1824).

11. Cf. Goethe's famous aphorism on "Symbolik" in which he says that the idea in the image remains ["infinitely effective and unattainable . . . one that, even when expressed in all languages, would remain inexpressible. . . ."]

12. *Noten und Abhandlungen zum Divan*, section headed "Eingeschaltetes."

13. ["That which speaks to feeling, the ultimate effect of all poetic structures, one, however, that presupposes the expenditure of the whole art. . . ."] ["Über den Dilettantismus], schema and notes compiled by Goethe and Schiller for an article for the *Propyläen*.

14. *Philosophical Lectures*, ed. Kathleen Coburn (London, 1949), p. 384.

15. "Thomas Mann and the Problem of Anti-Intellectualism," *Germanic Review*, XV (1940), 281. My italics.

16. "The Dance as Symbol and Leitmotiv in *Tonio Kröger*," *Germanic Review*, XXIX (1954), 286.

17. Goethe to Eichstädt, 15 September, 1804.

The Structure of Humor   Käte Hamburger*

Let the consideration of a hitherto little noted aspect of Thomas Mann's work serve as an introduction to this analysis of the Joseph tetralogy. It is that aspect that received its most distinct and most monumental development in "Joseph and his Brothers": the structure of humor. When I wrote the analysis of the work twenty years ago, I had already anchored it in this "structure" and tried to work out the "function of humor" for the purpose of "illuminating," in the true sense of the word, the multiple levels of that great biblical novel. But then Thomas Mann's work was not finished: the last decade of his life, a life that remained creative to the end, still gave us *Doctor Faustus, The Holy Sinner, The Black Swan*, the extensive continuation of *Felix Krull*, not to mention the essays, the wealth of theoretical pronouncements, and the collections of

*Translated by the editor from *Der Humor bei Thomas Mann: Zum Joseph-Roman* (Munich: Nymphenburger Verlag, 1965), 11–52. Reprinted by permission of Nymphenburger Verlag.

letters put out since 1945. It is only now that an overview is possible that spans the whole of Thomas Mann's creative work, and it is only now that its structural principles can be fully recognized and balanced against each other. If humor can be shown, through a textual analysis of the Joseph novel, to be a formative principle with a particular significance and function, then we must ask if and how far it is effective elsewhere in Mann's work and if and how it is connected with its other essential elements.

Humor, then, and not irony, is the aspect under which the work is to be considered here. It is important to stress that because, partly due to the pronouncements of the author himself but mainly to the strongly parodistic elements of the text that shade not only into comedy but also into caricature, elements that rightfully can be seen as expression and a narrative vehicle for an ironic stance, we are accustomed to interpret this work under the aegis of irony. Instead of examining more closely the numerous studies that have been dedicated to the problem of Thomas Mann's irony,[1] let us mention here only that structural element of the ironic phenomenon that more or less explicitly underlies these studies and that is also prominently reflected in the utterances of Thomas Mann himself. Irony is rooted in distance, that is, in a "critical" consciousness that never yields to appearances directly. It is no accident that Thomas Mann attributed irony in this fundamental sense to the "epic spirit of art" and expressed it metaphorically in the image of Apollo—"the god of distance, of objectivity, the god of Irony"—(*Die Kunst des Romans*, X, 353). The epic spirit of art is the spirit of irony because it "distances itself from things . . . it hovers above them and smiles down upon them . . ." (ibid.). Thomas Mann invoked irony frequently and applied this concept to the most manifold phenomena and attitudes. And everywhere where he does it, the structure of distance, of "ironic reserve" appears. As early as "Considerations of a Nonpolitical Man" (1918) he described the "middle and mediating position" of art "between intellect and life" as a "source of irony" (XII, 571). And this was possible fundamentally not because art "mediates," but because it opposes "both life and intellect" (ibid., 575), that is, because it does not ally itself with either, keeping a distance toward both sides. But the insight that "intellect" and "life" by their very nature stand to each other in an ironic relationship of distance belongs, as we know, to the fundamental problematics of Thomas Mann's work, of which I will speak further. For the moment I only wanted to point out Thomas Mann's frequent definitions of irony, which, however, do not need to be used as a basis in an examination of the elements of what we understand as Thomas Mann's ironic structuring of characters and language. This is so because irony can be an attitude defined, described, and even felt one way or another,[2] but it receives its literary expression only through the various means of the narrative, such as satirically exaggerated portrayal of characters, parodistic style, and others;[3] and it is by no means always clear whether the stance behind such presentation is more an ironic or a humorous one.

This problem is again first to be addressed with regard to Thomas Mann's own utterances. In his usage, he does not always distinguish between irony and humor, ironic and humorous. Thus, for example, he says of "the turn toward the democratic" that occurs in "Royal Highness" that it "actually is carried out only in a humorous manner, only ironice" (XII, 98). He also applies the concept of humor as well as that of irony to the narrative stance of the Joseph novel. It is also to be noted that he likes to accompany definitions of irony with the addition of "loving" or "warmhearted": irony, as reserve, "plays between the opposites, slyly and noncommittally, if not without warmth" (IX, 170). And, aware as he is of the stereotype of the ironist, he remarks explicitly that "epic irony" should not be thought of as cold and loveless, ridiculing or scorning. It is "instead an irony of the heart, a loving irony, it is greatness that is full of tenderness for the small" (X, 353). This comes close to descriptions of humor which, according to Jean Paul, lowers the great to set it beside the small and elevates the small to set it beside the great (*Vorschule d. Ästhetik*, #32). However, the concept of humor is almost totally consistent in Thomas Mann's usage when he is speaking of the Joseph novel. At the outset of working on it, in 1928, he announces that it would be the mission of the work "to prove that one can be mythical in a humorous way" (XI, 625), and he never calls it other than his "humorous novel of humanity"; it is precisely a device such as the built-in "biblical criticism" which could also be considered ironic that he describes as humorous (XI, 627, 655).

All of this is at least an indication that allows one to speculate that this "ironic German," the epic writer Thomas Mann, did in the final analysis count himself as one of the humorists of world literature, in a sense that was by no means superficial. This conjecture is supported by utterances widely separated in time. "The comic as consolation, the humorist as a true benefactor of humanity — the older I become, the more deeply I feel that it is so, and I felt it very early on," he wrote in 1926, savoring the memory of the "Stories" of the famous advocate Max Bernstein; then, however, he goes on into the realm of literature, from Hamsun to Shaw, and mentions the strong humorous tradition in England, "from epic burgher times," he adds, and with that has unexpectedly arrived at his own creative roots: "All my life, for me, the epic has coincided with the humorous almost exactly" (XI, 65), and doubtless nothing would have pleased and confirmed him more than the appearance at the time of an excellent study of the comic-humorous elements of his work by an Englishman — the scholar of German literature R. Peacock.[4] At the time, he admits that nothing made him prouder than the notes about humor that Schnitzler made while reading the *Magic Mountain*. Two years before his death, he distances himself with remarkable energy from being considered merely an ironist "without taking into account the concept of humor which after all, it appears to me, cannot be omitted totally in my case" (*Humor und Ironie*, XI, 802f.). He said this in a radio discussion, and, though it is true that such instantaneously formulated utterances cannot be considered wholly binding, the latter constraint would apply most to the definition of the difference between humor and irony that Thomas Mann gave at the time and which, in view of the situation probably did come out rather popularizing. "Irony, it would seem to me, is that spirit of art which elicits from the reader an intellectual"—later on the word is "erasmic"—"smile, while humor produces heartfelt laughter which I myself value more highly as an effect of art . . ." (ibid.). And when he does mention some humorous elements in his writing—the figure of Jacob in the Joseph tetralogy which, though full of "high pathos," is "surrounded by the aura of a peculiar kind of humor," or the "humorous idea, born of humorous intentions" of letting the biography of Leverkühn "be told by the good humanist Zeitblom . . . to pass the demonic through a decidedly undemonic medium" (ibid, 803f.), one has to admit that the definition of "heartfelt" or "welling up from the heart" does not quite apply to this humor, and the differentiation between irony and humor emerges even less clearly than before. Even granting the occasional nature of this pronouncement of the author's old age, and its informality, it should not be ignored totally. If not pertinent as a definition, it can be taken as an expression of Mann's understanding of himself that confirms the conception developed in this introductory chapter and which is to be fully justified in the analysis of the Joseph novel: the notion that Thomas Mann is one of the great humorists, the "superhumorists" of literature and, as such, and not coincidentally, also one of its great epic authors.

"Superhumor"—the concept does not originate with Thomas Mann; when, while reading *Don Quixote* with great pleasure, he speaks of the superhumorous style that could once more seduce him into considering humor an essential element of the epic (*Meerfahrt mit Don Quixote*, IX, 435), it indicates that he may have had that in his mind all along as a more telling definition than merely heartfelt humor or humor welling up from the heart. The Danish philosopher Harald Höffding coined that concept in his work *"Super-Humor"* (1916), still within the influence of the humor investigations of Kierkegaard and even more those of Jean Paul. However, in our connection and in view of Thomas Mann's humor, it is this concept itself more than Höffding's descriptions of it that is to be set up as a terminological standard. It should indicate that Thomas Mann's humor which is at issue here is a more covert phenomenon than those elements of parody, comedy, caricature, satire-irony that indeed, as R. Peacock quite rightly says, constitute the stylistic substance of most of Thomas Mann's works. I would say in anticipation that the latter may be used in the service of the superhumorous idea, but they also appear in texts where the latter is not present, as we will show. Because humor, superhumor, which is at issue here, is a structure that is not fully developed in all of Mann's work, and one that unfolds completely only in the middle period of his creation, in the twenties and thirties, the period of the Joseph opus, the central work not only of this era, but of Thomas Mann's production generally.

In order, then, to bring out the kind and structure of humor that reigns in these works, that constitutes them, we will not start with a defining concept, but rather begin, in an analytic and inductive manner, from the concrete, namely, at first with a minor work from the period of the Joseph novel, one that happens also to be located in a climate of ideas close to this central work and one that offers the simplest, most concrete starting point because of its drastic explicitness. This is "The Transposed Heads: An Indian Legend" (1940).

This is the "bloody and mindboggling" story of the two friends Shridaman and Nanda who, for the sake of the lovely-hipped Sita, lose their heads, each actually cutting off his own. Sita has become the wife of Shridaman, a young merchant from a Brahman family with the fine head of a thinker which, however, tops a somewhat flabby body, not lacking even a small potbelly. And though Sita knows that her husband's main feature is his head and not his body, her glances and thoughts still wander more often than permitted in the direction of Nanda's powerfully beautiful body above which this son of farm folk carries a rather ordinary, slightly goat-nosed and thick lipped though thoroughly nice peasant head, one that does not particularly detract from the main thing, his strong lovely body. The fine and noble Shridaman takes it upon himself to resolve the emotional confusion that comes about as a consequence between these three for the benefit of wife and friend, in that he cuts off his head in the temple of the great world mother Kali. Whereupon Nanda, seeing his friend in such a condition, does not hesitate to do the same. And Sita, faced with this "horrible mess," after some consideration of pros and cons, is just about to hang herself from a vine, when the rough but maternal voice of the great mother stops her and promises to reawaken the young men to life, if Sita will undertake to set the heads back up. "But do your job right and don't set up their heads backward in your silliness so they have to run around facing the back and become the laughing stock of people." (VIII, 765). Well, Sita sets them up wrong anyway, perhaps not quite from mere silliness and not in the manner feared by the world mother; instead, she sets Shridaman's fine thinker's head on Nanda's powerful peasant body and Nanda's peasant head on Shridaman's flabby merchant—and Brahman's body. A most happy exchange, the establishment of a harmony missing hitherto, one through which Shridaman, her husband, gains more than Nanda. And after a forest hermit has decided the rather ticklish question of marital rights that arises through this in favor of the head, Sita at first enjoys a time of perfect happiness with her husband who now is constituted capitally. For a while—because nature follows its own laws, those of biological adaptation, without bothering about ideals of harmony, so that Shridaman's powerful Nanda body becomes softer and flabbier under the influence of his thinker's head and the latter, in its turn, coarsens somewhat. Sita, disappointed again, and assuming that a favorable development in Nanda's case would correspond to Shridaman's unlucky one, sets out for the former. But after they have savored the short happiness of a night, Shridaman appears—not to avenge, but to sort out the confused relationships regarding the mixed-up feelings about head and body, thine and mine, me and he. This can only happen through the shared death of the three lovers at the stake, for Shridaman knows of no other choice and solution, only "to lay down our mixed-up separation and reunite our being with the All" (VIII, 802).

It may be evident from this short retelling that this bloody tale is not told "for its own sake." It can be seen from the events and statements cited that humor is in play and that it makes the story transparent for something else, something that stands behind it and that the telling is really all about. Let us stop for a while at the little word "really." It is suited to call our attention to the fact that it is not irony and also not, or not only, the comic, as it might seem natural to assume because of the exaggeratedly drastic events and the gaily parodistic narrative style—but that humor is the structural principle of this story. For this purpose a little conceptual analysis needs to be done, and to begin with we must register the opposite of the concept "real," or "authentic," that is, "inauthentic," for which we can use the approximation of "inadequate." The concept of the inauthentic or inadequate is our point of departure for this analysis, the phenomenology of humor, or more narrowly of the superhumorous type which is, in the final analysis, the one concerned in Thomas Mann's work. The element on which this humor structure is based is the recognition of something inadequate. This implies that an appearance does not correspond to what it is "really" intended to represent, that is, that something authentic has somehow been couched in an inauthentic form of appearance. Such a relationship of inadequacy, however, does not constitute the humorous stance alone; rather it is characteristic also for other attitudes toward phenomena in which it appears, for instance, as satirical, resigned, or even just moralizing. Molière judges his *femmes precieuses* satirically as ridiculous because their precious culture is not a real one, no real culture at all but rather one that is laughed at even by their servants. Rostand's Cyrano de Bergerac feels with pain and resignation that his great nose is ridiculous because it does not match a normal human face and, more deeply felt, his own serious personality. In such positions the inadequate is not only judged and evaluated as inadequate but beyond that as the worse, and as such it is despised or ridiculed or accepted with resignation. The humorist, however, does not take any of these judging positions. He does compare the inauthentic with the authentic that the former represents, or aspires to represent. But for him the inauthentic forms are inauthentic precisely because they are inauthentic forms of something authentic; that is, in the inauthentic, he still sees the authentic. Or, the other way around, he sees the authentic even in its least authentic manifestations—and it is for this reason that he does not judge but smiles.

Let us illustrate with what is surely the greatest example of humor in world literature. Don Quixote, who set out to actualize the world of the knightly romances in the reality of his poor life and in a time that was knightly no more, is merely an inadequate, merely a comic figure when he is measured against the standard of this reality. And it is as such a comic figure, such an object of satire that Cervantes meant him, a comic parody of the knightly romance. But when the point of reference for this inadequacy ceases to be a realistic one and—as it happens in this novel during which Cervantes changes from "a stepfather of Don Quixote to his real father"—becomes idealistic, then the standard shifts in favor of the knightly romances and, with them, of Don Quixote. Now the latter is an inauthentic figure precisely with reference to the authentic that he nonetheless embodies, namely, the ideals of bravery, helpfulness, morality, the inner nobility of true knighthood, ideals that still survive in the knightly romances. And Don Quixote is no more a comic figure but rather, as a reservoir of ethical values, a touchingly humoristic one. As far as the phenomenology of humor is concerned, it is not to be assumed from the great example of Don Quixote that the authentic must always be an ideal of this sort or another. We will have to denote it with a more general concept. But one essential constitutive element of humor does nonetheless emerge from Don Quixote. The condition for the production of the smile of humor from the discrepancy between authentic and inauthentic is that the authentic, the true meaning, still recognizable in its most inauthentic forms of manifestation, must be of an ethical-humane and not of an antihumane nature. It is impossible to imagine a humorous figure that, no matter how inauthentically, represents something antihumanely evil.[5]

We are now returning to Thomas Mann's work, and first of all to *The Transposed Heads*. It is thanks to the smile of humor that the Indian legend of the cut off and wrongly reattached heads reveals itself clearly, yes overly clearly, as the grotesquely inauthentic appearance of something authentic; it is this smile that can "resist the gruesome guiles of Maya," as we read at the outset in an assuaging sort of tone. But what then is this authentic quality? That, to be sure, is not evident at first glance, and, as far as this story is concerned, one has to look around carefully in the special world of Thomas Mann's thought. Then one will realize that the tale of the transposed heads is the humorous, or rather humorously resigned, answer to the problematic that governs Thomas Mann's early work, the *Buddenbrooks* period with "Little Herr Friedemann," "The Way to the Cemetery," *Tonio Kröger*, "Tristan," "Fiorenza," *Death in Venice*; the much debated problem of intellect and life which is truly resolved and put to rest only in the Joseph novel. Later, in the "Considerations of a

Nonpolitical Man," Mann came up with a formula for it—not only does intellect yearn for life, but life also yearns for its opposite—"two worlds whose relationship is erotic" and between which "longing . . . goes back and forth" (XII, 569). This longing was immediately stamped by Mann with the signature of irony, or what he then took to be irony, erotic irony. He called it irony because there is in it that reserve, that self-abnegation with which at least intellect confronts life for which it yearns yet without wanting to live it for its own sake, as Tonio Kröger, for instance, yearns for the "luxuries of the commonplace," the "blond and blue-eyed ones," the Hans Hansens and the Inge Holms. It is true that only the first part of the yearning-and-irony formula was actualized. Intellectuals reach out for life, with ironic yearning like Tonio Kröger, rebel against it grotesquely like Lobgott Piepsam (in "The Way to the Cemetery") and Detlev Spinell (in "Tristan") or perish like little Friedemann and Gustave Aschenbach, whereas the answering love of those who represent life toward the intellect is not thematized. When, however, Shridaman and Nanda "peered toward each other because of their diversity" (VIII, 715), when Shridaman with his spiritual head and feeble body has a liking for the rough Krishna nature of the thick-lipped Nanda with his powerful body, whereas the latter "was greatly impressed with [Shridaman's] noble head and his correct speech which is known to be associated with wisdom and insight" (ibid.), then this "reaching for the other" is doubtless the fulfillment of the formula of longing from the "Considerations," in which not even the component of ironic reserve is left out. Because, we read, "there was, in any case, some mockery in the affection of the one for the other" (ibid.). But there is an indication of a lighthearted undermining of these "inseparable" and different friends, an indication that the onetime formula for longing and harmony has become suspect (this might also be implied in Thomas Mann's writing, jokingly, after he finished the tale, in a letter of 18 June 1941: "Yes, Tonio, Hans, and Inge now have been united in a fiery grave. Peace to their ashes!"); and indeed the formula does get carried totally ad absurdum: precisely in that the slightly mocking sidelong glances of Shridaman and Nanda, and in each case after the main feature of the other, are fulfilled in an unexpectedly concrete manner. The idea of the harmony of body and spirit, intellect and life, is carried ad absurdum and canceled out (*aufgehoben*). But it is suspended or harmonized in the Hegelian double meaning of the word, destroyed and preserved at the same time—preserved in the sphere of humor that now begins its playing with the inauthentically authentic. For it is by no means the thoroughly natural friendship of the two young men in and of itself but the lovely-hipped Sita's attempt, so thoroughly failed, to combine the blessing from above with the blessing from below—to use the formula of the Joseph novel, and that not accidentally—to form that ideal harmony that could be called the ideal of humanity. But we know this idea only in its infinitely individualized and thus necessarily inadequate manifestations, as they are conditioned by the *principium individuationis* that the Brahman doctrine calls the veil of Maya. It is no accident that the narrative style, which has humorous touches from the outset, is reinforced most strongly by drastically comic tones at the moment when the legend reaches its high point in the decapitation and head-exchange scene in the temple of the robust world mother. The grotesque and "bloodily confusing" legend reveals itself as an image of human imperfection which to be sure is imperfect only with a view to a perfection, which is the idea, even the ideal of humanity. In the Indian legend the shortcoming of the individually finite and as such imperfect can only be suspended (*aufgehoben*) through the suspension (*Aufhebung*) of the *principium individuationis*. But the Western author makes sure that the idea of perfection is not totally destroyed after all but remains visible precisely as the source of the humorous play, in that it finds a necessarily finite but nearly ideal embodiment: in the little son of Shridaman and Sita who possesses the beautiful body of Nanda and who can only be educated in Shridaman's skill with the Veda because he does have a small defect after all—shortsightedness that "protected him from living too much in the body and turned his head toward the spiritual" (ibid., 806).

We had our reasons for starting out on our analysis of the humor structure with this small marginal text. For it is located at a certain intersection of relationships: on the one hand, it points back toward the problem circle of the first period of Thomas Mann's creative work; on the other, it stands in the space of the Joseph novel, which Mann called a humorous novel about humanity. Because what, in the "Transposed Heads," still remains hidden against the background of drastic grotesquerie—the idea of the human being—becomes the rich and clearly orchestrated yet at the same time complex and cryptic theme network of the great biblical novel that starts with the programmatic words that "it is the human being alone . . . whose mystery quite understandably makes up the A and O of all our talking and questioning . . ." (IV, 9). The following study concerns itself with the analysis of the biblical novel and hence with this idea. In it, the humor structure of the inauthentically authentic and the key function of humor will become recognizable in full clarity.

If the main humorous work is not included in this introductory consideration that is to lead up to it, then enough of the viewpoint of the humor structure has been indicated above to enable us to use it as a lookout point for seeing if and how other novels of Thomas Mann are also determined by it. In doing it, we will not follow the chronology of their origin but rather the extent of their determination by humor.

The most immediate, in this sense, is "The Holy Sinner," published in 1951, eight years after the completion of *Joseph*, six after *Doctor Faustus*, yet closer to the former than the latter, though the material, the legend of Pope Gregorius as told by Hartmann von Aue, does emerge precisely in the Leverkühn novel where Adrian Leverkühn reads it in the *Gesta Ro-*

manorum and then composes a puppet opera about which Zeitblom reports that the composer "had concentrated all the wit and horror, all the childlike urgency, imagination, and solemnity of musical illumination . . . on this exuberantly sinful, simpleminded and merciful story" (VI, 425). The author Thomas Mann, however, who takes up the theme belonging to the hero of his novel and treats it in his own manner, accents it differently: not with "wit" or yet "horror," but with a humor that announces itself from the outset in the serenely jocular narrative style and that sets the exuberance of sin and mercy in a cryptical, by no means immediately identifiable context. The sin in question was one that was of the most serious kind for medieval man and poet: double incest, in that Grigorss, later called Gregorius, offspring of the incestuous love of his princely parents, Sybilla and Wigilis, as Thomas Mann names them, compounds the sin by becoming the husband of his mother (as this legend is in the tradition of the Oedipus myth). But mercy is as extreme as sin, and it descends on the still "good sinner," as he is already called by Hartmann: first, the rescue of the highly born illegitimate child who has been set adrift on the sea and finally the advancement to the papacy (as you can check in the book), though this can happen only after the third of the extreme events, the seventeen-year penance on a bare rock in the sea.

If we disregard the narrative style for the moment, we should ask ourselves if a structure of humor is visible in this story as well, in that a relationship of inadequacy appears between appearance and idea. In any case, it is not as evident as in "The Transposed Heads" and *Joseph*. Here it seems that the "horrible and simultaneously uplifting story" with all its complications has itself elicited the humor of the teller: how the "child of shame, the husband of his mother, the son-in-law of his grandfather, the brother-in-law of his father, the abhorrent sibling of his children" (VII, 235) ends up in the chair of St. Peter, a pope of such holiness that all the bells of Rome start ringing by themselves. Thomas Mann has emphasized that the theme and meaning of his retelling of the old tale was the dispensation of mercy that follows "radical penance," even though "much travesty — not without love — intervenes" (XI, 690).[6] When the word "humorous" actually is mentioned, however, Mann does not name "The Holy Sinner." He does not even see in a humorous light the grotesque invention with which he considered it absolutely necessary to correct Hartmann — the explanation of the possibility of surviving on a bare rock in the sea for seventeen years at the mercy of the weather and with no other nourishment than the water trickling out of the rock. "That was impossible," he thinks, "and the patently impossible I could not utilize in my version of the story. I had to clothe it in a kind of illusory possibility . . ." (ibid.). What that is to be is, as we know, that Gregorius's body, in the course of the years, shrinks progressively until he is no bigger than a hedgehog, a clotted bristly object of nature, covered with moss that cannot be harmed by any weather, that spends the winter in the timeless sleep of a dormouse and, when it does not sleep, nourishes itself from a milky liquid that oozes from a few places of the earth, as the ancients have reported. The critic has licence to go beyond the author's own interpretation and to comment that the improbability of this illusory possibility is in no way less than that of Hartmann; indeed, that it even outstrips the latter, especially considering that this shrunken animal existence, after being discovered by emissaries from Rome and being given an infusion of wine and bread, recaptures his human size and beauty within two hours. The interpreter may recognize the smile of cryptic humor precisely in this extreme detail of the narrative that presents the legendary supernatural with the apparent seriousness of reality. The smile breaks through more distinctly as "the spirit of the tale" (of whom more presently) lifts a warning finger at the end, when everything is well: "Let none that enjoyed the story draw a false moral from it and think that it is no big deal with sin . . . Just spend seventeen years on a rock first, reduced to a dormouse . . . then you will see how much fun it is!" (VII, 260). The thoroughly jocular tone of this warning points to the source of the humor here. It lets you sense that the narrator is so to say not quite sure if the "moral" really is responsible for the great sinfulness of which he speaks, or if perhaps it is a completely different authority, namely, "Mother Nature." And this holds, it should be emphasized, over and above the theme that Thomas Mann incorporated into the story of his sinners and into the essence of their sin: that of the elitist superciliousness which particularly determines the consciousness of the noble siblings Sibylla and Wigilis, that excludes everyone else and enables Sibylla, even during her hard penance in the humble service of the sick and the beggars, not to consider herself a sinner but rather to believe that she, nobly born and fastidious, had every right to have a marriage partner corresponding to this rank, even if this happened to be her own brother, and, worse yet, her own son. Over and above this moral element that nonetheless does not prevent mercy, humor plays and lets this grandiose mercy appear in yet another light: namely, as a concession to nature. Is it not in fact nature that nurtures her great sinner from her "maternal source" of which we are told explicitly that this "earth-milk" "reached far down into the maternal organism" and to which the word mercy is applied (ibid., 192). But even at the shameful birth she appears in the guise of the splendid high-bosomed Dame Eisengrein who ministers with her midwifely services to Sibylla without bothering about the incestuous origin of the child. And, we read, "everything went so naturally and smoothly and without a hitch, as though the child had not been conceived in such sin at all, with one's own flesh and blood. . . . The women, then, totally forgot about sin . . ." (ibid., 53). There is also nothing wrong with the two daughters, named Humilitas and Stultitia, whom Sibylla conceives with her son and nephew. And the sigh of relief with which Pope Gregorius ascertains at the end that he at least did not enter into any forbidden relationships with these daughters, and that "everything has limits" (ibid.,

259) is truly a highly humorous recognition of the moral indifference of nature toward the ever so wicked moral or religious transgressions of love and conception. Surely incest is a grievous sin, and God's mercy is great when he elevates the child of shame to be his representative on earth. But "the spirit of the tale "is a waggish and clever spirit" (ibid., 58), and his waggish narration never lets one be completely sure whether God in all secrecy does not lean toward the mild and morally indifferent Mother Nature rather than toward the rigid prescriptions of morality and religion, and whether he does not elevate Gregorius and his bewitching mother, aunt, and wife because of the greatness of their love, no matter how earthly sensual and sinful it has been. For in the entrancing concluding scene where Gregorius is already speaking ex cathedra and old Sibylla confesses in front of her holy son, they smilingly admit to each other that in their innermost beings "where the soul makes no fuss" (ibid., 255) they must have known that they were mother and son. Humor breaks through with a smile and brings order into the whole unfathomable mess of good and evil, holy and sinful, guilt and mercy, and unmasks the extremely and horrifyingly inauthentic love and lust as a manifestation of something high and authentic, of love that is as eternal as nature and God's love.

If *Joseph* is indisputably the humorous masterpiece of Thomas Mann because, as will be shown, there the structure of humor not only determines the work's overall structure, but also is closely tied to the philosophical foundation of Thomas Mann, then "The Holy Sinner," even given the covert nature of the idea of humor in it, is a first-class work of humor in the more obvious sense of having a humorous style of narration. In this sense, it is even the most humorous of Thomas Mann's creations. Here, particularly, that narrative technique is employed to produce humor, which Thomas Mann believed he could already attribute to the Faust novel: the tale is told by a first-person narrator. Thomas Mann thought that in *Doctor Faustus* a comic effect was produced by passing the demonism, the life, and the figure of the great, lonely, and ahuman artist Adrian Leverkühn through an undemonic medium, the honest humanist and burgher Serenus Zeitblom. This contrast, however, does not rise to the level of humor because the object of the report is such that the smile of humor does not reach the undemonic medium either, and the relationship of inadequacy that exists here has at the most a parodistic accent. The Gregorius legend too is told by a first person narrator, the Irish monk Clemens. But even in terms of the narrative structure this is different from Serenus Zeitblom, even in this respect the monkish narrator is an element of the structure of humor. Unlike Zeitblom, he is not a true first person narrator who has experienced what he reports but a frame narrator who retells a tale handed down. But, as though Thomas Mann had wanted to emulate the literary theorists, he questions the frame story in a humorous, even flippant way — in having the narrator in the frame story reporting, for instance, what he could not possibly know as an individual — scenes, conversations between characters of the novel at which it was not present. Thus, in terms of narrative technique, the structure of the first-person narration disappears, and the "usual" telling of a third-person story takes over. Thomas Mann jokes playfully with this condition in that he, with witty ambiguity, "embodies" the narrative act that he calls the "spirit of the tale" into a first-person narrator. How this relates to the report in the Gregorius legend that at the entrance of the penitent elected Pope all the bells of Rome started to ring by themselves is one of the most delicious and refined inventions of modern narrative art, in itself a humorous travesty of the narrative problem:

> Who is ringing the bells? Not the bellringers. They ran out into the streets like everyone else because of this uncanny ringing. . . . Who then is ringing the bells of Rome? — *The spirit of the tale.* — It is he who says: "All the bells were ringing," and consequently it is also he that is ringing them. So spiritual is this spirit and so abstract that grammatically one can only speak of him in the third person, and it can only be said: "It is he." And yet he can also contract to a person, namely to the first person, and embody himself in someone who in this person speaks and says: it is I. I am the spirit of the tale who . . . is narrating this story in that I begin with its merciful ending and ring the bells of Rome, id est: report that they all as one began to ring by themselves on that day of the entry. (VII, 10)

With this narrator's joke, the tone is already set for the humor of the story, and this tone permeates the whole style of the tale, something that cannot be shown here in detail. It consists partly in the mixture of Thomas Mann's style with that of the medieval monk to produce the spirit of the tale. If Thomas Mann speaks like the monk (which includes the wittily interspersed Old French, English, dialect German montages), then the latter speaks like Thomas Mann too; in a sense, both narrators act out of character, and through the spirit of the tale their identity is at the same time affirmed as it is continually undone. If, then, the humor of the text is immediately evident through these narrative techniques, then the relationship of the narrative to the narrating medium itself is different from that in *Doctor Faustus*. Not only is the latter treated humorously, it is, as I tried to show, the subject of the report, the legend of mercy itself, whose ultimately serene meaning could become the object of the "enlightening" function of a humor that reveals the authentic even in its most inauthentic manifestation, repudiated by morality, religion, and society: it can see love even in incest.

Glancing back twenty-five years from "The Holy Sinner," we see that small autobiographically tinted novella *Disorder and Early Sorrow* (1926) which should be mentioned briefly because it too, even if in a very different way, contains the humorous structure of inauthenticity. For here a father experiences the apparent "infatuation" of his five-year-old daughter for a young man who had danced with her in a facetious way at a dinner dance given for her older siblings as an inauthentic manifestation of love, and sees her great suffering at the young man's subsequent lack of interest in her as a small and comic form of the pain of love that an unfaithful man can inflict upon a woman and yet, at the same time, as a form of what we might call the Medea pain. And the slightly nostalgic humor that colors the tale of this "early sorrow" flows from the father's knowledge that the true great sorrow of life cannot yet reach the soul of the little girl. "How fortunate, he thinks, that with every breath of her slumber Lethe flows into her little soul. . . . Tomorrow, for sure, the young fly-by-night will be only a pale shadow, incapable of upsetting her heart . . ." (VIII, 657).

Finally, we must still debate the question whether _Confessions of Felix Krull, Confidence Man_, in some ways Thomas Mann's most delightful work, merits being described as humorous. The delightful or amusing as such is by no means necessarily humorous, in our sense, superhumorous. And, if for no other reason than that the novel remained a fragment, it is impossible to decide on its humorous aspects. For only the finished work unlocks the intended meaning, and only that meaning can decide whether we can speak of a work truly structured by humor.

Felix Krull represents a special case first because of its origin. Started in 1910 (published in 1922 as book 1), continued 1951–54, the first conception was picked up unchanged in the last long fragment, and, in terms both of the character and development of the agreeable confidence man and of the style of his report, the unity of the parts which are separated by forty years is preserved. Yet this does not mean that the fragment of 1954 remained on the level of 1910. Instead, almost the contrary is true, that the contours of the figure sketched in 1910 only became fully clear when seen from the vantage point of the late continuation, and this is true because, ten years after the completion of the Joseph novel, _Felix Krull_ still in a sense belongs in the latter's space, and accordingly the confidence man, conceived originally parodistically, receives a ray of that humorous light in which "the little religious confidence man," the Joseph figure, stands—so that, when one looks at it from the vantage point of the longer fragment, the earlier conception takes on the shape of a preliminary form of Joseph.[7]

The delight of the early _Krull_, however, rests totally on the parodied figure that is ingeniously irridescent in many aspects. When Thomas Mann, in the _Considerations of a Nonpolitical Man_ of 1918, described the temporarily abandoned work as a parody of the German novel of education, he declared his participation in the "intellectualizing disintegration of the idea of Germanness, when the point had been reached before the war where one could parody the German novel of education and development, the great German autobiography, as the memoirs of a confidence man" (XII, 101). Yet one must admit that the notion of parody, stated in such an oblique intellectual way, in reference to a specific literary genre, does not do justice to the character and impression evoked by *Krull* and by virtue of which it is so thoroughly amusing. Without this pointer one would hardly read the novel as a parody of *Wilhelm Meister* or "Truth and Poetry," but first of all as a gay satire of the prewar era. In this respect, the form of the first-person narration already functions as a stylistic device because it alone can properly feature and parody the well turned, "chosen," and at the same time cliché-ridden style which belonged to the upper classes and the style of the "Gartenlaube" [sentimental nineteenth-century bourgeois style, editor] oʿ their reading (and, in this respect, perhaps indirectly also the outworn Goethe style of an epoch when in Germany classicism had faded to a bourgeois ideology and phraseology): "This was the home in which I was born on a mild rainy day in the merry month of May . . ." (VIII, 269); "It is merely that I sense in my reader's mien the worry that, with such varied interests, I might frivolously have completely forgotten the rather delicate question of my military situation" (VIII, 349). In all this, it remains uncertain to what degree Felix, as a child of his time and social level, might be simply using this style, and to what extent he—far removed from a naive common confidence man—is aware in the hidden parts of his being, or becomes increasingly aware, of exaggerating this style parodistically and, in doing so, playing a trick on this society and its bad-faith life and style, this bourgeois society with all its preference for imitation and falsifying that was still resting in the security of its superiority, its comfort. In this sense, Felix Krull's parental home, this "charming manor house" on the Rhine whose "sloping garden is generously decorated with dwarves, mushrooms, and all sorts of persuasively imitated animal life made of crockery," has a transparent connection with the fake "sparkling wine" in gorgeously decorated bottles thanks to which Felix's poor papa ends up in ignominious bankruptcy.

But if this beginning, which in a sense satirizes the era, explains Felix Krull's talent and career as a confidence man to a certain extent, it is still symptomatic or even symbolic of other contexts, constellations in which Thomas Mann wanted to set this figure. At the time of the first fragment, it was the artist problem of his own early period that he wanted to parody symbolically in the mirror image of the confidence man: "a new version of the motif of art and the artist, the psychology of a form of existence that is unreal and illusionary" (*Lebensabriss* [Sketch of my life], XI, 122). A "charlatan"—as he once said in a joking manner of the artist, the writer— a confidence man of the intellect: this is how the artist appears when one applies to him the attributes of the real confidence man, namely, that of a life dedicated to a false appearance, imitation, illusion, and fiction, for whose successful execution one needs the gifts of expression and transformation. A skilled charlatan and confidence man, in turn, can for the same reason appear like an artist—when one transfers the "unreal illusionary form of existence" of art, respectively the products of art, to him as a person. But if this was, according to his own words, the symbolizing intention of Thomas Mann, combined with the parody of the classic autobiography, then one may well suspect one of the reasons for the breaking off of the narrative at that time. The relationship of artist and confidence man, and the artist who serves here for the symbolic comparison with the confidence man, is thereby reduced too much to the actor, the artist of transformations and roles. And in the first *Krull* it is indeed this aspect that is explicitly stressed: from the emperor-playing of little Felix, the costumes in which he sits for his painter-godfather Schimmelpreester, his prodigy imitation on a fake violin, the ambiguously happy-disgusting experience with the actor Müller-Rosé (the double name being coined for that purpose) to his own art of fakery and simulation practiced from early on, his capacity to appear ill for purposes of school attendance, and, finally, in the highly famous faking of an epileptic attack at the draft board health examination. It is precisely here that the first fragment stops; and even though the main action of the continuation in the fragment of 1954, the Marquis de Venosta role, lies very much on the line of this symbolism, it is nonetheless already seen in a different light, and it is only here that we can see indications at least of the humorous structure of the inauthentically authentic.

It is again important to distinguish the shades of meaning here, even at the admitted risk of conceptual schematization and inadmissible compartmentalization of the text. The first Krull fragment with all its aspects of the parodistic, satirically comic, and symbolic, which could only be intimated here, is so amusing in a thematic and stylistic way that we do not hesitate to speak, in a direct and rather unreflective way, of a humorous novel. Yet it is only when one considers that early fragment not in isolation but precisely as part of the later one (about which, as we said, no final judgment can be made either) that the perception of humor acquires, or seems to acquire, the superhumorous structure of the inauthentically authentic. For the artist (actor) aspect is not enough in itself, it does not provide the background of meaning for the smile of superhumor. It is only in looking back from the continuation that the figure of the boy Felix, and with him the confidence game announced by the title, is placed in a wider network of relationships. First of all, this is true of that quality that the author intended, in the early conception, to be an important attribute of the lucky Sunday's child—his beauty. His special kind of confidence talent derives from the fact that he is as beautiful as a young god and that this is the fundamental orientation of his sense of existence. This is only supported by the talent for impersonation. And, if one looks at it more closely, this dissolves as a criminal category. After all, the first real confidence trick that he plays, involving the Marquis de Venosta, does not really belong on his account but on that of the young Marquis whom he does not cheat but whom he benefits immensely. The criminal classification and the burdensome tag of the title is dissolved against the background of a divine pattern that Thomas Mann favored greatly, that of Hermes. Shortly after the author had started *Krull*, Hermes appeared in Thomas Mann's work in the novella *Death in Venice*, for whose sake he interrupted and abandoned *Krull*; this is the first of his stories that sounds mythological motifs and builds them into the "secret" web of relationships as a suggestive sign. In the Venice novella the many-faced equivocal god of myriad aspects appears as Hermes Psychopompos, leading the dead to Hades, in various incarnations that Gustav Aschenbach meets: in the stranger who leans against the funeral chapel of the Ungerer cemetery in Munich, in a Hermes attitude, one foot crossed over the other; then as the sinister gondolier in Venice; and finally as the beautiful boy Tadzio himself, Eros the seducer who metamorphoses into the guide of souls, the Psychagogue before the fading eyes of the dying man on the beach. But it is a different matter in *Krull* where it is Felix Krull himself who begins to delineate himself as a Hermes type, in this case in the manifestation of the waggish delusive god of trade and of thieves who knows how to exploit the right moment and who precisely in this role is also a "Charidotes," a giver of joy and of the good, as Homer calls him. It goes with this image that he should wallow, with success and with that same sense of exploiting the right moment, in the realms of love; indeed, Hermes was even equated with Priapus and often connected with Aphrodite.

When we said that the Krull figure of the early fragment was clearly perceptible only from the vantage point of the later one, this is essentially connected with the invoking of Hermes. Essential here is the Madame Houpflé scene where the Hermes myth is parodied in a comic manner in that even the earlier jewel theft at the customs is "elevated" by the overexcited authoress to an act highly agreeable to her, one that she asks Felix to repeat in an escalating fashion, accompanied by all conceivable allusions to Hermes. And it is from here that a ray of Hermes reflects back on the nimble little chocolate theft that the boy Felix commits in the delicacy shop of his home town, taking advantage of the right moment. In short, it seems as though the intention was to mold the thoroughly pleasing figure of the confidence man into a more or less inauthentic manifestation of Hermes. After all, the fragment ends already with the first phase of Krull's trip as Marquis de Venosta in Lisbon. Whether and how far the prison stay that is already behind him as he writes his memoirs is to be blamed more on society, which is, after all, the object of irony in this novel, than on him, we do not know; but one may surmise that this too was not to be a criminal matter in the authentic sense. As we said, the fragmentary nature of the work prevents a fully valid interpretation. And for that reason we also cannot answer the question that arises here: whether the Hermes role of Krull in its turn could possibly still have been meant as a serene parody of that of Joseph, whether and to what extent the Hermes background, in the guise of the "roguish god" would have made a truly humorous novel of *Krull*. For an aspect of this multifaceted novel, a primary one that already appears in the first fragment, though not discussed heretofore, would fit here: that of the rogue, or picaresque, novel, a tradition in which *Krull* has constantly been put.[8]

In the attempt to portray Thomas Mann as a humorist epic writer we have stayed with texts that we believe we can describe as humorous in a determinate and binding way and avoided the less stringent, more or less indeterminate applications of the concepts of humor and humorous, as Thomas Mann himself also used them, for instance, in the above quotations. That is, only those texts are to be earmarked as truly humorous ones in which humor can be shown as a constellation of the inauthentically authentic, the smiling reflection of an authentic and hence in some way normative meaning in an inauthentic manifestation. Such a limitation and precision of the designation is required in order to separate humor from other categories contained in Thomas Mann's work, such as the comic, the parodistic, and the ironic. But even those of his novels that contain individual "humoristically" conceived figures, such as Tony Buddenbrook, or the Hofrätin Kestner in "The Beloved Returns," minor figures like Mr. Permaneder or the waiter Mager, a selection of characters in *The Magic Mountain*, including above all Hofrat Behrens and in some sense also Settembrini, are for that reason by no means humorous novels. And if one looks more closely, one finds that what one perceived as humorous in the case of these figures can more exactly be described by the concept of "loving irony" that Thomas Mann coined, and which, in reference to these characters, may denote the smiling sympathy with which their comic features are treated.

It is only at this point that the earlier question can be discussed, whether and to what extent the humorous aspect is detectible in the manner of presentation. Herman Meyer describes *The Magic Mountain*, for instance, as Thomas Mann's "first fully humorous work" because, in it — in the fashion of Fielding and Sterne, in his opinion — the author supposedly developed fully the "humorous narrative art" of the "subjective digressions, interruptions by the narrator, and reflections about the act of narration and time, in a manner of which he himself had at one time spoken about the 'humorously expansive style of the English' with which he says he rested in this novel from the strictures of *Death in Venice*."[9] Earlier Hermann J. Weigand in his book about *The Magic Mountain* (1933), had described the same phenomena as an expression of the "Ironic Temper," namely, the "spirit of sovereign play in which the author treats his theme, himself, and the reader."[10] Doubtless, in view of the representational-narrative means of this novel, the boundary between humorous and ironic treatment can hardly be drawn. For both of them, insofar as one insists on a distinction, are expressions of the same "epic spirit of art" of which Thomas Mann said that it "hovers smiling above it all." Novalis already had wanted to call Friedrich Schlegel's similar definition of irony as "the mood that surveys everything and that rises infinitely above everything that is determined including one's own art, virtue, or genius"[11] by the name of humor as "what Fr. Schlegel characterizes so distinctly as irony is in my opinion nothing but the consequence, the nature of composure, of the true presence of mind. It seems to me that Schlegel's irony is true humor. An idea benefits from having several names."[12]

Indeed subjective digressions and sovereign play with the narrative are in themselves not enough to attribute a humorous, ironic, or parodistic character to a narrative work. It is only the governing intention to which they are subordinated that decides that, and that also allows us to recognize the devices used in the representations as meant in one way or another. For that reason neither *Buddenbrooks* nor *The Magic Mountain* nor *The Beloved Returns* and not even such a fairy-tale happy-end novel as *Royal Highness* are humorous novels. They are, to be sure, as all of Thomas Mann's work, "enigmatical" and structured in multifaceted ways. But their enigmas are of a different sort; their structure is that of the *symbol*. That is to say, the represented realities of these novels point toward something other than what they are "in reality" — as a piece of colored material that "is" a flag points toward what it "signifies." They have been, as we showed, constructed on the principles of a "double optics,"[13] as for example the sanatorium in Davos is a symbol of the realm of the dead. Thus even the title *Lotte in Weimar* has a symbolic meaning and points toward the theme of the Goethe novel: the relationship between life and art in Goethe's existence in which Werther's Lotte is no more Goethe's Lotte, and the visit of the Hofrätin Kestner in Weimar is doomed to failure. But it does not fail in a humorous manner, not in the sense of authenticity still smilingly recognized in the inauthentic. Even though the touchingly comic arrangement of the old Lotte, to appear as Werther's Lotte in a white gown with pink ribbons at the dinner party of the Privy Councillor is such a comic humorous element, it merely emphasizes the nostalgically symbolic meaning of the visit — symbolic of the artistic existence of Goethe, that very higher symbolic life where one secretly means art when one urges love and is always ready to betray love, life, and humanity for the sake of art (II, 647f.). The "formal" and "representative" existence of the prince Klaus Heinrich is symbolic not only as a representation of his country, but it is also, in a wider sense, symbolic as a form of artistic existence. It is evident that symbol structure and humor structure are two different things. A tuberculosis sanatorium is not the inauthentic manifestation of the realm of the dead; instead the latter is "recognized," as another entity, in the former. And, in turn, the inauthentic manifestations in the humorous novels are not symbols of the authentic entities that live in them. These structures are so different that, with one exception, Thomas Mann did not use the structure of humor where he was using a symbolic structure, and vice versa. And only in one text are the two structures united to a far-reaching web of meaning. This is the Joseph novel which, then, for this reason also can be considered his central work.

Notes

1. Beda Allemann, *Ironie und Dichtung* [Irony and literature] (Pfullingen, 1956); Erich Heller, *Thomas Mann: Der ironische Deutsche* (Frankfurt, 1959); Eva Schaper, *Zwischen den Welten. Bemerkungen zu Thomas Manns Ironie* [Between worlds: remarks on Thomas Mann's irony], in *Literatur u. Gesellschaft* (Bonn, 1963); Reinhard Baumgart, *Das Ironische u. d. Ironie in den Werken Thomas Manns* [Irony and the ironic in Thomas Mann's work] (Munich, 1964).

2. With some justification Heller remarks that, in spite of the definitions of Schlegel, Hegel, Kierkegaard, and Thomas Mann himself, irony is inaccessible to a universal description because it is not a concept but an affect of conception like humor, love, or hatred (*Der ironische Deutsche*, p. 277). He believes that it demands that one discuss it ironically, and he believes that, in having tried to do that in the analysis of an individual novel, he has shown "what it consists of." If, in the final analysis, this means that irony does not really show itself, then it seems to me this is indeed a necessary outcome for irony as such clearly cannot be demonstrated but, as we saw, only manifests itself in its various nuances through its expressive means.

3. Cf. R. Baumgart, *Das Ironische*, and Hans Mayer, *Thomas Mann* (Berlin, 1950), chap. 14.

4. Ronald Peacock, "Much is comic in Thomas Mann," Inaugural Lecture Bedford College, London, 1963.

5. Cf. my essay "Don Quijote und die Struktur des epischen Humors" [Don Quixote and the structure of epic humor], in *Festgabe f. Eduard Berend* (Weimar, 1959), from which I took a shortened version of my determination of the structure of humor. It is no accident that it applies to Thomas Mann's superhumor as well as to *Don Quixote*, and it will be clarified in the following analysis.

6. But Hans Wysling too ("Die Technik der Montage: Zu Thomas Manns 'Erwähltem' " [The montage technique: about Thomas Mann's "Holy Sinner"] *Euphorian* 57 [1963]) writes that "it was perhaps less the motif of mercy than the linguistic experiment" that attracted the author to this, in his own words, "small archaic novel" (p. 156).

7. In a passage from a letter that has now been made available from the Zurich Archive by H. Wysling, Thomas Mann indeed says about Krull and Joseph: "The latter preexisted in the former, and now that one is Joseph redivivus" (H. Wysling, "Archivalisches Gewühle Zur Entstehungsgeschichte des Hochstaplerromans," *Blätter d. Thomas Mann Gesellschaft Zürich*, no. 5 (1965):38.

8. Regarding this, see especially Oskar Seidlin, *Pikareske Züge im Werke Thomas Manns* [Picaresque features in Thomas Mann's work], in *Von Goethe zu Thomas Mann* (Göttingen, 1963). Here, too, as in other relevant discussions, the connections between Krull and Joseph are touched upon. In the essay by Eva Schiffer, "Illusion u. Wirklichkeit in Thomas Manns *Felix Krull* and *Joseph*, verglichen" [A comparison of illusion and reality in Thomas Mann's *Felix Krull* and *Joseph*], *Monatshefte*, February 1963.

9. Herman Mayer, *Das Zitat in der Erzählkunst* [The function of the quotation in narrative] (Stuttgart, 1961), p. 209.

10. Hermann J. Weigand, *Thomas Mann's Novel "Der Zauberberg"* (New York, 1933), p. 95.

11. F. Schlegel's *Pros. Jugendschr.* (Minor), II, 189.

12. Novalis, *Schriften* (Kluckhohn), II, 20. Regarding the relationship of Thomas Mann's irony to romantic irony, compare my *Thomas Mann und die Romantik* (Berlin, 1932). On romantic irony, see Ingrid Strohschneider-Kohrs, *Die romantische Ironie in Theorie und Gestaltung* [Romantic irony in theory and application] (Tübingen, 1960).

13. Helmut Koopmann, *Die Entwicklung des intellektualen Romans b. Thomas Mann*

[Thomas Mann's development of the intellectual novel] (Bonn, 1962), employs the term that Nietzsche used for Wagner's art and that was taken up by Thomas Mann—"double optics" among other things also for the symbolic substance and method of Mann which, in this book, is justifiably profiled as the true inner form of his novelistic art that eschews any realism.

The Lord of Small Counterpositions: Mann's *The Magic Mountain*

R. P. Blackmur*

Prophecy, like revolution, is a convulsive or expressive reaction to what has already taken place, whether in the heart, in the actual world, or in a confusion of both. The truth of prophecy is therefore a matter of feeling or inspiration. Prophets rage in religion and politics; in the arts, prophets dramatize the conditions, the feelings, which underlie the rage. The rage of the priest comes about because he has to look ahead to salvation, and that of the politician because he has to look ahead to action, and neither priest nor politician can confront the terrible cost of salvation and action without the protective aid and personal momentum of rage. It is exactly those who must deal directly with the actual world who cannot stand it plain; they have to rely more upon inspiration than upon feeling, or they could not play the prophet's role at all. As George Herbert's poem has Christ ask of Judas: "Canst thou find hell about my lips? and misse / Of life, just at the gates of life and blisse?" Christ was more than a prophet, though he began in prophecy. The artist is always less than a prophet, though one of the high values that may be placed upon his work is that of prophecy. He does not look ahead to salvation or action; rather he dramatizes what is saved or lost, what acts or fails to act. He looks at the actual world with only a secondary regard to the terrible cost it exacts in religion and politics. Since he is not compelled to deal directly with that world, he can afford a plain vision of it with only the protection of his form. He relies upon his feeling, and, rather than needing inspiration himself, inspires others. In that inspiration which he creates, not that to which he pretends, is his power of prophecy; he prophesies, by giving form to his feeling of it, what we actually are.

It may be of course that he pretends more. Of all forms of purity the least possible is that a man shall be purely an artist, and that is especially so in an age like our own when we make so much more use of our artists than in ages just past; when, in fact, we pretend that our chief access to reality is in the aesthetic experience of it: that is to say, in experience

*Reprinted from *Eleven Essays in the European Novel* (Orlando, Fla.: Harcourt, Brace, Jovanovich, 1964), 75–96. Copyright © 1964 by R. P. Blackmur. Reprinted by permission of Harcourt Brace Jovanovich, Inc.

without responsibility. In such an age the temptation is great for the artist to pretend to the roles in which his audience casts him and to become the culture-hero to whom all things are possible. Perhaps temptation is the wrong word, it may be a contagious disease, of which the artist is only the alternate host, and for which he cannot be held responsible. At any rate, the masterpieces of our time gradually reveal themselves, by the uses to which we are forced to put them, as philosophies, religions, politics — and as the therapies and prophecies of these. This seems to have happened only partly in the sense that the arts have tried to take over the *functions* of these modes of the mind; it has happened much more in the sense that the *experience* of these modes of the mind has become the most pressing part of the subject-matter of the arts. It is not the artist's fault if his audience insists on confusing function and experience by the special arrogance of ignoring and the special vanity of uncommittedness in relation to existing society. The point is, our masterpieces are therapy and prophecy, though they cure nothing present and envisage nothing future. They see and state. And of course, with the formal advantages that go with the arts, they state better than they see.

These considerations ought to apply to almost any devoted reading that we do; it is almost an accident that they are meant here to apply to a re-reading of Thomas Mann's *The Magic Mountain*. It is less of an accident because these considerations have become natural *as a result* of the character of that book, together with its sequels. When first read, in the early twenties, one looked at it backwards through the war of 1914; now one looks at it through the second lens of the second war, and the double lens shows it in greater magnitude — so great, it looms the more the more it recedes. And this greater magnitude depends precisely upon that power of prophecy which comes to the artist who dramatises the actual thought — thought in all its senses — of his own time. It is this aspect of *The Magic Mountain* we here examine.

The artist of this kind shows us where we are ahead of ourselves; shows us with what in ourselves we have not yet consciously caught up; shows us, in short, as at the verge of a new shift, a new metamorphosis, of the old omniform which is our mind. It is ourselves — creatures, as we think, of the mid-twentieth century — whom we see in this legend of the *haut-bourgeois* at the climax of the nineteenth century; and we see all the clearer because the mechanisms and predilections are nineteenth-century, and we know how to discount them. It is not the nineteenth-century mind which Mann shows, but what had happened to it.

He shows it, of course, by a special twist; by the idiom of his sensibility; by establishing confines for his vision, outside which he will not look unless the pressure of his sensibility forces him to do so. It is the special twist body and soul take when they do not know where to lie. It is the idiom of an infected sensibility, with a polarity each extreme of which spreads like a stain into the other. The confines he sets for his vision are those of seemly obscurantism, which become, under pressure, the looming confines of the anonymous and the communal. This sequence is not a trick of the mind, it is a mode of operation common enough everywhere the bourgeois mind survives in its old honesty. It is a mind bent on protecting its certainty from its own restlessness and random anarchic promptings: hence the seemly obscurantism becomes unseemly, a demagogy of the soul addressing the soul, with a following tendency towards the intemperate, whether in discipline or the breach of discipline. But if the mind is honest in some dark corner it finds it cannot abide on its own practice; its obscurantism becomes indeed unseemly — the protection of something intolerably smothering; and the anonymous and communal, if the pressure of honesty is great enough, break through and see the mind again upon its task of making full assent to the conditions of life with will and choice, with reason and imagination. The story of Hans Castorp is told according to this sequence; but what happens to him is not that he takes up the mind's task, but that his example (the confines in which he is envisaged) shows us, the readers, that the task is there but cannot be taken up, at least not by the kind of man this young engineer stands for in any society he can comprehend. In the actuality of Hans Castorp's predicament is Mann's prophecy: where it works we have a feeling that reality itself is mired in the predicament; where it fails is where the terms of the predicament seem to have mired, not reality, but some human idiopathic horror of it.

That horror of reality — that cultivation of hallucination and fantasy — is what revulses us in the book, and one would like to believe it merely some way-station on a route we need not travel; yet it seems also the positive, ever-tempting escape of suicidal shame. The rate and scope of prophetic power in the arts vary. It may be that we have left behind Mann's vision without, yet, the power of seeing how we have done it or where we are. Mann's vision is gloomy: of an illness so uncopeable that it must somehow be identified with life: the vision of a society composed at every articulate point, of outsiders to that society. The gravity of our disorder seems plain in the fact that we do not think the heroism of the outsider or of the artist unnatural, but in the right course of things. Thus we resort to private force as if it were evangelical; to private absolutisms as if they were magnanimous; to panaceas as if they were specific. This is our own form of the suicidal shame which overcame the world of the magic mountain, and which Hans Castorp, though he could not handle it, could in the end see straight, see through, and reject. It was not his disease after all, this shame of the surface convulsion — of the Blue Peter and the Silent Sister — but a deep parallel to it, at the very bottom of the anonymous and the communal.

It is because we can recognize that this is so — so of Hans Castorp; so of us — and because we can use Mann's novel about Hans Castorp as also about us, and therefore as both an instance and a part of the act of recognition — it is because of these things that we may yet escape the stop-short predicament of Hans Castorp. To recognize, to say, is almost everything in the life of the mind. What we say, what we master in the saying, is our creation; and what we create is necessarily what we are. We create, in the end, only what we potentially are. Creation is discovery.

It is in the arts above all that creation is discovery. Every form of the imagination belongs to the heuristic mode of the mind. Better, the heuristic mode belongs to the polymorph of the imagination. Better still — and here is where the adventures of Hans Castorp come in — the use of the imagination prevents us from the seemly obscurantism of thinking we already know what we are, and what others are, by compelling us to find out, in the instance, as an exemplum, and by an act of recognition. That is what we do symbolically in the arts, and that is what, by the symbols they make, the arts do in us. And there is this blessed difference between our relation to the arts and to other modes of the mind: the heuristic imagination is always a renewable act and can never pretend to be complete. America must always be rediscovered, because *this* America was never discovered before, though of course, as we like to reassure ourselves in the dark, it was always there.

It was always there; and, as always, it must be found when not being looked for; it must be a true discovery and yet must seem an accident; otherwise one would reject it in advance as being either incredible or intolerable. *It was always there*, and whatever it was, it was what the settled forms of knowledge either excluded or converted into an institutional mystery. Only the charlatan and the quack got at it as a regular thing. Only in dreams did it invade the ordinary nineteenth-century individual. Therefore, if the spirit was quickened or agitated enough — restless enough without force, dubious enough without reference to conviction — one turned to the charlatan and the quack, to the unseemly, the illicit, the shameful, the equivocal, one turned and thought the turning a part of the process of rebirth; for so to turn was to come on the missing half of reality, *to what was always there all along*. One thinks of the French symbolists, of the less energetic hedonists, of art for art, of pure poetry: one thinks of the biography of the artist from 1800 to 1900, of the biography as a kind of standard for subject-matter, and how what was at first appropriate to the biography finally came to be the subject-matter itself: the artist against society. It remained for the artists of the twentieth century to show, on the model of the bohemian artist, the ordinary man against society: man devouring himself in the effort to renew himself, to come on the thing, still alive, *that was always there*.

Mann's *The Magic Mountain* is a legend of how such an ordinary man tapped the resources within him of charlatanry and the equivocal, and came, by the growth of his sensibility, upon what it was that made charlatanry possible and the equivocal inevitable as the mode and the result of experience. Where the artist takes hold of his material expressively and molds as much of it as his form will take, the ordinary man is taken hold of by the material as far as he can be reached. The chief conceptual form of Mann's novel is the relation between Hans Castorp and his experience, and the relation is predicated more or less equally by the simplicity of Hans at an intellectual level and by the equivocalness of the experience at the level at which it is felt. The relation, then, is the stress between the simple and the equivocal; and the progressive epiphanies of that stress constitute the movement of the book. Everything that works towards these epiphanies — and everything that can be *converted* from a less to a more available phase — adds value to the conceptual form. Everything that works against — everything that hides or obviates — these epiphanies detracts from the value. Everything merely intellectual, for example, must either be converted into, or deeply allied with, the sensibility. Hans must never lose his naivety, no matter how high a value is assigned to it. On the other hand, as the experience represented takes up more and more of the intellectual burden of the modern mind, it must always be brought back to that equivocal status in which it had appeared in the first place in the mind's history.

This is, of course, one way of getting at the problem of remaking culture, and it is interesting to note that society should have gotten into such a situation that a novelist would tackle the job from a point of view so near the amorphous, so anxious for metamorphosis, certain only of the polymorphic: as if culture were again embryonic, but with a prospect, not of original birth in sin or imperfection, but of rebirth in disease and shame. As readers, we need keep the problem of remaking culture only in the background, precisely as Mann may have kept it only for future consideration. The conceptual form of the stress between the simple and the equivocal, especially when exhibited in terms of a pattern of rebirth, is an extraordinarily powerful instrument with which to compose a novel. As a form it cannot help putting into relation what it takes hold of, and it has the great advantage that it works as well no matter in which direction the stress is set up. In Mann's story of Joseph, it is the hero himself who is equivocal, and his experience one simple blow after another. In the story of Hans Castorp the direction is opposite. But in both stories the conceptual form is identical and bears the fullest possible burden of the experience of culture as it actually is: what *occupies* the relation between the hero and his world.

The weight of culture and its reformation is imponderable and ever-pressing. Let us take it here only as a novelist's subject. Let us see how Mann went about making his subject malleable, keeping it plastic, letting happen to it what must, under the force of his strict conceptual form. It is the form — such is the seriousness of the novelist — that stands for the weight of the culture, stands for it with a kind of ascetic abandon. The novelist plays it for all it is worth, but binds himself not to exceed that worth.

Therefore he takes precautions. He makes his hero not only simple but ordinary, and he makes the experience of his hero not only equivocal but also an extension of ordinary experience—the little expected, but always astonishing and puzzling extension from a particular health to its corresponding disease. The words are all familiar, but the accents come in new places; there is either more emptiness or more thickness between the syllables. The more one knows what is going on, the more one is disconcerted; precisely because it is the familiar that has been converted into the strange, and never—here is where the asceticism comes in—the strange that has become familiar.

The sequence in which Mann leads his readers to receive these impressions, constitutes another precaution. Hans is felt as ordinary before he is discovered as simple, but the experience is emphasized as equivocal before it is discovered as familiar. Only the achieved simplicity can cope with the familiar. Had Mann reversed his sequence—had he led from the simple to the ordinary, the familiar to the equivocal—the relation between them would have existed, but only at a minimum stress, like a ghost at high noon, and been immediate prey to the nearest intellectual formularization. That is why, as a further precaution, Hans does not come to us with much useable intellectual furniture; the lack of it not only prevents him from substituting formula for response, it also hinders the reader from doing so. It is the sensibility stands between, for Hans, and for ourselves.

There are more precautions, but we do not need to examine them. Let us touch rather on some of the forces Mann risks letting loose on Hans without precaution just to see what they will do. As Mann is far from an economical writer there are a great many of these forces that cluster about Hans; if he is not furnished with ideas he is furnished with a multiplicity of attributes, and the meaning of many of them is not fixed but floating. Thinking of all these attributes together, one concludes that Hans is representative but not himself the thing—perhaps not even a part of the thing—he represents, though touched by it. He is bourgeois, but he is haut-bourgeois, that is to say, the lever but not the substance of the characteristic phase human power took in the nineteenth century. He is the conservator of something no longer there to conserve; rather like the eighteenth-century gentleman in nineteenth-century England or America. He belongs to that aristocracy which, unless it has individual talent or predatory ability, is without function beyond the preservation of ritual against a better time. Mann puts it that he is mediocre, but in an honourable sense. He is a man disinclined to active life or any function of it. Trained as an engineer, he can feel no calling in it, and cannot open his great textbook on steamships. But he puts a good face on it; he will appear active, and will live with what good face can go without a good heart. He is something of an artist, but only in the sentimental sense where talent is not an issue; he neither takes nor gives authority in his relations to the arts, but bemuses them to his own less than conscious purposes. He takes care about eating and drinking and smoking his Maria Mancinis, about his clothes and all creature-comforts, and about music of the kind that heightens or obviates creature-comforts. He has even a kind of taste in all the arts that protect and occupy his indolent repose. In short, he is representative rather than conscious of the weaknesses of the age he feels so little a part of. He is his own foil; he shows off clearest against himself. Yet in some sense he could see that there was no positive reason why he should exert himself; he seemed to know that incentive and motive must come from outside — and the outside gave no sign. Hence, in Mann's view, he is not quite mediocre. He is therefore a possible victim of a spiritual and physical palsy of doubt and discontent in a world which gave no answer to ultimate questions. The ritual of his being craved a little the substance of conviction. He could not, like the extraordinary man, conquer an alien world by "moral remoteness and single-mindedness" or "exceptionally robust vitality." But in his mediocrity, he might, under the right circumstances, find out what things are; and in that possibility lies his honour. We see at once that he is one of those young men who are to be occupied with a search without entirely knowing that he has undertaken it. It will be more as if the search had undertaken him. He will respond more with his sensibility than his mind, yet his mind will shift with his sensibility, a kind of permanent reserve accommodation ready at no matter what destination. But it is the sensibility, not the mind, we see shift as he moves from the role of life's delicate child, who can practice only seemly obscurantism, to the role his mistress assigns him of *joli bourgeois à la petite tache humide*, in which he finds he can sink into obscurity itself, thence to his third role, where he re-emerges as life's delicate child but at an infinitely higher rate of value.

When he comes, this pretty bourgeois, to the magic mountain, it is partly to visit a sick cousin, and partly to give himself a change of air, a vacation, an interlude, before taking up the serious business of life. Thus the trip combines duty with license; it is a legitimate extravagance of spirit — a confession that life rests on something other than its settled forms, an avowal that there must be an occasional respite from virtue to make it regularly tolerable. The bourgeois, by inventing the idea of vacations, made only one in the long series of devices men have made to maintain themselves in an intolerable society; and his further step is to have made the vacations themselves intolerable. Hans Castorp's experience on the magic mountain follows the pattern of vacations, with the difference that it lasted longer than expected and discovered new modes of the intolerable.

The difference is because he takes his vacation among men and women of all races of Europe, all young, all in the service of death, and all fevered. The youth counts more than the death, and the fever counts more than either. Fever is that shifting standard by which things are never right. In fever, though the old things happen, they do not happen at the same rate, in the same relation, nor with the same result. In fever even the most ordinary things are equivocal. The magic mountain is inhabited by the youth of Europe at fever-pitch, and serves as a kind of excess paradigm — a prophecy in darkness — for William James' speculation that if you raised the body temperature a degree you would change the human race. The fever is the sickness that accompanies the change — the *process* of a shift in phase; when the fever goes, stable phase will have been reached, the phase either of a new thing or of death, there is no telling which. Fever alters, fever cleans, and it burns up what it cleans; fever is like spirit in Santayana's phrase, it chills the flesh and is itself on fire.

At first, so to speak, Hans is feverish but does not have fever. He has feelings of extravagant joy, of reckless sweetness; he sees the advantages of shame over honor, and he has, rather feverishly, the characteristic need of the bourgeois for the illicit when the law has gone (as, up here, it has gone) bad: the illicit is a restorative and it shows as the blessedness of the seductive. The push for the unseemly replaces the practice of seemly obscurantism. When he identifies his interest in Clavdia Chauchat with an unseemly boyhood experience his interest turns to infatuation with her reckless flabbiness and diseased flesh, and he produces, as the act of communion, a genuine fever in himself. Thereat, the two doctors make him one of them; the chief doctor assures him he has a talent for illness, and the other — that lover of disease to whom disease is love — shakes him warmly by the hand. It is a conquest.

It all goes back to that special characterization of Hans as mediocre: a product of an age he is discontented with; without moral remoteness or unusual vigor; without effective education either of past ages or of his own; a lover of death (that is of a stability not vital) and of his own ease. What should he want more than to prolong a holiday which has trapped him with both its actuality and its ceremony: compared to which his previous life and its ceremonies were only laid on. Now that he had the fever he had the sense of reality. Yet this mountain only showed the life below with the palsy to which it was by nature prone, and with its shame a little nearer the surface. Here everything was infected with itself. Ideals, intents, motives which had become pretenses of themselves were the first to suffer change to their true phase. Disorder, confusion, disease had become the immediate order of nature.

But if the story of how Hans developed a fever goes back to his mediocrity, it also goes forward — or inward — to something else. If the disease is seen straight for what it must be — Hans' moist spot *cannot* be tubercular, as his soul *cannot* be bourgeois — if his novitiate is truly passed through, it will be because there is a magnetism under the magic of the mountain, some attractive or propulsive force, something which when recognized as well as felt will seem a principle of order, clarity, health. Whatever it is, it will be whatever has made all this disturbance take place by the mere rise of a degree of temperature. At the moment when Hans has affirmed the rise—a little over a quarter of the way through the book—the disturbance is convulsive, a war of the equivocal which has not yet forced upon Hans' mediocrity the increment of simplicity but which has rather only immersed him in the half-awareness of elated abandonment. Nothing has moved towards clarity, let alone order and health; the magnetism is still magic, the force still seductiveness, the principle still contradiction. In Joachim Ziemssen, Hans' sick cousin, there is one remnant of the old world, the soldier's avowal of glory in death, but this Hans does not share. In Behrens, the medical director, there is the uncertainty and the humor of the question whether the disease comes to the mountain or the mountain makes the disease. In Krokowski, the psychiatrist, there is half a charlatan, but the other half is force, of darkness in light: of disease as what shines in the light. In Settembrini, the humanist, there is half-pretence and wayward emotion in the masquerade of order—the organ-grinder's order in the shape of a dancing monkey—but the other half is the force of aspiring rational will. In Madame Chauchat there is a tainted place—the taint of a cat always half in heat—but she is also what is tainted, or at least the sentiment of it: the vitality of the other thing, possibly shameful but in essence the very thing Settembrini would dignify if he had in reality the power he strove so feverishly to represent. To all these, Hans abandons himself with triumphant laughter and dreadful anticipation, and builds a double infatuation: with Clavdia Chauchat—sex as disease; and with death—life as a sickness, an infection, of matter; each in its most voluptuary form. That is what happens to the bourgeois who has conjured, or found, in himself, and thereby in his world, a rise of a degree or two of temperature: a passion for the moribund.

Only scorn—that earliest form of criticism—can momentarily pull him back. When Madame Chauchat scorns his hysterical advances, his temperature drops to normal; when she accepts him in manner it rises; when she accepts him in full—on carnival night when the Thou holds sway—he goes into delirious rhapsody of the shameless and the sacred. But it is only scorn of sex and death that has this reactive power. The scorn of Settembrini the humanist, the furious rebel of reason, only drives him on, a kind of unconscious devil's advocacy of further abandonment. Hans may be, as Settembrini calls him, life's delicate child; he is also more European than Settembrini thinks. Europe is not all Mediterranean, neither all reason nor all latinity. Nor was latin reason ever enough. It had always to be founded on something not itself, and commonly discovered that by itself it made life unbearable. The world was not yet ready for the atheism of reason, no more for Settembrini than for Hans; both served forces of an occult character, and Hans knew this better than Settembrini, for he had little protection—only the power of engorgement—against the primitive things which continually assaulted him. On the other hand he did not know enough to use Settembrini in fullness—for his dream of history and the noble lies by which the fragments of life are put together; he knew only enough to quote him and misuse him — which is what the bourgeois has chiefly done with the classical tradition. Settembrini was right, with the rightness of tragic insight that takes up the impossible role of evangelist and teacher; Hans Castorp was life's delicate child, and it was up to him to teach Hans the mature form of the European tradition: not what brought it to life but what permitted it to survive, what kept it alive, plastic, possible, plausible, prophetic.

But just as Settembrini did not have the effective scorn of Clavdia Chauchat, so he did not himself represent the whole of what he wished to teach; there was not enough in him to make a true simple. He needed the help of his rhetorical enemy the absolute will. This we get at once in the sickened, corrosively ugly, puny, and fashionably dressed figure of the Jewish Jesuit Naphta. The two argue, and in a peculiar sense complete each other, by confusing themselves. Hans, listening, takes up the attitude in which — in this Circe's palace — he had drawn pigs, and decides that Naphta is not a true Jesuit but a *joli jésuite* with a *petite tache humide*. Time passes, Joachim goes, Hans, alone, stays forever, and continues listening to argument after argument between the rational humanist position and the super-rational absolutist position. The one sees life philanthropically, the other sees life as a disease; they push into each other, and bind, like the dovetail joints of a box, until their friction is maximum. It makes little difference where the arguments take off, the result is the same. The crucial argument, for example, starts over capital punishment, and ends up with the will behaving like reason, and reason asserting itself wilfully. The argument has reached the merging point where nobody knows who is devout and who free-thinking. Mann's imagination is right. Surely the rational humanist is devout. Surely the Jesuit who will sacrifice everything to blessedness is a free-thinker. Surely he who would build a tolerable universe is devout and praises God. Surely he who insists on an intolerable universe at any cost is a free-thinker and blasphemes God with the degraded remnants of his faith.

It is a real question — the kind that forces such ordinary souls as Hans to simplicity as the only response to the equivocal — the question which is the greater temptation: to insist exclusively on that which is possible to know, or to insist wholly on the force of that which it is impossible to know. Each temptation leads to reckless omnicompetence and disaster; which is why each not only consents to, but invites the intervention of the terror. Perhaps the temptation *is* the invocation of terror, the one in the form of the eagle treading the dove, the other in the form of invoking the devil as incentive to God; the one by Revolution, the other by Inquisition. Here is the terrible dilemma, in Eliot's phrase, of the incredible public world and the intolerable private world: the dilemma of the impossible choice between doing good even though evil come, and doing deliberate evil in the hope that after the destruction good may have a chance to supervene. Either choice is heresy, one the heresy that goodness leads to blessedness, the other the heresy that good may be force. Mann did not invent this dilemma. To the ordinary mind everywhere, but especially to the mediocre mind of the disinherited bourgeois who has any sense of simplicity at all, it is the central form of the struggle between the tolerable world and the intolerable world as ideals for action. It is the struggle between the fool of virtue and the ascetic libertine. The pity is that there is no escaping action, and the curse is that action cannot escape the infection of thought. In this argument which sprang from a difference about capital punishment, we see how thought becomes action and how action takes resource in thought. The more other-worldly the source of power, the more the power seems to withdraw itself, the more the devil is uncovered and the more the power takes the all-touching, all-penetrating form of the terror. Total security would be total terror: the savage absolutism of the advantage of mankind seen in kingdom come, or the savage absolutism of rational truth as moral law: absolute spirit or absolute man.

Hans makes his spiritual exercises listening to all this. He has not mind enough to know how *little* mind is in Settembrini's reason or how *much* there is in Naphta's absolutism; how little the one, how much the other created in his own image. Naturally, therefore, when he tries to choose between the "all-consuming all-equalizing chaos, that ascetic-libertine state" and "the 'critical subjective' where empty bombast and a bourgeois strictness of morals contradicted each other," he tends towards Naphta's "morally chaotic All." All Clavdia Chauchat represented: abandon, adventure, sin, shame, elation: all this tended that way. Hans understood very well the *petite tache humide* of extreme submission and even better the palsy in his neck and chin. Thus he took his spiritual exercises. Life's delicate child stretched his sensibility in terms of the Operationes Spirituales of the diseased Jesuit.

But he is not done stretching, and each further stretch is either in parallel or developmental response to this spiritual exercise. Here we will limit ourselves to the dream in the snow and the adventure of Peeperkorn, for in these two we have at the maximum the relation between the simple and the equivocal which is the conceptual form of the book, and have also the maximum reach of this novel as prophecy, both in relation to the polarity of Settembrini and Naphta. The chapter called Snow is a dream — part waking, part sleeping, part hallucinated, and part reawakened — in five parts. The first is Hans' innocent impulse to try the lion's maw, the sea's depth, the desert place, the winter wildness of the snow: by submitting consciously to nature he might find out the rank and stature of *Homo Dei*. In the second part, his heart struggles alone in the icy void, and he escapes his impulse by finding himself back at the hayhut where he had started, deliberately lost. In the third part, as he forces himself to wander on, ethics and religion, the will of the mind and the narcosis of the body, struggle to possess him. So begins the danger state in which abasement is the right action: he thinks of death in formal splendor, of Naphta's knout of discipline, and — while there intrudes a hallucination of Settembrini with a horn and a handorgan — of Clavdia Chauchat. Hands pull him to lie down in the snow. But he stands — there must be no coying with the bride of the storm — letting only his head droop. At once he is below, on the plains, their fragrant abundance, birdsong and rainbows, the climate of the living. Here, with the unbearable purity of an Italian tenor's voice, begins the fourth part of the dream. Spread before him is the pastoral of Mediterranean metempsychosis, full of sweetness and light and ceremony and maternity. Hans feels an unscrupulous outsider till he follows the gaze of a lovely boy within a temple. There two hags dismember and devour a child — life's delicate child — and he wakes, wrapped in the cold whispered brawling of their curse upon him, lying in the snow. The fresh strength of withdrawal from fatal sleep gives him, in the fifth part, the power of waking vision. He knows that it has been the great soul dreaming in him the anonymous and communal dream of human hope and its cost.

In this dream is the paradigm for Hans' conversion; it is also the point where Mann pushed his prophecy beyond the discovery of the actual into the revelation (that is, the pushed vision) of the real; and it should be noted that both for paradigm and prophecy Mann sticks to the conceptual form of the stress between the simple and the equivocal. In his dream Hans reaches that simplicity which absorbs the equivocal. It is, for him, the great man's dream, and while it still presses on his mind he not only knows the task of the mind but feels, in his healthy exhilaration, potent to perform his part in it. It is as if the fever had dropped and the future had *come again* upon the anterior state of what it always was. For the moment Hans is both morally remote and exceptionally robust, and he has that sense of conclusion that goes with necessary action. He has known reason and recklessness, all of man — flesh, blood, disease, death — and knows the name for all: the human being, the delicate child of life. He knows that behind enlightened man lies the blood sacrifice; and he knows that this is better than either the pennypipe of reason or the *guazzobuglio* of God and the Devil. He sees that if man can keep a little clear in the head and keep pious in the heart, then disease, health, spirit, nature are not themselves problems. "The recklessness of death is in life, it would not be life without it — and in the centre is the position of the *Homo Dei*, between recklessness and reason, as his state is between mystic community and windy individualism. . . . Man is the lord of counterpositions, they can only be through him, and thus he is more aristocratic than they. More so than death, too aristocratic for death — that is the freedom of the mind. More aristocratic than life, too aristocratic for life, and that is the piety of the heart." So for the access of moral remoteness. With the new exceptionally robust vitality he sees one more thing: that love and death do not couple, but that love is opposed to death. "From love and sweetness alone come form and civilization—but always in recognition of blood sacrifice. . . . I will keep faith with death in my heart, yet well remember that faith with death and the dead is evil, is hostile to humankind, so soon as we give it power over thought and action. *For the sake of goodness and love, man shall let death have no sovereignty over his thoughts.*"

Hans thinks that he will know all this forever. But this great man's dream cannot last in this middling young man, at least not as a force, only as a change in the beat of his heart, and as the sense of a mystery lost, held as a memory of rapture and as an incentive to gallantry. Though the dream had faded and the thought was no longer clear after dinner that night, it was with that memory and that incentive (that remoteness and that vitality) that he could see his dead cousin's face smile in its warrior's beard and could meet in full faith the extra-human vitality (without remoteness) of Mynheer Peeperkorn. Before both this life in death and this supererogation of life, Hans was himself a little lord of great counterpositions, owing and giving allegiance that shifted, but always the allegiance of self.

Almost he loses that allegiance when he is confronted with Peeperkorn. Peeperkorn wears a clerical waistcoat and checkered tails; he is Naphta and Settembrini together, without the emphasis of either, and with a tremendous blurred personality lodged in gin, wine, coffee extra-strong; in a voice of high moment but without matter or sequence but with a speaking gesture that made good what he did not say. He might be the lord of counterpositions, but he is more likely a torrent, the thing in man like a mountain, a waterfall, or the sea. Nobody like Peeperkorn can last very long in our lives nor can such men often last out their own lives. The pitch is too hard to keep and we are mostly unequal to the demanded effort of its example. Yet it is the pitch of life as force, force as fever—the pitch of the life force—of the going-on-ness without some pressure of which, some shifting stage of which, we should all stop; but it is a force converted too far beyond the human phase—even though it is what humans are made of. So converted, it is destructive force; in serving it we are destroyed by it if we do not protect ourselves from it, just as Peeperkorn, when love and alcohol fail him, destroys himself. Surely that is what is meant when his death is called abdication: he is the king of all those parts of ourselves we cannot be and live. Yet, as we are human, we yearn to serve his force even more than we dread his apparition. We seek what we must shun, as Melville said of Shakespeare; and we organize what we shun in order to go on seeking it. In armies we organize it as discipline and in religion as ritual, though we know that the act of war is beyond any discipline and that the act of religion is beyond any ritual. In the lesser creations of ordinary life we think we purge such apparitions, by toadying, by indifference, by ridicule, by thought—but if we stop thinking we feel the force within us.

That is what happened to Hans when confronted with Mynheer Peeperkorn. When he stops toadying and stops thinking he feels Mynheer Peeperkorn within him. That Clavdia Chauchat has returned to the mountain as Peeperkorn's mistress — attached to him because of his feeling for her and the anguish of that feeling — does nothing to bring about Hans' discovery of full feeling, but her presence makes a true contrast to that discovery. As she had become Thou to him on the night of the carnival of fever, so she is no longer so after the moment in the new carnival of feeling when Peeperkorn and Hans become — precisely in their struggle over her — blood brothers, become Thou to each other, and the reign of Thou holds full sway. Hans learns that Peeperkorn is human too; more human than anybody: the all-too-human we cannot be is human too: human on the grand scale, that scale which has the long perspective we call tragic when we do not call it love, but which taken out of scale, taken close, is holocaust. But here are Peeperkorn's own words, when he reprehends Hans for glibness over their relations to Clavdia. They are drinking wine by twilight, the old man abed, Hans at his side. "Feeling, you understand, is the masculine force that rouses life. Life slumbers. It needs to be roused, to be awakened to a drunken marriage with divine feeling. For feeling, young man, is godlike. Man is godlike, in that he feels. He is the feeling of God. God created him in order to feel through him. Man is nothing but the organ through which God consummates his marriage with roused and intoxicated life. If man fails in feeling, it is the surrender of his masculinity, a cosmic catastrophe, an irreconcilable horror." It is on this basis that the Thou holds sway between them. Yet, as they separate in the dark, Hans imagines Settembrini coming in suddenly and turning on the light, to let reason and convention reign. In the dark, alone, feeling becomes that wholly human, wholly intolerable creation: that thing out of the womb we call hysteria. Perhaps that is why, in the next chapter, after raising his voice, half man of sorrows and half sybaritic rogue, to harangue the waterfall ("that long catastrophe of foam and fury") he kills himself that night. It is not possible to convert nature into one's own hysteria, and if you try life becomes intolerable.

No matter. Such a push of hysteria is possible of actual experience at any time — it is the terrible temptation in the exercise of human powers of creation, and to feel it is to come on the quick of our disease, our ultimate giddiness. After his exposure to this temptation, Hans falls successively under the spells of the Great God Dumps, Music as the means of self-re-creation, Traffic with the questionable morass of the subhuman or unclean traffic with one's own nature, the General Contagion of rancor and hysteria ending in Naphta's suicide in the duel where Settembrini fires in the air, and lastly the spell for the coming war and Settembrini's death. Then Hans goes down into battle and vanishes. Living or dead, says Mann, his prospects are poor. Yet he had known in the Spirit what in the flesh he could scarcely have done: in moments — out of death and the rebellion of the flesh — a dream of love: that is to say the Reign of Thou over all the counterpositions of the human spirit. Mann addresses Hans, in closing, with the Thou of love and allegiance. Hans was indeed a small Lord.

Thinking of all this we see that Mann is indeed the innerly twinned child of Dostoevsky and Nietzsche. He springs from the human depths and also from those depths which are all-too-human. He understands the Apollonian and the Dionysiac, also the Inquisitor and the Galloping Troika (Dostoevsky's image of Russia, an image which Clavdia Chauchat had on her cigarette case): four precarious roles all resting on a surface which convulses, through the anonymous and communal, with its own appropriate terror, its underlying moral chaos and orgiastic freedom. He knows that terror intervenes because we forget it is there, a part of ourselves, into which we slip with dismay; but he knows too, that we can recast ourselves, if we will, if we remember and do not deny what lies under us, without the intervention of terror. But since it is not done, since terror does come, it is his business to prophesy what ought to have been remembered. He shows us therefore upon what violence, and at what extremities, the Thou comes to hold sway: by carnival, within the presence of personality, at death, and at war: in each case in response to a breakthrough.

In the simple, but mutually reversed, dualism of Naphta and Settembrini — that is, in the stress of Hans' relations to it — it is not so much their confusion that is shown, as that the conditions they have to meet are shown breaking through. The part of the mind that makes choice has still the old choice to make: namely, choice of the method of protection and control. The moist spots in each are in their attempts to replace the conditions of existence with themselves. The difference between them is that where Settembrini seems to ignore the abyss of feeling within him, Naphta, seeming to know it, does no more than create a false abyss of his own. In the structures of the mind there can be no sharper difference. Yet the current temptation will always be to take Naphta's invention of the private abyss as a real solution, needing no transformation, never seeing how relatively easy it is to make up for Settembrini's deliberate failure of vision as a mere oversight.

As a clarifying example, consider how Naphta could do nothing with Clavdia Chauchat, no matter how far you pushed him; yet Settembrini could, with but the restoration of his original insights (those in Hans' dream), do anything with her: her abyss is the real one: she is the force of it, as she tells Hans, which is why Hans changes his Thou from her to Peeperkorn. Both rest upon Clavdia as the sacred condition of life. As it is, both Peeperkorn and Hans feel Settembrini's prejudice against Clavdia somehow justified, as in her own way Clavdia does too. He is not "hu-man," she says, but she knows he understands the human, in her as well as elsewhere. It is Settembrini alone among all these diseased and defective figures who comes to his end as a part of human life, not by disappearance or self-destruction; and it is only by thinking of Settembrini that we understand the tragic failure of Peeperkorn's hysteria of the human: to remake the conditions of life in his own image. It is only Settembrini who suggests that man can still be lord of counterpositions.

What are they—these counterpositions? Do we not come at them in this novel which hints at reality by showing the actuality of all those conditions of life which it is the constant task of our waking moments to accommodate, expiate, and refresh? They are the golden eagle overhead, the anonymous and communal within ourselves. They are the actual of what one already knows, the reality that was always there.

Aspects of Parody in the Works of Thomas Mann
Hans Eichner*

There are not very many subjects to which Thomas Mann has referred as frequently in his writings of the last four decades as that of parody, and there is none which has been so persistently ignored by his critics; yet the author's remarks on this subject are not only of great interest in themselves, but form an invaluable commentary on his narrative technique and on his position in German literature.

As the most revealing discussions of the nature and function of parody are to be found in Thomas Mann's most recent novel, *Doktor Faustus*, this work provides the most convenient starting-point for an analysis of his use of this term.

When the hero of *Doktor Faustus*, Adrian Leverkühn, is exhorted by his teacher to take up music as a career, he pleads that he lacks the right attitude; all the conventional works of art, he complains, appear to him parodistic of themselves, all the devices and conventions of art appear to him to be suitable nowadays only for parody.[1] He feels that the traditional methods and conventions on which all art depends have become outworn and banal, that they are no longer in tune with the spirit of the time, and that modern society, highly critical, self-conscious and haunted by the spectre of its own dissolution, no longer provides a secure foundation for the artist to build on. Tormented by his own keen sense of criticism and by his awareness of the unprecedented difficulties which beset the path of the contemporary artist, he has come to doubt the possibility of great artistic achievement in his own day.

Leverkühn's friend and biographer, Serenus Zeitblom, comments on these doubts and misgivings as follows:

*Reprinted by permission from *Modern Language Review* 47 (1952):30–48.

[There is much illusion in a work of art, one could go further and say that it is illusory in itself, as "work." It desires to make us believe that it was not made but came about and sprang, like Pallas Athene in all the glory of her chiselled weapons, from Jupiter's head. But that is a pretence. No work ever came about that way. It is work after all, a working at art for the sake of illusion—and the question is whether, given the state of our consciousness, our knowledge, and our sense of reality, this game is still permissible, still intellectually possible, still to be taken seriously; whether the work as such, a structure that is self-sufficient and harmoniously enclosed upon itself, still has any legitimate relationship to total insecurity, problematic nature, and lack of harmony that characterizes our social conditions, whether not all illusion, even the most beautiful, and precisely the most beautiful, has today become a lie.]²

He quotes Leverkühn's remark, ["Illusion and play are opposed today by the conscience of art. Art wants to stop being illusion and play; it wants to become insight"]. And he comments:

["And whenever something ceases to coincide with its definition, does it not cease to exist? And how is art to live as knowledge? . . . [I ask myself with profound worry what strains, intellectual tricks, indirection, and irony will be needed to save it, to reconquer it, and to attain a work that, as a travesty of innocence, would admit to the state of consciousness that had made it possible"].³

The nature of these intellectual tricks and the doubts concerning the vitality of the artistic traditions of the bourgeois epoch which lead to them are further illuminated in Leverkühn's dialogue with the devil, who reminds the young composer of all his difficulties and sums up: ["What is to be sacrificed to criticism is the illusionary character of the bourgeois work of art in which music participates, even though it makes no image. . . . The conventions assumed to be required and binding that guaranteed the freedom of play have been done away with"]. Leverkühn retorts that one could know that and yet recognize the conventions in a sphere beyond all criticism ("jenseits aller Kritik"): ["One could raise the game to a higher power by playing with forms, knowing that their vitality has vanished"]. And now the devil supplies the name for the form of art which plays with outworn forms: ["I know, I know. Parody. It could be fun if it were not quite so dismal in its aristocratic nihilism"].⁴

Thus it appears that parody is the only way of composing which is left open to Leverkühn—at least without the aid of those states of frenzied inspiration which sweep away his critical objections and which are due to the artificial stimulus of disease, but which Mann condemns, on the symbolic plane of the novel, as a gift of hell. The dialogue in which this gift is offered to Leverkühn is timed so as to take place in the year 1911,⁵ a fact which is not without significance. It was about this time that the expressionist movement was coming to the fore in German literature—in the previous year, for instance, the first three expressionist magazines had been founded — and Thomas Mann has condemned expressionism — "all art which is not controlled by the intellect" — as "black magic"[6] a phrase which at once reminds us of *Doktor Faustus*. But the year 1911 was also a turning-point in Thomas Mann's own life. In that year he began to work on the first of his many novels which exhibit those very features which he has described in *Doktor Faustus* as parodistic — *Bekenntnisse des Hochstaplers Felix Krull*. In fact, there are no less than six works, which completely dominate the four decades from 1911 to the present day, to which he himself has applied such terms as parody or persiflage — *Bekenntnisse, Der Tod in Venedig, Gesang vom Kindchen, Der Zauberberg, Joseph und seine Brüder*, and *Doktor Faustus*.[7] Thus we have the following situation: in 1911, it is finally made clear to Mann's fiction-hero that the artist of his day is faced with the alternatives of either abandoning all intellectual control, a procedure which is "black magic," or resigning himself to the mode of parody. At about the same time, and in real life, the German writers of Leverkühn's own generation[8] came out in favour of irrationalism. And in the same year Thomas Mann himself, whose humanistic ideal of a synthesis of reason and instinct is directly opposed to an expressionist theory and practice, began to follow up the other alternative, that of parody.

Before the elements of parody in Mann's works can be illustrated, it will be necessary to make clear his highly specialized usage of this term. The passage which is most illuminating in this connexion occurs in a review of a little-known novel by Hatzfeld, *Die Lemminge* — a review in which Mann himself exhibits that inclination to regard works of art as if they were parodistic of themselves of which Leverkühn complains so bitterly in the pages of *Doktor Faustus*.

In this review, Mann quotes the following sentence of Hatzfeld's novel: ["Iwan Wagner spent one of the last spring days in a small town of that hilly terrain that, in light and serene undulations, extends to the foothills which form a connection with the higher and more impressive mountain ranges of Allgäu"]. Innocent as this sentence may sound, Mann comments on it as follows:

[This is pure parody. It is as though today someone began: "The Rhineland . . . that favored stretch of land without roughness in its weather conditions as well as the quality of its soil, richly settled with small towns and localities and gaily populated, must belong to the most attractive spots of inhabited earth." It is funny, playful, and fictive. The voice of the second, interposed author, of "the writer of these lines" who is pleased in parading the most literary expressions is beguilingly oldfashioned and naive to the point of drollery. But when it gets serious, when things are expressed through the medium of the epic writer himself, then it is different: "Then a car raced through the night. The moon suddenly soared, sank, squares swayed out. — Forests attacked it

like lustful dogs, and fell back again. Bluish glassy silence. Iwan Wagner
was fleeing, fleeing Leoni." That is something else. It is the voice of the
real, undisguised author, a new story with a strong dash of what one
calls Expressionism. No trace of the pleasant observer with his well
constructed relative clauses and his "serene undulations."][9]

As this passage suggests, the term "parody" is used by Mann to denote a
work of art whose old-fashioned or out-worn technique creates a humorous effect. Parody in his sense of the word, is closely related to irony, but
the two terms are not synonymous, parody being used by him exclusively
with reference to matters of technique, form or diction. Unlike irony, it
has as its substance an artistic tradition whose idiom has become antiquated. Mann's terminology is perfectly consistent and will be adopted for
the remainder of our analysis.

It should be realized that Mann does not, as has been suggested,
"show disapproval by parody."[10] The truth is the very opposite. Mann
himself explains his inclination to parody as a result of his lack of genuine
naïveté ("Mangel an eigentlicher Naivität"), and concludes that the
mainspring of his use of parody is to be found in devotion — ["Love for an
art in whose possibility one no longer believes"].[11] The tradition to which
Mann refers in this passage, and which is the most important model of his
parodies, is that of Goethe.

In his autobiography, Thomas Mann tells us that he was inspired to
write the Bekenntnisse des Hochstaplers Felix Krull, the first of his works
in which a parodistic technique is used, by reading the memoirs of
Manolescu, and adds: ["I received a fantastic intellectual stimulus from
the parodistic idea of transcribing a part of beloved tradition — the
Goethean autodidactic, autobiographical, aristocratic confessional — into
the realm of the criminal"].[12] Felix Krull, the retired swindler of Mann's
fragmentary novel, looks back on his career of fraud and deceit with the
same detached and loving appreciation with which Goethe writes of his
own life in Dichtung und Wahrheit. The shafts of Mann's irony, however,
are not only directed against certain features of autobiography, but even
more so against an aspect of fiction, the "illusionary character of the work
of art" which is discussed so extensively in Doktor Faustus. An excellent
example of the manner of the fragment — of the ["intellectual tricks,
indirections, and ironies"] about which Mann writes in connexion with
Leverkühn's compositions — is provided by the very first passage of the
novel:

[At the moment of grasping a pen, in complete leisure and solitude —
healthy by the way, even though tired, very tired (to the extent that I
will only be able to proceed in short stages and with frequent periods of
rest) — in getting ready then to confide my confessions in that clean and
pleasing handwriting that is characteristic of me to the patient paper, a
fleeting reservation sneaks in as to whether I am equal to this intellectual enterprise in terms of my prior education and schooling. But then,

since all that I have to report is composed of experiences, mistakes, and passions, and thus I am in full command of my material, that lingering doubt could at the most refer to the tact and decorum of expression that I possess, and in these matters, according to my opinion, regular and successfully completed studies are less important than a natural talent and a good upbringing.][13]

The devices which Mann named in his review of Hatzfeld's novel can be recognized at once. Here are the "well-constructed relative clauses" — so many of them, in fact, that the "writer of these lines" has to repeat himself and to employ brackets to ensure the clarity of his sentences. Here are the "most literary expressions" — "the patient paper" / "this intellectual enterprise" / "tact and decorum of expression." Moreover, while it is perfectly fitting that Krull, the retired swindler, should ask himself whether he possesses the necessary qualifications for the composition of the book, the reader who enters into the spirit of the passage will bear in mind that the burden of authorship is really placed on shoulders very well equipped to bear it; again, when Krull avows that the narrative consists of his "most personal and immediate experiences," the reader may well interpret this avowal as an allusion to the fact that by writing Krull's memoirs Thomas Mann also symbolically portrayed his own experiences; for the illusionary form of existence ("unwirklich-illusionäre Existenzform") which is typical of the swindler is equally typical of the author.[14] Krull protests too much — a few paragraphs further on he goes so far as to insist that the only moral value of his account lies in its absolute truthfulness — and the reader is unable to suspend his disbelief precisely because he is so often implored to do so. The decisive difference between the *Bekenntnisse* and the ordinary Ich-Roman is that the reader of the former is expected to keep in mind that the interposed narrator is a fictitious personage.

Bekenntnisse des Hochstaplers Felix Krull is a work of unusual charm and freshness, and one could fill pages with amusing illustrations of its technique. As the parodistic devices employed in it are, however, not essentially different from those of *Doktor Faustus* and *Der Zauberberg*, which will be discussed in greater detail, we may now consider the next work in which Mann himself has pointed out parodistic features, *Der Tod in Venedig*.

Der Tod in Venedig deals with a writer of outstanding achievements who has become a representative figure in public life. In order to lend such dignity to his work as would reflect the character and position of its hero, Mann aimed at a close imitation of the sovereign style of *Die Wahlverwandtschaften*.[15] Although he had already begun to work on the *Bekenntnisse*, he must have been hoping for a while that it would be possible, after all, to continue the tradition of Goethe in a straightforward manner, as is suggested by the optimistic prediction of a new classicism he made at that time.[16] Some four years after the completion of *Der Tod in Venedig*, however, we find him considering ["how all stylistic adaptation always touches upon parody and becomes parodistic"];[17] and in the light of this remark it is hardly surprising that he should have reached the conclusion that the 'Meisterstil' of his tale was "Anpassung, ja Parodie."[18] The reader may find it difficult to subscribe to Thomas Mann's verdict on his own work. It cannot be denied that the diction of *Der Tod in Venedig* occasionally borders on the archaic, but this is so perfectly attuned to the atmosphere of the story that its author has remained the only critic to find in it the seeds of mockery. Yet, if Mann's judgement is unlikely to be accepted, this can only increase its value as an indication of his attitude towards art; once again, we see that he himself has that fastidiously critical outlook, that dread of the remotest suggestion of triteness and cliché, and that tendency to regard works of art as if they were parodistic of themselves, of which his fiction-hero Leverkühn has so much cause to complain. It is well to remember, as is suggested in *Doktor Faustus*, that these qualities also have their advantages, that they alone will provide that constant urge to find new ways without which art would cease to develop, and become stagnant.

From the time of *Der Tod in Venedig* onwards, Mann has avoided the form of the modern realistic novel in his major works.[19] Before these can be discussed, however, a few words must be said about the hexameter idyll, *Gesang vom Kindchen*, which precedes them. The avowed model of this poem was Goethe's *Hermann und Dorothea*, with which it shares the background of "Krieg und Völkersturm"[20] and — a detail Mann does not mention — the division into nine *Gesänge*. Mann first became acquainted with the form of the hexameter as a child, when he read Homer in German translation,[21] but the verse of *Gesang vom Kindchen* is modelled on Goethe's rather loose hexameters rather than on those of Voss, who tried to imitate the classical metre as closely as possible. In fact, when the metrical defects of his poem were pointed out, Mann promptly countered with a reference to Goethe: ["The bumpiness so often mentioned by the critics is to the best of my knowledge only apparent. If one reads the rhythms not as hexameters but freely, then, as people with a fine sensitivity to language have confirmed to me, they read well. Besides, I like to remember in this connection how Goethe had begged old Voss to mark the bad hexameters in "Hermann und Dorothea," and how he received the answer that, to Voss' regret, they would all have to be marked"].[22]

I doubt whether Thomas Mann's critics were much impressed by this rebuff, but it gives rise to an amusing speculation. As Thomas Mann knew of the elder Voss's comment on *Hermann und Dorothea*, it seems likely that he also knew of the conversation between Goethe and the younger Voss, in which the poet refused to emend the famous line with a supernumerary foot, the "siebenfüßige Bestie."[23] "Ungerecht bleiben die Männer, und die Zeiten der Liebe vergehen" ["Men remain unjust, and the time of love is gone"].[24] This would account for the fact that *Gesang vom*

Kindchen also contains a line of seven feet: "Unter dem seidenen Gezelt von meerwinddurchatmeter Bläue" ["Under the silken tent of a blue breathed through by seawinds"].[25] If Mann had intended the extra syllable to be slurred, he would probably have written "seidnen" or "seid'nen." As it stands, the line may well be interpreted as a humorous allusion to *Hermann und Dorothea.* The contrast between the heroic metre and the homely subject-matter which prevails in large parts of Goethe's poem — a contrast which, to be sure, only adds to its charm — foreshadows the parodistic elements of *Gesang vom Kindchen.* Thus the descriptions of the cart-horses as "Hengste," "schäumende Rosse," etc., in contexts which sustain the reader's awareness of the bourgeois setting, are plainly mock-heroic, and the paraphrase of "he began to speak" in the line "Da versetzte der Vater und that bedeutend den Mund auf" ["Then the father spoke and opened his mouth with meaning" is certainly a parody rather than a straightforward continuation of Homer.[26]

In *Gesang vom Kindchen* parodistic features are both more frequent and more noticeable. The most striking instances are those in which modern scientific terminology occurs side by side with words that are obsolescent:

Dürftig nährte der Deutsche sich, da feindliche Kriegsmacht
Ihm die Zufuhr sperrte; es fehlte an Fett und an Eiweiß.

Fluß des Mittelohrs, also lautet' betrüblich sein Wahrspruch.
Da galt es pfleglich vorzugehen und nach der Verordnung:
Wasserstoffsuperoxyd, das dumpf and brodelnd im Ohr braust,
Einzulassen. . . .[27]

[Poorly was the German nourished, for enemy strength
Barred his transport; fat and protein were lacking.

Fluid in the middle ear, thus worrisomely his prophecy.
It was a matter of care then and following orders:
Hydrogen peroxide that muffled and bubbly rushes in the ear
To introduce. . . .]

Passages such as these may produce a smile, but they remain on the purely verbal plane, and do not compensate the reader for the defects of the poem. Mann's parody is at its best when it transcends the verbal plane, when the humorous effect of the startling, slightly unusual and sometimes deliberately precious *mot juste* is supported by sly thrusts at the central and most indispensable conventions of the art of storytelling, as is the case in *Der Zauberberg.*

In the contemporary realistic novel, the events portrayed "sing themselves out through the medium of the epic poet," to use the phrase coined by Mann in his review of *Die Lemminge.* The narrator is invisible and omniscient, he carefully avoids anything which might in any way remind the reader of his existence. The events of the story are, on the whole, presented directly, without the aid of an interposed narrator, and the question of their reality is never raised. This mode of presentation is employed in the bulk of Thomas Mann's work up to the time of the *Bekenntnisse*.

In the novel of the eighteenth and early nineteenth centuries, the method of presentation is usually very different. Thus Heinse, in the preface of *Ardinghello*, gravely informs the reader of the circumstances under which he found the manuscript of which the novel purports to consist. In other novels, there is a narrator, usually the real author himself, who continues the tradition of the story by word of mouth and of whose presence the reader is almost continually aware. The narrator often addresses him directly, adds personal comments to the events, refers to the characters of his story by such tell-tale phrases as "our friend" or "the hero of our tale" and attempts to convince the reader of his veracity by accounting for his knowledge. It is this type of narrative which Thomas Mann parodies in *Der Zauberberg*. Needless to say, he is by no means the first to have done so; he had countless predecessors from the time of Cervantes onwards. Wieland's *Agathon*, to name as an example the earliest of the series of *Bildungsromane* to which *Der Zauberberg* belongs, purports to be based on a diary of its hero, of which the author himself suggests in his preface that it does not exist. Thomas Mann himself points to the tradition in which *Der Zauberberg* has its place when he calls it ["a story that . . . strangely, ironically, and almost parodistically undertakes to renew the old German novel of education in the manner of Wilhelm Meister, this product of our greatest bourgeois epoch"].[28] Among the many novels in this tradition, it is *Wilhelm Meister* itself, a work which Mann has singled out as "the representative novel of the Germans,"[29] to which *Der Zauberberg* is most closely related in its content. As regards the parodistic aspects of Mann's novel, they form so close and natural a continuation of the technical tradition of *Wilhelm Meister* that the assumption of any other model seems superfluous, though some of Mann's critical comments plainly show the influence of F. Schlegel's theory of Romantic irony. A brief survey of the narrative technique of Goethe's novel will enable us to illustrate this point.

The narrator of *Wilhelm Meister* makes his presence felt for the first time towards the end of the first, very short chapter. When Wilhelm and Mariane meet and embrace, we read: ["Who would dare to describe the scene, who has the right to express the bliss of two lovers!"].[30] He refers to Wilhelm as "unser Held," "unser Freund," etc.[31] His knowledge of all that concerns his characters appears to be unlimited at first. He is able to portray thoughts and feelings as well as actions and conversations. A particularly impressive example is the description of Wilhelm's changing emotions in the night in which he discovers Mariane's presumed infidelity. Elsewhere, however, when it is evident that certain actions take place without a witness, he carefully phrases his statements so as to imply his uncertainty: ["When he [Wilhelm] was quite alone in the evening and did not need to fear being disturbed, he used to wear a silk sash around his body, and at times he is supposed to have . . . stuck . . . a dagger behind his belt"].[32] In a similar case later on in the book, the narrator forestalls the reader's question as to the source of his knowledge by humorously accounting for it: ["Sleep would not come; he put the slippers on his table, walked up and down, occasionally stopping by the table, and a roguish genius who was spying on him insists that he spent a great part of the night busying himself with the most darling little shoes"].[33]

In later parts of *Wilhelm Meister*, especially in the *Wanderjahre*, Goethe observes the restrictions imposed by his method of narration more carefully: inconsistencies are rarer, and the narrator is at pains really to account for his knowledge. He pretends to have made inquiries with regard to the past history of Hersilie's uncle ["What we could find out follows"]);[34] and hints darkly at unspecified sources of information about the "Mann von fünfzig Jahren" ["The secret story tells us . . ."]).[35] On one occasion, he pretends to have been informed of the events he narrates stage by stage, in the order in which they occurred, just as we might hear of the fate of an acquaintance whom we only meet very occasionally: ["We will gladly admit, that, in the course of finding out about these events, we were somewhat worried . . ."].[36]

Another feature which is characteristic of the narrative technique of *Wilhelm Meister* but is largely absent from the modern realistic novel is the narrator's comment on his own procedure. At the beginning of the chapter which follows Wilhelm's discovery of Mariane's presumed un-faithfulness, for instance, Goethe explains in some detail why he does not provide an account of the time in which Wilhelm mourned her loss.[37] On another occasion, he searches for the right word, as it were, in the presence of his readers: ["She was what I would call with one word an 'empathizer'—someone who flatters a friend by paying attention to his ideas as long as possible, then just shows ecstasy"].[38] In the *Wanderjahre*, the narrator increasingly restricts his activities to those of an editor. A very large portion of the work consists of letters and documents, and repeated reference is made to Makarie's archives and Friedrich's minutes. Passages in which Goethe comments on his method of presentation or asks the reader's leave to include a poem or story become more frequent. An example of the latter feature is the introduction of the song of the "pilgernde Thörin": ["Since one later had reason to believe that this burlesque romance had some intimate connection with her, you will excuse me for including it here"].[39] A similar preamble precedes the 'Mann von fünfzig Jahren', and in the body of this tale the narrator interrupts his story and comments: ["Our readers will surely be convinced that, from here on, we must proceed with our story by narration and contemplation rather than by depiction"].[40]

Towards the end of *Wilhelm Meister*, the narrator even writes about the difficulties of his task:

> Here, however, the duty of reporting, portraying, execution, and combination becomes increasingly difficult. Who does not sense that this time we are approaching the end where we are in a quandary between the fear of losing ourselves in details and the desire to leave nothing unexamined. The dispatch that just arrived did, to be sure, inform us of many things, but the letters and the many attachments contained various things that were not exactly of general interest. Thus we tend to combine that which we knew then with that which came to our knowledge later and to conclude confidently in this way the serious business of faithful reporting that we undertook.][41]

This passage is interesting also from another point of view. As the narrator says that "we" had been informed of diverse matters by the messages which had just arrived, he must have been present on the occasion. This is the only passage in the novel in which the personal presence of the narrator at the scenes portrayed is explicitly claimed.

Another passage implies the identity of the narrator with Goethe. When Wilhelm is told why the dramatic arts are not tolerated in the Pedagogic Province, a comment is added by the narrator which contains a reference to Goethe's past: ["Let the editor of these pages confess himself here: that he included this strange part with some reluctance. Has he not also devoted more of his vitality and powers to the theater than was reasonable? And could one easily convince him that this has been an unpardonable error?"].[42] Apart from confirming an assumption which the reader would be unlikely to doubt in any case, this passage is of course a further illustration of the pretence, so important for the structure of the *Wanderjahre*, that Goethe merely acts as an editor and has no control over the happenings of his story.

In most of the examples which I have quoted, Goethe employs the conventions of the narrative technique he has chosen in a straightforward manner. Occasionally, however, he uses them as a humoristic device, for instance when he uses the convention of the limited knowledge of the narrator in order to tease his reader. Thus, he conceals the identity of Wilhelm's nocturnal visitor in the fifth book of the *Lehrjahre*, and speculates about it in a later chapter, pretending to be ignorant in order to arouse the reader's curiosity: ["the conjecture that the visitor of the night before had been Philine was strengthened by that, and we too see ourselves forced to join that opinion, especially because we cannot discover the reasons that made him [Wilhelm] doubt it and that must have filled him with a strange suspicion"].[43] We are only told at a very much later stage that the visitor really was Philine.

On another occasion, precisely the opposite course is adopted towards the same end. The narrator knows what profession Wilhelm intends to take up and what the fetish is that Wilhelm always carries about with him, but only uses his knowledge in order to tease the reader by refusing to share it with him. In the report of Wilhelm's talk with Jarno about his future, his plans are referred to as ["a certain business"], ["a useful art"], ["his goal"], ["the confidentially expressed purpose"], ["the plan once formulated"], etc., and the fetish – the instrument case of Natalie's doctor – is referred to as "etwas . . . das halb wie eine Brieftasche, halb wie ein Besteck aussah" – a description which looks sufficiently like a clue to set the reader guessing, but does not really give the secret away. The narrator adds drily, "was es aber gewesen, dürfen wir dem Leser noch nicht vertrauen." [but what it was we can still not reveal to the reader.][44] When, in the second part of the *Wanderjahre*, the reader's suspense as to Wilhelm's choice of profession might have subsided, a similar device is employed to restore it. We are told that an important event provided Wilhelm with an opportunity to make use of the skill he had only recently acquired, but Goethe adds again that he must not reveal any further details: "Welcher Art aber dieß gewesen, dürfen wir im Augenblicke noch nicht offenbaren."[45]

A rather more unusual example of the use of the conventional pretence of ignorance on the part of the narrator in order to mystify the reader is to be found in the "Mann von fünfzig Jahren." The hero of this tale wishes to return the embroidered portfolio which has been lent to him with a few lines of thanks, and thinks of Ovid's couplet, "Nec factas solum vestes spectare juvabat, / Tum quoque dum fierent; tantus decor adfuit arti," but decides against using these lines, for reasons which Goethe sets out at length. We are told that he decides on a course of action, which is, however, not revealed to us: ["How the friend got himself out of such a predicament is not known to us, and we must count this case among those over which the Muses themselves cunningly throw their veil"].[46] Now Goethe either held the key to the solution of his hero's problem and deliberately kept it from the reader, or failed to reveal it simply because he had not worked it out himself; but in either case, he only arouses the reader's curiosity in order to leave it unsatisfied, and the "Schalkheit" of which he writes is not the Muses', but his own.

There are also a number of passages – most of them in the *Wanderjahre* – which admit of two interpretations, one of which is straightforward, while the other is parodistic. At least one such passage, however, can be found in the *Lehrjahre*. Mariane has fallen asleep while Wilhelm tells her of his early passion for the puppet theatre. At the conclusion of his hero's narrative, Goethe expresses the wish ["that our hero may in the future find more attentive listeners for his favorite stories"].[47] Perhaps these lines only express the narrator's wish that his hero should find more sympathetic listeners in his later life; in this case, the passage is a straightforward application of the convention according to which the narrator claims, in the interest of the illusion of reality, to lack both foreknowledge of and control over his hero's fate. But the narrator does in fact provide for the audience which he wishes Wilhelm to find by letting him tell his story, as it were, in the presence of his readers, and the passage therefore implies the wish that the readers should follow the narrative attentively and thus be the "aufmerksamere Zuhörer" that he desires Wilhelm to discover.

Another similarly ambiguous passage occurs in one of Hersilie's letters. Having just told Wilhelm about the young hawker who brought her Felix's message, she adds that there was something mysterious ("etwas Geheimnißvolles") about him and comments: ["Such things are inevitable in novels these days, should we be encountering them in life?"].[48] It is quite possible, of course, to read this passage naively, but the critical reader will be inclined to regard it as a parodistic thrust at the illusionary character of the novel: if it is natural for Hersilie to distinguish between the hawker, whom she meets "im Leben," and the host of mysterious characters which were created by German novelists under the influence of Mignon and the harpist, it is equally natural for the reader of the *Wanderjahre* to reflect that he meets the hawker just as much "im Roman" as he does the others.

A last quotation will illustrate this point from another angle. When Goethe praises the work of the painter who accompanies his hero to Italy, he wards off the suspicion ["as though we were trying to pass something off on our gullible readers with the help of general statements that we cannot demonstrate"], by printing, in quotation marks, ["the judgment of a conoisseur who was to spend several years admiring these and similar [paintings]"].[49]

Surely the make-believe is here carried to an extreme. If the reader is inclined to think that the painter in question is an invention, his suspicions will not be allayed by the testimony of an unnamed critic who is just as likely to be an invention; and the reader who is not prepared to take Goethe's word for the quality of those paintings is just as unlikely to take the word of a critic whom Goethe specially created for the purpose. I do not profess to know what Goethe had in mind when he penned the testimonial; but the most natural interpretation of the passage seems to be that of high comedy. When similar passages occur in the novels of Thomas Mann, internal evidence and the author's own critical comment leave us no doubt that they must be interpreted in this light.[50]

The first paragraph of *Der Zauberberg* is a stylistic *tour de force* designed to make the parodistic intention of the novel clear from the outset, a method which is also employed in the *Bekenntnisse* and in *Doktor Faustus*:

[The story of Hans Castorp that we want to tell — not for his sake (for the reader will find him to be a simple though appealing young man), but for the sake of the story itself that to us appears worth telling to a high degree (though we should still remember in Hans Castorp's favor that it is his story, and not every story happens to everybody): this story stems from long ago; one might say that it is already quite covered with a historic patina, and must absolutely be reported in the tense of the deepest past.][51]

The narrator brings himself to the notice of the reader in the very first sentence of the book, directly refers to him and immediately begins to comment on his own procedure—features which would be quite out of place in the modern realistic novel—thus establishing the place of *Der Zauberberg* in the narrative tradition of *Wilhelm Meister*. A few lines further on, he refers to himself explicitly as 'der Erzähler', just as Goethe calls himself "der Redacteur dieser Bogen" or "ein treuer Referent."[52] In the context of Mann's novels, these conventions, however, undergo a slight transformation. The leisurely periodic diction of these works closely resembles the diction of *Wilhelm Meister*, as well as, for instance, that of the English novel of the eighteenth century, but its features are deliberately exaggerated. The reader of the opening sentences of *Der Zauberberg*, the first of which is so long that brackets have to be used to ensure its clarity, is bound to realize that Mann wrote them with his tongue in his cheek. They are full of the "wohlgefügte Relativsätze" whose parodistic effect is pointed out in his review of *Die Lemminge*, and such figures of speech as that of the "historischer Edelrost" supply the "höchst schriftstellerische Ausdrücke" mentioned in the review. When, in the following pages, further parallels between *Wilhelm Meister* and *Der Zauberberg* are pointed out, this element of parodistic exaggeration will be noticed time and again.

Like Goethe in *Wilhelm Meister*, but far more frequently, Mann lets the reader share in his search for the right expression: ["The high degree of pastness of our story stems from its happening before a certain turning point and boundary that was to divide life and consciousness. . . . It takes place, or, in order to studiously avoid any use of the present tense, it took place and had taken place in earlier times, in the old days, in the world before the Great War"].[53] Often he adds an explanation to a term he has chosen, or warns the reader that a term he has employed is not entirely appropriate:

[In an unrestrained manner, it was very much part of Hans Castorp's intention that she should notice some, yes, as much as possible, of it. We call it unrestrained because he was fully aware of the irrationality of his case.]

[Such a little verse decidedly did not suit him and his relationship to Madame Chauchat—the word "relationship" is to be chalked up to him, we refuse any responsibility for it.][54]

The question of the source of the narrator's knowledge is not nearly as important as in *Wilhelm Meister*. All the events of the story occur in the presence of Hans Castorp, and, with the sole exception of this character, the thoughts and feelings of the persons in the novel are not portrayed by the narrator unless they can be inferred from their gestures or facial expressions. With Castorp, however, the narrator is united by a special bond; his complete and unexplained knowledge of everything that concerns his hero is made the subject of ironic comment: ["You will protest that the narrator is spreading it on thick and romantic when he connects the name of tedium with that of the demonic and ascribes to it the effect of mystical dread. And yet we are not fabricating but sticking precisely with the personal experience of our simple hero which we know in a way that unfortunately cannot be examined and that clearly proves that tedium under certain circumstances can acquire such a character and cause such feelings"].[55] This passage may very well be a hint that Castorp's experiences symbolically represent the author's spiritual development, as has been suggested by Professor Weigand;[56] what concerns us here, however, is its parodistic aspect. In the very sentence in which the narrator casts doubt on his knowledge of Castorp's experience by refusing to account for it, he uses it in order to prove something else.

The fact that the bulk of *Der Zauberberg* is based on the assumption of the narrator's complete awareness of Castorp's experiences does not prevent him from pleading ignorance when it suits his purpose, as Goethe does with regard to the identity of Wilhelm's nocturnal visitor in the *Lehrjahre*. Thus Mann deals with the question of what his hero discusses with Dr. Krokowsky in the latter's consulting room by advancing a few suggestions and adding that these are mere "Vorschläge und Vermutungen." [propositions and guesses.][57] On other occasions, however, Mann takes the opposite course, letting the reader know that he could, if he chose, set his mind at rest as to the precise nature of an event of which only a hint is offered, but using his knowledge in order to tease him with a succession of further hints. This device, which we have met in the pages of *Wilhelm Meister* in connection with the profession Wilhelm intends to take up, is used by Mann with particular poignancy with respect to the fateful events of the night of the *mardi gras*: the narrator breaks off when Clavdia leaves the parlour, and in the sequel Mann drops inconclusive hints on at least five different occasions before setting the reader's mind at rest.[58]

A further parallel with *Wilhelm Meister* is provided by Mann's habit of utilizing the continued presence of a narrator in order to explain his method of presentation. Such comment is particularly frequent with regard to the "double time of narrative" the difference between the time it takes the reader to read the account of an event, which Mann calls "musical time" and the time taken up by the event itself, which Mann calls "imaginary time."[59] Mann reverts to this subject repeatedly, explaining that the ratio of musical time to imaginary time must, according to the rules of narrative, rapidly decrease in the later stages of the novel. The resultant disproportion, the rapidity with which imaginary time passes in the second half of the novel, is illustrated and parodied with such delightful humour that one example at least may be adduced in the present connection. Chapter VI of the *Zauberberg* begins as follows:

> [But, as far as the valley was concerned, the thickly snowcovered wintry valley . . . its ridges . . . had been covered with snow for six unthinkable but fleeting months, and all the guests were declaring that they could not bear to see the snow any more, it made them sick, for their requirements in this direction the summer had been enough. . . . And they put on colored glasses — green, yellow, and red, to protect their eyes but even more for the heart.
>
> Valley and mountains under snow for six months already? For seven! Time passes while we are telling our story.][60]

Thus one month has passed in Castor's life in the musical time taken up by a few sentences.

In the major work on which Thomas Mann embarked after the completion of *Der Zauberberg*, his parody of the illusionary character of the work of art takes a somewhat different form. The vast structure of *Joseph und seine Bruder* is really based on a foundation of legend and history. In contrast to the normal practice of historical novelists, Mann has made the criticism and collation of his sources an integral part of his narrative,[61] the text of the Joseph novels abounds with such phrases as ["according to the claims of tradition"] or ["that should be taken with some skepticism"].[62] Where his sources differ, Mann likes to tell the reader why he prefers one to the other; where he diverges from all his sources, he likes to present his reasons. Now Mann's erudition is vast and genuine, and his reconstruction of early Hebrew and Egyptian society, of the religious life and the psychology of the period, commands the admiration of the scholar as well as of the literary critic;[63] but his procedure is still further removed from that of the historian than from that of the ordinary historical novelist. The tradition of legend and story provides hardly more than the bare outline of what is, in the best sense of the word, a work of the imagination, and Thomas Mann makes the same claim to scientific accuracy for the freely invented parts of his novel as he makes for those parts which are really based on sources of one sort or another. Needless to say, all the protestations of historical accuracy, even when they are not wholly unfounded, are phrased in such a manner as to prevent the reader from taking them seriously. As the author tells us in his introduction, "the exactness, the realism are fictional, they are play and artful illusion. . . . The reasoning is also playful, it is not really the language of the author but of the work itself, it has been incorporated into its linguistic sphere, it is indirect, a stylized and bantering language, a contribution to the pseudo-exactness, very close to persiflage and, at any rate, to irony.[64] How far this persiflage goes becomes immediately obvious from the treatment of events which occur without a witness. On such occasions, Goethe in *Wilhelm Meister* displays uncertainty or has recourse to such obviously ironic phrases as that of the "schelmischer Genius" who spied on Wilhelm rehearsing his parts; Thomas Mann boldly and paradoxically insists that he knows what happened. When writing about Joseph in the well, for instance, the author stresses the hopelessness of Joseph's situation and adds: ["It might seem even more surprising that the dread of his own fate still left room in his soul for pity with his murderers"]. The reader would be unlikely to reflect that Thomas Mann could not have known, and any comment can therefore only detract from the illusion of reality. Thomas Mann nevertheless makes such a comment: ["But this is nonetheless the proven situation"].[65] The same procedure is adopted in portraying the scene in which Jacob sees Joseph's coat of many colours and infers that his son has been killed: ["It is a sure fact that Jacob fell over at the sight of the coat, in spite of all foresight. Yet no one saw how it happened"].[66]

It is perhaps this undercurrent of humour and mockery, together with the author's desire to make us realize that he is dealing with persons who are, in spite of the remoteness of their times, not so very different from ourselves, which is responsible for one of the less pleasant features of the Joseph novels — the jarring juxtaposition of antiquated terms, adapted to the setting of the story in place and time, and modern vernacular, apparently introduced in the interest of increased vigour. Thus Joseph's presumed death is expressed by the phrase ["that Dumuzi is no more and the spoiled darling is gone"],[67] and the porters of Pharaoh's palace say about Joseph and Mut-em-enet, ["the mistress is hot for the young steward, but he avoids her. What a mess!"].[68]

Thomas Mann had turned from the unfinished *Bekenntnisse* to *Der Tod in Venedig* partly because he had found the parodistic style of the former work "schwer durchzuhalten." [hard to keep up.][69] A similar need for change may have contributed to Mann's decision to turn to *Lotte in Weimar* before he had completed the Joseph novels. By virtue of the masterly adaptation of style to subject-matter and the prominence of dialogue and inner monologue, which reduces direct narration to a bare minimum, the technique of this work also deviates considerably from that of the ordinary historical novel, but it must nevertheless be regarded as the only larger novel Mann wrote after 1911 in which he did not employ a parodistic technique. He returned to this method, however, for the first larger work which he wrote after the completion of *Joseph und seine Brüder*, *Doktor Faustus*. Having explored the parodistic possibilities of the fictitious autobiography in the *Bekenntnisse*, of the technique of *Wilhelm Meister* in *Der Zauberberg* and of the pseudo-scientific mode of presentation in the Joseph novels, Thomas Mann now devised a fourth possibility — the fictitious biography. In *Doktor Faustus*, the outstanding feature of the fictitious autobiography, that the interposed narrator is a character of his own story, and the outstanding feature of the technique of *Wilhelm Meister*, that the narrator has to account for his knowledge, are combined. The personality of Serenus Zeitblom, the "biographer" of *Doktor Faustus*, is designed to meet widely different purposes. As a man of sober temperament, intellectual integrity and humanistic convictions, he can provide the commentary on the story and act as a foil to his more gifted and less scrupulous friend. As an educated man who is an amateur in the art of writing, he makes an ideal narrator for a parodistic novel. His eagerness to perform his task well, his dissatisfaction with the results of his efforts and his habit of apologizing for errors of composition instead of correcting them provide the foundation of the parody. It will be remembered that in the pages of this novel the charge is levelled against the bourgeois work of art that it purports to have come into being of its own accord, to be ["not made, but come about"], whereas it is really ["labor, labor of art for purposes of illusion"]. In a sense, *Doktor Faustus* is exempt from this charge: time and again, the reader is presented with the amusing spectacle of the fictitious narrator groaning under his task; but this of course only removes the objection one stage further. Behind the labours of the interposed biographer, the labours of the real author are hidden all the more inscrutably.

The style of *Doktor Faustus* is once again the deliberately old-fashioned style which is described as pure parody in the review of *Die Lemminge*, and the first page is once more designed to bring the parodistic intentions of the novel home to any but the dullest reader: Zeitblom loses himself in a maze of interjections and subsidiary clauses and has to repeat part of his sentence before he can bring it to an end. He tries to improve on himself or add some further remark for which the construction of his sentences, already overloaded, does not allow, so that he has to introduce his afterthought with a "will sagen" [what I mean] or "ich sage besser" [I should say]. His eagerness to say everything at once leads to such "highly literary expressions" as "langjähriges Studierzimmer" or "herzpochendes Mitteilungsbedürfnis" and to his description of Adrian's death as leading him "aus tiefer Nacht in die tiefste" [from deep night into the deepest], which is incomprehensible to the reader, who does not yet know that Adrian's death is preceded by insanity. Furthermore, the first paragraph of the book already contains the first ironic play with the illusionary character of the work of art. The interposed author expresses his concern at the impossibility of having Leverkühn's biography published — a remark which will be received by the reader with the mental reservation that the real author was aware that it would be published immediately upon completion; and he calls a "first and certainly very preliminary biography" what is, in fact, irrefutably final for the simple reason that it is not a biography at all.

The second paragraph brings Zeitblom's first apology for a supposed deficiency of style: ["I read over these lines and cannot but note a certain uneasiness and an irregularity of breath"].[70] And the fourth paragraph brings his first apology for a supposed fault of composition: ["Here I interrupt with the shamed feeling of an artistic failing and lack of control. Adrian himself would hardly have . . . let such a theme emerge before its time"].[71]

It is interesting to compare these lines with a similar passage in *Wilhelm Meister*. The interposed narrator of "Nicht zu weit" interrupts his narrative with the following remark: ["As can be seen strikingly at this point, we have, in arrogating to ourselves the rights of the epic poet, only too quickly drawn a favorable reader into the middle of a passionate scene"].[72] In both cases the supposed fault of composition has been committed deliberately; if Goethe had really felt that he had carried the reader with him too quickly he would have rewritten the passage instead of apologizing for it. In both cases also a narrator is interposed between the reader and the real author. This latter feature, however, is without any significance in "Nicht zu weit." Goethe makes no concessions to the personality of the narrator, and writes in his usual style; he does not even make allowance for the fact that this particular story is supposed to be told by word of mouth. The reader, hardly aware that there is an interposed narrator, will therefore be likely to accept the apology at its face value, regarding it as a typical feature of Goethe's conscious and sovereign art of story-telling. Thomas Mann, on the other hand, has adapted his style to the personality of Zeitblom, and the reader is neither allowed to forget that the passage is supposed to have been written by Zeitblom, nor that this supposition is fictitious: Zeitblom, like Krull, "protests too much." The reader will therefore be aware that the indiscretion for which Zeitblom apologizes has been committed deliberately by the real author, for the sake of the subsequent apology; thus, in Mann's hands, Goethe's straightforward device has become a means of parody.

Another connexion in which Mann adopts in a spirit of parody Goethe's habit of explicitly commenting on his own methods is the division of his story into chapters. Zeitblom feels that no chapter should exceed a certain length, so as not to tire the reader, but holds that every chapter should be homogeneous in its subject-matter and deal with it completely — conflicting demands which he is quite unable to resolve. The apologies and desperate remedies to which the unfortunate author resorts have a most humorous effect. Thus, when Zeitblom discusses Leverkühn's great oratorio, "Doktor Fausti Weheklag," considerations of unity prevent him from dividing his criticism into different chapters, but the length of the single chapter that would result if he were not to divide it all would be altogether excessive; he cuts the Gordian knot by dividing it into three sections and then restoring the lost unity by the chapter headings "XXXIV," "XXXIV Fortsetzung" and "XXXIV Schluß" — a truly Solomon-like compromise! Elsewhere, when he has strayed from his subject at the very beginning of a chapter, he places three asterisks under the passage and explains with naive complacency: ["Little stars too refresh the eye and senses of the reader; it does not always have to be the more strongly separating impact of a Roman numeral, and I could not let the above digression . . . acquire the character of an independent piece . . ."].[73]

The question of the narrator's knowledge occupies a special position in *Doktor Faustus*. In the *Bekenntnisse*, this problem does not arise, as the interposed author is writing about his own experiences; in *Der Zauberberg* it is solved by the assumption of a special bond between narrator and hero; in the Joseph novels it is absorbed in the pseudo-scientific method of the work; but in *Doktor Faustus* the narrator, who is a close friend of Leverkühn, limits himself almost exclusively to the report of facts of which he can reasonably claim to have knowledge. Zeitblom has to be credited with a phenomenal memory, but the verisimilitude is supported by all the devices, the references to hearsay evidence, notes and documents, and the occasional display of uncertainty, with which the reader of *Wilhelm Meister* is familiar.[74] Even so, the restrictions imposed by the form of the novel could not always be observed. On one occasion, Zeitblom leads up to a discussion of the problem, but loses the thread again.[75] And twice, when an intimate conversation has to be reported of which neither of the participants could conceivably have supplied Zeitblom with a verbatim account, his explanations are far from convincing: ["What happened between Adrian and Rudolf Schwerdtfeger, and how it happened—I know it, and let it be protested ten times that I could not know since I had not "been there," but today it is a spiritual fact that I have been there, for, when one experiences again and again a story such as this, one becomes through his horrible intimacy an eye and ear witness of its hidden aspects too"].[76]

A passage such as this contravenes the restrictions Mann has imposed on himself, and does not make entirely happy reading. Such inconsistencies are, however, very rare indeed, and on the plane of purely technical achievement, though perhaps not as a whole, the novel ranks very high among Thomas Mann's works. By selecting the form of the fictitious biography for his work, the author achieved a number of purposes apart from that of parody. As Zeitblom writes the biography during the last years of the war and describes the circumstances under which he is working on it, Leverkühn's gradual approach to insanity and the climax of the irrationalist orgy in Hitler's Germany of which this is a symbol are placed simultaneously before the reader's eyes, so that this novel, in a unique manner, contains its own interpretation. And although Zeitblom appears to be exclusively concerned with unfolding the life-story of his much-admired friend, he reveals so much about himself that he emerges finally as a more convincing and moving figure than the avowed hero of the novel. This impression is further increased if the reader realizes that, amongst the many passages in which the real author seems to watch

Zeitblom's labours with an amused smile, there are some in which he seems to address his public directly and with a tragic earnestness, and to use the thin disguise of the interposed author only in order to be able to speak more freely, without the bitterness which has so often blurred the message of his more personal utterances outside the realm of fiction in recent years. Viewed in this light, the passage towards the end of the novel[77] in which Zeitblom writes about his estrangement from Germany and the loyalty which he has proved by devoting himself to the writing of Leverkühn's biography is among the most moving Thomas Mann has written.

In spite of all this, the contemporary reader, with the events of recent history fresh in his mind, may well ask himself whether parody is really the appropriate form for so tragic a content, and whether Mann would really have chosen this form in this particular instance, were it not, in words he himself used of the young Leverkühn, that parody was ["in reality the proud evasion of the sterility that threatened a great talent through skepticism and an intellectual chastity, through the sense for the deadly extent of the kingdom of the banal"].[78] As he himself avowed while working on *Doktor Faustus*, parody was the only stylistic mode which he still felt able to use.[79]

The bearing which these considerations have on Mann's historical position as a novelist is obvious. It may be that the reconquest of the myth for the novel, in which, as he was well aware, his works play a leading role,[80] will inaugurate a new phase of achievement, but in matters of form his parodistic works stand at the end of a long line of development. He has often expressed the conviction that the bourgeois epoch, with which his work is indissolubly associated, is drawing towards its close, and if, through the lips of Goethe, he defined culture as "Liebe und Parodie,"[81] he was well aware that such culture, admirable as it may be, was the product of an age which was heading towards dissolution. Here, too, as in so many other ways, Mann felt that he was following in the footsteps of Goethe; for it is in words ascribed to Goethe that he sums up, in *Lotte in Weimar*, the historical position of parody: ["Parody . . . I like to ponder that most of all. The gentle thread of life gives occasion for much thought, much brooding, and of all the ponderings that accompany art, this one is the most oddly serene and delicate. Devoted destruction, smiling leavetaking . . . Conserving succession that is already a joke and an insult. To repeat the loved, sacred, old, the supreme model on a level and with a substance that puts the stamp of parody on it, and approximate the products of late, already mocking structures of dissolution such as the post-Euripidean comedy . . ."].[82] As for the works of his own maturity, he himself has called them, in words previously used by Harry Levin of the works of James Joyce, "novels to end all novels."[83]

Thus, in view of the historical position of parody, Leverkühn's tempter may be right, in a sense, when he calls it ["doleful . . . in its aristocratic nihilism"]. If the novel is to survive, it will have to find other ways of avoiding banality that those chosen by Thomas Mann. But to suggest that his vast achievement is the last of its kind is only to underline its greatness.

Notes

1. *Doktor Faustus* (Stockholm, 1947), p. 209.

2. Ibid. p. 280.

3. Ibid. p. 281

4. Ibid. pp. 373 f.

5. Zeitblom writes, op. cit., p. 326, that the dialogue took place either in the first or in the second summer Leverkühn spent in Italy, that is, either in 1911 or in 1912 (p. 344). The second of these dates must be rejected. The 24 years of the pact date from Leverkühn's infection in May 1906 to the outbreak of insanity in May 1930 (pp. 238, 356, 384, 745), and the dialogue took place almost five years after the conclusion of the pact (p. 355), that is, in 1911. Thomas Mann repeatedly made "zeitliche Berechnungen" when working on the novel (*Die Entstehung des "Doktor Faustus,"* Amsterdam, 1949, pp. 31 and 100), but he must have miscalculated by a few months; according to the devil, the dialogue took place *almost* five years after May 1906, that is, before May 1911; according to Zeitblom, however, Leverkuhn arrived in Italy only in late June (p. 326).

6. *I Believe. The Personal Philosophies of Twenty-Three Eminent Men and Women of Our Time* (London, 1940), p. 221.

7. *Der Zauberberg* (Stockholm, 1946), vol. I, p. xiv; *Betrachtungen eines Unpolitischen* (Berlin, 1922), pp. 60 and 78; *Rede und Antwort* (Berlin, 1922), pp. 358 f.; *Forderung des Tages* (Berlin, 1930), p. 47; *The Theme of the Joseph-Novels* (Washington, 1942), pp. 6 f.; *Die Entstehung des "Doktor Faustus,"* ed. cit. pp. 32, 37, 68.

8. The year of Leverkühn's birth is given as 1883. F. Kafka and E. Stadler were born in 1883, Sternheim, Unruh, Trakl, Heym and R. Goering all between 1878 and 1887.

9. *Bemühungen* (Berlin, 1925), pp. 306 f. The passage which Mann quotes in order to illustrate the comic effect of the sentence from Hatzfeld's novel is taken from his own novel, *Bekenntnisse des Hochstaplers Felix Krull, Buch der Kindheit* (11.–15. Tausend, Stuttgart-Berlin-Leipzig, 1924), p. 7.

10. Berthold Biermann, "Thomas Mann and Goethe," *The Stature of Thomas Mann* (New York, 1947), p. 249.

11. *Rede und Antwort*, ed. cit. p. 359.

12. "Lebensabriß," *Die neue Rundschau*, Jg. 41, vol. I, pp. 751 ff.

13. *Bekenntnisse des Hochstaplers Felix Krull*, ed. cit. p. 5.

14. Cf. "Lebensabriß," *Die neue Rundschau*, Jg. 41, vol. I, p. 751.

15. See Otto Zarek, "Neben dem Werk," *Neue Rundschau*, Jg. 36, p. 621.

16. "Uber die Kunst Richard Wagners" (1911), *Rede und Antwort*, ed. cit. p. 363.

17. "Der Bildungsroman," *Vossische Zeitung* 4 Nov. 1916.

18. *Betrachtungen eines Unpolitischen*, ed. p. 78.

19. *Lotte in Weimar* may be considered as the exception which proves the rule.

20. *Rede und Antwort*, ed. cit. p. 358.

21. *Herr und Hund. Gesang vom Kindchen. Zwei Idyllen* (1919), p. 143.

22. *Rede und Antwort*, ed. cit. p. 357.

23. *Goethes Gespräche*, ed. Biedermann, vol. I, pp. 385 f.

24. *Gesang vom Kindchen*, ed. cit. p. 170.

25. *Goethes Werke, Hgg. im Auftrage der Großherzogin Sophie von Sachsen* (Weimar, 1887-1912), I, vol. 50, p. 204.

26. *Weimarer Ausgabe*, I, vol. 50, pp. 189, 242 f., 227.

27. *Gesang vom Kindchen*, ed. cit. pp. 156 and 166.

28. *Die Forderung des Tages*, ed. cit. p. 47.

29. *Weimarer Ausgabe*, I, vol. 21, p. 6.

30. Ibid. p. 96.

31. *Weimarer Ausgabe*, I, vol. 21, pp. 43, 68, 82, 123, etc.

32. Ibid. p. 87.

33. Ibid. vol. 22, p. 197.

34. Ibid. vol. 24, p. 120.

35. Ibid. vol. 24, p. 267.

36. Ibid. vol. 24, p. 328.

37. Ibid. vol. 21, p. 117.

38. Ibid. vol. 21, p. 169.

39. *Weimarer Ausgabe*, I, vol. 24, p. 78.

40. Ibid. vol. 24, p. 334.

41. Ibid. vol. 25i, pp. 259 f.

42. Ibid. vol. 25i, p. 22.

43. *Weimarer Ausgabe*, I, vol. 22, p. 214.

44. Ibid. vol. 24, p. 56.

45. Ibid. vol. 25i, p. 32.

46. Ibid. vol. 24, p. 308.

47. Ibid. vol. 21, p. 43.

48. *Weimarer Ausgabe*, I, vol. 25, p. 36.

49. Ibid. vol. 24, p. 366.

50. In my interpretation of this novel, I am greatly indebted to H. G. Weigand's book, *Thomas Mann's Novel "Der Zauberberg"* (New York and London, 1933). Many of the passages from the novel which will be quoted below are discussed in this study. Professor Weigand mentions many points of contact between *Wilhelm Meister* and *Der Zauberberg*, but seems to regard the mode of narration employed in the latter novel as essentially romantic: "While the 'Zauberberg' derives from the realistic tradition in some of its surface aspects (and would be unthinkable without it)," he writes, op. cit. p. 67, "it stems in its essence from the tradition of German Romanticism." If we consider the influence of *Wilhelm Meister* to be more important, this is not to deny the many similarities between Mann's parodies and romantic irony as practised by the Romantics, who were also influenced by *Wilhelm Meister*.

51. *Der Zauberberg*, ed. cit. vol. I, p. 1.

52. *Weimarer Ausgabe*, I, vol. 25, i, pp. 22 and 260.

53. *Der Zauberberg*, ed. cit. vol. I, p. 1.

54. Ibid. pp. 210 f. and 208.

55. *Der Zauberberg*, ed. cit. vol. II, p. 437.

56. Op. cit. p. 73.

57. *Der Zauberberg*, ed. cit. vol. 2, p. 35.

58. Cf. H. J. Weigand, op. cit. pp. 75 ff.

59. *Der Zauberberg*, ed. cit. vol. 1, pp. 275 f., vol. II, pp. 300 ff.

60. Ibid. vol. II, p. 4.

61. Cf. Käte Hamburger, *Thomas Manns Roman "Joseph und seine Brüder"* (Stockholm, 1945), pp. 31 ff.

62. *Die Geschichten Jaakobs* (Berlin, 1933), p. xiv.

63. Cf. Karl Kerényi, *Romandichtung und Mythologie* (Zürich, 1945).

64. *The Theme of the Joseph-Novels*, ed. cit. pp. 6 f.

65. *Der junge Joseph* (Berlin, 1934), p. 230.

66. *Der junge Joseph*, p. 298.

67. Ibid. p. 291.

68. *Joseph in Agypten* (Vienna, 1936), p. 672.

69. *Der Zauberberg*, ed. cit. vol. I, p. xiv. The same phrase is used in *Doktor Faustus*, ed. cit. p. 326, of Leverkühn's comic opera on the subject of *Love's Labour's Lost*, on which the composer is working at roughly the same time (1910 or 1911): 'Die parodistische Künstlichkeit des Stils war schwer durchzuhalten.'

70. *Doktor Faustus*, ed. cit. p. 9.

71. *Weimarer Ausgabe*, I, vol. 25, p. 195.

72. Ibid. pp. 11 f.

73. *Doktor Faustus*, ed. cit. p. 272.

74. Cf. *Doktor Faustus*, ed. cit. pp. 13, 190, 204 f., 244, 343 f., etc.

75. Ibid. p. 231.

76. Ibid. p. 661. Cf. p. 673.

77. Ibid. pp. 764 f.

78. Ibid. p. 235.

79. See his quotation from his own diary in *Die Entstehung des Doktor Faustus*, ed. cit. p. 51.

80. Cf. K. Kerényi, op. cit. p. 31.

81. *Lotte in Weimar* (Stockholm, 1946), p. 291. Cf. ibid. p. 310.

82. Ibid. p. 355.

83. *Die Entstehung des Doktor Faustus*, ed. cit. p. 83.

84. *Doktor Faustus*, ed. cit. p. 374.

Myth Versus Secularism: Religion in Thomas Mann's *Joseph*

Henry Hatfield*

When Thomas Mann chose a Biblical subject as the theme of a major work, he exposed himself to legitimate questions about his own religious point of view. Had he abandoned the attitude of such earlier work as *Buddenbrooks*, in which the Christian figures are at best pathetic, or of *Der Zauberberg*, where the only avowed Christian is the basically unpleasant Naphta? Such questions are relevant in Mann's case; for except in a few stories and such relatively minor books as *Die vertauschten Köpfe*

*Reprinted from *Festschrift für Bernhard Blume* (Göttingen: Vandenhoeck & Ruprecht, 1967), 271–79, by permission of Vandenhoeck & Ruprecht.

and *Der Erwählte*, he was never a practitioner of *l'art pour l'art*. Even *Felix Krull* implies a moral standpoint, a Weltanschauung. Various critics have attempted to describe Mann's religious attitude: Anna Hellersberg-Wendriner, for instance, senses a ["Mysticism of divine absence"] in Mann;[1] Ronald Gray, very recently, has maintained that Mann really has no religious or ethical orientation: his whole attitude, Gray believes, shows his ambivalence, his nihilism, or both.[2] Although Mann himself, like many other humanists, moved towards a united front with Christianity during the Nazi period, he claimed even then to be endowed with no more than a certain religiosity.

In a sense it is paradoxical that Mann worked with religious (or quasi-religious) materials in the Twenties and Thirties, in decades when he was particularly fascinated by the ideas of Sigmund Freud. Freud after all considered religion an illusion and maintained in one of his last works that Moses was an Egyptian. Intrigued and impressed though he was by the importance of myth as a key to the unconscious and to primitive thought, Freud utterly rejected a mythical approach in dealing with contemporary affairs and personal matters. In a most friendly letter to Mann on the occasion of the novelist's sixtieth birthday, he extended no congratulations, for, he stated, "the bestowal of wishes is trivial and seems to me a regression to an era when mankind believed in the magic omnipotence of thought."[3] This seems unduly austere, but it makes Freud's own position completely clear: to think mythically in the twentieth century would be neurotic.

On some levels, the reasons for Mann's evocation of the world of the Old Testament are clear enough. We know that he planned, around 1926, to write an introduction to a book of illustrations of the Joseph story, and that he was intrigued by Goethe's remark in *Dichtung und Wahrheit*: ["This natural tale has great charm, but it seems too short, and one feels called upon to depict it minutely"].[4] Above all, Mann wished to break a lance for the Jews, the people who primarily represented *Geist* to him, in a time seething with anti-intellectualism and racial hatred. A shibboleth of the pseudo-romanticists of those days was myth, interpreted to make the term appear as the opposite of civilized thinking. Myth, then, was a major weapon of reaction disguised as progress.[5] Mann believed, however, that genuine romanticism implies faith in the future.[6] Characteristically, he decided to rescue the myth from the fascists and protofascists. In his *Joseph* he created a humane myth, a symbolic story of the upward development of man and his concept of God. As the tetralogy proceeds, however, its thrust from the mythic dimness of the patriarchal world to the clear light of Joseph's realm becomes increasingly evident. Perhaps this thrust from myth towards reason may also be read as a transition from theism to secularism.

Before taking up the religious and mythical aspects of the *Joseph* novels, however, I should quickly note that they have other important facets—political, social, autobiographical, and of course formal. Perhaps the comic element is as important as any other. In a highly suggestive, beautifully written essay, Mark van Doren has considered *Joseph* as a comedy in four parts. Van Doren notes its brilliant conversation; its relaxed, leisurely handling of time; and Joseph's failure, despite all his preternatural intelligence, really to understand himself and his own limitations.[7] Mann's skepticism is interpreted as a concomitant of his universality:

> The genius of Mann is skeptical in the finest sense of an often misapprehended term. It was not that he believed nothing: he believed everything; he liked ideas, and could live with all of them at once. No sooner did one start up in his brain than another came to reinforce, illuminate, or check it. This was why he could turn so soon from tenderness to pathos, and why he could mock the very man he loved the most. These transformations of his mood will bewilder anyone who does not comprehend how serious at last the comic spirit is. Nothing in man is more serious than his sense of humor; it is the sign that he wants all the truth, and sees more sides of it than can be soberly and systematically stated; it is the sign, furthermore, that he can remember one idea even while he entertains another, and that he can live with contradiction. It is the reason at any rate that we cannot take seriously one whose mind and heart have never been known to smile. The gods do not weep; they smile. Eternity is something like the sun.[8]

Returning to the immediate theme of this paper, I should like to examine first the introductory chapter of *Joseph*, ["Journey into Hell"]. (It is typical of the benign irony of the work that there is nothing infernal about this descent.) As has been noted, ["Journey into Hell"] serves as a quasi-musical overture to the tetralogy. Opening with the magnificent statement ["Deep is the well of the past"], it also functions as an introduction to the depths of time and to the mythical mode of thinking. Of at least equal importance in the interpretation of the novel are the few pages[9] devoted to retelling the Gnostic myth of the fall of the soul. In Mann's adaptation, the soul—"*die* Seele"—became enamored of sheer, unformed matter; God then created the world of forms so that "she"[10] might mingle with it and thus form living men. In her infatuation, she forgot her divine origin. To redeem the soul, God sent a messenger spirit— "*der* Geist," *Logos*—his mission was to destroy the physical world. Both life and death would then cease to exist, and the soul, free of her earthly entanglements, would return to heaven like a prodigal daughter returning to her true home. The spirit however in turn falls in love with the soul, despite or because of the fact that she has been interfused with the material element. Both literally and morally, the spirit and the soul have fallen: they are, or seem to be, alienated from God.

From this myth—which of course has striking analogies with the fall as related in Genesis, Mann boldly infers that the story of man is older than the material world.[11] Spirit and soul,[12] in their involvement with matter, must be images of man, that two-souled, problematic creature who is irresistibly attracted by both the sensuous and the divine. Yet God deeply loves man, is fascinated by his dual nature, and finds him far more interesting than those representatives of pure spirit, the angels. (Naturally enough, the angels — who refer to man sarcastically as "das Engeltier" — bitterly resent this, as does a recent commentator.)[13]

To press the argument a step further, I suggest that the "romance of the soul" mirrors the action of the novel as a whole, just as ["the Lament of Doctor Faustus"] is a mirror and symbol of *Doktor Faustus*, as ["Before the Law"] is a miniature recapitulation of Kafka's *Der Prozeß*. As I shall try to show, the spirit in Mann's myth plays a role analogous to Joseph's own. Mann wittily compares the spirit's romance with the soul to the case of an ambassador who becomes so entranced with another nation that he betrays his own:

["The intellect's fate in this mission is much like that of the emissary of one kingdom to another, enemy one, who, if he has to stay away for long, is ruined for purposes of his own country in that he, unawares and by way of naturalization, adaptation, and gradual contamination glides into the attitudes and interests of the opposition to the extent that he is no longer suited to represent the interests of the home country and must be recalled"].[14]

Similarly, Joseph's role as the mediator between Pharaoh and the people suggests the spirit's mediation between God and matter; as "metatron" or second in command in his realm, he also recalls the Gnostic demiurge. Like the spirit, he leaves his home for a lower realm — to his father, Egypt is a sort of hell — and lingers indefinitely in a world which attracts him sensually and intellectually. Even in the Bible, we remember, Joseph remained in Egypt and was buried there.[15] Again like the spirit, however, he is not deprived of his higher nature, nor does he forget his native land. And Egypt is by no means a hell, any more than the world in Mann's very anti-Gnostic variation of the myth is really evil. God can never have seriously intended to destroy it.[16] Mann's interpretation of the "romance of the soul" reminds one of Robert Frost's lines:

> But God's own descent
> Into flesh was meant
> As a demonstration
> That the supreme merit
> Lay in risking spirit
> In substantiation.[17]

In character as well as role, Joseph reminds us of the spirit. A mixture of savior and rogue, he reflects spirit fused with ensouled matter. He is *tâm*[18] — a combination of "Yes" and "Yes-No." The "lower" aspect of his blessing, the Biblical "blessings . . . of the womb," links him to the flesh and the senses. Joseph's wittiness is one of his major attractions, and wit itself is a messenger, the ["mediator between the father's and the mother's heritage"],[19] reconciling the principles of light and dark. (Wit is conceived in the novel largely in its older meaning of skill in forming ingenious intellectual combinations.)

Actually, his secular, humanistic endowment is closer to Mann's taste than is the purely spiritual blessing which Judah finally received. Similarly, as we have seen, Mann's God prefers men to angels. His God is as genial and tolerant as is the God in Goethe's ["Prologue in Heaven"], a deity wittily compared to Old King Cole by Oliver Alden in Santayana's *The Last Puritan*. Indeed, the angels believe that God has a less serious attitude toward the moral realm than does the fallen angel Semael, the Mephistophelean but hardly Satanic champion of evil;[20] and these jealous servants of God even hint that He himself contains an element of evil:[21] in other words, He is *tâm*.

In evoking the world of Jacob and his ancestors, Mann took great pains to elucidate the mythical way of thought. He explains elaborately how "moon grammar" reduces the three modes of time to an eternal present, and how patriarchal figures identify themselves with their archetypical predecessors. Napoleon's identification of himself with Julius Caesar and Seneca's line "Medea nunc sum!" are examples of this sort of mythical thinking, which still occasionally persists. Mann's own sense of *unio mystica* with Goethe, and Hitler's apparent obsession with Wagnerian heroes, are twentieth-century examples. As the long novel proceeds, however, ["moon grammar"] is increasingly replaced by the clear light of day. Once he has matured, Joseph thinks and acts realistically and logically. Freud would have approved.

Moreover, various antimythical forces operate throughout the tetralogy. Characters are psychologically analyzed and 'unmasked' with a subtlety which owes much to Nietzsche and Freud. Thus Isaac becomes blind *so that* he can give the blessing to Jacob rather than to Esau, and Joseph seems to want unconsciously to anger his brothers. There is a wealth of realistic detail, recalling Mann's statement: "Ohne Realismus geht's nicht. Es ist der Rückgrat und das, was überzeugt." [you can't do it without realism, that's the backbone and that which persuades.][22] Occasional flashes of irony or parody distance us from the realm of myth: the scene in an Egyptian border fortress recalls a modern customs and immigration inspection; Egyptian nationalism suggests German chauvinism. It is even said that God has "a great theological career" before him. In the fourth volume, Joseph's sense of acting out a story planned long before by God becomes increasingly obvious. At the end, the fairy-tale note provides a culminating *Verfremdungseffekt:* ["And thus ends the pretty / story and God-invention of"]. What a myth, but alas, only a myth! to paraphrase Faust's exclamation.

The reciprocal relation between Abraham and God is complex and subtle. On the one hand, Abraham has no doubt that God objectively exists; on the other, he realizes that he is himself "to a certain extent" "God's father." God needs Abraham and the other prophets to help Him develop from a crude tribal divinity to a genuinely monotheistic deity. The narrator neither affirms nor denies God's objective reality, but possibly *Das Gesetz,* a pendant to *Joseph,* affords insight into Mann's attitude.[23]

Paradoxically, the novel's very wealth and richness of mythological reference have a relativizing effect. That Joseph's life reflects the myths of Osiris, Adonis, Dionysus, and other gods, and that it anticipates the crucifixion and resurrection of Jesus Christ, may suggest that all such accounts are only mythically or symbolically true. If the mysterious messengers who frequently appear throughout the novel are mythically both angels and the god Hermes, perhaps *de facto* they are neither. And it is by no means clear that Pharaoh Ikhnaton's monotheism is inferior to Hebrew religious concepts.

Since *Das Gesetz* was written immediately after the completion of *Joseph* (in 1943) and plays in the same Hebrew and Egyptian milieu, one may turn to it for additional illumination of the novel. As Mann characterized it as on the whole a ["lightweight improvisation"],[24] one should not overemphasize its significance; but precisely because it is a not too seriously intended work of art, Mann felt himself free, I believe, to express his personal opinions. Here mythical thinking is not practiced; the author is much more outside—and above—the story. Aside from its immediate function as propaganda against the Nazis, the story is interesting largely in its concept of God and its portrait of Moses as the artist; the two elements are closely interrelated.

Moses is seen as a sculptor of human beings: he molds the Hebrew people, which has become crude and demoralized in its long Egyptian captivity. By providing the erring nation with a code of moral and practical behavior, he instills conscience into it. Later, after inventing the Hebrew alphabet, he hews out the Decalogue, twice, illuminating the letters with his own blood. (The Bible states expressly that the commandments were written down by God's finger.)[25] Half an Egyptian,[26] he has the necessary artistic distance from his human raw material. He is passionate and sensual, but, as in Judah's case, precisely his passions make him "hunger and thirst after righteousness." Moses' great creation however is not the Decalogue or the molding of the Jewish people but—God.

Such an interpretation may seem startling or worse, but it is in line with the skeptical, downright Voltairean tone of the work. All the miracles are rationalistically explained; the Hebrews behave at least as badly as the Egyptians; and Moses, soon to be the transcriber (or author) of the commandment forbidding adultery, has a lush Moorish concubine, since his wife no longer appeals to his senses. In fact, 'God' (Moses' conscience or unconscious?) never forbids anything Moses really wants. In recounting Moses' proscription of incest, Mann includes the outrageous, or outrageously amusing, clause: ["You are not even allowed to sleep with your aunt . . ."].[27]

Revealingly, Moses often links himself most intimately with God: he tells the people that ["Jahwe and I"] want them to behave decently.[28] Other turns of phrase are even more significant. When Moses castigates the mob for attributing salvation to the golden calf (in *Das Gesetz* it is a sexual symbol, a golden bull), he states that he alone led the people out of Egypt [" – the Lord speaks"].[29] The following sentence is the most explicit of all: [" 'I am the Lord your God,' he said, at the risk of their taking him for that in actuality . . ."].[30] In forbidding false witness, he employs the threat ["I want to devour him"];[31] later, after the affair of the golden calf, God threatens to devour the whole nation of backsliding Hebrews.[32]

Res ipsa loquitur: 'God' is a projection of Moses' own imperious will. Yet Moses is by no means a hypocrite; rather, he has, like all Mann's artists, an "all-too-human" side. Nor is Mann nihilistic or basically cynical here: he upholds the Decalogue and the symbolic validity of God, though only at the cost of sacrificing God's actuality. 'God' knows that men will not keep the commandments; 'God'-Moses knows all too well that he has broken at least two of them himself. But Moses has learned the hard way that violation of the moral code imbues the sinner with the "ice-cold" sense of anxiety and guilt – ["and it would be better for him not to have been born"].[33]

To return to *Joseph*: we recall that it traces God's development and "great theological career": it is in that sense, as in others, a *Bildungsroman*. But educational novels end, and whatever has developed will presumably decline. We note also that Joseph himself is really far closer to Hermes than to Jehovah; and Hermes is of course only a charming symbol. Yet Joseph is not a "debunking," antimythical novel. As Käte Hamburger well says: ["The story of Joseph . . . is only a hint, a beginning, a vague reflection of the myth of the gods, but it is precisely still such a hint, beginning, and reflection"].[34]

While Thomas Mann believed – symbolically – in many gods, he believed in them only to the extent that they represented to him a humane, rational ethic and view of the world. To him, intellect and wit were an essential part of humanity; as Aristotle said, a stupid person cannot be good. That Mann preferred Erasmus to Luther is relevant here. Mann was far too conciliatory and too courteous to proclaim shrilly that "God is dead"; his God is a construction, a projection of the best in man, a beneficent fiction. He writes in *Joseph* of a God of the future, but he may well have envisioned a future without God. Here a quotation from Harvey Cox is very relevant to an "urban-secular" writer like Mann:

> The central question is: What are the sources of meaning and value by which man lives his life? Are they created and imposed by God, or does man invent them himself? It is characteristic of urban-secular man that he perceives himself as the source of whatever significance the

human enterprise holds. His perception is confirmed by modern cultural anthropology and by the sociology of knowledge. Symbol systems, the constellations of meaning by which human life is given value and direction, are seen as projections of a given society. They change when the society changes and in predictable ways. There is nothing timeless or divine about them.

But does not this theory of the source of meaning in human life rob God of His divine prerogative? How can we accept this grandiose assessment of man's place in the universe without at the same time limiting or degrading God?[35]

How indeed? — and Mr. Cox never really answers his own rhetorical question; far more than Mann he wants to have the best of both worlds, avant-garde and theological. Not at all cynically, Mann implies that "an honest God's the noblest work of man." Many may find this frivolous, but Mann gave in *Joseph* his aspect of truth — next to love the highest of our values. As Peter Gay notes in his splendid vindication of the Enlightenment: "In their more pacific, generous moods, the philosophers conceded to the pious man his share of honesty, but they considered him incapable of pursuing an inquiry to its end — the man caught in myth must make the myth, not the truth, his final value. . . ."[36] If I understand Mr. Gay correctly, he implies that myth and symbol have great value, but that a man must decide whether or not they should prevail over rational truth: he *cannot* have it both ways. The kingdom evoked in *Joseph* is secular, a kingdom of man at his best, in which human beings err, as in *Faust*, but in which human adventurousness, inventiveness, and above all, human love are decisive. *Joseph* is a statement of a paradoxical faith in man, doubly paradoxical when one thinks of the dark times in which it was written.

Notes

1. See *Mystik der Gottesferne* (Bern and München, 1960), *passim*.

2. See *The German Tradition in Literature 1871–1945* (Cambridge, 1965), esp. pp. 105–223.

3. Letter to Thomas Mann [c. June 6, 1935], in Sigmund Freud, *Letters* (New York, 1960), p. 426.

4. *Johann Wolfgang Goethe* (Gedenkausgabe), X (Zürich, 1948), p. 157.

5. *Gesammelte Werke* (Frankfurt a. M., 1960), X, 258 f. Hereafter this edition will be cited only by volume and page.

6. X, 267 *et passim*.

7. At the end of the novel — to disagree with one point while agreeing with the rest — Joseph does understand his own limitations, I believe.

8. "Joseph and His Brothers: A Comedy in Four Parts," in *The Happy Critic* (New York, 1961), p. 74.

9. IV, 39–49.

10. The fact that "spirit" is masculine and "soul" feminine in German is of psychological, mythical, and perhaps even philosophical importance.

11. IV, 39.

12. Mann speaks of a "higher identity" of spirit and soul, and seems to hint that the future will make this clear.

13. Cf. Gray, pp. 185–207, esp. p. 187.

14. IV, 43.

15. Genesis 50:26.

16. Also, since Mann calls *Geist* the "second ambassador," God must have intended the soul to behave as "she" did. (IV, 42, 45 f.)

17. Frost, *In the Clearing* (New York, 1962), unpaged dedication (in part).

18. Käte Hamburger, *Der Humor bei Thomas Mann* (München, 1965), p. 203. This book is a revision of Frau Hamburger's *Thomas Manns Roman "Joseph und seine Brüder." Eine Einführung* (Stockholm, 1945).

19. Cf. Hamburger, *Der Humor*, 200.

20. V, 1284.

21. V, 1287.

22. Mann, *Briefe 1948–1955* (Frankfurt a. M., 1965), pp. 231 f. (Letter to H. Hatfield, 19. XI. 1951).

23. The story, not one of his major achievements, will be briefly discussed below.

24. In *Die Entstehung des Doktor Faustus* (Amsterdam, 1949), p. 20.

25. Exodus 31:18.

26. See Freud, *Der Mann Moses und die monotheistische Religion* (1938) and Käte Hamburger's introduction to her edition of "Das Gesetz" (Frankfurt a. M., 1964).

27. VIII, 850.

28. VIII, 851.

29. VIII, 872.

30. VIII, 850.

31. VIII, 851.

32. VIII, 873.

33. VIII, 875.

34. Hamburger, *Der Humor*, p. 147.

35. *The Secular City* (New York and London, 1966), p. 72.

36. *The Enlightenment: An Interpretation*, I (New York, 1966), p. 151.

The Second Author of
Der Tod in Venedig

Dorrit Cohn*

I

In his review of a now forgotten contemporary novel Thomas Mann draws the following distinction between the author and the narrator of a fictional work: ["Narrating is something totally different from writing, and what distinguishes them is an indirection in the former . . ."]. This indirectness, he goes on to explain, is most slyly effective when it veils itself in directness: when the author interpolates between himself and his reader a second voice, ["the voice of a second, interposed author," "as when . . . a gentleman announces himself and makes speeches who, however, is in no way identical with the epic author but rather an invented and shadowy observer"].[1] Clearly Mann does not have in mind here a simple ["first-person narrator"] who tells his own life in the manner of Felix Krull, or even the peripheral type of first-person narrator who tells the life of a friend in the manner of Serenus Zeitblom. The reader needs hardly be told that a narrator so spectacularly equipped with a name, a civic identity and a body of his own should not be confused with the author of the work in which he appears. It is primarily when a narrator remains a truly ["shadowy observer"], a disincarnated voice without name or face, that the reader will be inclined to attribute to him the mind, if not the body, of the author whose name appears on the title page. This is especially likely to happen with a teller who intrudes loudly and volubly into his tale, as the narrators of Mann's own third-person novels almost invariably do. Like so many of his comments concerning the works of other writers, the distinction Mann draws in the passage quoted above looks suspiciously as though it were meant primarily *pro domo*.

In recent times, with our consciousness raised by modern literary theory, we have learned to resist the tendency to equate that authorial narrator — as we now generally call Mann's "second author"[2] — with the author himself. At least in theory. In critical practice the distinction has been slow to sink in, perhaps because it has never been freighted sufficiently with demonstrations and qualifications. The author-narrator equation has been peculiarly tenacious in cases where a narrator takes earnest moralistic stands on weighty problems of morality; the reader then is given to extending the narrator's authority in matters of fictional fact onto his normative commentary. When his tone is more jocular, and

*From *Probleme der Moderne: Studien zur deutschen Literatur von Nietzsche bis Brecht. Festschrift für Walter Sokel*, ed. Benjamin Bennett, Anton Kaes, and William J. Lillyman (Tübingen: Max Niemeyer Verlag, pp. 223–45. Reprinted by permission of Max Niemeyer Verlag.

especially when he plays self-conscious games with the narrative genre, it seems easier to grant him a personality of his own. This may well be why Mann's narrators in *Der Zauberberg* and the Joseph novels have long since been recognized as "second authors," whereas the seriously perorating monsieur who narrates *Der Tod in Venedig* has almost invariably been identified with Thomas Mann himself.

Nor can we automatically assume that this identification is incorrect. But since it has decisively affected interpretation of Mann's most enigmatic novella, my contention is that it needs to be questioned once and for all.[3] In taking up this problem I follow a general directive provided by Franz Stanzel in his *Theorie des Erzählens*. Having reminded us that the separation of the authorial narrator from the personality of the author is a fairly recent narratological acquisition, he states: ["One must start with the assumption that the authorial narrator is, within certain limits, an autonomous figure . . . which thus is accessible to the interpreter in his own personality. It is only when this kind of an interpretative attempt has proved conclusively negative that we can assume the identity of the authorial narrator with the author"].[4] I assume from the wider context of his *Theorie* that Stanzel would insist that such interpretive assays be carried out intra-textually, without regard to evidence that might be gathered about the author from outside the text. My own intention, at any rate, is to perform my experiment with *Tod in Venedig* as far as possible *en vase clos*.[5]

My principal focus will be the relationship of the narrator to his protagonist, such as it emerges from the language he employs in telling the story of Aschenbach's Venetian love and death. This story itself must of course be attributed to the invention of its author; the narrator, for his part, recounts it as though it were historically real.[6] We can therefore hold him accountable only for his narrative *manner*, not his narrative *matter* (or, as the Russian Formalists would say, only for the *sujet*, not for the *fabula*). It follows that his personality — his "Eigenpersönlichkeit" — will stand out most clearly at those textual moments when he departs furthest from straightforward narration, when he moves from the mimetic, story-telling level to the non-mimetic level of ideology and evaluation.[7] In this respect, as we will see, the narrator of *Tod in Venedig* provides a profusion of data for drawing his mental portrait: generalizations, exclamations, homilies, aphorisms and other expressions of normative subjectivity. These will ultimately allow us to assess his objectivity, to decide whether he is, ideologically speaking, a reliable narrator, and thus a spokesman for the norms of the author who has invented both him and his story.[8]

II

In briefest summary the relationship of the narrator to his protagonist in *Tod in Venedig* may be described as one of increasing distance. In the early phases of the story it is essentially sympathetic, respectful, even reverent; in the later phases a deepening rift develops, building an increasingly ironic narratorial stance.[9] In this regard Mann's novella evolves in a manner diametrically opposed to the typical Bildungsroman, where we usually witness a gradual approach of the mind of the protagonist to that of the narrator. Here the protagonist does not rise to his narrator's ethical and cultural standards but falls away from them. The events of Aschenbach's final dream, we are told ["left behind the cultivation of life annihilated, destroyed"] (516),[10] and subsequently, as he shamelessly pursues Tadzio through the streets of Venice, ["the monstrous appeared promising to him, and the moral law appeared invalid"] (518). The narrator meanwhile — as the words he uses here to describe Aschenbach's moral debacle indicate — remains poised on the cultural pinnacle that has brought forth his protagonist's own artistic achievement.

It should be noted from the outset, however, that this bifurcating narrative schema unfolds solely on the ideological or evaluative level of the story, without in the least affecting the point of view (in the technical sense of the word) from which the story is presented.[11] On the perceptual level the narrator steadfastly adheres to his protagonist's perspective on the outside world; from the initial moment when he observes the strange wanderer standing on the steps of the funeral chapel to the final moment when he watches Tadzio standing on the sandbar we see the events and figures of the outside world through Aschenbach's eyes. The narrator also upholds from start to finish his free access to his protagonist's inner life (whereas he never so much as mentions what goes on in the mind of Tadzio). In sum, the narrator maintains his intimacy with Aschenbach's sensations, thoughts, and feelings, even as he distances himself from him more and more on the ideological level.[12]

Now to follow this relationship through the text in greater detail. The most obtrusive indicator of the narrator's personality — and of the fact that he *has* a clearly defined personality — is the series of statements of "eternal truths" he formulates.[13] There are in all some twenty glosses of this kind scattered through the text, and they express a consistent system of values. This narrator is for discipline, dignity, decorum, achievement and sobriety, against disorder, intoxication, passion and passivity. In short, he volubly upholds within the story a heavily rationalistic and moralistic cultural code, most strikingly in the maxims that culminate many of his statements *ex cathedra*:

[For it is dissolute not to be able to want a wholesome disenchantment. For human beings love and honor each other as long as they are not capable of judging each other, and longing is the product of a lack of understanding. (496)

. . . for passion paralyzes the sense of fastidiousness and lets itself be drawn into dealing with charms that sobriety would take humorously or reject with indignation. (506)

He who is beyond himself detests nothing more than to have to return
into himself. (515)

With their causal inceptions (*denn*) these sententiae profess full account-
ability for the case under discussion. They embed Aschenbach's story in a
predictable world, a system of stable psychological concepts and moral
precepts.

That the narrator's code of values in fact closely matches the
protagonist's own before his fall can be seen from the flashback on
Aschenbach's career as a writer provided in chapter II. As others have
noted, this summary biography sounds rather like a eulogy penned in
advance by the deceased himself. The narrator clearly takes the role of
apologist, and his gnomic generalizations — more extensive here than
elsewhere in the text, and all concerned, as the subject demands, with the
psychology and sociology of artistic achievement — serve only to heighten
the representative import of Aschenbach's existence. With one notable
exception — to which I will return below — they unreservedly enhance the
laudatio (see e.g. the passages starting with the words ["For an important
intellectual production"; "A living, intellectually uncommitted concreteness;" "But it seems that there is nothing against which a noble and
diligent spirit"] (452–55).

The ideological concord between the narrator and Aschenbach continues into the narrated time of the story itself: in the starting episode, the
voyage South, the early phases of the Venice adventure authorial generalizations are barely differentiated from figural thoughts. During Aschenbach's introspection while he awaits his Munich tramway: ["he had reined
in and cooled off his feelings because he knew that he had an inclination to
be content with a gay approximation and a half perfection. Was it now the
enslaved emotion that was avenging itself by abandoning him, in refusing
to bear and give wings to his art . . . ?"] (449). Note that tensual sequence
in the first sentence: Aschenbach *knew* what the narrator *knows to be*
true. Note also that the second sentence may quite as validly be read as a
question Aschenbach puts to himself (in narrated monologue form) and as
a question posed by the analytic narrator. Or take the scene where
Aschenbach first perceives Tadzio in the hall of the hotel and wonders why
he is allowed to escape the monastic dress code of his sisters: ["Was he ill?
. . . Or was he simply an indulged favorite child, elevated by a partial and
capricious love? Aschenbach tended to believe the latter. *Almost every
artist has a voluptious and treacherous tendency to approve the injustice
that brings about beauty and to greet aristocratic favoritism with understanding and respect*"] (470; my italics). The narrator's speculation about
artists flows from Aschenbach's speculations about Tadzio as smoothly as if
the latter had self-indulgently accounted for his own reactions. Again,
during Aschenbach's first contemplation of the ocean, narratorial comment dovetails with figural emotions:

[I will stay then, thought Aschenbach. Where could it be better? . . . He loved the sea for deep reasons; out of the need for peace of the hard working artist who wants to rest from the demanding multiplicity of appearances at the breast of the simple, the immense; "out of a forbidden penchant for the unstructured, immeasurable, eternal, for nothingness, a tendency that was directly opposed to his calling and for that very reason seductive. *He who labors at the production of the excellent longs to repose in the perfect; and is nothingness not a form of perfection?* But, as he was dreaming away into the emptiness. . . .] (475; my italics).

Fused almost seamlessly at both ends with Aschenbach's oceanic feelings, the narrator's intervention creates not a trace of distancing irony. This is true despite the ominous notes he sounds: ["at the breast of . . . the immense," out of a forbidden . . . seductive tendency to nothingness"]. Aschenbach is still ["the hard working artist who struggles to produce the excellent"], and who may be allowed — by way of vacation — a temporary indulgence in thanatos.

This entente cordiale between authorial and figural minds is disrupted at just about the mid-point of the Venetian adventure in a scene to be considered in detail below. From this point on the authorial commentary becomes emphatically distanced and judgemental. A clear example is the scene where Aschenbach, having followed Tadzio with the "salutary" intention of striking up a casual conversation with him finds himself too strongly moved to speak:

[Too late! he thought at this moment. Too late! But was it really too late? The step that he neglected to take could very possibly have lead to something wholesome, light, and serene, to a healthy sobriety. But it must have been a matter of the aging man not wanting sobriety because the intoxication was too precious for him. *Who is to unravel the essence and character of the artist! Who can comprehend the deeply instinctual fusion of discipline and licentiousness on which it rests. For it is licentious not to be able to want a wholesome disenchantment.*]

The narrator distances himself from Aschenbach explicitly and immediately when he questions the directly quoted ["too late!"]. He now provides his interpretation for the failed action, which he attributes to a weakening of willpower, a falling away from the unquestioned values of health and sobriety. The exclamatory authorial rhetoric subsequently reinforces the critical analysis, grounds it in generalizations concerning the moral lability of artists, and caps it with the sententious final judgement. Then, returning to the individual case at hand, the narrator explicitly excludes Aschenbach from this authorial wisdom: ["Aschenbach was not in the mood for self-criticism any more"].

There are numerous instances in the later parts of the story that follow this same general pattern: an inside view of Aschenbach's mind, followed by a judgemental intervention cast in gnomic present tense, followed by a return to Aschenbach's now properly adjudged reactions. To quote one further example: when Aschenbach reads about the Venetian plague in the German newspapers,

> ["One should be silent," Aschenbach thought excitedly. . . . But at the same time his heart was filled with satisfaction about the adventure that wanted to descend upon the world outside. *For passion, like crime, does not thrive in the secure order and comfort of the commonplace. Instead, it must welcome any relaxation of civil order, any confusion and affliction in the world for it can vaguely hope to gain some advantage for itself from it.* So Aschenbach felt a dark satisfaction about the officially concealed events in the dirty alleys of Venice] (500; my italics).

Again Aschenbach's response (this time plainly immoral) is instantly denounced and explained by the narrator, and in the severest terms. Even a shade too severe, perhaps. The unwonted analogy between passion and crime makes it appear as though the narrator were bent on imposing his moral standards with the utmost rigidity. At the same time the syllogistic "So . . ." with which he reverts to Aschenbach's sinful thoughts maintains the sense that he is a perfectly dispassionate analyst.

A further device that underscores the narrator's progressive disengagement is his increasingly estranging and negative way of referring to Aschenbach. In the early sections distancing appellations appear sparingly and remain neutral and descriptive: ["the traveller," "the waiting one," "the resting one"]. After the narrator parts company with his character, ideologically speaking, we find on a regular basis the more condescending epithets ["the aging man," "the lonely one"]. And at crucial stations of his descent Aschenbach becomes ["the afflicted," "the stubborn one," "the crazed one," "the besotted," "the confused one," "the one who has gone astray"], and on, in a more and more degrading name-calling series that leads down to the final ["degraded one"]."

So far the schismatic trend I have been tracing has, to all appearances, its objective motivation in the story's mimetic stratum. Faced with a character who manifests such progressively deviant behaviour this severely judgemental narrator can hardly be expected to react differently. Even so, the smugness and narrowness of his evaluative code in the passages already cited may cause some irritation in the reader, akin to that nauseated intolerance Roland Barthes attributes to the reader of Balzac at moments when he laces his novels with cultural adages.[15] Perennial reactions of this type aside, however, there are at least two of the narrator's interventions in *Tod in Venedig* that give one pause on more substantial grounds. In these two instances the narrator indulges in a kind of ideological overkill that produces an effect contrary to the one he is ostensibly trying to achieve. It is to these two moments in their episodic context that I will now turn for close inspection.

III

As previously mentioned, the turning point in the relationship between narrator and character on the ideological level roughly coincides with the midpoint of Aschenbach's Venetian adventure: the pivotal scene when the enamored writer for the first and last time practices his art.[16] Before this point is reached however, a long section (480–492) intervenes where authorial generalizations have disappeared from the text altogether; this section comprises mainly Aschenbach's abortive attempt to leave Venice (end of chapter III) and the first quiescently serene phase of his love (beginning of chapter IV). In these pages the narrator goes beyond adopting merely Aschenbach's visual perspective, he also emulates the hymnic diction (complete with Homeric hexameters), the Hellenic allusions and the mythical imagery that properly belong to Aschenbach's consciousness. This stylistic contagion — technically a form of free indirect style — has often been mistaken for stylistic parody, an interpretation for which I find no evidence in the text.[17] The employment of free indirect style, in the absence of other distancing devices, points rather to a momentary "sharing" of Aschenbach's inner experience by the narrator — as though he were himself temporarily on vacation from his post as moral preceptor.

This consonance reaches its apogee in the moments of high intensity that immediately precede the writing scene, when the Platonic theory of beauty surfaces in Aschenbach's mind as he watches Tadzio cavorting on the beach: ["Statue and mirror! His eyes took in the noble figure over there at the edge of the blue, and, with rising ecstasy, he felt he was encompassing with this same glance beauty itself, form as divine thought, the one and pure perfection that lives in the spirit . . ."] (490). Both the initial exclamation in this quote, and the final present tense (*lebt*) indicate the extent of the narratorial identification with the figural thoughts. The Platonic montage that now follows (combining passages from the *Phaedrus* and the *Symposium*) is largely cast in narrated monologue form, fusing the narrator *verbatim* with Aschenbach's mental language. An intensely emotive tone thus pervades the text as the narrator, in concert with Aschenbach, approaches the climactic writing scene. His sudden *change* of tone in the course of narrating this episode is therefore all the more discordant.

The scene opens with a strikingly balanced gnomic statement: ["The happiness of the writer consists in the thought that can fully become feeling, in the feeling that can fully become thought"] (492). No other narratorial generalization in the entire text is as harmoniously attuned to the mood of the protagonist. Its syntactical symmetry reflects with utmost precision the creative equipoise Aschenbach himself seeks between thought and feeling. But already in the next sentence, even as the narrator grants Aschenbach this supreme ["happiness"], he begins to withdraw from the miraculous moment: ["It was such a pulsing thought, such a precise feeling that belonged to and obeyed *the lonely man then*. . . . Suddenly, he wanted to write"] (492; my italics). Both the estranging epithet and the distancing adverb underline the narrator's disengagement from the creative act that will ensue. Other even more strongly alienating phrases follow presently: the writer is called ["the afflicted one"], the moment of writing ["at this moment of crisis"], the object of his emotion ["the idol"], and so forth.

When we consider the radical nature of Aschenbach's creative performance in this scene, it is hardly surprising that the narrator refuses to follow him in silent consonance: ["And it was his desire to work in the presence of Tadzio, to use the figure of the boy as a model in his writing, to let his style follow the lines of this body . . . and to transport his beauty into the spiritual"] (492). As T. J. Reed has pointed out, Aschenbach here tries to enact (literally and literarily) the truth Diotima imparts to Socrates that Eros alone can serve as guide to absolute beauty.[18] In this light his act of "writing Tadzio" can be interpreted as his attempt at gaining direct access to the realm of Platonic ideas. But this mystic creative urge is of course in flagrant violation of Aschenbach's own past aesthetic credo, a credo that the narrator had explicitly endorsed. Its dominant principle, as we recall, had precisely been that the artist can *not* create in the heat of emotion: ["he had reined in and cooled off his feelings because he knew that he tended to be content with a gay approximation and a half perfection"] (449). Aschenbach's scriptural intercourse with Tadzio thus clearly contradicts the ethos to which he has dedicated his creative life. And beyond that it also countermands the entire process of mimetic art, the patient art of the novelist who had woven ["Maja" — "the novellistic tapestry rich in figures that brought together such a multiplicity of fates in the shadow of an idea"] (450), as the narrator had admiringly described it. These horizontal images of shadow and carpet point up the radical contrast between the reflected phenomenal world Aschenbach had formerly created, and the direct vertical ascension of the Platonic writing act he presently performs.

But if all this helps to explain why the writing scene brings about the sudden change in the level-headed narrator's attitude toward Aschenbach, it also draws attention to his limitations. These come to be clearly in evidence in the drastic distancing move he undertakes in the immediate aftermath of Aschenbach's scriptural act, when he momentarily, but quite literally, steps out of and away from his story. Not the least shocking aspect of his breakaway is that it breaks all the unities — of time, place, and action — to which the novella so classically adheres from the moment of Aschenbach's arrival in Venice. Flashing forward to the public reception the writer's creative offspring will receive, the narrator at first describes it with unrestrained admiration as ["that page and a half of consummate prose . . . whose purity, nobility, and soaring emotional tension was soon to arouse the admiration of many"] (493). The comment that now follows, however, deflates both the writer and the writing in almost brutally sobering terms: ["Surely it is good that the world knows only the beautiful work but not its origins or the conditions for its creation; for knowledge of the sources from which the artist's inspiration flowed would often cause confusion and repulsion and thus cancel out the impression of excellence"] (493). This is in every respect the least motivated, most jarring and disconcerting of the narrator's interventions. It almost seems as though he were taking headlong flight onto familiar ground—the psychology of the reading public—from the mysteries of a creative process that is beyond his comprehension. The substance of his comment itself raises several questions. Is it not, within its context, plainly contradictory? Having just revealed the sources of Aschenbach's newly created piece, what is the sense of now declaring that these sources had better remain hidden? Finally, is not the attribution of "confusing" and even "repulsive" effects to Aschenbach's sublimated "Platonic" procreation excessively moralistic and unnecessarily aggressive?

These questions will, in my view, inevitably arise in the mind of a reader who dissociates the narrator from the author of *Tod in Venedig*. And since this, the narrator's most questionable intervention, is located precisely at the point of origin of the ideological schism in the story, it tends to reduce the trustworthiness of his distancing comments from this point forward. At the very least the reader's allegiance will henceforth be divided between the narrator and his protagonist. I would even suggest that Mann may have designedly made his narrator jump the gun: his overreaction within an episode that still clearly belongs to, and indeed climaxes the Apollonian phase of Aschenbach's erotic adventure welds the reader's sympathy more firmly to the protagonist than if the narrator had waited with his distancing move until after Aschenbach had begun his Dionysian descent.

IV

A second, even clearer, instance of evaluative overstatement occurs in the scene where Aschenbach reaches his nadir: the paragraph-long sentence that introduces his second Socratic monologue (in the scene that immediately precedes the death scene). I cannot demonstrate its rhetorical impact without quoting it in full:

[There he sat, the master, the artist who had achieved dignity, the author of "The Wretch" who had renounced gypsy instincts and turbid depths in such exemplary and pure fashion, who had broken relations with the abyss and rejected depravity, the high-climber who had overcome his own knowledge and left all irony behind and grown accustomed to the amenities of popularity, he whose fame was officially endorsed, whose name had been titled and whose style boys were encouraged to emulate—there he sat, lids closed, with only an occasional, quickly suppressed mocking and perplexed glance flitting forth sideways, and his drooping lips, cosmetically enhanced, formed a few words from the strange dream logic of his half slumbering brain.] (521)

The most obviously "destructive" aspect of this passage is of course the grotesque ["falling distance"] it builds between the before and after, the former self-image and the present reality. The elevation itself is constructed by sardonically piling up phrases we have heard before in a different context: they are the very phrases the narrator had employed in the laudatory curriculum vitae of the summary interchapter. What is perhaps less obvious is that this sentence parodistically echoes that earlier chapter's opening sentence. The syntactical analogy becomes clear from a skeletal alignment of constituent parts:

(A)	(B)
[*The author* of . . . the prose epic about the life of Frederick of Prussia;	There he sat, *the master the artist* who had achieved dignity
the patient artist who . . . wove the novellistic tapestry "Maja"	
the creator of that powerful tale titled "The Wretch"	*the author* of "The Wretch"
the writer finally . . . of the impassioned	*the high-climber* who, free from his own knowledge and all irony . . .
essay about "Intellect and Art"	
Gustav Aschenbach, then (405)	he, whose . . . whose . . . he sat there . . . (521)]

As Oskar Seidlin has pointed out, the four nominal clauses of the earlier sentence (A) mark the steps of Aschenbach's artistic achievement—["The four stages . . . of creative life"].[19] In the later sentence (B) we again have four nominal clauses, with the first three very nearly corresponding (but in reverse order) to those in (A). But with the fourth—["the high-climbing one"]—(B) begins to climb hectically, finally culminating in three elaborate genitive constructions. Note also that the nominal series of (A) no longer stands up independently in (B) but is framed by the verbal phrase ["he sat there"], so that the inflated "master" is now subordinated to the disreputable state in which he "sits there."

Another, even more striking modification is that while (A) pairs each of the four epithets with one of Aschenbach's major works, (B) reduces him to the authorship of a single work, the story "Ein Elender." The reason for singling out this work is immediately apparent: unlike Aschenbach's other heroes, the protagonist of "Ein Elender" is an anti-hero, the anti-type of his creator's mature self who represents everything Aschenbach has wanted to reject. This despised figure, so the narrator's verbal irony implies, is precisely what the Aschenbach who "sits there" has now become. But the language employed to evoke this identity in turn associates the narrator with the writer who has created this repulsive character. For he applies to the degraded Aschenbach the same unequivo-cally negative rhetoric that—according to the narrator's own earlier description—Aschenbach had applied to his degraded creature: ["The force of words with which depravity was rejected here spoke for the renunciation of all moral doubt, of any sympathy for the abyss, the refusal of the easily compassionate expression that to understand all meant to forgive all"] (455). The fact that the narrator now applies these same phrases to the author of "Der Elende"—["who . . . had refused the turbid depths, renounced sympathy with the abyss, and rejected the depraved"] (521)—confirms that he continues to emulate the values for which Aschenbach had opted at the pivotal moment of his career when he had created his story.

The entire weighty sentence finally leads up to the inquit phrase signalling the quotation of Aschenbach's monologue: ["his drooping lips, cosmetically enhanced, formed a few words from the strange dream logic of his half slumbering brain"] (521). The fact that the narrator quotes his character's thoughts directly on this occasion is in itself significant: no other mode of presentation could have disengaged him as effectively from the ensuing discourse. But the terms he uses to introduce it—["slumbering brain," "dream logic"]—are of course even more alienating; they disqual-ify its meaning in advance, as much as to warn us that the words we are about to hear will be errant nonsense.[20] When one examines the actual content of Aschenbach's slumberous mind however one is forced to conclude that his dream-logic produces nothing less than the moment of truth toward which the entire story has been moving: a lucidly hopeless diagnosis of the artist's fate.

Aschenbach's Socratic address takes us back again to the Platonic doctrine of beauty as found in the *Phaedrus* and the *Symposium*. But he now turns this doctrine to profoundly pessimistic account—at least so far as the poet is concerned; ["we poets"], he tells Phaedrus ["cannot follow the path of beauty . . . without having Eros join us and set himself up as the leader, . . . for passion is our exaltation, and our longing must remain love—that is our happiness and our shame"] (521 f.). Having acknowl-edged the poet's defeat on the Platonic path to the higher realm, Aschenbach now denounces with particular bitterness his own erstwhile pedagogic pretensions, with words that clearly echo Plato-Socrates' ulti-mate decision (in Book X of *The Republic*) to exile the poet from the ideal state:[21] ["The masterly posing of our style is a lie and a foolishness, our fame and standing a farce, the trust the public has in us is highly ridiculous, and the notion of educating the people and the youth through art is a risky undertaking that ought to be prohibited"] (522). Isn't Aschenbach saying here exactly the same thing the narrator has just finished saying in his introduction, and in almost identical terms? His self-criticism is, if anything, even more biting than the narrator's sarcasm — which now appears as gratuitous aggression, merely intended to add insult to injury.

When we come to consider Aschenbach's despairing statement concerning the constitutional immorality of the poet at the conclusion of his monologue, the narrator's prefatory venom takes on an even more dubious air. To understand this we must briefly turn back to an earlier moment of his rhetoric. In the interchapter the narrator explains — in entirely approving terms — why Aschenbach had, at a decisive point of his artistic development, renounced his youthful indulgence in immoral "psychologism" — ["the indecent psychologism of the times"] (455) — and had opted for a disciplined and dignified pursuit of beauty. At this point the narrator queries — in the form of three elaborately phrased rhetorical questions — whether this "moral decisiveness" of the mature master might not in turn lead him back to immoral behaviour. The exact terms of his predictive speculation (see the quotation in note)[22] are less important for our purposes than the fact that he dismisses it indecisively with a decisive shrug of the shoulder — ["Be that as it may"] — and then immediately calls on a philosophical adage — ["A development is a fate"] — to lead him back to and on with his admiring account of Aschenbach's development as an artist.

Now it is precisely to this crossroads in his career — the point when he made his decisive choice against "psychologism" and in favor of purely aesthetic values — that Aschenbach returns at the conclusion of his monologue. And as he does so, he repeats almost verbatim the account the narrator had previously given of this crucial moment. Except that now, far from shrugging off the question of the artist's immorality, as the narrator had done in the interchapter, Aschenbach provides it with an unequivocally affirmative answer: ["Form and detachment, Phaidros, lead to intoxication and desire, . . . to horrifying emotional outrage, . . . they lead to the abyss, they too lead to the abyss. They lead us poets there, I tell you, because we cannot manage to elevate ourselves but only to dissipate"] (522). For all its dream-logic, this conclusion to Aschenbach's monologue is tragically clear (as well as clearly tragic): the poet at the crossroads is forced to choose between two paths that both equally lead to the "abyss." In evading one form of immoral behaviour he inevitably falls into another. In short, Aschenbach's retrospective cognition exactly confirms the narrator's prospective suspicion. How, in view of this, are we to understand the destructive rhetoric with which the narrator introduces Aschenbach's articulation of the dark truth?

Inevitably, if one equates the narrator with Thomas Mann one is forced to find reasons to denigrate Aschenbach's famous last words. Critics have generally done so. They have understood his monologue as an inauthentic self-justification: instead of facing up to his individual guilt — his false choice at the crossroads — Aschenbach attributes his abysmal end to the fate of poets generally, the generic ["us poets"]. One critic puts it this way: ["The tendency to the abyss is not an essential part of the determination of beauty, as Aschenbach would have it, but the result of a false life"].[23] In my opinion this interpretation cannot be substantiated on the basis of the text itself. Within its boundaries only two paths are open to the artist, and both lead to the same abyss. To open an alternate, "moral" path for Aschenbach one has to look outside the text: to Mann's other, more optimistic works (*Tonio Kröger*, the Joseph novels), or to certain of his autobiographical pronouncements.[24]

On the other hand, if one dissociates the narrator from Thomas Mann one is free to denigrate his introduction to the monologue, and to understand Aschenbach's last words for what they are: his (and the story's) moment of truth, which the narrator is unwilling or unable to share to the bitter end. It is surely significant that only Aschenbach can sound this truth, that he can sound it only with lips drooping under his make-up, and only after these lips have taken in the fatal germs of the plague. In this light his monologue takes on the meaning of an anagnorisis, the expression of that lethal knowledge the hero of Greek tragedy reaches when he stands on the verge of death. The irony the narrator directs at Aschenbach in this moment can then be turned back on its speaker — by a reader who, for his part, is willing and able to share the tragic truth *the author* imparts to him with this story.[25]

V

To this point my argument for the "second author" of *Tod in Venedig* has rested solely on what the narrator says and how he says it. But what he leaves unsaid is equally important for my case. To this other, tacit half of his story I now turn to complement and complete the tell-tale evidence.

It is tell-tale in the literal sense: for with *Tod in Venedig* Mann (though not his narrator) gives us — among other things — a *fantastic* tale. His vehicle is of course the population of uncanny figures Aschenbach encounters on his lethal journey. These figures acquire their ominous meaning less by way of their individual appearances — though their death-and/or devil-like features have often been noted — than by way of their serial *re*appearances. The unlikeliness (on realistic grounds) of their uncanny likeness suggests cumulatively that they all represent the *same* sinister power, a power relentlessly bent on driving Aschenbach to his ruinous end. Now these hints of supernatural doings, which even a first reader finds too strong to miss and dismiss, are never picked up by the narrator himself. Though he meticulously describes each individual stranger, he passes silently over their obtrusive sameness, to all appearances studiously closing his eyes to it. This wilful blindness is the natural counterpart to the moralistic, realistic, and rationalistic world view he voices throughout.[26]

Yet for all the narrator's closely woven cover-up on the non-mimetic level of the text, the underlying mystery on the mimetic level keeps shining through the causal fabric. And these abysmal glimpses into a covert realm make the reader feel increasingly uneasy with the overt explanations he is offered. The narrator's silence, in short, speaks louder than his words; it perhaps undercuts his trustworthiness even more effectively than his normative excesses. For nowhere else does it become quite as evident that the author *behind* the work is communicating a message that escapes the narrator he placed *within* the work. The exact content of this message — whether it signifies otherworldly, cosmic powers or the powers of the individual unconscious, myth or (depth-) psychology or, as is most likely, both at once[27] — is less important in the present context than the fact that it refers to a realm that escapes the narrator. Escapes him precisely because he is bent on ignoring all questions that point above or below his plane conception of the world and of the psyche. In this respect his disregard of the demonic figures corresponds exactly to his rhetorical stand-off from Aschenbach's mental experience at both its zenith (the writing scene) and its nadir (the final monologue).[28] By the same token, the demonic figures themselves reinforce the truth value of Aschenbach's anagnorisis in the latter instance; for what can their dark presence in the story intimate, if not that a fateful force is at work in the universe, a force that irresistibly draws those who strive for beauty down into the abyss — ["down to the abyss, they too down to the abyss"].

But the fantastic undercurrent in the *fabula* of *Tod in Venedig* also has an essential aesthetic function. As Christine Brooke-Rose has recently suggested, every good story needs to keep back something: "whatever overdetermination may occur in any one work . . . , some underdetermination is necessary for it to retain its hold over us, its peculiar mixture of recognition-pleasure and mystery."[29] In Mann's novella it is clearly the series of mysterious strangers that creates underdetermination, counterbalancing the narrator's *over*determination on the ideological level. In terms of Roland Barthes codes, to which Brooke-Rose refers in the same essay, these strangers would have to be assigned to the story's hermeneutic code, the enigma-creating code that the narrator disregards and that the text leaves unresolved. The *fact* that it remains unresolved tacitly ironizes — behind the narrator's back — the univocal interpretation he tries to impose on Aschenbach's story.

VI

At this point I call my intra-textual "experiment" to a halt. Not, needless to say, because I have arrived at a complete or completely new interpretation of Mann's novella but because I feel that I have provided sufficient evidence to confirm my starting hypothesis: that the narrator of *Tod in Venedig* is not identical with its author. But before closing I want to turn back on my experiment to face a crucial methodological question: granted that the positing of a "second author" may explain in a plausible manner certain discrepancies between the narrator's commentary on Aschenbach's story and this story itself, is this the *only* plausible way to account for these discrepancies? Is it even the *most* plausible way?

My answer is: yes — but with one very important provision: if, and only if, we grant (or assume, or believe) that *Tod in Venedig* is a flawless work — flawless in the sense that it perfectly achieves its author's intentions. As soon as we abandon that assumption an alternate way becomes available to us: namely to attribute the narrator's shortcomings to Thomas Mann himself: more precisely, to the peculiar circumstances — personal, historical, etc. — that attended the composition of this work and that made him fall short of his creative goal.

Now this is precisely the way taken by T. J. Reed in his book *Thomas Mann: The Uses of Tradition*. To my knowledge Reed is the only scholar to have squarely faced the problems raised by the narrator's ideological excesses toward the end of *Tod in Venedig*. Referring specifically to the sentence that introduces Aschenbach's final monologue (discussed in section IV above), Reed points up the narrator's "emphatic judgement," and adds: "It is a shade too emphatic for the reader accustomed to Mann's ironic temper. Where are the reservations usually felt in every inflection of his phrasing? The finality with which Aschenbach's case is settled is positively suspicious. . . . Is it not crudely direct beside the informed survey of Aschenbach's development in Chapter Two . . . ? There are depths to be sounded under the polished surface of the story."[30] These words serve as the opening gambit for a probing investigation into the genesis of Mann's novella. They clearly indicate that Reed's admirable study is a specific attempt to account for the "positively suspicious" nature of the narrator's judgemental rhetoric. Significantly Reed pursues his genetic interpretation without ever questioning the reliability of this narrator, whom he seems to identify automatically with the author.[31] What he questions instead is the coherence and aesthetic integrity of the work itself: by following through the stages of Mann's creative process he reveals what he finds concealed beneath the "polished surface" of the final product — that Mann has superimposed "a moral tale" on a text he had originally conceived "hymnically" (pp. 151–154).[32] This "diametrical change" explains for Reed what he describes as the novella's ambiguity in the word's more dubious sense: . . . uncertainty of meaning, disunity" (p.

173). Mann has "sought to work out a changed conception in materials and language ideally suited to an earlier one" (p. 174). And although Reed has by this point shifted the ground of his critique from the narrator's narrow moralism to what he calls the story's "disharmony between style and substance" (p. 176), the fact remains that it was the vexing narrator who sent him on his way in the first place—sent him, that is, outside the text to probe the vagaries of its composition.

On the face of it Reed's extra-textual approach to the textual ambiguities in *Tod in Venedig* would appear to differ radically from the intra-textual approach I have followed in this paper. Yet from a certain theoretical perspective these two approaches can be related, if not reconciled, with each other. We owe this perspective to a recent article by Tamar Yacobi where the problem of fictional reliability is discussed on the basis of a reader-oriented theory of literary texts.[33] According to Yacobi, a reader who attributes unreliability to the narrator of a work of fiction is merely choosing one of several "principles of resolution" potentially available to him when he is faced with the "tensions, incongruities, contradictions and other infelicities" of a literary work (p. 119). A rival principle, equally available to him, is what Yacobi calls the "genetic principle" which places the blame on the biographical-historical background of the work. These two principles of resolution have in common that they "both resolve referential problems by attributing their occurrence to some source of report." The difference between them "lies in the answer to the question: who is responsible . . . ?" (p. 121). The reader who calls on the genetic principle will answer: the author. The reader who calls on the unreliability principle will answer: the narrator—which signifies, in the case of an authorial third-person text like *Tod in Venedig*, that he refuses to regard the narrator as the mouthpiece of the author.

From this theoretical vantage point, then, Reed's genetic explanation appears—even to myself—no less (and no more) valid and plausible than my "second author" explanation. But my equanimity gives way when I return from the plane of abstract generality to the concrete singularity of Mann's novella. For within the interpretive arena of an individual text these two explanations are mutually exclusive, and the reader is forced to choose between them. Which brings me—at the risk of stating the obvious—to mention some of my reasons for preferring my perspectival over Reed's genetic resolution.

I have already alluded to what is no doubt my primary reason: the severance of the narrator from the author seems to me a necessary interpretive move for a reader bent on affirming the aesthetic integrity of Mann's novella.[34] Obviously one's willingness to make this move will depend to some degree on one's estimation of Mann's œuvre as a whole. And it is no doubt because my own high esteem is due in large part to the complexity of vision I find incarnated in his other major narrative works— though not always in his extra-literary pronouncements—that I am unwilling to ascribe to Mann the ideological simplicities voiced in *Tod in Venedig*. The fact, moreover, that these pronouncements address the subject of Mann's deepest concerns and most differentiated views — art and the artist — reinforces my reluctance. In his other novels and novellas Mann always approaches this subject obliquely, most obliquely of all in his only other full-fledged tragedy of a creative artist, *Doktor Faustus*. I take it to be no mere coincidence that Mann here reverts — three decades later — to the same basic narrative indirection I attribute to him in *Tod in Venedig*.

Admittedly the ironic interval that separates Mann from Zeitblom is far more blatant than the interval that separates him from the teller of the earlier work. Yet the proximity of the narrative situations in these two works offers a kind of proof by the absurd of my "second author" hypothesis: for is it not equally difficult to imagine the narrator of *Tod in Venedig* to be the creator of Aschenbach as it is to imagine Zeitblom to be the creator of Adrian Leverkühn? Only a mind capable of Mann's famous ["irony in both directions"] could have conceived both members of these pairs in dialectical unison.

Notes

1. *Gesammelte Werke in zwölf Bänden* (Frankfurt, a. M. 1960), X, pp. 631 f. The novel under review is Adolf von Hatzfeld's *Die Lemminge* (1923).

2. The term was first proposed by Franz Stanzel in *Die typischen Erzählsituationen im Roman* (Vienna, 1955).

3. A number of critics of *Tod in Venedig* have recognized the narrator-author differential as a factor that must be taken into account, but without drawing the interpretive consequences that it implies. See esp. Hans W. Niklas, *Thomas Manns Novelle Der Tod in Venedig* (Marburg, 1968), p. 87; Herbert Lehnert, "*Tristan, Tonio Kröger* und *Der Tod in Venedig*: Ein Strukturvergleich," *Orbis Litterarum*, 24 (1969), pp. 298–304; Josef Kunz, *Die deutsche Novelle im 20. Jahrhundert* (Berlin, 1971), pp. 154, 161. The closest approach to an interpretation based on the narrator's separate personality is found in Inge Diersen, *Untersuchungen zu Thomas Mann* (Berlin, 1959, 1965), pp. 122–128. Overstressing as she does the political implications of the narrator's ideological conservatism Diersen arrives at conclusions that I find difficult to substantiate on the basis of the text; some of her remarks on the narrator's role are nonetheless valid and insightful.

4. Franz Stanzel, *Theorie des Ezrählens* (Göttingen, 1979), p. 27 f.

5. Given Mann's ambivalent views concerning art and the artist during the time of writing, as well as his contradictory self-interpretations of *Tod in Venedig*, extra-textual evidence concerning authorial intentions is notoriously inconclusive. See Herbert Lehnert, *Thomas Mann: Fiktion, Mythos, Religion* (Stuttgart, 1965), pp. 120–139; Hans Wysling, "Ein Elender": Zu einem Novellenplan Thomas Mann," in Paul Scherrer and Hans Wysling, *Quellenkritische Studien zum Werk Thomas Manns* (Bern, 1967); T. J. Reed, *Thomas Mann: The Uses of Tradition* (Oxford, 1974), pp. 119–143. Reed's genetically oriented chapter on *Tod in Venedig* (pp. 144–178) will be discussed in my conclusion.

6. This most general and most basic distinction between novelists and their narrators is pointed up by Wolfgang Kayser in his classic essay "Wer erzählt den Roman?" (*Vortragsreise*, [Bern, 1958], p. 91). The distinction is discussed in a more modern theoretical vein by Félix

Martínez-Bonati in *Fictive Discourse and the Structures of Literature* (Ithaca, N.Y., 1981); see esp. pp. 77-96.

7. For the differentiation between mimetic and non-mimetic language in fiction, see Martínez-Bonati, pp. 32-39. Mimetic language is "as though transparent; it does not interpose itself between us and the things of which it speaks"; the non-mimetic parts of a narrator's discourse, by contrast, "refer us back to his presence, since they . . . are *his* language, his acts *qua* narrator, his perceptible subjectivity" (pp. 36 f.).

8. I here use the term "reliable narrator" in the sense defined by Wayne Booth: "I have called a narrator *reliable* when he speaks for . . . the norms of the work (which is to say, the implied author's norms), *unreliable* when he does not" (*The Rhetoric of Fiction* [Chicago, 1961], p. 158 f.).

9. The growing separation of the narrator from Aschenbach has been previously noted by Burton Pike ("Thomas Mann and the Problematic Self," *Publications of the English Goethe Society*, 37 [1967], p. 136; see also Diersen, p. 124.

10. Page numbers in the text refer to *Gesammelte Werke in zwölf Bänden* (Frankfurt, a. M. 1960), VIII.

11. In this respect *Tod in Venedig* is a remarkable illustration for the "nonconcurrence of points of view articulated at different levels" that Boris Uspensky discusses in *A Poetics of Composition* (Berkeley, 1973), pp. 101-108. Uspensky's recognition that "point of view" is a composite concept that must be divided into several discrete "levels" is therefore essential for the correct description of the narrative situation in Mann's novella. Failure to distinguish between these discrete levels in *Tod in Venedig* seems to me the reason why its narrative structure has been characterized in such widely differing ways, ranging from those critics who see the narrator as the "mirror" of Aschenbach (Fritz Martini, *Das Wagnis der Sprache* [Stuttgart, 1964], p. 210) to those who see him as taking an ironic stance from beginning to end (Reinhard Baumgart, *Das Ironische und die Ironie in den Werken Thomas Manns* [Munich, 1964], pp. 120 f.).

12. In his discussion of Pike's article (see note 9 above) Lehnert denies the mounting distance between the narrator and Aschenbach on the grounds that ["the narrator keeps alternating between an internal and an external perspective"] (*Thomas-Mann-Forschung* [Stuttgart, 1969], p. 139). It is apparent that Lehnert confuses different point-of-view levels here. A narrator's free access to a character's mind — "Innensicht" — by no means necessarily coincides with sympathy (identification), nor "Außensicht" with irony (distance). This confusion also affects his analysis of the narrative structure of *Tod in Venedig* in his article (see note 3 above). Neither the perennial ["interplay between the inner perspective and a more distanced biographer's perspective"] (p. 301) that he considers characteristic for this work nor the "Perspektiven-Ambivalenz" to which he relates this alternation seem to me accurate descriptions of the overall narrative structure.

13. The narrator's ideological commentary is also stressed by Niklas (pp. 91 f.) and Kunz (p. 154).

14. Several critics have remarked on these distancing epithets (e.g. Lehnert, *Thomas Mann*, p. 116, Niklas, p. 90, Kunz, p. 155), without however clearly recognizing their evolving function.

15. Roland Barthes, *S/Z* (Paris, 1970), p. 104.

16. Cf. Kunz (p. 158) who also regards this scene as the ["point of division"] between the ascending and descending movements of the story.

17. The principal advocate for the "parodistic idiom" in *Tod in Venedig* is Erich Heller (*The Ironic German: A Study of Thomas Mann* [Boston, 1958]; see esp. p. 99). Heller qualifies his thesis somewhat in the later essay "Autobiographie und Literatur," in *Essays on European Literature*, eds. Peter Uwe Hohendahl *et al.* (St. Louis, 1972), esp. pp. 92-97. Peter Heller has recently revived the parodistic interpretation in "*Der Tod in Venedig* und Thomas Manns Grund-Motiv" in *Thomas Mann: Ein Kolloqium*, eds. Hans S. Schulte and Gerald

Chapple (Bonn, 1979); see esp. pp. 69–72. A forceful argument against the parodistic intent of *Tod in Venedig* is provided by Hans Rudolf Vaget in " 'Goethe oder Wagner': Studien zu Thomas Manns Goethe-Rezeption, 1905–1912": in H. R. Vaget and D. Barnouw, *Thomas Mann: Studien zur Frage der Rezeption* (Bern, 1975); see esp. pp. 40–55.

18. Reed, p. 160. The Platonic import of Aschenbach's creative moment is disregarded by Pike who takes its diminutive yield—"anderthalb Seiten"—as an ironic comment on Aschenbach's artistic potential (p. 135).

19. *Von Goethe zu Thomas Mann* (Göttingen, 1963), p. 151.

20. The dream concept bears emphatically negative attributes throughout the narrator's discourse. See e.g., ["with confused dream-words"] (461), ["comically dreamlike adventure"] (484), ["dream-spell"] (510), and of course ["the horrible dream"] (515) that leaves Aschenbach ["helpless in the demon's power"] (517).

21. Cf. Erich Heller, *The Ironic German*, p. 114.

22. ["But is moral decisiveness on the other side of knowledge, of disintegrating and hampering realization—is this not again a simplification, a moral reduction of world and soul, and thus also a strengthening in the direction of evil, of the forbidden, the morally impossible? And does form not have two faces? Is it not at the same time moral and immoral—moral as the result and expression of discipline, immoral, or even amoral, insofar as it by its very nature includes a moral indifference, yes in that it even strives to subdue the moral faculty under its proud and unrestricted scepter? Be that as it may! A development is a fate"] (455).

23. Niklas, p. 14; see also p. 81. Similarly Diersen, pp. 113, 121.

24. See, *inter alia*, Pike, p. 133: "Considering Mann's attitude toward art as it emerges *in his other writings*—fiction, essays, and letters—is not an art which so peremptorily excludes sympathy with the abyss incomplete?" (my emphasis). Niklas (p. 14) even calls on Goethe (!) for a positive conception of art that shows up the shortcomings of Aschenbach's.

25. I cannot resist breaking my self-imposed interdiction against extra-textual evidence at this juncture. The one point that remains constant in Mann's notoriously self-contradictory comments on *Tod in Venedig* through the years is that Aschenbach's final monologue articulates the truth of the story. He pronounced on this, so far as I can gather, in four different places. First in a letter to Elisabeth Zimmer, dated 6. September 1915: ["I intended to render something like *the tragedy of mastery*. You seem to have understood that as you consider the speech to Phaidros as *the core of it all*"]. Next in *Betrachtungen eines Unpolitischen* when he speaks of a past work ["where I *let* a 'dignified artist' *comprehend* that his kind *necessarily* remain disreputable and adventurers in feeling"]—whereupon he goes on to quote verbatim further phrases from the monologue. Then in the comments on *Tod in Venedig* in the Princeton address "On Myself" (1940): ["The artist, imprisoned in the sensuous realm as he is, can really never become dignified: this fundamental conviction imbued with a bitterly melancholy skepticism toward all artists *is expressed in the confession* (shaped to follow Plato's dialogues) that I *gave* to the hero as he was near death"]. Finally in a letter to Jürgen Ernestus dated, 17. Juni 1954, where he again quotes and paraphrases the monologue, and then adds (this time with a shade of reserve): ["All this skeptical and suffering pessimism has much truth in it, perhaps exaggerated truth and hence only half true"]. All the above quotations may be found in *Thomas Mann*, Teil I: 1889–1917, *Dichter über ihre Dichtungen* 14/1 (Munich, 1975), respectively pp. 406, 411, 439f., 448. All emphases are mine.

26. In this regard the narrator may be taken as a forerunner of Zeitblom, who closes his eyes equally tightly to the supernatural motivations of his protagonist's fate. Curiously Diersen, who draws the analogy between the two narrator's on different grounds (p. 126f.), fails to mention this important link.—I take the narrator's two references to a "Dämon" (502, 517) as purely rhetorical tropes, unrelated to the fantastic figures in the story.

27. The "bifocally" mythic and psychological meaning of the stranger-figures is stressed by André von Gronicka ("Myth Plus Psychology: A Stylistic Analysis of *Death in*

Venice," in *Thomas Mann: A Collection of Critical Essays,* ed. Henry Hatfield [Englewood Cliffs, N.J., 1964], esp. pp. 51–54).

28. Aschenbach himself, while he never relates the stranger-figures causally to his fate or to each other, does on several occasions reflect on them with puzzlement. See esp. 446, 461, 468, 515.

29. "The Readerhood of Man," in *The Reader in the Text,* eds. Susan R. Suleiman and Inge Crosman (Princeton, 1980), p. 131.

30. Reed, p. 149.

31. Except perhaps toward the end of his discussion when he states rather cryptically: "It has proved possible to detach Mann from the emphatic condemnations of the later pages. These formulations . . . are Mann's concession to more confident moralists than himself" (p. 173). Is he suggesting here that the moralistic narrator is a kind of hypocritical role that Mann adopted for public consumption? This seems to me a highly unlikely interpretation.

32. The terms ["moral fable"] and ["hymnic"] are used by Mann himself to contrast the final product with the original creative impulse. See his letter to Carl Maria Weber (4. Juli 1920) — the crown witness for Reed's genetic argument.

33. "Fictional Reliability as a Communicative Problem," *Poetics Today,* 2 (1981), 113–126.

34. It is interesting to note in this connection that a number of recent critics have felt it necessary, and for the same reasons, to sever the narrator from the author of another famous work of fiction: *Die Wahlverwandtschaften.* The operation is performed most boldly by Eric Blackall in *Goethe and the Novel* (Ithaca, N.Y., 1976). According to Blackall, Goethe's narrator "throughout the novel . . . is trying to describe something that is really beyond him" (p. 172). Charging this narrator with "conventional platitude" (p. 184) and even incompetence" (p. 186), Blackall concludes that Goethe employs his services to create "an expressive tension between what is told and the telling" (p. 187). See also Jane K. Brown, "*Die Wahlverwandtschaften* and the English Novel of Manners," *Comparative Literature,* 28 (1976), 97–108, esp. pp. 105–107. In view of Mann's confession that he read *Wahlverwandtschaften* no less than five times in the course of his work on *Tod in Venedig,* one suspects that Goethe's interpolation of an unreliable narrator in this novel may have contributed to Mann's choice of an analogous device.

Thomas Mann's Conception of the Creative Writer

Peter Heller*

The Pattern of Balanced Ambivalence

A study of Mann's conception of the man of letters and of the literary artist is necessarily an enquiry into his entire philosophy of life, for to Mann "art is the quintessence of humanity and the artist the most human of men."[1] Because of Mann's perennial and conscious preoccupation with intellectual and artistic creativity, his views on the writer reflect most of

*Reprinted by permission of the Modern Language Association of America from *PMLA* 69 (1954):763–96.

the shifts and oscillations in his career. The present essay does not encompass all of these changes in accentuation and tonality.

It will be recalled that the unpolitical young man of the Wilhelminian era who established his reputation with the *Buddenbrooks* (1900) gave way during the First World War to a sophisticated conservative and to an effective, if ambiguous, propagandist for the cause of the Fatherland. The author of *Der Zauberberg* (1924) assumed the role of a literary spokesman for the Weimar Republic. Through Hitler's accession to power, the narrator of *Joseph und seine Brüder* (1933 to 1943) became an exile, an expatriate, and a leader in the literary campaign against National Socialism. As a confirmed internationalist, Mann contributed to the anti-German propaganda of the Second World War. At the same time, he worked on his most German novel, *Doktor Faustus* (1947). Finally, as an American citizen and left-wing liberal, he apparently turned again to Europe.

It is true that throughout the vicissitudes and triumphs of his career, Mann's work and general outlook have retained an amazing degree of homogeneity and even of uniformity. Though after 1918 Mann did undergo a gradual transformation which had a lasting effect on his views, he always sought to avoid a complete break with his former convictions. He changed his emphasis. He announced that a qualified affirmation had been modified to a qualified rejection, but he was not compelled to abandon his basic categories, and he never changed his basic mood. Nonetheless, a selective analysis of Mann's *Weltanschauung* must have its center of gravity in one definite phase of development. The present examination is concerned primarily with Mann's explicit deliberations during the period of the Weimar Republic, though references to earlier and to later views of the author seemed in order to indicate either a significant continuity or a metamorphosis in his thinking. Since the essay is an enquiry into Mann's ideology rather than into the more comprehensive symbols of his art, paraphrases and English translations were substituted for the original,[2] a procedure which has its value in focusing attention on the intellectual content even though it does not do justice to formulations which themselves partake of the nature of artistic creation.

The structure of Mann's ideology is determined by his need for emotional oscillation. Mann's ambivalence is balanced. It requires a constant ironical movement between antinomies. Torn between opposing emotions directed toward the same object, he desires mediation; yet the partial resolution of a conflict immediately reactivates his ambivalence. The conceptual structure within which the ambivalence expresses itself is symmetrical. In Mann's metaphysics, the Spirit is hostile to, and yearns for, Nature.[3] Nature is hostile to, and yearns for, the Spirit. It is the cosmic role of man, and, specifically, of art and the artist to mediate between the opposites. The ultimate synthesis, the complete merging of Spirit and

Nature, is to Mann an infinitely distant goal. Yet humanity should approximate it.

Mann's entire theory of the artist could be treated in terms of this bare framework, that is, in terms of almost mathemathical plus-and-minus relationships between Spirit, Nature, and the intermediary, art. However, Mann's comprehensive abstractions and metaphysical entities are unreliable, and, while they recur in most of his works, they frequently trap the interpreter in a tangle of contradictions. The general categories always become highly suggestive within the context of one given essay. They assume a specific character by virtue of descriptive attributes which lend the color and shape required for the particular occasion; but from one work to the other the most imposing general terms are likely to shift their meaning. Hence they elude precise definition. The characteristic and durable elements in Mann's ideology are closer to the level of common usage, closer to the pictorial and to the impressionistic than the academic idiom suggests.

The impassioned juggling of philosophical concepts is nonetheless significant. For it shows that Mann is most at ease when he can split the world into opposites, and then proceed to mediate between them. In his fiction he prefers a position that will enable him to reject and to love at the same time. This problematic relationship has always been his first choice. It required strong outside pressures, a direct attack on fundamental beliefs and loyalties of the author, to provoke him to an unqualified rejection of one alternative and to an almost equally simple acceptance of the other. He could be unambiguously positive in his declarations only when they were directed at an external opponent, when they took on the form of aggressive counter-attitudes. Through the immediate contact with National Socialism Mann's pros and cons were placed at a wider distance from one another than ever before: "Yes, we have learned once more to know good from evil. For evil has revealed itself to us in a naked crudity which has opened our eyes to a simple dignity and beauty of the good. We have laid hold upon it; and think no shame to our sophistication to admit the fact. Again we dare to take upon our lips such words as freedom, truth, and justice; being weaned from our embarrassment and scepticism by the sight of so much baseness" (*Ord*, 237).

Neither the First World War nor the conditions prevailing in the initial years of the Weimar Republic — nor the present world situation — could induce Mann to refrain to such an extent from the attempt to mediate. The *Betrachtungen* of 1918, though heavily weighted in the direction of nationalist conservatism, remained a debate with his brother, and with the other half of the author's own self.[4] Conservative progressivism, the synthesis between East and West, between the individualistic tradition of Weimar and the socialist idea, between romanticism and rationalism constituted the program of the author in the early democratic

phase. And yet Mann's ideology contains a core of unambivalent sentiments and of unambiguous convictions. This core is rarely revealed, but
without a center of uncorroded beliefs, Mann could not have maintained
his balanced ambivalence. For no man can endure an all-pervasive
emotional relativism.

The Aristocracy of Nature and the Nobility of the Spirit

Mann's enjoyment of the dialectical movement between opposites is
illustrated to perfection by his essay on Goethe and Tolstoi who, according
to the author, represent the *naive* (unconscious, spontaneous) genius in
contradistinction to Schiller and Dostoevski, the representatives of the
sentimental (the reflective, analytical) type.[5] As others had done before
him, Mann equated his Schillerian distinction with other pairs of opposites, such as the classical and the romantic spirit, *Plastik* and *Vision*, the
epic and the apocalyptic mood. The naive authors are said to have an
affinity to reality, realism, objectivity, evolution, rooted conservatism,
and, of course, to Nature. Their antipodes are inspired by idealism, by the
dream, by subjectivity, by revolutionary zeal, by rhetorical activism, in
short, by the Spirit. In characteristic fashion, the author thus forms two
clusters, each of them allegedly indivisible and antithetical to the other.

The naive genius — to put the matter in the most extreme form —
cannot love anyone but himself (*Ess*, 175). At least in his youth, he is
blindly egocentric, living like young Joseph, under the dangerous assumption that his fellowmen must love him more than they love themselves.[6]
However, this self-love is more than mere complacency. It is creative of a
life "full of romantic happenings," and at the root of "all autobiography."
It may appear in a highly sublimated form as the humble veneration and
awe of man for the mystery of his own being (*Ess*, 101).

The "grateful and reverent self-absorption of the darling of the gods"
explains the "absence of customary reserve, discretion, decency, and
shame." The naive genius makes an "absolute claim" on the love of the
world. Hence he will reveal his vices as generously as his virtues. "He
craves to be known and loved, loved *because* known, or loved *although*
known. . . . And the remarkable thing is that the world acknowledges
and honors this claim" (*Ess*, 100 f., *Bem*, 20 f.).

Even more remarkable is the fact that, according to Mann, this
egocentric eros is "not to be divorced" from a genuine love for humanity.
In the early twenties, Mann was still convinced that there was an
inevitable connection between "*Selbst- und Menschenbildung*" (*Bem*,
115). On his quest for self-improvement and self-completion the naive
genius is led eventually to shape and to form the lives of other humans. He
conceives of his own being as a cultural task to be pursued in incessant and
arduous labor, and he is rewarded for his zeal by gaining, almost as though
by accident, an "educational influence . . . , and the joy and dignity of a

leader and former of youth" (*Ess*, 160). This harvest—again we think of Joseph, the charming young parasite and exhibitionist who turns into a provider—marks the high point in the life of a productive human being. It is a spiritual triumph which exceeds by far "all ordinary human joys of love and fatherhood" (*Ess*, 160).

Nonetheless, the naive genius, as Mann describes him, remains close to the earth, in loving unison with his physical appearance and his vital impulses. The sensuous and the sensual are his domains. As he is fond of his own body, so he is preoccupied in his art with the concrete human figure. His sharp senses, his strong eroticism, his sensitiveness to natural phenomena, his concern and intuitive sympathy with the organic derive from the same source. Goethe's and Tolstoi's charm, their love of sports and games, their sense of well-being were manifestations of a zest for life. The naive genius approves of, and enjoys, his own being. Hence he accepts and appreciates reality, and he observes it with sympathetic precision. "The truth, the power, the calm, and the humility of Nature," Mann observes, will never be reconciled to the "disproportionate, fevered, and dogmatic presumption of [the] Spirit" (*Ess*, 118).

Like Antaeus, the naive genius draws strength and instinctive security from the soil. Rooted, without programmatic pathos, in his native ground, he has little talent for rebellion. His self-esteem is described as a "pride in his [own] earth-bound aristocracy" (*Ess*, 120). Goethe possessed a "deep metaphysical certainty" that under no circumstances he could be "other than favored and privileged, ever other than well-born" (*Ess*, 125). Refusing to distinguish between good fortune and achievement, he calmly spoke of "inborn merits" (*Bem*, 58).

This paradoxical term, Mann claims, anticipated Schopenhauer's distinction between man's transcendental freedom in the *esse* and man's absolute bondage in the *operari* (that is, in the deterministic world of phenomena). It was, at the same time, an expression of metaphysical arrogance. It implied contempt for the less fortunate. It favored the notion that men are born unfree and unequal, that their will is but part of their being, and, consequently, that individuals are not responsible for what they make of themselves but can be praised or condemned only for what they are. In contrast to this aristocratic consciousness of innate rank, Mann's spiritual artist cultivates the ethos of the self-made man. It is significant that Goethe and Tolstoi were of genteel (patrician and aristocratic) birth, while Schiller and Dostoevski were of humble origin. The spiritual artists attain nobility through effort, discipline, conscious will, and activity. They are proud of their freedom. For freedom and Spirit are one. They signify "release from Nature, rebellion against her" (*Ess*, 121). To the spiritual artist, the dignity of man does not consist in the *reality* of his being, but in his striving for the *ideal*.

Mann's typology refines upon familiar notions concerning the happy, well-adjusted children of the world and the dispossessed fanatical dream-

ers and idealists. Goethe's or Tolstoi's astounding gifts—he observes—
merged with a radiant vitality to inspire the feeling, "the man is like God"
(*Ess*, 105). Schiller or Dostoevski never impressed their visitors as god-like.

And yet, Goethe, according to Mann, looked like a "comfortable
farmer," or a "staff-officer in mufti." Tolstoi expressed "a banal interest in
cock-fights and boxing-matches" (*Ess*, 128 f.). Both were often unfriendly
or embarrassed in receiving visitors, and never likely to utter "great words
and thoughts" to those who came to pay them homage (*Ess*, 106). In fact,
the worldliness of the naive artists usually disappointed their admirers
while the sons of the Spirit made personally a spiritual impression, as the
hopeful average man would expect those who were "soul-shakers" to do
(*Ess*, 129). The "lofty, pallid, suffering-saint and criminal look of Dostoevski," the "mild, intrepid, fanatical, and equally ailing physiognomy of
Schiller" corresponded satisfactorily to the accepted pictures of the Russian and the German genius (*Ess*, 129). What, then, accounted for the
personal attraction of Goethe and Tolstoi? What made the pilgrims troop
to Weimar and Yasnaya Polyana? According to Mann, the power of
personality is not of the mind. It is an "elemental" mystery of the vital
sphere (*Ess*, 106 ff.).

Now this is not to say that the balance is in favor of the naive artists.
Mann is most anxious to establish an equilibrium of pros and cons, not
only in his own attitude toward the antithetical types, and in the attitudes
which he attributes to their public, but also in the distribution of virtues
and deficiencies which characterize the internal economies of his ideal
protagonists, and in the forces of attraction and repulsion which govern
their mutual relationship.

He exposes the vanity of his naive heroes in order to justify it on a
higher plane. He celebrates their exalted position in order to expose its
dubious and ridiculous aspects. He praises their vitality to point out its
frightening and disastrous consequences. For with all their godlike radi-
ance, Mann's Goethe and Tolstoi appear, among other things, as oppres-
sive misfits and as tortured devils. As for the *sentimental* heroes, it will be
seen that they are altogether wretched in their glory.

To turn to Mann's naive genius first: It is true that in his maturity he
desires to help and to teach, to love, and to be loved by, his fellowmen, but
at the same time he is the victim of his own amoral neutrality, and
condemned to suffer under his own contempt for all human beings.
Despite their unsuspecting mediocrity, the ordinary people are aware of
this Janus face of their idol, and, consequently, they develop an ambivalent attitude of their own. They venerate the genius; and yet they feel
oppressed by his superhuman or inhuman traits. They are deeply grateful
for the existence of the vital giant; and yet they are glad to be rid of the
monster. Mann's Goethe is the object of a cult; but he remains isolated. He
lives in disharmony with the circles of servants and flatterers which he has
drawn around his ego. In *Lotte in Weimar*, Mann exposes the empty

rituals, the sensationalism, the stiffness, the gossip, the pomposity which emprison the old Goethe. He satirizes the stage-world of celebrity and its snobberies. He dwells at length on the vain, uncomfortable, and—at times—rather cynical histrionics of his hero. To be sure, Goethe moves continually in an aura of greatness, and so does Mann in describing him. Historical importance is attached to every word and gesture of the idol. An overwhelming difference in rank separates the chosen man from the crowd. However, even while he restores and propagandizes the religion of genius,[7] Mann humanizes and deflates the myth.

According to Mann, the naive and the spiritual genius alike are subject to conflicts and weaknesses in so far as they do not represent fully and harmoniously man's intermediary position. "Effortless Nature . . . is crude. Effortless Spirit is without root or substance." For man is "a lofty encounter of Nature and Spirit as they mutually yearn toward each other" (*Ess*, 151). Since both the vital and the spiritual man fall short of the perfect balance, they cannot live in simple harmony with their endowments. ["Spiritualization! is the sentimentive imperative of the favorites of nature, just as that of the sons of the spirit is embodiment"] (*Bem*, 101).

The native genius is subject to the "Faustian conflict." He is torn between the impulses of a strong animal constitution and the yearnings for the lofty regions of man's spiritual ancestry (*Ess*, 133). Goethe sought to transform himself from a product of Nature into a product of culture. His self-abnegation, restraint, and discipline remain exemplary for those who strive for the synthesis (*Ess*, 132). In Tolstoi, who was too much of a barbarian to conceive of the balanced ideal of culture, the struggle against the "natural man" (*Ess*, 151), against the body, and specifically, against sexual impulses, led to distortions and painful inconsistencies. Tolstoi's forced hostility toward the organic was pathetic and ludicrous, for he remained the "darling of the creative impulse of organic life" (*Ess*, 131).

Yet all naive geniuses are forced to fight their own inclinations. Their efforts at spiritualization are in conflict with a somewhat passive and recalcitrant temperament. Unlike the spiritual type, Mann's naive genius is not a man of unilinear action, of abstract programs, and inflexible purposes. He is embedded in his physical being, dependent on his moods and surroundings, open to many influences, and in need of love, encouragement, and prodding.

Since the Faustian conflict implies a purpose and at least the desire for a goal, it is not—in Mann's view—the deepest source of unhappiness for the naive genius (*Bem*, 73). His most terrifying and truly catastrophic experience is a complete denial of all purpose and a destructive indifference toward all goals. While the inertia or hesitancy, "[das] tief Zögernde" in the naive man may make for organic growth and for productive slowness of creation, it may be equally conducive to indolence and to "willenlose Schlenderei" (*Lei*, 78). Similarly, the abundant vitality of the naive man alternates with the most radical depressions (*Bem*, 70), and his intellectual humility has a reverse side of absolute skepticism and total negation. "It is pure error to think that conflict and complexity are things of the Spirit, while nature's kingdom must be all brightness and harmony." The children of Nature lack unity with themselves, and the peace of mind which alone can bring happiness. "Nature herself appears to weave in their being a questionable strand, an element of contradiction . . . an all-pervasive doubt which, since it cannot conduce to goodness, cannot conduce to happiness either. Spirit is good. Nature [is] . . . neither good nor evil, she escapes definition, as she herself refuses to define and judge; . . . and as this indifference of hers appears subjectively and spiritually in her children" it becomes a source of torment, of evil, and of dire confusion (*Ess*, 133; *Bem*, 72 f.).

Thus Goethe and Tolstoi were compelled to torture themselves and others with a radical lack of faith. Tolstoi was plagued with a "terrifying nihilism" which sprang from boundless despair (*Ess*, 134). Observers of Goethe noted his "deep irony" toward all human affairs (*Bem*, 79). Tolstoi's malice, Mann declares, was nothing but "tortured spite" against those who fancied they held the secret of clarity and truth. It was a disbelief in clarity and truth (*Ess*, 134). Tolstoi suspected, at times, that no man was ever sincere, and that all sentiments were lies (*Bem*, 75). Goethe was "tolerant without being mild." His icy neutrality was beyond the pale of the human. It was either something godlike or something devilish (*Ess*, 137).

It is evident that, according to Mann, a genius can never be "normal, healthy and according to rule." His physical constitution is likely to be "delicate and irritable, prone to crises and to disease." Some aspects of his psyche will always be foreign to the average man, and close to the psychopathic, though it is not for the Philistine to say so (*Ess*, 152). In fact, Mann usually treats artistic creativity as a product of decadence, or rather, genius in Mann's world arises at a point in the sequence of generations where ordinarily the mere *décadent* would make his appearance. Instead of exemplifying the decrease in vitality, the genius, standing at what is conceived of as a *late* stage of (biological and spiritual) development, summarizes the heritage. A dazzling and admirable phenomenon, the genius remains perilously close to decay, and even shows symptoms of decadence himself.

And yet, according to Mann, the type of genius exemplified by the children of Nature is exuberantly healthy and wholesome in comparison to the nobility of the Spirit. The latter are the "great sinners" and the damned, the religious sufferers of holy disease. Though Mann speaks of them with eloquent love and irony, he claims that these figures inspire a "mystic, silence-enjoining awe."[8] For the spiritual genius "in whom saint and criminal are one," is more than endangered. His strength can be measured only by the disease which he transforms into a stimulant.[9] He develops in a productive intimacy with his own afflictions. His sickness—

like that of Adrian Leverkühn in *Doktor Faustus*—becomes inseparable from the roots of his being, and a driving force to sublime achievement. In the spiritual genius, disease appears as an "artistocratic attribute of heightened humanity" (*Ess*, 108).

For like all of Mann's major categories, disease "has two faces, and a double relation to man." By throwing its victim back upon his body, disease has a dehumanizing effect. By intensifying man's conflict with his animal nature it may recommend itself as a "highly dignified human phenomenon." "Spirit is pride; it is a wilful denial and contradiction of Nature; it is detachment, withdrawal, estrangement from her. Spirit distinguishes from all other forms of organic life this creature man, this being which is to such a high degree independent of Nature and hostile to her. Hence the question, the aristocratic problem: is man not all the more human the more detached he is from Nature, that is to say, the more diseased he is? For what would disease be, if not disjunction from Nature?" (*Ess*, 108 f.; *Bem*, 34).

The spiritual artist conceives of man as "the romantic being." For he believes that as a spiritual entity man stands outside of Nature, and transcends her dominion. In this emotional separation from her, in this double essence of Nature and Spirit, he finds both his own importance and his own misery (*Ess*, 110). The deep human sympathy of the *sentimental* genius stems from his realization that man is inevitably involved in tragic antinomies.

The mutual relationships between Mann's two types of artists are subject to the same intricacies and governed by the same ambivalence which obtain between Nature and Spirit. The initial reaction is hostile. Goethe objected to the abstract ethical rigor and to the strenuous intellectualism of Schiller while the conscious, reflective genius could not altogether suppress the "idealistic malice of Spirit against Nature" (*Ess*, 120). The amoral vitality and childlike unconcern of the natural man (e.g., Goethe, Tolstoi) elicited the irony of the knowing and penetrating moral judge (e.g., Schiller, Dostoevski). However, Schiller and Goethe became friends. Spirit and Nature are in need of one another. Through a Hegelian trick of the world-spirit the naive genius is endowed with a yearning for spiritualization. As he matures, he learns to admire the conscious energy and moral force of his antipode. As for the spiritual artist, he becomes, like Schiller, the servant and suitor of the naive man. For with all his critical distance he yearns for Nature, and is in love with her. He is the sentimentalist to whom all of nature seems beautiful and worth preserving (e.g., Rousseau), the moralist who admires simplicity, the holy man irresistibly attracted to the divine. Eros, "the ironic god," determines this "peculiarly absolute judgment of values" on the part of the spiritual artist. For Spirit enters into a relationship with Nature "which is in a sense erotic," and governed by the polarity of male and female. In his capacity as a sublime lover, the Spirit can dare the ultimate in self-abasement and self-surrender without resigning his own nobility. Indeed, this love of the Spirit for Nature, and of the spiritual man for his naive counterpart, "will always retain the accent of a certain tender contempt" (*Ess*, 123).[10]

Creative Egocentricity

While the types defined in "Goethe and Tolstoi" illustrate Mann's view of the artist as a messenger, intermediary, or guide who travels between the spheres of Nature and Spirit, they do not represent rigid alternatives. Mann has portrayed a great number of creative men who do not fit into either pattern. Ranging from Wagner to Lessing, from Fontane to the Biblical prophets, from Whitman to Novalis, from Freud to Frederick the Great, he always sought for ancestral and mythical models to lend him support in his own existence and work. Divergent as these model figures were, Mann, at one time or other, treated each of them as a norm and type.

With ease, intuitive skill, and considerable sleights of hand, he conjured up parallels and correlations between all representatives of creative endeavor. His treatment of Wagner may serve as an instance.[11] He equated his image of this cunning and subtle artist with Zola and Ibsen. He wrote of Wagner, Nietzsche, and Schopenhauer that "the three are one" (*Bet*, 46). He identified this trinity with the *Nineteenth Century* and with *Romanticism*. He claimed of Wagner and of the entities equated with Wagner that they were but modern manifestations of the ethical, pessimistic, and bourgeois mentality which he designated as the *German spirit*. Wagner, finally, appeared as a conscious and European representative of the medieval — or was it the perennial? — German *Meister*, the representative of an archetype which the author described in the *Betrachtungen* of 1918 as if he had perceived it in a vision: "I see a face inclined slightly to the side and forwards, a countenance . . . unmistakable in national character, somehow archaic, and old-fashioned, somehow reminiscent of a Nürnberg burgher, and human in an unheard-of, and unique sense, ethical and spiritual, hard and gentle at the same time — the eyes looking inward and beyond things, not fiery, rather a little tired and languishing, the mouth firmly closed, and signs of exertion and strain on the wrinkled forehead which is careworn but not morose" (*Bet*, 88).[12]

This type, in turn, is related to Mann's Dürer, to his Lessing, and to his modern *Leistungsethiker*, to the desperate men of achievement such as Thomas Buddenbrook, Aschenbach, and Leverkühn. It is related to Mann's Schiller,[13] and, above all, to Mann himself. On closer acquaintance with the author's fiction and essays, we discover that the maze of equations and affinities ever increases in size until the correlations become so comprehensive that they lose all specific meaning. There is, apparently, no system that would include all of Mann's models. What is significant is the author's habit of relating all figures to himself, his effort to discover himself under the disguises of distant ages and personalities.

Indeed, Mann is always concerned with himself. He always wishes to judge, to criticize, or to praise himself in others. He is ever in search of his own roots, and always compelled to compare the works he discusses with his own products. He is never isolated within his own world; but his interest, his empathy, his insight are always directly connected with a consuming concern for his own being. Whatever the topic, every single essay Mann has written contributes to an analysis of Mann's own works. Hence it is hardly surprising that Mann should be preoccupied with egocentricity, also in his own theories of the artist. It will be recalled that self-love was the distinctive characteristic of the naive type. As such it was juxtaposed to the disease of the spiritual man who seemed to lack this positive narcissism. However, Mann's own interpretation must be supplemented. For the fundamental categories applicable to Mann's theory of the artist, that is: naive self-love, spiritual disease, and pervasive ambivalence, are more closely related to one another than they appear to be on first sight.

The disease of Mann's spiritual artist never comes merely from the outside. To call it self-inflicted is to simplify matters unduly, though Mann always hints at this possibility. Moreover, as a disciple of Schopenhauer, Mann has always been inclined to assume that a man's fate — though he might seem to be exposed to the blind chance of the *operari* — merely reveals what he metaphysically wills to be or what he *is* essentially (namely, in the metaphysical realm of the *esse*). Thus Adrian Leverkühn, the hero of *Doktor Faustus* (1947), neglects his infection deliberately, if not quite consciously. Gustav Aschenbach in *Der Tod in Venedig* (1911) deliberately disregards the many warnings against his passion and against the epidemic. He must eat the poisoned fruit. Hans Castorp in *Der Zauberberg* (1924) is soon drawn to the community of the sick, and, later on, he is strangely reluctant in his efforts to regain his health. Dostoevski's epilepsy, Mann claims, was the result of sexual repression, in fact, his disease was a kind of orgy.[14] While they need not be conscious of it, Mann's sick artists enjoy their afflictions, or, at least, they approve of them. They experience their disease as a form of self-destruction or self-punishment, as a source of excitement, as a sin, as guilt, or excess, and as a source of superiority. The pathological genius yearns for self-dedication to danger and evil. However, self-destructiveness, the "gloomy joys of self-hatred,"[15] are — just like self-love — aspects and consequences of egocentricity, insofar as that term denotes a strong concentration of feeling on the self. In Mann's description of the two artistic types, self-love and disease point to opposite tendencies, to an antithesis; but it is an antithesis *within the larger orbit of egocentricity*. Both tendencies together, that is: the tenderness and the cruelty, the gentle care and the torture, the love and the hatred bestowed on the self, reveal, in turn, a significant and, perhaps, the basic aspects of Mann's ambivalence. To turn with a yes-and-no, with love *and* hatred toward everything in himself and, subsequently, toward everything in the outside world, this is the fundamental tendency of Mann's writer and artist. Ambivalent egocentricity is his chief problem. To restrain, to socialize, to sublimate this basic tendency must be his main task. The temptation of the artist is not only that of self-indulgent vanity but equally the lure of self-destruction.

This interpretation — though not Mann's own — merely makes explicit what the author's comments imply. Egocentricity is not at the root of the naive genius but it is, to Mann, at the root of all creative effort. The reader of the *Betrachtungen*, he fears, will object to the author's excessive sense of self-importance. "I can only answer that I never have lived, and I never could have lived, without taking myself seriously." Spiritual and intellectual achievement, arts and ethics, "everything that seems good and noble to me" is the result of man's capacity to take himself seriously. ". . . all I ever accomplished, and all I ever produced (down to the effect and attraction of the smallest units, of every single line, of every expression), my entire life-work — as much and as little as that may mean — is exclusively the result of my taking myself seriously" (*Bet*, xvii). Thoroughness and conscientiousness are but products of intensive interest in one's self, and these traits, be they ever so close to pedantry, form, according to Mann, the very essence of his own artistic nature and of his moral being (*Bet*, xvi).

Mann derived his very definition of the poet's gift from his concept of creative egocentricity. The poet, he maintained in 1906, attaches importance to himself, and hence to events outside himself which he can relate to his ego. No matter whether he turns to a traditional tale or to live reality, "it is not the gift of invention, it is the gift of animation [*Beseelung*] that makes the poet." And what is animation? It is "the penetration and impregnation of the subject-matter with that which is the poet's own," that is, with the poet's own personality. It is the subjective intensification imparted to a copy or image of reality. "All the figures in a work of literature — be they ever so hostile and opposed to one another — are emanations of the creative ego" (*Red*, 8 f.). Whatever the merits of the familiar and sweeping attack on German "egotism" may be, Mann's self-judgment, his views on creativity and cultural achievement, and — if we may anticipate a further range of Mann's enquiry into egocentricity — his specific evaluation of German culture, come close to a corroboration of Santayana's thesis.[16]

Curiously enough, the alleged connection between egocentricity and creative effort emerges most clearly from Mann's portrait of Lessing who, as an artistic and playful thinker, as a sober and reasonable poet, as an antipode of the romantic Wagner, became the model for Mann's own essayistic and polemical efforts during the twenties. Like Mann himself — so the author implies — Lessing was restricted to a rather narrow range of subjects, but he possessed the art "to swell out a single seedcorn so as to make of it a play of inexhaustible interest" (*Ess*, 193). He was self-centered not merely in the sense that he knew how to cultivate and how to exploit his own garden. His egocentricity took on the form of self-criticism and self-surveillance. His "proud economy of output" — the "opposite to unintelligent productivity" — was the result of his shrewd self-awareness, of his pride and critical dignity (*Ess*, 194). He did not rage against himself as the pathological artist would, but he was well acquainted with a sublimated and comparatively bourgeois form of self-torture: He was merciless toward his own work. His autobiographical tendency and his frankness combined with the urge to hold judgment over himself. In Lessing, self-punishment — that is, negative egocentricity — assumed the guise of "critical self-surrender" (*For*, 81), and self-irony. It was he who furnished his critics with all their weapons, who said "the best things about himself," who spoke the truth as he saw it, however bleak and forbidding (*Ess*, 192).

Indeed, Lessing himself insisted that he was not a genius. Speaking *pro domo* as well as for Lessing, Mann disagrees with this self-depreciation. He rebukes the critics who — with a "jaundiced eye" — would exclude the "classic of the poetic intellect" from the "sacred sphere of the poetic afflatus." The typically German insistence on a rigid separation between profane writing and inspired creation was due, Mann claimed, to a mixture of "piety and spitefulness." It was the sign of a "provincial and sentimental stuffiness." It was a judgment motivated by a secret, reactionary, and anti-intellectual tendency. "The antithesis posited by the conservative critics is untenable, since the line between creative authorship and mere 'writing' runs . . . not outwardly, between the products, but inwardly, within the personality itself. . . ." Within the same person the impulsive and driven "writer" may gloriously combine with the clear-eyed and calm poet (*Ess*, 191 f.).

While Mann himself was concerned with the distinction between the poet and the man of letters,[17] he wished to mediate between these antithetical terms, and he was suspicious of invidious comparisons. To Mann, the creative process always required passionate self-involvement. The degrees of consciousness, and the elements of purposive effort, which attended this self-involvement he would treat, at times, as variables. "An art whose medium is language will always show a high degree of critical creativity, for speech itself is a critique of life": it names, it "hits," it characterizes, and judges the very objects it brings to life (*For*, 78). The hymnist Hölderlin spoke of a sacred sobriety. Perhaps he felt that the poet should gain mastery over an initial state of intoxication. Instead of a simple alternative, Mann conceived of a sequence with subtle alternations between rational and non-rational states of mind. Sobriety and detachment, he observed in 1929, were, of course, not productive, but perhaps creative productivity and artistic craftsmanship must alternate in the genesis of a work as two stages "united by an act of cool objectivation."

The "enthusiasts of simplification" failed to realize "how the conscious and the unconscious overlap in the domain of the productive, how much of the naive, of the unconscious, of the demonic—to use . . . their favorite word—enters into, and determines, all conscious action" (*Ess*, 192; *For*, 78).

Strain and labor are to Mann indicative of moral strength. He likes to quote Lessing's famous admission that he had to produce everything through "pressure and pipes" (*For*, 79, 268).[18] Nonetheless, Mann feels, the artist must not be too purposive, too rational, and too conscious. He must not deny the nightside of his being. Heroic constraint, rigid discipline, active effort, as well as self-consciousness, self-awareness, self-criticism, and the virile conscience tend to produce a tense and all too virtuous state of mind in which the access to the vital regions is obstructed.

> The moral imperative of the artist [Mann wrote in 1909] is to achieve collectedness of mind. The ethics of the artist require the power for egotistic concentration, that is, the determination to achieve form, the will to limitation and to concreteness. The artist must renounce freedom, infinity, slumber, and indeterminate motion in the unlimited realm of sensation and feeling. The morality of the artist is the will to create a work. But ignoble and immoral, bloodless and repellent is the work which was born out of the cold, the clever, the virtuous, and closed self-sufficiency of an artistic temperament. The morality of the artist demands dedication, error, self-abandonment, and loss of self. It requires struggle and misery, vivid experience, and passion. (*Red*, 397 f.)

Social Reality

These elements are opposed to egocentric self-absorption. For, true to his ambivalence, Mann now praises, now condemns the asocial isolation and autarky of the artist. Should the artist be *good* or *evil?* Is it "truly ethical" to preserve one's purity, or to abandon oneself to destructive forces? The great moralists who explored the depths of the ethical universe usually had been great sinners too (*Red*, 318). Even in Mann's latest novel, the *Holy Sinner* (1951), the sinner became a saint.

Somewhat earlier, *Doktor Faustus* (1947) gave rise to a significant misrepresentation. Some readers saw in the symbolic fate of Adrian a justification—and thus, almost, a glorification—of Germany's own pact with the devil, of its self-abandonment to sin and evil. Was not the contrast between Zeitblom and Leverkühn a variation on the theme of Mann's *Betrachtungen* of 1918? There the demagogical *Zivilisationsliterat* of the Western World had been confronted with the inward German, the man of music and culture. If the genius Leverkühn was diseased, the pious humanist Zeitblom was downright ridiculous or, at any rate, a much smaller man than the tragic representative of Germany. Had Mann not made fun of his own role during the last war against Germany when he put his own sermons for democracy in the mouth of Zeitblom? Did not the author imply that the very pact with the powers of evil was the necessary prelude to a subsequent ascension? Surely, the sins of Germany had predestined her to a far more fertile and demonic humanism, to a far greater destiny than was in store for those who, in their pettiness and cowardice, had avoided evil.

I repeat that this was a misrepresentation. Whatever the parallel between Germany and Adrian, Mann's portrait of the unhappy genius was not intended to exonerate the regime which brought the nation so close to its ruin. The author maintained his dual allegiance to darkness and to light. He believed that the descent into the abyss could bring about an enrichment of human consciousness if, and only if, it did not lead to the total loss of the rational personality. While the case-history of the syphilitic musician did not conceal the author's passionate concern with death, sickness, and isolation, Mann's development ever since the twenties left no doubt that he demanded of the artist an increasing acceptance of the social aspects of life, an increasing identification with the concerns of his community. Read without a bias, the message of *Faustus* was directed against arrogant seclusion, and against *ascetic-orgiastic* self-destruction.

Even so, there is a certain ambiguity in the novel. While the positive attitude towards the social sphere had become dominant in Mann's philosophy of life, the opposite trend remained present though recessive. The significance and extent of this development in Mann is somewhat obscured by the author's habit of expressing his philosophy in large metaphorical abstractions. In 1909, Mann praised the men who remain loyal to the night and yet perform the mightiest works of the day (*Red*, 399). In 1924, he defined the poets as problem-children prone to abandon themselves to sickness and death, yet destined to kindness towards life (*Bem*, 339). In 1948, he advocated a humanism which, having passed through the depths, would accept the knowledge of the "infernal and demonic," and incorporate it into its tribute to the human mystery.[19]

These generous statements — heartfelt, reasonable, and non-committal as they are — have a wide appeal, for they can be made to cover a multitude of divergent creeds. Yet, one might ask whether the mediation between night and day in 1909, or between death and life in 1924, or the inclusion of the demonic into the new humanism of 1948 revealed anything beyond the author's recurrent longing for a peaceful conjunction of opposites. Actually, Mann's commonplaces arise from a maze of specific conflicts. To discover their dynamic content, one must descend into this maze. What, then, are the antagonistic powers which the artist must face?

The renunciation of egocentric isolation, of narcissistic forms of attachment, and of bohemian freedom must take place, first of all, in the domain of personal relationship. The abyss which, according to Mann, attracts all artists and esthetes is that of a sterile and dangerous libertinism, a deeply pessimistic and orgiastic form of existence. Its perfect symbol is homoerotism, a form of love which negates "all that marriage stands for." It is opposed to "the laying of a foundation, to settlement, procreation, the sequence of generations, and to responsibility." It is essentially opposed to the enduring "loyalty" which constitutes the ethical and the vital foundation of family life (For, 173). In his youth, Mann observed in the late twenties, he himself had presented a negative view of marriage and fatherhood. Thomas Buddenbrook had expressed the author's own sentiments: "I need no son! Where shall I be when I am dead? I shall be in all those who ever said, and say, and shall say 'I,' and especially in those who express this 'I' fully, with strength, and good cheer. . . ." However, this turning away from the idea of a family and from the continuous unfolding of the family tree, this escape into metaphysics was a symptom of disintegration.[20] "Always," the author claims, "did the concepts of individualism and death merge into one for me. Always" — yet here one has reason to doubt the accuracy of Mann's memory — "did I associate the concept of life with the ideas of duty and service." Thomas Buddenbrook and Aschenbach, Mann explains, are dying men, "escapists from the discipline and the morality of life, Dionysians of death" (For, 174f.).

In Mann's early works, the artist is ever conscious of his asocial nature, and aware of his culpable isolation. He feels akin to the outcast, the gypsy, the criminal, and the impostor. Even the respectable Tonio Kröger finds it natural that he should be suspect to the police.

> A poet [Mann wrote in 1907] . . . is a fellow completely useless in all fields of serious activity, a man interested in nothing but tricks and nonsense. He is not only of no profit to the state but positively rebellious. He need not even possess special intellectual endowments. He can have a mind as slow and as dull as mine has always been. Incidentally, he is inwardly a childish charlatan, tending to debauchery, and suspect in every way. He should not (and does not) expect anything from society . . . but silent contempt. [And yet] . . . society gives this type of man the opportunity to earn respect, and to lead a supremely comfortable life in its very midst. (Red, 387)

The protagonists of Mann's early Novellen, or figures such as Hanno Buddenbrook and the poet Axel Martini in Königliche Hoheit, suggest that this is not a mere parody on the Philistine critique of the artist. The subtler irony of the passage lies in the fact that the author himself cannot deny its truth. By the twenties, Mann's artist has subdued his bad conscience, but it has not disappeared. Joseph's trickeries and the punishment of pit and prison still point to the former obsessive sense of guilt which had found its most radical expression in the author's identification with the swindler Felix Krull.[21]

Mann's artist begins his career with the tacit assumption that society is of no concern to him. To himself he is, in a sense, the only genuine human being on the surface of the earth. Hence he must learn that reality is real. He must persuade himself to take it seriously. In the twenties, Mann described the stages in this belated process of maturation. "To the dreamer," he wrote, "reality is more dreamlike and more flattering than any dream. But often, to live, to become real also seems to us like a betrayal . . . of our youth which was pure and free from reality. Indeed, . . . we were unstable, pure, and free, full of pride and shyness, and without faith that reality in any case would once be 'our due.' And yet life brought its realities, one after the other. Shaking your head, you remember them" (Red, 227). Mann tells of his inner rebellion against "deeds done by those closest to us, and marked by the severity of life, without a trace of humor, and terribly final." He recalls that he too has "become real" through "work and dignities, house, marriage, and child." Only in secrecy could he retain "some faith in the freedom and alienation of former times."

> Fantastic, unsuspected reality, we do not mistake your deadly serious-
> ness! For in whatever guise and gestures you may appear — whether pale
> with passion or humanly comfortable — all your figures, as they have
> appeared before our incredulous eyes to amuse us or to agitate us deeply,
> have something terrifying, and reveal a sacred menace. The eyes of all
> these shapes betray that they are related to the last in the sequence
> which, in the end, will also be "due" to us. Their family resemblance to
> death is unmistakable. Indeed, finally we shall enter death, and we shall
> bear the dignities of death's reality. Who would have thought it
> possible — Yet all reality, whether pale or gay, wears death's features.
> (Red, 228)

All of this is beautiful and true, but by a typical Mannian twist, reality and social functions which had been part and parcel of life have now become associated with the serious dignity of death. For Mann distinguishes between two aspects of death, and — as might be expected — he is ambivalent towards both. He praises or condemns death both as a denial of life and as its ultimate climax.[22]

Since the artist, as Mann sees him, never doubts the importance of his own fantasies but rather must make an effort to assume a positive and receptive attitude toward reality, the experiences and gratifications which are generally held to be most natural and pleasurable assume for him the character of ethical achievements. The artist considers it creditable and almost a self-conquest if he can engage in intimate human relationships and in a career. Instead of having spontaneous emotions, he mingles affections with the pride in being able to produce them. He is somewhat like a half-cured neurotic who boasts that he can now behave as normally as any well adjusted person. Thus Mann is pleased to find that, according to Hegel, he chose the most ethical road to marriage. His own capacity to found a home, and to adjust to it, he attributes not simply to inclination or to an emotional need, but to an "honest goodwill towards life," "the psychological formula of all morality and sociality" (For, 175 ff.). During the twenties, Mann seemed to feel that he must prove to himself and to his audience that he was working as diligently at living as any model student might work on his assigned task. Even in attending the celebrations in honor of his fiftieth birthday, Mann felt that he performed a moral feat (cf. *For*, 9 f.).

The postulate of *lebensgutwillige Bravheit*, of sympathy with and friendliness toward life, seemed to Mann as applicable to public affairs as it was applicable to the sphere of private relationships. Formerly, he had believed that intellect and politics endangered the soul and threatened the continuity of culture. Now, after the First World War, he felt that the only possibility for the survival of culture consisted in the synthesis between soul and intellect, between *Kultur* and *Zivilisation*. In response to the threat of fascism, he became increasingly convinced that the age demanded of the writer an active participation in the socio-political issues of the day. He discovered that his sense of isolation had been due to a self-deception characteristic of the early phase in the life of an artist. Works of art, he asserted now, were not only enjoyed socially, but the very act of artistic conception was a social event.

The act of creation "takes place in a deep adventurous . . . solitude" which is, actually, a special form of social intercourse, a "social loneliness." As he matures, the artist discovers that he has always fulfilled a social function though he did so at first in such a rebellious, dreamy, and playful fashion that he could not be aware of it. "Creative literature is an organ of national life, not only according to the official phrases but in all truth" (*For*, 16).

Mann immediately generalized on the basis of his personal experience. He found that, like the religious man, the man of culture thought only of himself, that is, of his own salvation. His goal was the perfection of the inner man in a purely humanistic, ethical, and esthetic sense. While the man of culture might hope that his work of self-sanctification would contribute ultimately and in some mystical fashion to the welfare of the world, this contribution was not the direct and avowed aim of his efforts (*For*, 190).[23] German culture at large — Mann asserted in the twenties — had sinfully neglected the social aspects of life. Unless this deficiency was remedied, it would be destroyed by the modern, victorious, and revolutionary "idea of community." In the late twenties, Mann felt that the time had come for an alliance between socialism and the conservative-romantic tradition. "Karl Marx" was to "read Friedrich Hölderlin," and vice versa (*For*, 195 f.).

In a summary of his development as a political thinker written in 1939, Mann pointed out that he had had to acquire the basis for his allegiance to democracy by way of a conscious reorientation. For the fundamental conviction underlying democracy — namely, that "the political and social are parts of the human" — was foreign to his "bourgeois-intellectual" upbringing (*Ord*, 228). To the traditional German type whom Mann associates with the mood of "the cross, death, and the grave"

(*Ord*, 232), culture meant music, metaphysics, psychology, "a pessimistic ethic, and an individualistic idealism" (*Ord*, 229). This had been Mann's own conviction in *Betrachtungen* of 1918. It implied an aversion to the "indecent optimism" of democracy, to its demagogues who preached the gospel of progress, and, indeed, to politics as a whole (*Ord*, 232). For democracy was simply "the political aspect of the intellect, the readiness of the intellect to be political" (*Ord*, 228).

As Mann changed into a man of social conscience, the former virtues assumed a sinister aspect. To be unpolitical and antidemocratic was now — in the thirties and during the Second World War — a great crime, and equivalent to a "suicidal position" of the mind (*Ord*, 231). By virtue of an antidemocratic pride in pure culture the German spirit had become the enemy of humanity. Barbarism was the fruit of Germany's esthetic bourgeois culture (*Ord*, 236).

However, involvement in the issues of the day inevitably raised the question in Mann's own mind whether the artist was qualified for the role of the politician. In what manner was he to participate in the struggle? Mann did not question the *unconscious* bond between the writer and the age. The poet's life "is symbolic," he "only needs to speak of himself, and whether he wants to or not, he will speak in the name of his age, in the name of all. Taking their place, he bears the sufferings of others and gives expression to them, as Goethe once did with the sorrows of Werther."[24] Art itself is symbolic territory. The difficulties and obstacles which the musician Leverkühn encounters in his efforts at composition mirror the desperate struggles for the achievement of a new socio-political order. However, this connection is involuntary, figurative, and fraught with mystery. Mann's essays, on the other hand, were conscious attempts to deal explicitly with contemporary problems. With all his intuition, the artist might lack the skill to give a rational analysis of political issues. Mann himself had claimed in 1920 that the prophecy and leadership of the artists was something "organic" and nondiscursive which had its proof in "being and doing," while in the form of direct doctrine it always ran the greatest risk of becoming coarse, superficial, and devoid of spiritual substance (*Red*, 308).

And yet, Mann felt increasingly that it was impossible to maintain neat distinctions between the modes of communication. The arts were in a violent crisis which could lead to death or to the birth of entirely new forms. The writer, Mann observed in 1924, could no longer exist as a pure artist or esthete, just as the politician could no longer afford to be ignorant of spiritual matters (*Bem*, 240). Menacingly and with greater urgency than at any other time, the problem of man itself confronted all who lived seriously (*Bem*, 240). Since every issue pointed to a central dilemma, the spiritual man had to assume greater responsibilities than ever. The tensions and complexities of the age exercised a heavy pressure, and subjected the writer's temperament to a severer discipline. Mann envisaged a new spiritual type, distinguished by caution, presence of mind, and dignity of thought. Lightheaded bravado would be as foreign to him as mere despondency.

The artist, Mann wrote in 1930, now experienced moments when the general distress and crisis made art "a mental impossibility," when the "happy and impassioned preoccupation with eternally human values" seemed ephemeral and superfluous (*Ord*, 47). Still, he could not subscribe to a "remorselessly social point of view." He could not look upon art as a private pastime and "put idealism on the level of frivolity." For artistic form "is akin to the Spirit." Art, that is, partakes of the force that leads to the improvement of the human condition; and in the sphere of art "the conflict between the social and the ideal" is resolved (*Ord*, 46 f.).

Mann pointed to Lessing and to the prophets of the Old Testament in order to show that the artist could be belligerent without betraying his art, that he need not be a simpleton to be used as "a front by wickedness and self-interest," nor subservient to "our beloved 'things-as-they-are.' " It did not degrade the artist to recognize stupidity and corruption, and to vent his anger (*Ord*, vii). "The Hebrew prophets, wrathfully warning and admonishing their people, were poets too, and mighty ones, though their poetry took [on] critical form; and prophecy" — Mann claimed — "as sensitive anticipation, [as] suffering and clairvoyant perception of the age and the future" has always been an essential element of truly creative writing (*Ord*, viii).

Art and Truth

Mann's decisions have rarely been final. In the fight against National Socialism he did assign the writer the task of teaching, of communicating insights which referred directly and unambiguously to the problems of external and public reality. However, he was never quite convinced that the artist could be trusted with this assignment. No matter how dignified and worthy an artist might be, his veracity was open to doubt. The relation between art and truth was, inevitably, a highly problematic affair. At the most — it would seem — Mann could claim that there were compensations for the artist's basic lack of seriousness, that the artist was, after all, not necessarily less reliable as a guide than other fallible humans.

Man, according to Mann, could attain perfection only in art (*Red*, 104), for only the artist anticipated the synthesis between Nature and Spirit. However, this anticipation of a final harmony was playful. It was merely imaginary. It lacked the solidity of the ultimate unification. Indeed, art lacked the concreteness of any realistic achievement, be the latter ever so inferior in perfection to the fictitious miracles performed by the dreamers. Art was essentially a — very serious — game. Reality, on the other hand, was always imperfect. Hence the artist's admiration and contempt for reality should be matched by the realist's admiring contempt for art.

However, the problem that troubled Mann was not, primarily, the dichotomy between reality and ideal. Apparently, he was never tempted to engage in direct action. The artist might be a teacher of practical truths, a judge of reality, without being an activist, if only he could maintain a stable and positive relation to the data of the real world, if only he could reconcile art and truth. On this antithesis Mann insisted, and, as always, he wished to mediate between the antinomies which he himself had established as such.

As early as 1906, Mann wrote that Nietzsche, the "German lyricist of cognition," had founded a European school in which the concept of the artist merged with that of the man of knowledge. The writers of this school wanted to know *and* to create, to gain deep insight *and* to achieve esthetic perfection of form (*Red*, 13). They derived their ethical inspiration from the patient and proud endurance of their twofold sufferings as poets and as thinkers. They had to bear "the spasms . . . of creative labor" as well as the pains that accompanied "the artistic form of insight commonly called observation." For they experienced observation as "a passion," as "torture, martyrdom, and heroism" (*Red*, 13).

Though he recognized the "fine, sensual delight" of observation (*Red*, 104), Mann generally associated observation, criticism, and theoretical insight with a sublimated, if somewhat tortured, aggression. The feeling that consciousness and insight *kill* the object of perception is probably at the root of all metaphysical systems in which the Spirit (intellect) appears as hostile to Nature (or to the soul). These systems, so common in the romantic and neoromantic literature of Germany, attribute sentiments which accompany the process of thinking to the nature and to the effect of thoughts and insights as such. It will be recalled that in "Goethe and Tolstoi" — or in the *Joseph Novels* — Mann modified this metaphysical mythology in order to state explicitly that the Spirit played a double role as an enemy and as a lover of Nature. However, the earlier Mann was inclined to emphasize the rigorously hostile objectivity[25] of the spiritual observer. The artist's eyes, he asserted, were both "colder and more passionate" than those of ordinary men. In his private life, a writer might be "good, tolerant, loving," and given to "uncritical approval"; as an artist he was forced to "observe with lightning speed and to perceive with painful malice." He had to notice every characteristic detail, every indication of race, social milieu, or psychological condition, to register them "ruthlessly, as if he had no human contact with what he saw." Together with the refinement of the observing sensory apparatus, the artist's capacity for suffering increased until every experience became a torture. The artist's "only weapon is expression. He can describe, define, and characterize. . . . [That is] his sublime . . . revenge on his own experience. The more sensitive the perceptive instrument affected by the original impression, the more violent will be the revenge. This is the mainspring of that cold and pitiless accuracy, this is the drawn bow, the trembling string from which the arrow of the word is launched, the sharp, winged arrow of the word that whirs through the air" and pierces the eye of the target (*Red*, 15).

Here, artist and thinker are brought together quite closely. However, the fact that an intellectual or spiritual element was a necessary ingredient in every artistic expression did not settle in Mann's own mind the problem of the artist's relation to truth. Art, he knew, admitted varying degrees of consciousness and spiritual awareness. Some artists lacked all sense of intellectual responsibility. Perhaps even the classics of the poetic intellect — like Lessing — had a claim to poetic rank only because they had imposed certain limitations on their truthfulness, seriousness, and spirituality.

It will be recalled that Mann was eager to come to the rescue of Lessing. In particular, he defended Lessing's irascibility (*For*, 84 f.), for, in accordance with Mann's equation between intellect and aggression, the most conscious art was distinguished by the "hankering after a fight," the love of controversy for its own sake (*For*, 84 f.). The polemical element put the "salt and pepper" into Lessing's works, and, at times, so dominated the author that he found the merely creative "flat and insipid" (*For*, 84 f.).

Mann spoke of the "combatant" character of his own controversial production in a similar vein, but then he immediately contrasted it with the "dream life of the imagination." He clearly implied the troublesome antithesis when he observed that his own wish to contribute to "the enlightenment of the world had been, though not a profounder, at least a warmer and more passionate feeling than the careful, patient devotion to the weaving of epic music" (*Ord*, v).

Once more, artistic and intellectual productivity seem far apart. Once more they are brought close together in the definition of the poet as *irritabilis vates* (*Bem*, 339), as a man endowed with an aggressive and thin-skinned sensitivity. For Mann claimed that the source of his own pugnacious essays was none other than this poetic nervousness and irritability of perception (*Bet*, xi). Mann's concept of sensitivity provides a clue to his views on the function of the artist, and on the artist's relation to the fluctuating human truths. The later Mann thought of sensitivity as the basis for man's greatest virtue. Only the sensitive individual could be attentive and obedient to the *world-hour*.[26] In the Joseph novels the author showed that insights and attitudes which had been correct and justified at one time became atavistic, sinful, and criminal when they were no longer in accord with the age.[27] Similarly, Mann felt during the twenties that his own position in the First World War had not been a mistake or a sin but that it had become sinfully inappropriate only after the war, because the historical situation now demanded a different orientation. In an age of transition, a stubborn loyalty to set convictions could be a fault and a crime while the ability to change might become a virtue. This belief of Mann was facilitated by his ambivalence. Since few of his sentiments and convictions were absolute, he could adapt and modify his position without great difficulty. He experienced his conversion after 1918 as a mere shift in perspective. By obedience to changing historical needs he did not mean flattery of the masses or subservience to the demands of their rulers. However, a certain moral relativism seems inherent in his historical view of human values. For the historically sensitive man, for the time-server (if this term may be used in a higher, and, indeed, in an ideal sense) the truth of today may be the lie of tomorrow.

In short, in Mann's dynamic and dialectical universe, truths have no absolute status. He felt, at times, that the singleminded cult of one exclusive perspective was tantamount to a self-hypnosis which would lead to death or to a "dignified state of petrifaction," that he needed new truths as a fresh stimulus to life (*Ord*, 22). Even in his rationalistic mood, when he praised precision and identified beauty with objectivity (*Red*, 370), Mann did not abandon his relativism. Lessing, the model of those who strive for truth, lived and thrived, according to Mann, on scepticism and doubt. They were his "native heath," and his "religion." Doubt as a form of faith, scepticism as a positive passion—that was quite genuinely the paradox of Lessing and of the classic type he established. It was "a paradox of the heart and not of the understanding," and it implied a conception of truth and a feeling for truth unique in its freedom and beauty (*Ess*, 197).

Mann's Lessing found "the criteria of truth" in the personality of its spokesman rather than in the particular statement upheld as true (*For*, 80). This relativization and humanization of the concept of truth explains why he preferred the striving for truth to truth itself. According to Lessing, man "proves his worth not in the possession or the supposed possession of truth, but in the sheer pains he takes to come at it. That"— Mann continues—"is to subjectivate the value of truth and almost truth itself. It implies a profound philosophical doubt of the objective together with a passion for research. The ethical human element . . . [Lessing] recognizes only in this passion" (*Ess*, 197; *For*, 86).

The dangers of this attitude are evident. It corrodes the faith in reason and research as effective tools for obtaining truths, and substitutes for it the high evaluation of impassioned intellectual effort as such; not because this endeavor leads to convincing or useful results but because it is creditable in itself. An emotional faith in the intrinsic nobility of cerebral activities is coupled with the most thoroughgoing scepticism concerning the ends served by this activity. Santayana pointed out that Lessing's preference for pure striving, if it was to be taken literally and seriously, would necessarily transform the pursuit of truth into the pursuit of any fresh idea. For the possession of truth was no longer wanted, and, indeed, truth was no longer discoverable. "Any idea will do, so long as it is pregnant with another that may presently take its place; and as presumably error will precipitate new ideas more readily than truth, we might almost find it implied in Lessing's maxim that, as Nietzsche maintained, what is really good is neither truth nor the pursuit of truth (for you might find it, and what would you do then?), but rather a perpetual flux of errors." Santayana objected to the subjectivism in Lessing's famous statement,[28] and saw in it the seeds of both transcendentalism and nihilism. He considered nihilism a variant of subjectivism, and he attacked the philosophical subjectivism of the Germans in all its phases as a manifestation of egotism.

A reference to this critique is relevant in the present context, not because we are concerned with its validity but because of Mann's own preoccupation with egocentricity, and because of the fact that Mann too seemed to have in mind similar connections and a similar charge when he felt it incumbent upon him to defend Lessing's dictum. "How false it would be," Mann exclaimed, to confuse Lessing's philosophic doubt in the possibility of true insight or in the accessibility of truth with "nihilism" or with "intentional malice" (Ess, 197). However, the protest contained an admission.

For Mann too believed that an element of subjectivism and of relativism, a tendency to nihilistic denial of absolutes were inherent in Lessing's attitude, not because Lessing anticipated the cardinal sins of German idealism or because he was inclined to make a transcendental *ego* the arbiter and creator of the universe, but because he was an artist. As shown above, Mann too accused the German cultural heritage at large of an asocial individualism, subjectivism, and egotism. However, egocentricity remained to him, first of all, the problem of the artist.

According to Mann, Lessing played with thoughts, he indulged in "dialectical virtuosity." That is decisive, even though Mann takes pains to distinguish this deeply serious, passionate, and touching virtuosity from cold and vain sophistry (Ess, 198; For, 88). Mann holds that the artist is never completely reliable as a thinker. Even if he is of the serious and intellectual type, he remains an artist only "by virtue of the playful passion" — the delight in form — "which constitutes the organic secret of art" (Ess, 198 f.). In art the statement is subservient to the end of a sublime play.

According to Mann, Lessing was capable of taking a stand, of conveying a message, not because he had firm convictions but because he was benevolent and kind.

> This great controversialist . . . did not become nihilistic, he did not "leave the battlefield with a burst of mocking laughter." He was kindly. And this his nation and all the nations should count his highest claim to praise. He pondered long and deeply. That he then made play with the conclusions to which he came was not done for the sake of play. His was a spirit as full of faith, love, and hope as any that has lived and taken

thought for the lot of man. He, the manliest of spirits, had faith in a future manhood and maturity of humanity. (*Ess*, 200; *For*, 92)

The passage is characteristic of Mann, and it is fitting that it should conclude with the thought of future maturity. For what is maturity to Mann's artist, or, rather, what is the attitude that leads to maturity, to a positive rootedness in reality? It is the attitude of *lebensgutwillige Bravheit*, and in describing the intellectual virtues of the Lessingian type Mann merely describes the form which this solid benevolence toward life assumes in the realm of cognition. It will be recalled that, according to Mann, the artist — the dreamer — considered it a positive ethical achievement if he could accept reality. Likewise, he considers it an ethical achievement if he can affirm a truth. The humble fellow beings of genius, in turn, have to be grateful for the fact that the great man endorses reality and truth. If we reflect upon this a moment, does it not seem to us that Mann's demand is as presumptuous as it is childish? The artist himself — we might say — should be grateful for his capacity to establish contact with a world which exists independently of his fantasies. He alone should be grateful for being able to cling to some truths instead of being immersed in eternal doubt and vacillation. Or is the artist endowed with potential omnipotence? Can the creative ego abolish or smash reality and truth? Is it not infantile to expect the "nation and all the nations" to reward and to admire you for having refrained from mischief, to expect the world to see your greatest virtue in the fact that you abstained from futile cynicism and were not malicious enough to create confusion for confusion's sake? Is the artist a child who should be commended for his behavior in the world of grownups?

Indeed, Mann's artist remains bound to a sphere of immaturity, to a realm where truth and reality are denied in favor of playfulness and imagination. It is the same realm in which the ego, the majesty of the self continues to reign supreme. It is the dubious paradise of narcissistic egocentricity.[29] Hence Mann repeatedly paraphrases Nietzsche's description of the artist as an "excessively vain, excessively sensual monkey" (*For*, 306). He points out that "the histrionic, the apelike, the blague, and the fraud" are the roots of acting and the theatre, just as the desire to brag (*For*, 307) is the primitive basis for the narrative arts.

The frivolous, childish, and the childlike traits are most pronounced in a lecture on Wagner which Mann gave in 1933. There he defined the artist as a human creature inclined — at bottom — to merrymaking, an instigator to all kinds of festivities, in healthy contrast to the man of intellect, knowledge, and austere judgment, to the human being possessed of the absolute seriousness of a Nietzsche (*Ess*, 329). The artist is always concerned with the production of effects, and, generally, with enjoyment. It matters little whether he composes a tragedy or a farce, for it merely requires a change of perspective, a different illumination, to turn one into the other. "The farce is a hidden tragedy, the tragedy—in the last analysis—a sublime . . . joke" (Ess, 329). To be sure, the artist has a seriousness of his own, his seriousness in playing—that purest, loftiest, and most moving manifestation of the human mind—is beyond all doubt (Lei, 125); but his intellectual conscience is a subject "to ponder—and perhaps to shudder at" (Ess, 329). The artist believes in his truths "just so far as he needs in order to give them the fullest expression" and to produce with them the deepest impression. Consequently, he is very serious about his truths, serious even to tears—but yet not quite serious—and hence not serious at all. His intellectual seriousness is only "seriousness for the purpose of the game" (Ess, 330; Lei, 126). And since the artist is necessarily somewhat irresponsible, he is not fully accountable for what he does. The critics are mistaken when they attribute conscious fraud or sinister intentions to the creator, "as though there could be a kind of artist to whom his own effectiveness was a sham, instead of being, as it always is, an effect first of all upon himself. . . . Innocent may be the last adjective to apply to a certain type of art"—e.g., to the art of Wagner— but the artist himself is always innocent (Ess, 344). He is innocent as a child, and therefore under no compulsion to treat himself as an entirely serious and consistent character. He can make fun of himself as the composer of Parzival did when he signed his manuscript of the opera, "Richard Wagner, Oberkirchenrat" (Lei, 126), or when, "by way of relaxation," he talked "nonsense and told Saxon jokes" which made Nietzsche blush for him (Ess, 330).

Even the most solemn artist can never be quite as restrained and objective as adults are expected to be. All artists, for instance, have an insatiable greed for the first place. The saying, "Pereant qui ante nos nostra dixerunt," and Goethe's question, "Lebt man denn, wenn andere leben?" express a mood that has been felt by all of them (Ess, 331). For the artists are immoderate and shameless enough to give in to their jealousy and to their intolerance of all competitors and rivals. The desire to be indisputably superior to all others, to be, in fact, the continual center of attention and admiration, may not be always apparent but, in Mann's estimate, this boundless claim can never be foreign to the artist.

What, then, on the basis of this survey, is the artist's attitude toward knowledge? Can he be a reliable guide to the truths of his age? Mann's answer is ambiguous and inconclusive. From Nietzsche and Freud he has learned that virtues and capacities grow out of the refinement of primitive tendencies. It seems to be Mann's opinion that the artist who has come to master the vain and sensual monkey within him, and who has found the way to his human community, may take upon himself the burden and honor of spiritual leadership. At the same time, Mann continues to entertain grave doubts concerning the trustworthiness of the poet. However, he seems to feel that similar doubts are applicable to all men. In one respect at least the artist is forced to be more truthful and more severe with himself than other human beings. In his art, he cannot dissemble. In his art, he does what he is. For "art is truth — the truth about the artist" (*Ess*, 346).

SUMMARY AND INTERPRETATION

The preceding enquiry into Mann's views on art and truth demonstrated once more that the sphere of ambivalent, and, indeed, of infantile egocentricity constitutes the chief area of conflict in the author's image of the writer. The artist — as conceived by Mann — must come to terms with the child within him. This child or infant is extremely self-centered and fascinated by his own being. He lives in a world beyond the laws of the grownups. In his own sphere, the artist-child is omnipotent. There he alone determines what is true or false. In his *innocent* games, he can destroy or create the cosmos at will. Hence he finds it difficult to take the outside-world seriously, and when — like a good child — he makes an effort to accept reality and truth, he expects a special reward.

Fortunately, the child is not autonomous. He demands absolute and undivided love. This demand, though unrealistic in itself, draws him towards the outside world. As yet, he cannot tolerate rivals. He must see himself as the infinitely charming and bewitching center of festive occasions. However, this need can never be fully appeased. It is now rejected, now satisfied. This alternation between frustration and fulfillment reenforces a basic ambivalence in the child. Henceforth, he must turn toward the outer world as well as toward himself with simultaneous (or nearly simultaneous) feelings of love *and* hatred, of guilt *and* pride.

In Mann's world, the artist wants to repress, to modify, to sublimate his egocentricity as much as he wants to assert and to satisfy it. He wants to overcome the childish and childlike within him as much as he is drawn towards it. Hence the desire to return to youth and childhood, and the fear of such a return, are an ever recurrent theme of Mann's books. This is, so to speak, the archetype and the psychological source for all other recurrences in the author's works. It is the psychological source of the technique of varied recurrence, of the Leitmotiv in the narrowest, and in the most inclusive sense.[30] The return to childhood and to ancestral models inspired Mann's early epic of his family traditions (*Buddenbrooks*), and his subsequent treatment of myth with its ever recurrent human figures and constellations (*Joseph und seine Brüder*). Tonio Kröger witnesses the *return* of Hans Hansen and Ingeborg Holm, the beloved and the symbols of his youth. Hans Castorp experiences a similar return of his early friend Hippe in the shape of Clawdia. Joseph playfully re-enacts and relives the entire conflict and story of his youth when he brings about his reunion with the long-lost family. The *Return of the Beloved* shows Lotte's primitive attempt to achieve the recurrence of a glorious and problematic past in contrast with the far more vital and spiritual forms of recurrence which

Goethe achieves through his artistic creations. Finally, the hero of *Faustus* attempts to return to exactly the same conditions as those of his childhood. He duplicates the landscape, the household, and the very details of his early life. His return to the mother, consummated in the second infancy of insanity, reveals an ominous, pathological variant of the wish for recurrence.[31]

The author's equation between the conservative and the infantile[32] suggests that the same, invariably ambivalent, attitude toward the return and the regression is implied in Mann's favorite abstractions. He demands, for example, that men should assist the new without destroying the old, or that they should help the future without surrendering the loyalty to the past. The effective investment — the emotional meaning — which these commonplaces have to Mann derive, in part, from the author's attachment to his own roots. To what extent — he asks — should man abandon, or cling to, the egocentric paradise and hell of childhood?

Considering the importance which the theme of egocentricity has for Mann, it is not surprising that the author's ideological development can be summarized in terms of his self-estimates. In the earlier phase of his career, Mann presented the writer as a man who had to struggle less against a world which rejected him than against his own self-rejection. He was keenly aware of the *malheur d'être poète*, and, though he took pride in his very misery, his consciousness of creative power was overshadowed by a sense of guilt. Correspondingly, the self-estimate of Mann in the period preceding the First World War remained modest. At times, he spoke rather disparagingly of his achievements. This attitude, utterly unlike that of young Joseph (and of Mann's naive type in general), was not destined to become a permanent characteristic of the author. As Mann remarked of Wagner, "depressive self-deprecation" gradually gave way to "dictatorial self-sufficiency" (*Ess*, 319).

To be sure, feelings of inferiority and superiority are closely related in the ambivalent character. The self-effacement of the young artist hides his self-esteem. The self-esteem of the aged celebrity conceals the persistent doubt. Mann himself has always asserted and questioned his own greatness. He has never ceased to take his own measure. He has never been at peace with his own self-estimate nor has he ever been unconcerned with the question of his own rank.

Nonetheless a distinct change in Mann's self-estimate became evident in the twenties. It accompanied the author's increasing demand for adjustment to, and recognition of, reality. At the time when Mann told his readers how the artist lost his feeling of being unique, how he entered the community, and discovered that he was much like other humans, he himself lost his bad conscience. Thus, at the very time when Mann underwent and proclaimed the experience of socialization, he became increasingly fond of veiled comparisons between himself and Goethe. His former envy of the healthy commonplace men gradually gave way to a benevolent, if faintly contemptuous, condescension. As part of the human community, the author began to speak in the name of the German artist and of the artist in general, or, rather, in the name of Germany and, subsequently, in the name of mankind. In turning from the individual to the bourgeois, from the bourgeois to the timelessly human, Mann raised the stature of the artist and his own stature to mythical proportions.[33] And yet, in the major work of his old age, Mann identified himself with an artist who never indulged in social forms of vanity but who cultivated all the more his self-destructive and arrogant isolation. Adrian Leverkühn seemed to possess the love of the author to an even greater extent than did young Joseph. In his old age, Mann seems to have returned once more to his early self-identification with the problematic spiritual men.

However, in the inner recesses of his creative imagination, Mann has always wavered between Joseph and Adrian, between positive and negative egocentricity, between the naive and the sentimental type. He praised this indecision. The ironical reservation of judgment was the "really fruitful, the productive, and hence the artistic principle" (*Ess*, 173).

He wavered between antithetical types; but he was not bound to any rigidly defined polarity. He experienced the world in terms of antinomies and saw himself as a mediator; yet this was an instinctive dialectical method which enabled him to come to grips with a multitude of distinct and divergent experiences. His system of Nature and Spirit, precisely because it was far too vague to provide a reliable frame of reference, did not restrict him in his exploration of the world.

Similarly, Mann's egocentricity did not seriously narrow his scope. He discovered everywhere new elective affinities and new ancestors in whom he could recognize his own traits and who would justify his own existence. Just as he transformed the compulsive need for oscillation into a strategy for mental conquest, he transformed and utilized his egocentric doubt until it became a formidable source of energy for his creative efforts.

It would be pointless to blame the author for his need to see the human universe in explicit relation to his own existence. Egocentricity provides the form and mould in which Mann's great capacities unfold themselves. His curiosity and his astounding gift of observation, his empathy and his unfailing psychological intelligence, his gift to present whatever he sees as a unified configuration, and even his detachment and his objectivity are all inspired by the Sisyphean task of self-evaluation, self-knowledge, and self-projection.

As Mann points out, the decisive question is what an author does with his self-concern, how he expands his ego, how he relates the world to it. To Mann, artistic production is rooted in man's capacity "to take himself seriously." To him, egocentricity is the source of thoroughness, economy, "animation," and self-criticism. He defines the will to create a work as "egotistic concentration," and if he sees the secret of inspiration in self-abandonment, he means by this the capacity to surrender the conscious to the unconscious self.

He asks whether the rational or the non-rational processes are to be called truly artistic, and he associates this problem with his enigma of ethics, that is, with the question whether true virtue consists in rational self-preservation or in passionate self-surrender, that is, in self-torture and in self-destruction. Carefully mediating between the abyss of death and the sane sphere of life, between beauty and bourgeois virtues, between homoerotic libertinage and the affirmation of the family, Mann gradually comes to demand of the artist that he carry the burdens and enjoy the benefits of social responsibility. The conservative loyalty to a purely individualistic, self-centered, and asocial *Kultur* now appears as the sin of the German artist, and of the educated German bourgeoisie at large. However, it still remains dubious to what extent the artist can or should become responsible and reliable. The dual image of bow and lyre, the dual emphasis on the artist as a severe man of knowledge and on the artist as a playful child of Nature raises the question whether the creative writer is fit to communicate directly and unambiguously the truths and precepts which the men of his age require. The artist, though an *irritabilis vates*, can never quite forsake the plays of an egocentric fantasy world. And yet, Mann feels that the writer who has achieved a measure of self-conquest can impart the verities of his epoch and lead the way toward an uninhibited and mature humanity. This belief is not based, primarily, on faith in man's reason. It is rooted in the conviction that the great artist — fully aware of the complexities, dangers, and conflicts inherent in the human condition — is ultimately destined to benevolence and to kindness. The great artist has a sympathetic understanding of life, a gift of greater value than the rational empiricism of the scientist or the irrational élan which characterizes the protagonists of the demonic forces.

The very playfulness of the artist — problematic as it is — has its sublime aspect to Mann. He calls the artist's "seriousness in playing" ["the purest and most affecting form of human nobility of mind"] (*Lei,* 125) insofar as it is playfulness in Schiller's sense, that is, insofar as it is the perfect expression of an equilibrium and a synthesis between the sensuous and the spiritual endowments of man. For Mann remains, in a sense, enough of a romantic to understand why the child should be called the father to the man, though he is also enough of a realist to understand why the child must grow into a man. To put this again in terms of the triad that has fairly dominated German literary thought ever since Schiller's essay on naive and *sentimental* poetry: the unity of the naive harmony, disturbed by conscious and fragmentary awareness, by restlessly purposive activity, and by the rigor of ideal demands, must be regained at a higher level where instinct and spontaneity would be in unison with the demands of physical and social realities, and with the commands of the ideal. To

Mann, the creative artist is ever at work on the task of inspiring the strenuous achievements of the *man* with the ease of the child's spontaneity, and of sublimating the unheeding self-centered games of the *child* so that they may express the consciousness, responsibility, and ethical discipline of the man.

Unlike the insights gained from a rare depth and a still rarer clarity of introspection, Mann's metaphysical notions are eclectic, deceptive, and inconsistent, now too elusive to be defined, now too crude and simplistic to be taken at face value. They have done damage to the author's reputation as an artist. Moreover, the later Mann appears, at times, in the guise of a somewhat complacent humanist. The heaping of antitheses, the ironical dialectics, the oscillations, and ornate rhetoric of the author are nonetheless inspired by an ideal of unity and integration which is deeply felt precisely because Mann is continually aware of the conflicting trends within him, because he is Adrian as well as Zeitblom, and because Adrian is anything but complacent. Mann desires a balance which would not omit or oppress any part of the human but would include all its elements, and bring them into lively, vibrant, and fruitful communication with one another. This intuitive ideal is similar to Hesse's vision, but the equilibrium conceived of by Mann is weightier and closer to the earth, less ethereal and more energetic than Hesse's dream. Mann was often extravagant as a thinker. As an artist he has always built on the foundations of a thorough realism.

Notes

1. J. G. Brennan, *Thomas Mann's World* (New York: Columbia Univ. Press, 1942), p. x. Even where Mann's concern with this topic is not apparent, as, e.g., in the Joseph novels, he himself insists that he traced the development of the "artistic ego." Cf. Mann's essay, "The Joseph Novels," in Ch. Neider, ed. *The Stature of Thomas Mann* (New York: New Directions, 1947), p. 228.

2. In quoting from Mann, I made ample use of Mrs. Lowe-Porter's translations. Wherever I disagreed with her renderings, I took the liberty to revise them. Note the following abbreviations of Thomas Mann's works: *Bem* for *Bemühungen, Gesammelte Werke*, Vol. X (Berlin: S. Fischer, 1925); *Bet* for *Betrachtungen eines Unpolitischen* (Berlin: S. Fischer, 1922); *Ess* for *Essays of Three Decades*, tr. H. T. Lowe-Porter (New York: A. A. Knopf, 1947); *For* for *Die Forderung des Tages* (Berlin: S. Fischer, 1930); *Lei* for *Leiden und Grösse der Meister* (Berlin: S. Fischer, 1936); *Ord* for *Order of the Day* (New York: A. A. Knopf, 1942); *Red* for *Rede und Antwort, Gesammelte Werke*, Vol. IX (Berlin: S. Fischer, 1925).

3. Since Mann's Spirit and Nature are metaphysical entities, i.e., more than mere concepts though less than gods, I have capitalized these terms.

4. A residue of Mann's characteristic ambivalence became manifest even in the author's campaign against National Socialism. Cf. the essay in which he treats Hitler as another hostile brother, and thus as another *alter ego* ("A Brother," *Ord*, 153–161).

5. "Goethe and Tolstoi," 1922 (*Bem*, 9–140; *Ess*, 93–175).

6. "The Joseph Novels," p. 228.

7. Cf. E. Zilsel, *Die Geniereligion* (Wien: Braumüller, 1918).

8. Mann, "Dostoevski — in Moderation," in *The Short Novels of Dostoevski* (New York: Dial, 1945), pp. vii f.

9. Loc. cit. Disease, Mann holds, is not of value to everyone. It all depends on who falls sick, whether a Dostoevski, a Nietzsche, or *"ein Durchschnittsdummkopf"* (*Neue Studien*, Stockholm: Bermann-Fischer, 1948, p. 90).

10. Aschenbach's love of Tadzio in *Der Tod in Venedig* is a symbol for the sentiment Mann ascribes to the spiritual genius in his relation to the naive man — though it must be a more sublimated passion than Aschenbach's if it is to receive the explicit approval of the author.

11. For the following, cf. the two Wagner essays in *Ess*, 307–371; also *Lei*, 90 f.; *Bet*, 39 f.; *Red*, 360–363; *For*, 273–277, 396–399.

12. Though it has few characteristic details, this woodcut might be taken for an idealized self-portrait of the author. In his physiognomy and in his character, Adrian Leverkühn appears as a direct descendant of this same "metaphysical craftsman" (*Bet*, 88). Leverkühn is a contemporary projection of the "mittelalterlich-nürnbergisch Gesicht" (*Bet*, 89).

13. Cf. "Schwere Stunde" (1905) in *Königliche Hoheit und Novellen* (Berlin: S. Fischer, 1928), pp. 721–728.

14. *Neue Studien* (1948), pp. 82 f.

15. The expression is Hermann Hesse's. Cf. "Tractat vom Steppenwolf," p. 21, in *Der Steppenwolf* (Zürich: Manesse, n.d.).

16. George Santayana, *Egotism in German Philosophy*, first published in 1916 (New York: Scribner, 1940).

17. Cf., e.g., *Herr und Hund, Gesang vom Kindchen, Zwei Idylle* (Berlin: S. Fischer, 1919), pp. 141–143.

18. For another similar statement quoted by Mann, cf. *Red*, 238.

19. Mann, *Nietzsche's Philosophy in the Light of Contemporary Events* (Washington, D.C.: Library of Congress, 1947), p. 36.

20. "The same process," Mann continues, "this dissolution of the discipline of life, this return to the orgiastic freedom of individualism I once more portrayed in *Death in Venice*, in the guise of pederasty" (*For*, 174). Note how the same connections between death, isolation, individualism, and the homoerotic recur in *Faustus* (cf. the relationship between Adrian and Schwerdtfeger).

21. T. Mann, *Bekenntnisse des Hochstaplers Felix Krull* (Amsterdam: Querido, 1937), now continued in *Die Begegnung* (Olten: Oltner Bücherfreunde, 1953).

22. For the two aspects of death, cf., e.g., the scene on Jaacob's deathbed and the subsequent funeral in *Joseph, der Ernährer* (Stockholm: Bermann-Fischer, 1943), pp. 602–639.

23. Note the parallel to the egotism of the naive man. Now, in the later twenties, Mann was evidently more severe than he had been in the essay on Goethe and Tolstoi written in 1922.

24. Quoted by F. Strich, *Der Dichter und die Zeit* (Bern: A. Francke, 1947), p. 380. Mann's apologetic introduction to the *Betrachtungen* also indicated the role of the poet as a representative sufferer, by way of a quotation from Claudel's *Violane*, "Why did my body have to labor in the place of Christendom?" (*Bet*, xv).

25. The paradox of a hostile objectivity is implicit in the basic assumption of an antagonism between Spirit and Nature. For, according to this premise, the so-called neutrality of dispassionate intellectual observation is necessarily charged with the *ressentiments* of the Spirit.

26. "The Joseph Novels," p. 229.

27. Cf. also, loc. cit.

28. Santayana, p. 112. However, Santayana's criticism was not directed primarily at Lessing himself but rather at his dictum. "Lessing had said that he preferred the pursuit of truth to the truth itself; but if we take this seriously (as possibly it was not meant) the pursuit of truth at once changes its character" (p. 111).

29. The *naturelbische Indifferenz* of the naive type, his spirit of doubt and contradiction, and his nihilism are closely related to the intellectual nihilism which endangers the Lessingian writer. In turn, the writer's ambivalent egocentricity is connected with both doubt (i.e., the danger of total nihilistic negation) and artistic playfulness. Concerning the latter, it is well to realize that Mann himself has always played with ideas both in his essays and in his fiction, and that, ultimately, it has always been more important to him to convey vital experiences than to make *valid statements*.

30. Cf. P. Heller, "Some Functions of the Leitmotiv in Thomas Mann's Joseph Tetralogy," *GR*, XXII (1947), 126–141.

31. It seems that Mann himself has gone back to the world of his youth. *Faustus* is the first step on this way back to German settings, and, beyond the *Buddenbrooks*, to the German past, to a world of guilt, sacred disease, and holy sins. *Die Betrogene* (Frankfurt: S. Fischer, 1953), and the work on the old fragment of *Felix Krull* also point to the author's earlier spheres of interest.

32. For Mann's equation between the infantile attitude—as a regressive identification with a father-image—and the clinging to conservative, ancestral, or mythical patterns, cf. F. J. Hoffman, *Freudianism and the Literary Mind* (Baton Rouge: Louisiana State Univ. Press, 1945), p. 220. It should be emphasized that Mann frequently uses the term *infantil* in a positive or neutral sense without pathological or pejorative implications.

33. Cf. "The Joseph Novels," and Mann's dictum, *"Wo ich bin, ist die deutsche Kultur,"* quoted by Heinrich Mann in "Mein Bruder," *Die Neue Rundschau, Sonderausgabe zu Thomas Manns 70. Geburtstag*, June 1945 (Stockholm: Bermann Fischer), p. 3. Cf. also Mann's "novel of a novel," *Die Entstehung des Doktor Faustus* (Amsterdam: Bermann-Fischer, 1949).

Much Is Comic in Thomas Mann   Ronald Peacock*

It is a privilege to succeed to a Chair held previously by two such well-known and respected scholars as J. G. Robertson and Professor Purdie. I never knew Robertson personally, but of course his name and work were familiar to me from my student days, and they still have meaning and influence in the world of German studies after more than a generation. He was a great pioneer of his subject in England. Professor Purdie carried on with devotion the work he began here in this College. At the present moment I remember with pleasure how, when I was still a beginner and only on the most junior terms of acquaintanceship with her, she had, with her characteristic generosity, a warm and appreciative word

*An inaugural lecture held at Bedford College, University of London, in March 1963, and printed on behalf of the college in a limited edition. The lecture is reprinted here with the permission of the College Council. Original quotations from Mann in German (cited in the notes) have been omitted.

for something I had written. J. G. Robertson and Professor Purdie, over a space of no less than fifty-three years, made the Department here a focal point for the study of German literature in this country, and conferred great distinction on this Chair. In one sense this is daunting for me; in another, comforting, because the accumulated capital reserves are so great that they will support us for many years to come, covering with an easy generosity our own liabilities.

I propose in this lecture to talk about some aspects of the comic in Thomas Mann's novels. My starting-point is a very strong feeling that the critical writing on Mann has taken its cue too exclusively from his basic philosophical themes, and not enough from his textures. Reviewing the criticism that has heaped up since the thirties one observes that a vast amount of work has been expended on interpreting Mann's novels as analyses of modern European man trapped between nihilism and ruthless ideologies. It is of course true; the weighty novels, at least from *The Magic Mountain* on, have opened wide horizons of cultural *Problematik*. There can be no doubt of the importance of Mann's work from this point of view. Nevertheless, a number of problems concerning the imagination at work in his novels, as distinct from their ideas, have been neglected; and in my view one of these problems concerns especially their comic elements. Of course, most people have realized that Mann's last, and unfinished, novel written in his late seventies, about an elegant-minded confidence man and embezzler, is indeed a comic novel. But apart from that one finds really only passing remarks about humour in Mann. In a well-known and sizeable collaborative book, teeming with famous names and excellent articles, *The Stature of Thomas Mann*, a book in which his reputation was sacramentally monumentalized, one cannot help but feel that there is very little occasion for laughter. And yet its subject wrote in a letter to his daughter Erika, about a new novel — it was in fact the first volume of the Joseph series: — "It is rather grand, and, as always, much is comic. . . ."[1] These words, from which I have derived my title, fall simply and casually from his lips, but their meaning is enhanced by what they take for granted in the intimate understanding between father and daughter. To be strictly accurate, Erich Heller and Käthe Hamburger, and others after them, writing about the Joseph novels, do take some account of the humorous element in the figure of Joseph, but they also keep it very firmly geared to a serious, lofty, quasi-theological interpretation of the work. Neither they nor anyone else to my knowledge, in published work, has considered the comic as "always present," as a central, constant feature of Mann's imagination, and attempted to assess it on a scale suitable to its role throughout his work. A recent book about him, for instance, by Anna Hellersberg-Wendriner, is called *Mystik der Gottesferne* (the Mysticism of the Divine Absence), and in relation to *Felix Krull* it makes a steady use not of the word "comic" but of the word "tragic." Or we have the line of argument that makes a passing reference to Mann's humour, only to write off the works in which it is more prominent as *minor* ones. Thus Hans Eichner, in his *Thomas Mann*: "If," he writes of the Holy Sinner, with a strange Puritanism, "one is willingly disposed to allow oneself to be amused . . . then *The Holy Sinner* is amusing as only *Felix Krull* otherwise — which (he goes on) is equivalent to saying, however, that it does not belong to Mann's significant works" (p. 108). Everyone, of course, has talked about irony, but philosophically, not aesthetically, as a matter of conflicting attitudes and concepts, not of imagination. Let me repeat: philosophical interpretations of Mann are important; but they are not in themselves complete.

When I first read Mann, the early stories and *Buddenbrooks*, what impressed me immediately were the brilliantly perceptive, vivid psychological line-drawings of half-way artists, decadents, charlatans, and ineffective intellectual types. I enjoyed the comic and grotesque figures and the irrepressible irony. But also I enjoyed the style, which now appears, when compared with the average prose style of novelists at the turn of the century, as extremely original and advanced, a style in which a merciless descriptive lucidity co-exists with musical rhythms and animation. One can perceive in it already the virtuosity that was ultimately to bring every shade of verbal skill and rhythmic vitality to bear on Mann's subjects and the expression of his complex mentality. In my view two predominant components of Mann's art have always been the presentation of comic material and the cultivation of a style and composition of great formal and musical beauty. This is in fact a piquant and strange combination, because the one tends to be more intellectual, and the other more emotional. But I can only speak about one thing this afternoon, and so I want to maintain that the comic belongs essentially to the imaginative substance of most of Mann's work. I had thought there was no study devoted entirely to Mann's humour, and this in spite of a bibliography published in 1955 by Jonas and running to over five thousand books and articles, all of which I have of course read in preparing this lecture. However, there does now exist a doctoral thesis of this University, by Mavis Beale, on Mann's irony and humour. It is a lengthy work, and in many ways good. Yet Miss Beale, like others, allows the problem of irony to dominate, and discusses irony more in relation to Mann's ideas than to his comic imagination. In consequence, her thesis, specialized though it is, leaves me with a fairly free hand for the theme I have adopted.

Thomas Mann himself has frequently spoken of humour in his work, linking himself particularly with the north German humorist Fritz Reuter, and the later Fontane; and it really is rather surprising that not more than passing remarks have been made by scholars. In a radio discussion in Zürich in 1953 about humour and irony he protested good-naturedly against so many critics having always spoken excessively of his irony, and never about his humour. He said he had a higher regard for "das herzaufquellende Lachen" (the warm surge of laughter from the heart) than for "das erasmische Lächeln der Ironie" (the thin smile of intellectual irony).[2] Speaking about how to read to an audience an early story, *Der Kleiderschrank* (The Wardrobe), he says it should not be taken too seriously or sadly; one must bring out the grotesque humour and at certain points the audience must *laugh*. (Letter to Kurt Martens, 15.XI.99). An appealing passage in *Lotte in Weimar* is the one in the long morning soliloquy of Goethe, where Goethe praises Schiller for having been always ready to laugh. "Er hat mitgelacht" (he laughed at the things I laughed at). And now that he is dead: "Es lacht sich mit niemandem mehr." (There is no one to laugh with any more.) From the recently published letters we can see how much Thomas Mann himself wanted to laugh and be laughed with. If we glance rapidly over Mann's novels what do we find? The early stories are mostly studies in caricature and the grotesque. *Buddenbrooks* and *Dr. Faustus*, in spite of their serious themes, have extremely strong comic threads in them. *Königliche Hoheit* (Royal Highness) is a sort of fairy-tale comedy. *The Magic Mountain* is one vast macabre comedy. The *Joseph* Tetralogy is a humorous transposition of Biblical myth. *Lotte in Weimar* is an elaborate witticism. *Der Erwählte* (The Holy Sinner) is a transposition of a medieval legend into humanist comedy. And *The Confessions of Felix Krull* is a sophisticated, modern version of the picaresque tale. What is left? Only a few wholly serious long-shorts — very beautiful works, but few in number. The very first scene of his first novel is a charming episode of child humour — little Antonie Buddenbrook reciting an article from the newly revised catechism, to the laughing delight of her agnostic grandfather, whose own speech is a mirth-provoking mixture of French and low German dialect. And the second chapter follows up quickly with little Christian Buddenbrook, who will end up in an asylum, giving his first performance as a mimic — the first of many — with an imitation of his schoolmaster.

The word "irony" has without doubt been overworked in connexion with Mann. Nobody can really be blamed, because his writing is obviously and richly ironical. And it is true that much of his humour is of the playfully ironical kind. But not all of it, and the one word has been used indiscriminately to describe what is really a group of effects and tones of expression. In talking only about the *serious* side of his irony, abstracting it from its humorous context and seeing it simply as a dilemma between principles or ideas, critics have overlooked the *range* of humour in Mann, in which irony *may* be an ingredient, but also may not. Mann can see the funny side of anything, without needing to be ironical. The story about a railway accident (*Das Eisenbahnunglück*) is a model of comic focusing, showing the most masterly control of a near-farcical tone amidst essentially catastrophic incidents. *The Holy Sinner* is a more elaborate exercise of a similar kind, a sublime and miraculous subject being treated in a consistently humorous manner. There are plenty of examples both of a good-natured humour, gay and cheerful, and of rollicking farce to be found. For instance, not just irony, but an indulgent humour plays round the figure of Antoinette Buddenbrook, whose naive vitality and moral buoyancy are unimpaired amidst all the constant ill-luck that befalls her in her unfortunate marriages to very dubious characters. Or again, in *Lotte in Weimar*, how charming the delicate humour in the sixty-four-year-old Lotte; she has come after forty odd years to Weimar to see the author of *The Sorrows of Werther*, who had once made love to her and incorporated her in his novel. And as she remembers across those years Goethe's kiss, she mixes it up in her memory with the passionate description of Werther kissing Lotte in the novel and she is now unclear as to which was which and whether it was quite the same thing. There are countless innocuously funny passages, in the story about the dog, for instance (*Herr und Hund*), or incidents like Castorp, in *The Magic Mountain*, discovering he has a temperature, or the description of Krull's first theft of chocolate in the grocer's shop. As to farce, most people would recall at once the scene where Felix Krull simulates an epileptic fit before the panel of military doctors in order to evade service, or his elegant mingling of love-making and necklace-snatching in the Paris hotel bedroom. But there are numerous others in most of the novels; for example, to mention only one, the visit of the red-haired, thick-lipped, freckled Miss Cuzzle to Lotte on her arrival in Weimar, with her Irish gift of the gab and her folio of crayon portraits of famous people from the life, including — the year was 1816 — Napoleon, the Duke of Wellington, Prince Metternich, Talleyrand, Blücher, and others; for her artistic efforts, to win attention at all, needed the added interest of the famous subject. There are many episodes of this kind, perfect bits of comedy or farce beautifully executed.

Apart from such purely humorous features there are other tones in Mann that are not really ironical though they are taken for that. He often indulges in forms of friendly mockery that are pleasing and harmless. He has command of all the nuances of pleasantry, of waggishness, of persiflage, of the whimsical and amusingly fanciful, the facetious and the playful.

With regard to irony proper, it should be stressed that irony with Mann is *in the first place* not a literary figure but a matter of temperament. Mann's irony is primary; he was born ironical. And of course irony of this kind is usually linked very closely in the personality with great reserve of feeling, and scepticism. Mann is deeply acquainted with the flight from feeling that takes place in the fastidious character. He has a horror of crude feeling, of emotions in their raw state. He is no partisan of popular or mass emotion. You cannot see Mann, for example, sitting in the circle round the camp fire, his open mouth emitting melodies in happy unison with his fellows. Where you can see him is with a friend, giving an enormously funny account of a camp-fire sing-song he had *witnessed*. He does, of course, share the common sentiments of humanity, but he rarely presents them in direct expression. When he does he skirts the sentimental.

He was, without doubt, fundamentally a sceptic, given by nature to noncommittal attitudes, and taking a cool and detached intellectual view of people and their circumstances, adopting by instinct the superior vantage-point, from which inconsistency, folly, and inadequacy are unerringly picked out. And since not a soul exists who is not in some way inconsistent and inadequate, Mann finds plenty to be amused at. These are the complex sources of Mann's irony and his highly-developed sense of the ludicrous, the incongruous, the absurd, the grotesque. Out of these basic traits of temperament came the urge to comedy, and the imaginative fulness of his picture. His ideas, his philosophical dilemmas, are the conceptual superstructure of what his imagination, rooted in deep instinctive reactions, showed him first.

In his book on the English Comic Writers, Hazlitt devotes a chapter to the Periodical Essayists. He comments thus on their method: "These last applied the same unrestrained expression of their thoughts to the more immediate and passing scenes of life, to temporary and local matters; and in order to discharge the invidious office of *Censor Morum* more freely, and with less responsibility, assumed some fictitious and humorous disguise, which, however, in a great degree, corresponded to their own peculiar habits and character. By thus concealing their own name and person under the title of the *Tatler*, *Spectator*, etc., they were enabled to inform us more fully of what was passing in the world, while the dramatic contrast and ironical point of view to which the whole is subjected, added a greater liveliness and piquancy to the descriptions." This is a useful pointer to Thomas Mann's character as a comic writer. If we think of his novel writing as a whole, it appears as the work of a spectator-commentator — I mean it literally: someone who observes and comments — with an infinite capacity for description, portraiture, mimicry, and sly comments on life, all communicating a vast amusement at men and things, starting with himself. In the earlier stories and *Buddenbrooks*, Mann still keeps to a conventional style of story-telling. But gradually he finds his special manner. In *Royal Highness* it is becoming clearer, and he establishes it firmly in *The Magic Mountain*, displaying it from then on in its most splendid forms. He is not one of those novelists who project their panorama of story or drama and disappear behind it. He is always very much present. "For here I sit and dispose myself to tell a story at once horrible and edifying. But it is most uncertain in what language I shall write, whether Latin, French, German or Anglo-saxon . . . one thing is certain, however: I write prose, and not little verses, for which on the whole I have no exaggerated respect. On the contrary, in this matter I subscribe to the tradition of the Emperor Carolus, who was not only a great lawgiver and judge of his peoples, but also the protector of grammar and assiduous patron of correct and pure prose . . ."[3] Who can mistake it? Mann's Narrator, whether it is himself, or himself in disguise, always steps before his audience with a pronounced tone of voice and a certain deliberate address to the reader. And his manner, his Narrator's gesture, is such that it carries everywhere innuendo, as it creates arabesques of amused comment playing over the human scene. His descriptions of people are always, in one act, both visual creation of a character, and simultaneously an unmasking of it. And in the dialogue, the character, as he speaks, is always shadowed by the author's mockery, like the shading that gives depth to capitals in certain types of printing. In his later works, Mann sometimes doubled up on this hyper-conscious method by insinuating himself into a fictive character who assumed the role of narrator, as in the Irish monk who tells the story of Gregorius, and Serenus Zeitblom who tells that of Adrian Leverkühn in *Dr. Faustus*.

Scholars mostly speak of Mann's parody in connexion with this aspect of his story-telling, following hints from Mann himself; and the tendency is to jump straight to philosophical interpretations of this parody, treating it as another symptom of our twentieth century culture in despair. This is no doubt apposite in certain instances, but parody is an aesthetic phenomenon, and Mann's covers far more things than cultural despair. I am not even sure that one needs necessarily to know *what* is parodied. *Felix Krull*, for example, is said, on Mann's own authority, to be a parody of Goethe's autobiography. I think it would be a poor prospect for *Krull* if its enjoyment depended on awareness of this reference. As with irony, I would like to go behind the parody, which is an external result, to what I think is a basic phenomenon in Mann's make-up as an artist. And that is mimicry. There is a potential mime in Thomas Mann. He transposes mime into a verbal form. All his play with mock-styles derives from this—the mock-biblical, mock-medieval, mock-Goethean, the mock-learned and so on. And just as, when we watch a miming, at the ballet for instance, we are aware of a certain elaborate way of pointing meaning with gesture, so Mann's narrative voice is highly self-aware, and easily contains an element of mockery and self-mockery; the more it succeeds the more it points to its own miming and its own success.

It is worth remembering that Mann always insisted that all artists had something of the actor in them, and remembering, too, that he himself was highly interested in reading his stories aloud. When he did so he shed his natural diffidence and became an actor. It would in fact be a fruitful study to examine Mann's descriptions of people systematically in order to show how much of the theatrical they contain, especially in connexion with comedy. One observes repeatedly how, when describing comic characters, he pinpoints essential or typical features and gestures, presenting them economically and sharply as the caricaturist does with a few simplified, strong lines. This, for instance, is how he introduces Makler Gosch in *Buddenbrooks*: "His smooth-shaven face was distinguished by a hooked nose, a long, pointed chin, sharp features, and a wide mouth, which he pulled downwards, pressing the thin lips together in a drawn malevolent expression. It was his endeavour, in which he fairly succeeded, to show to the world the countenance of a scheming villain, fine, savage, and diabolical."[4] Or take the banker Kesselmeyer, from the same work: "The trimmed white side-whiskers which covered his cheeks, leaving the chin and lips free, stood out sharply against the redness of his face. He had a mobile, droll little mouth, which contained but two lower teeth. As Herr Kesselmeyer, with his hands thrust straight down into his trouser pockets, stood there, confused, absent-minded, and pondering, he placed these two yellow, tapering canines against his upper lip. . . . Finally, he took his hands out of his pockets, bent forward, let his lower lip hang open, and laboriously unravelled a pince-nez cord from the general tangle on his chest. Then, with a sudden, swift movement, he raised his pince-nez to his nose, making the strangest grimace, surveyed the married couple, and remarked: 'Aha.' "[5] Such descriptions could be taken as blue-prints for comic acting.

Mann always creates a highly *personal* Narrator. Either he himself assumes ostentatiously the role of narrator, investing him, of course, with his own singularities and interests, thus giving the narrative decisive slants and colours in the manner suggested in the passage I quoted from Hazlitt. Or he impersonates a character, as with Zeitblom; and then, of course, the effects are incredibly intricate, because sometimes you hear Zeitblom speaking fully in character, sometimes you hear him speaking with Mann's voice, and sometimes you hear from his manner Thomas Mann telling you what he thinks about Serenus Zeitblom. Mann creates in this way a diabolically subtle and amusing mechanism of oblique comment, which is, however, only an extension of his own natural voice.

That is another important feature; Mann's narrative manner is always that of a voice talking. Amidst all the virtuosity of his elaborate style and formal structure (of sentence, paragraph, and chapter) the conversational echoes are never lost. The voice always cultivates the intimate note, it draws constantly on familiar, even slangy, idioms, it is the instrument of an elaborate gossip, it is always roping the reader into disclosures, and there will almost certainly be laughs in them. There will inevitably be things of common interest to the narrator and his reader as average sinners, eager to enjoy some slice of wickedness. When people laugh, they look at each other, sharing the joke. This gesture is incorporated into Mann's style. Admittedly, this voice can become wearisome; its effectiveness lies in its singularity, and like all singular things it may become monotonous if you try to take too much at a time.

I used the word mechanism a moment ago. Mann's "Voice" is, in fact, more than just style; it is a marvellously effective "convention"; one of those procedures that artists and poets use in order to liberate a particular view of, or comment on, the world. Mann establishes his narrator, fixes the tone and manner of his voice, and sets it talking; and everything else is generated and bodied forth within this enveloping stream of talk—the visible world, people, dialogue, events, ideas, and musings; their outlines all emerge gradually and brilliantly clear from the sumptuous billowing talk and they are all lit in a new and original way by the tone. In this respect he is reminiscent of Rabelais, a mind with a colossal capacity for playful comment and movement, disporting itself in a riot of verbal creation. Mann creates a convention in the same sense in which the interior monologue of Joyce, or the curious dialogue of Ivy Compton-Burnett, are conventions. They are procedures which, seemingly quite artificial, paradoxically reveal more of nature and reality. To create mechanisms of this kind is the distinction of great as against minor artists. They constitute, in fact, one of the meanings of what we call unity of form and content, because the thing seen or meant or stated, the aspect of life or reality observed, cannot appear except by means of the artifice; it is inseparable from it, and remains hidden unless liberated by it. What Thomas Mann reveals with his convention, his deeply resourceful, mimicking, echoing voice, are the deep perspectives of reference and cross-reference in the natures and preoccupations of his main persons — as with Castorp, Joseph, Goethe, or Krull — in a given space within which the meanings of their actions and talk are linked in clear circuits of reverberation. Philosophical meanings are intensified thereby, and a transparency is created for one wave of disclosure and illumination after another.

I would like to give at this point one or two examples in which Mann's powers of comic observation and description are used in a framework of complex reference in a most brilliant manner. It is not easy to find quotations conveniently brief — Mann needs great breadth for his presentation; you have to read several pages before settling into his key, on which everything depends. However, here is one, which I hope will do, from *The Magic Mountain*. It contains a slightly gruesome element — Mann doesn't respect the taboos of sentiment or propriety. If this disturbs you, perhaps you can just concentrate your attention on the climax at the end. I choose this passage because in a few lines it focuses three central themes of the novel — death, disease, and love — in a sequence of visual images. The young hero Hans Castorp walks along a corridor in the sanatorium, at which he has just arrived to visit his cousin, feeling the gruesome fascination of the oxygen flasks outside some of the doors, which indicate the hopeless cases nearing the end. He meets the doctor, Behrens, who exchanges a cheerful word, before entering one of the rooms, and tells Castorp he is surprised he only wants to stay eight weeks. When Castorp says not eight, but three, he exclaims that that isn't worth taking one's coat off for. Castorp should stay for the winter, because the international *haute volée* doesn't come till then. He ought to see the boys on their skis! And the women! Like birds of paradise, and enormously amorous (mächtig galant). I quote:

"But now I must go and see my moribundus," said he, "in No. 27 here. Final stages, you know. Going straight out. He's tippled off five dozen flasks of oxygen yesterday and today, the old boozer. But by noon I should think he'll be home. Well, Reuter my lad" he said as he went in "what about opening another bottle. . . ." His words were lost behind the door, which he pulled to. But for the space of a moment Hans Castorp had glimpsed, in the back of the room, on a pillow, the waxen profile of a young man with a light beard on his chin, who had slowly rolled his very large eyeballs towards the door.

It was the first moribundus Hans Castorp had ever in his life seen. . . . How dignified the head of the young man had lain on the pillow with the little goatee sticking up! What immense significance there had been in those large, large eyes, as he had twisted them slowly towards the door! Hans Castorp, still immersed in the fleeting glimpse, attempted, quite involuntarily, as he went towards the staircase, to make his own eyes as big, as significant, and as gravely revolving as those of the moribundus, and these eyes he turned on a lady who had come through a door behind him and passed him at the top of the stairs. He did not immediately see that it was Madame Chauchat. She smiled softly at the eyes he was making, patted the plait at the back of her head into position, and descended the stairs in front of him, noiseless, lithe, her head held slightly forward.[6]

The passage is only a page long but it contains a whole range of comic tones. Castorp's morbid mustering of the oxygen bottles; the simple geniality of the doctor and his cheerful treatment of the place and the patients; his professionally callous jocoseness about the moribundus; the humorously evasive Latin phrases; the momentary macabre physical sight through the half-open door; the comic intensity and self-forgetfulness of Castorp's pre-occupation with what he had seen; the grotesque mimicry of the rolling eyes; and then the ludicrous climax, Castorp's meeting, at this very moment, with the woman who was the object of his erotic desires, and who mistakenly thinks he is making eyes at her — this woman whose function it is in the novel to focus the deep relationship of love, disease, and death. This is a comedy of misunderstanding, with a macabre surface and profound references, a complexly significant moment. The creation of such moments in which a number of cross-references are held in a marvellous focus is visionary; it is not a matter of incidental humour, or passing irony, or an act of intellectual calculation. Such moments cannot be thought up; they are *given*. And in Mann they are given, and this is my point, as visions of a comic imagination.

My second example is the climax of *The Holy Sinner*.[7] This is the story, you remember, of Gregorius, who was the child of an incestuous union of brother and sister, and later unwittingly married his mother. On discovering this he had himself taken by a fisherman far away to a desert rock in the middle of a vast lake, there to do penance. The scene I am referring to is too long to quote in full; I shall have to give a mixture of synopsis and quotation. At a time when the papal chair is vacant, Probus, a noble Roman, and Liberius, a Cardinal, have each in the same hour an almost identical vision, in which a heavenly lamb reveals to them where a new Pope, by name Gregorius, is to be found, and exhorts them to undertake the arduous journey to the far north and fetch him. With the help of the old fisherman, who seventeen years before had taken Gregorius to the wild rock in the middle of the lake and left him there with his feet locked in an iron clamp, they make their way to it, as the lamb had instructed them; and there they look for the object of their search, the man to be elected Pope. They see only a strange little creature, scarcely bigger than a hedgehog—for Gregorius during his penance had shrunk to this size for lack of proper food—trying to hide from them. Liberius, the priest, considers their mission to have failed. But Probus persuades him to approach the creature. To their astonishment they hear a human voice issue from its hairy mouth: "Be gone! Do not disturb the penance of God's greatest sinner!" Probus speaks on, telling of their mission, and of their present disappointment at not finding the Pope elect. At this they see tears roll down the curse-marked, deformed face. The creature tells them of its baptism and its name, which is Gregorius. The priest protests in horror that it is Satan's mockery and a snare of Hell! "Fugamus!" he cries, "We are the devil's own sport. God has not chosen a prickly creature of the fields to be his bishop, and even if it does bear the name of his chosen one a hundred times over! . . ." The priest turns to hurry away. Probus holds him back. And behind them they hear a modest little voice saying: "I studied in my time grammaticam, divinitatem, and legem. . . ." This rather shatters them. But the priest still resists: "Am I to return home with this creature—crown it with the tiara, place it on the Sedia questatoria, and expect Rome and the world to revere it as their Pope? . . ." And again the modest little voice comes: "Do not be put off by my appearance. Childish sustenance and exposure to the weather reduced me to what I am. Adult proportions will return to me." Finally Probus asks it if it is willing to accept election, and, quite without fuss, it indicates assent. Whereupon Liberius gives it the key found in the fish's belly: — "Et tibi dabo claves regni coelorum" he murmurs and kneels before the creature. The latter, taking the key, presses it with its shrunken arms to its matted bosom. "Dear parents," it says, "I will redeem you."

The story is of a great sinner who later became God's elect and a great Pope. At its heart is the miracle of his penance and survival, and his discovery by men of the Faith directed by a vision. To agnostics, or to believers who for a moment divest themselves of sentiment, a miracle is by its very nature bound to have its funny aspects. Mann sets his focus on everything that is laughter-provoking in the realities of this situation, and never falters; a false move, a change of tone at the wrong moment would ruin everything. And with great tact he sees the comedy, to the verge of farce, without reducing it to vulgarity. It is a sublime event; he sees the funny sides of it; but it remains the moment of miraculous proof. The details of the visual scene are extremely comic: the tall, thin priest, and the little fat citizen (an old comic gag), both elderly, and almost overcome by physical strains — face to face, if that is the right expression, with the hairy little thing that is the elect of God. Comic, too, the unfolding of the conversation — the doubts, shocks, surprises it brings, putting pride and faith to a severe test. But beneath this near-farcical surface is the firm pattern of the divine plan, brought to focus simultaneously by various signs and references so that the full depth of the story is presented to the mind: thus, the finding of the clamp-key in the belly of the fish, of the clamp itself at the edge of the rock, the human attitudes of the weird creature, the name Gregorius, the creature's dramatic answer in the language of theology to the priest's accusation that it is all the work of the devil, the perfect correspondence of the evidence with the instructions of the lamb in the dream, the simple, sublime readiness of the creature to accept the Papal office, and the touching rightness of his first promise — to redeem his incestuous parents. The passage as a whole, like the one from *The Magic Mountain*, shows again a sequence of comic images focusing profound references. I would say that this work is the least understood of Mann's novels. Some dismiss it simply as a farce. Professor Pascal calls it an overdone joke. The difficulty, no doubt, is that it seems to make gratuitous fun of a Christian legend. I do not think it does. Mann conveys a humanist's version of the Christian material. The implication in his treatment is that the tortured complications suffered by the victims — such as Gregorius — of life's horrible situations can be redeemed by charity, by gentleness, by humane indulgence, in which piety and humour play their part. And this is the agnostic's, or humanist's, equivalent of redemption from evil. In this story a profound sense of the potential despair in life is treated with a miraculously light touch, the humour and the comedy embodying an assenting faith to man and life even in the face of horror. And the serenity that in the Christian legend derives from faith in redemption appears in Mann's story as a philosophical serenity expressed as humour.

Turning to another aspect of Mann's comedy, we remember that the Spectators and Tatlers, though not satirists of Swiftian severity, had at least a vein of indulgent satire. They were also wits. So it is with Thomas Mann. His caricatures sometimes verge on the satirical; sometimes they are just ludicrous. Often it is not so much satire as an unmasking scrutiny, truth-seeking rather than fiercely ethical. There is more lynx-eyed interest than *saeva indignatio*. Fundamentally, Thomas Mann is human and benevolent, and his malice usually more mild than ugly. He is, nevertheless, the man with an eye for one's weakness, and he commands the ruthless word to describe it. In physical appearance he will never fail to see the wart first, the little deformity, the abnormality that lets you down, and makes you an object of mirth; on this he will centre his description. It may seem merciless, but it is in fact based on a sense that life itself is cruelly unjust, and he is veritably obsessed with the refusal to beautify. Scorching truth is one of his pre-occupations; better the ludicrous that is true than the fair that is an illusion or a sentimental deception. Here are, then, some of the sources of his caricature. He exploits, it has to be admitted, the funny side of people's weaknesses, yet on the whole he is careful to do this only when physical deficiency is allied in some way to a general inadequacy that offends the reason. This combination produces his numerous portraits in a vein of the grotesquely comic, where bodily oddity on the one hand, and vanity, or silliness, or a foolish lack of self-criticism on the other, enhance each other. I will take one example from a multitude of possible ones. It is the introductory description of Spinell, the neurotic, self-styled author in the story *Tristan*: —[8]

> Imagine a dark-complexioned man in the early thirties, of tall stature, with hair noticeably grey already at the temples, but whose round, pale, slightly-puffed face shows not the remotest evidence of beard. It was not shaved—one would have recognised that; soft, blurred, boyish, there was on it only here and there an odd, downy little hair. And that looked really most peculiar. His shiny brown, doe eyes had a gentle expression, his nose was squat and a little too fleshy. Furthermore Herr Spinell had an arching, porous upper lip of Roman character, large decayed teeth, and feet of rare dimension. . . . He was usually well dressed, and fashionably, in a long black coat and spotted waistcoat. He was unsociable and sought no one's company. Just now and again a condescending, affable, expansive mood could seize him, and that happened whenever Herr Spinell fell into an aesthetic state of mind, as the sight of some beautiful object, a harmonious conjunction of two colours, a vase of noble form, or the mountains lit by the setting sun, sent him into loud transports of admiration. "How exquisite!" he would then say, dropping his head to one side, drawing up his shoulders, spreading his hands, and puckering his lips. "Heavens, just look, how exquisite!" And in the emotion of such moments he was capable of blindly falling on the necks of the most distinguished persons, whether men or women. . . .

Later in the story, this character is made to strike the most ridiculous attitudes in his sterile, precious veneration of the consumptive woman who plays Chopin's nocturnes and Wagner's Tristan music to him.

Mann says things about Spinell that are in some ways true of all artists. But he is mainly an example of failure. He is the pretentious aesthete, imitative, superficial, sterile, and essentially vulgar. He is one of Mann's "warnings," like Christian Buddenbrook. He is the full physical realization of the dubious and spurious side of artists and aesthetes. It is not enough to say, as critics often do, that he is treated ironically, because that does not do justice to the art of comic description here at work. He is a masterly caricature, in whom the physically comic is linked pointedly with the theme of fatuous aestheticism, to give the picture an edge of satire. There is a whole gallery of such types, which include from the early work the relatively innocuous and amusing little drawing of the infant prodigy at the piano, Bibi Saccellaphylaccas, Christian Buddenbrook (perhaps the most often quoted example of Mann's decadents) and the banker Kesselmeyer, and from the later work more developed figures like the doctors and numerous patients in *The Magic Mountain*, or the impresario Fitelberg in *Dr. Faustus*, a highly elaborate study of a farcically funny personality.

A word now on Mann as a wit. Some of the best examples of this aspect of his humour are in *Lotte in Weimar*. This novel is indeed, taken as a whole, a great *jeu d'esprit*, besides being in its details a long string of jokes, witticisms, bits of comedy, and amusing fantasy, with here and there the usual tedious stretches, but on the whole remarkably sustained. There are occasional elements of farce, and caricature, as in the previous works, but there is here a finer point on everything, as an intelligence both artistic and learned makes play with the subject from Goethe's life. The basic situation is fertile: Lotte, the youthful love of Goethe and the prototype of the Lotte in his *Werther*, ventures at the age of sixty-four, with an uncontrollable trembling of the head, to visit the poet again; she is willing to face all the risks of such a delicate undertaking, which is fraught with absurd possibilities. In the presentation of Goethe himself Mann's trick is to present him as his daily, real, and private self, rather in the manner of Shaw's exposition of genius, in Caesar or St. Joan, working from a commonsense view of the natural person set against the conventional stereotypes of reputation. This gives rise, of course, to endless little shocks of a comic kind, and opportunities for oblique shafts of wit against both Goethe and his entourage. A fine passage, I always think, is the one in Goethe's morning monologue about growing old, in which Goethe, after running morosely and anxiously over his ailments, praises age, its superiority and its capacity for adjustment, and looks on youth and its insignificant experiences with tolerant contempt; and one feels in all this a man singing in the dark to comfort himself. The ambiguity is exquisite: to the irony of the thought in itself is added the pleasant irony that Thomas Mann, who was into his sixties by then, is uttering it on his own behalf as well as Goethe's, and it enhances the comedy of humanizing the Olympian personality of legend. A bit of fine, feline wit is where Adele Schopenhauer, talking to Lotte, comments adversely on Goethe's tyrannising over literary taste and his attempts to prevent the younger generation from getting a hearing; without success, however, for she and like-minded friends read Uhland and Hoffmann in spite of his hostility. And Lotte, comically naive and self-important as she thinks of the world-renowned work in which she herself figured, suggests that these authors could not possibly match the author of *Werther*. Thus Mann lets a clever woman put Goethe in his place, and then a simple woman put the clever one in *her* place. And that, perhaps, is a charming oblique tribute to the Eternal Feminine in one of its energetic manifestations.

The voice of Mann as narrator develops as Mann develops. Experience, knowledge, ideas accumulate behind it, and it is in the very nature of this voice to draw on all its stores. In consequence, if you read all his works, and chronologically, you will observe and share in Mann's own process of moral evolution and self-humanization. In answer to his early scepticism and the pessimistic sense of the inadequacies of human beings he forged for himself a creed on the basis of reason and charity. In Mann we have an example of a sceptic taking himself in hand and working out valiantly a philosophy of humanism, an example of moral pedagogy exercised on himself in benign self-criticism and self-mockery. This progress towards a faith redeems what there is of bitterness and melancholy in the earlier stories. But also, by a wonderful paradox, it allows him in the sequence a still greater liberty of comic and satirical effect. From his firm base in piety he can make daring sallies into irreverence. The expansion of his world of thought and his view on to life give an ever wider field of implication and reference. No wonder, then, that he can draw so richly on so many tones of the comic — mockery, sarcasm, caricature, the sardonic, the grotesque, the ludicrous, the macabre, irony, wit, persiflage, raillery, the simply humorous and funny, the humour in extravagance, the picaresque, the farcical, indulgent amusement, the comedy of character and of situation.

Behind all the particular conflicts of principles in Mann's work, the dichotomies of art and life, mind and nature, the individual and the collective, culture and civilisation, democracy and fascism, and so on, one can discern a fundamental anxiety about *order*; and I myself would add to this another anxiety, which has not to my knowledge been observed. It is a concern for a certain kind of *success*, of which order is the outward sign; biological success, intellectual success, ethical success, and also aesthetic success; moreover, all of these may interfuse in a cultural process. The central feature of most of those queer people in the early works is that they are failures; figures for contempt, if you are severe and Puritanical; for mockery and comedy, if you are humane. And his bourgeois types, if not always failures, are one-sided and incomplete. Aschenbach, a tragic figure, is also a failure. There runs through these works a current of horror at the idea of being a failure.

At this early stage Mann has no positive working philosophy. His attempts to move forward, to search for a successful order, a synthesis of spiritual and vital energies, in a spirit of cautious optimism, begin to be apparent first in *Tonio Kröger*, and then more decisively in the themes of *Royal Highness*, which many think is a weak novel but which is highly symptomatic of the development Mann experienced. Here he looks for the first time beyond the problems of his own personal situation as an artist-intellectual at odds with "life" and the bourgeois ethos to problems that touch the family, society, and politics. Its central character, Klaus Heinrich, a ruling prince, strives to find amidst his purely formal existence as Prince a real, personal life and also a living, real relationship to his people. He is helped by love, by his love for Imma Spoelmann, in whom Thomas Mann has drawn a charming picture of a new type of woman, brilliant mathematician and shrewd observer of politics rolled into one. Science, government, and the love of a man, coalesce fruitfully in this wonderful girl, who appeared to Thomas Mann's imagination, by a deep and happy coincidence, in the same year in which this College received its Royal Charter to provide for the higher education of women. *Royal Highness* shows Mann beginning to take up the wider-based themes of his later novels. Looking at his work as a whole, earlier and later together, one sees the ancient strife between order and disorder as the problem lying at the heart of everything—of the defections of the phoney artists; of the fall of the Buddenbrooks from the mercantile ethos; of the sexual degradation of the hero of *Death in Venice*; of the libidinous temptations of the Magic Mountain; of the papal sinner-saint; of the mediation of the Hebrew patriarchs; of the pact of the tainted Faustian genius; and of the artistic and aristocratic criminality of Krull.

This opposition may be seen as the broadest basis of his comic forms and it gives a place, a large place, in his work to all the comic effects arising from forbidden fruit, from the forbidden subject, the taboo. Mann, as Spectator-narrator, rarely loses an opportunity of letting the naughty child, and the child in the adult, and the natural man in the adult, take over and make uninhibited observations. This is, of course, one of the oldest sources of the comic, from Aristophanes to Rabelais, Cervantes, Molière and their successors. Licentious humour belongs to this and Mann includes it, though he screens it with mock modesty for the Puritan censorship. A highly original slant is the way he saw disease and decadence as agents releasing the natural and physical man, setting him free from all restraints. Hence the devastating and lurid comedy of the *Magic Mountain*, of the sanatorium as the arena of the forces of disintegration, breaking down all that is civilized, except for the thinnest of appearances, in an uproarious riot of dissolution. For nearly ten years after his first success with *Buddenbrooks*, Mann was not sure what subjects to take, or what new line to develop. Then, round about 1912, he toyed with the Krull subject, but left it on one side. About the same time, he found the sanatorium subject. I am convinced that he held on to this and elaborated it at great length not simply because of its significance as a focus for ideas and culture-criticism but because his comic imagination saw here, with the certainty of genius, its great opportunity—to portray men and their minds comically involved with, and betrayed by, physical nature. After that he only turned rarely to exclusively serious treatments. And it was clearly logical for him to come back in the end to Krull.

Thomas Mann's humanist creed cannot as such claim any great originality. But it gives him a firm base from which to work as Spectator-novelist. He does what, after all, comic writers have always done; he works from the golden mean of reason. He uses his humanist faith as the point of reference for his view of the comic fall from grace. I have tried to indicate briefly how wide a range he has and how varied his effects are, from the ruthless portraits of decadents at the beginning of his career to the benevolent and serene comedies of later years. Here his genius unfolds its real originality, which lies not in the humanism as a set of ideas, which after all he shares with others, but in the comic forms created by his imagination, and in that Spectator's voice which, never at a loss for sensationally precise words for things observed, records endlessly, like a long-playing disc, a vast and benign amusement.

Notes

1. "Der Jakob las mehrmals aus seinem neuen Roman vor, — es ist sehr großartig und etwas komisch, wie immer." An Erika Mann 15.11.31. *Briefe 1889–1936* (Fischer-Verlag 1961). p. 303.

2. "Humor und Ironie," in: *Nachlese* (S. Fischer Verlag, Berlin und Frankfurt am Main 1956).

3. *Der Erwählte* (S. Fischer Verlag, Frankfurt am Main 1951). pp. 15–6.

4. (*Buddenbrooks*, Vierter Tiel, drittes Kapitel).

5. (*Buddenbrooks*, Vierter Teil, sechstes Kapitel).

6. *Der Zauberberg* (S. Fischer, Berlin 1930). pp. 179–80.

7. The central passage referred to is to be found in the section entitled "Die Auffindung."

On the Political Development of an Unpolitical Man
Hans Mayer*

"But how can I surrender my whole self without at the same time surrendering the world which is my idea? My idea, my experience, my dream, my pain? I am not talking about you, not at all, rest assured of that, only about me, about me. . . ."

These sentences, written as early as 1906, appear in the study "Bilse and I" that is polemical and autobiographical at the same time and in which the author of *Buddenbrooks*, much attacked as the writer of an alleged roman à clef, tries to distinguish himself from one Lieutenant Bilse, the author of an authentic roman à clef rescued from oblivion through this very exposure. Here the Schopenhauerism of the young Thomas Mann can be felt as well. The world is described as "my idea." But then, further in the 1906 essay, the world is not merely "my idea," but "my

*Translated by the editor from *Thomas Mann* (Frankfurt am Main: Suhrkamp Verlag, 1980), 348–69. Copyright © 1980 Suhrkamp Verlag Frankfurt am Main.

experience, my dream, my pain." Even then the thirty-one-year-old author formulated this self-analysis with unusual insight: literature as self-portrayal, and particularly as the representation of that which is experienced, dreamed, and suffered. If one considers the life's work, it proves to unite, in a unique manner, in a constant sequence of self-representations precisely this: experience, dream, and pain. Yet these are not modes of feeling or realms that are separated from each other. Like the pain, the dream originates in experience.

Another example, this one from 1939: from the novel *Lotte in Weimar*. August von Goethe asks his father who has received him peevishly, almost reluctantly, what he is engaged on at present—the "life story" perhaps, that is *Truth and Poetry*? Thomas Mann has his Goethe answer: "Incorrect. It's always life story." With Thomas Mann himself, too, it was always life story.

Hence the difficulty of rendering a self-contained conclusive portrayal of the political development of this man. There is no dearth of publications about the politician Thomas Mann, his relationship to politics, even the political relevance of the novels and stories. The famous epic writer and Nobel laureate has been analyzed as subject and object of politics. Thomas Mann and his opposition, the politics of an unpolitical man, phases of development as well as continuities, all of it has been treated in the secondary literature. It was not without justification that the French Germanist Edmond Vermeil in 1938—thus at a time when Thomas Mann was in exile and there could be no doubt about his political position—in his comprehensive overview of intellectual forerunners of the German nationalism of the twentieth century, named not only the likes of Spengler and Ernst Jünger or Moeller van den Bruck but also the philosopher Walter Rathenau and Thomas Mann as the author of *Considerations of a Nonpolitical Man*.[1] There is the 1947 essay by Max Rychner about "Thomas Mann and Politics" that Mann himself still read and endorsed pensively; Klaus Schröter has analyzed the political essays of the twenty-year-old beginner; Erich Heller as well as Roman Karst and Kurt Sontheimer have occupied themselves with this problem.

Still, questions remain. Does it not appear as though everything were becoming less clear the more impressively the documentation accumulates? Let us look at the probable reasons for this. An examination of Thomas Mann's political development is faced with *two methodological possibilities*. The usual procedure is to stick with the immense supply of Mann's own pronouncements—"It's always life story." Thomas Mann at all times had a predilection for seeing himself as it were historically: to do this, he invested heavily in periodizing his literary development and tried to accommodate highly contradictory positions and opinions through gentle adjustment to achieve a mediated congruence. If one imitates him in this endeavor by producing something of a secondhand secondary literature, after the primary author has shown himself only too willing to contribute a firsthand secondary literature, then everything is nicely in order. One takes the author's word for it, one takes him literally, maps the avenues, names the dead end streets and the wrong paths—always in agreement with the author.

One could talk to him easily about venial things. When I took over the task of putting together a twelve-volume edition for Mann's eightieth birthday (in 1950) for Aufbau in East Berlin, two difficulties could be seen from the beginning: what does one do with *Considerations of a Nonpolitical Man?* How does one choose from a magnitude of essays, reviews, occasional speeches, and miscellaneous items that could barely be surveyed? I had intended to sacrifice the "Considerations." They would have required a volume for themselves, one that could more usefully be filled with other texts. As the whole edition had been prepared very thoroughly in conversations by Lake Zurich as well as in letters, quick agreement could be reached about this. Thomas Mann had not the slightest reservations about leaving out the *Considerations* for the time being, especially as it had been proposed to publish that giant essay of 1918 later in a supplementary volume. He too seemed to consider it more important to present the radio speeches addressed to German listeners, as well as the diaries "Suffering for Germany" ("Leiden an Deutschland") or the great political speeches after the end of World War II.

There was, then, general agreement with Thomas Mann's opinions and actions since approximately the year 1922 when objections were raised against the articles from the early period of World War I: from those "Thoughts in Wartime" of September 1914 which have not been reproduced until today either in East Berlin or in the posthumous Frankfurt edition, up to the *Considerations* from the last year of World War I.

Still, all this is not satisfactory. If one believes every word of his author, the indefatigable autobiographer, one can sketch the political development rather sharply. In that case, there are two texts that mark a break and are intended to accentuate it: the 1922 speech "The German Republic" and later the famous New Year's letter of 1 January 1937 to the German philologist Franz Obenauer, then dean of the Philosophical Faculty at Bonn, who had informed Thomas Mann of the withdrawal of his honorary doctorate.

The speech "The German Republic," given in October of that same year in the presence of President Friedrich Ebert and of the author Gerhart Hauptmann to whom the text was to be dedicated on the occasion of his sixtieth birthday, was intended and received as a new confrontation of Thomas Mann with the *Considerations of a Nonpolitical Man* that had appeared four years before. The speaker knew it. He had willed and provoked this confrontation. Yet at the same time he attempted, in a strange foreword that he added to the speech for publication, to explain his World War I allegiance: the contrast between then and now, he indicated, was not all that great. "If the author, then, partially advocates ideas other than those in the 'Nonpolitical Man,' then the fault lies in the contradiction between ideas and not one in the author. He has remained the same, at one with himself in his essence and meaning, so much so that he may answer those who praise him for his 'change' as well as those who accuse him for it as a traitor of the German idea: this republican exhortation continues the direction of the 'Considerations' exactly and without a break into the present, and its attitude does not alter or renounce that of the earlier work: one of German humanism."

This is equivocal and formulated with conscious ambivalence. What is to be relativized: the earlier nationalism or the present bourgeois democratic republicanism?

In the *Considerations of a Nonpolitical Man*, Thomas Mann made yet another attempt at infusing meaning into his youthful turn-of-the-century dreams. By 1918, however, he must already have sensed that his examples and polemical antitheses had not been chosen very fairly. Political enlightenment is not coextensive with the type of the civilized man of letters ("Zivilisationsliterat") of the d'Annunzio type; questionable as it may have been in its own development, one can not do away with bourgeois democracy in all its scope and extension by citing Dostoevski's ridicule of the "little town of Paris" as the midpoint of European upheavals. In his later speeches and texts, Thomas Mann recognized and portrayed the advantages of bourgeois democracy and emancipation, human rights and theories of social innovation too clearly to allow himself to remain in agreement with the absolute judgments of this earlier work.

These infusions of meaning and positive accents, however, with which Thomas Mann at that time (1918) strove to expound and transfigure German cultural reality were even more important than the negative attitudes. The world of romanticism is invoked: the charming, socially alienated, and "unpolitical" figure of Eichendorff's "Good-for-Nothing"; the culmination of Schopenhauer's philosophy; the rejection of society in Hans Pfitzner's *Palestrina*; Friedrich Nietzsche's interpretation of the prelude to the first act of the *Meistersinger* as a supposed German answer to the political stance of the non-German, Western world. All this is to be seen as proof that the German attitude to politics must of necessity be ascetic, lacking in understanding, apolitical, the relationship of a spiritual and for that reason socially alienated people. For in the sense of Nietzsche and Wagner's music, of this equation of spiritual existence and social solitude, the highest form of intellectual refinement must coincide with the most rigid encapsulation against social process. This is said to be the German mission and the German reality.

We need not disprove any of this. The later Thomas Mann has himself revised everything from the ground up. It was yet again an ironic fairy tale, a musically rhapsodic fantasy that was offered, similar to the ironic wedding of our "Royal Highness" with the "dollar princess." How little Wilhelminian Germany really corresponded to that delusion constructed of Nietzsche aphorisms and *Meistersinger* chords, of Eichendorffian romanticism and spiritual refinement, to what extent the politicians and generals of Wilhelm II fought for extremely real goals, is a circumstance well known and repeatedly stated by Thomas Mann later.[2]

The first public *critical distancing* from the world of Wilhelm II, this "talent," as Thomas Mann remarks mockingly, occurs in the speech "The German Republic": "We smiled and bit our lip as we watched, we searched the expressions of the other Europeans and tried to read in them that they did not hold us responsible for the comedy, which they did anyway; we wanted to hope that they distinguished between Germany and its representative, something for which they were hardly equipped — and then we turned our attention to cultural matters again, permeated with the melancholy feeling of the God-given nature of tradition, of the disintegration of political and national life." A remarkable confession. After all, it obliterates the whole reduction of what is "German" in the "Considerations of a Nonpolitical Man." In 1918, "cultural matters" were to be revealed "as the true substance of German national life": precisely because they were *not* "political." In 1922, it is admitted that this dogma, motivated as it is by love for Germany, originates, like all Eros, including the pedagogical kind, in the consciousness of a deficiency. Because intellectual and political life were separated by an abyss in the age of Wilhelminian imperialism, Thomas Mann, in time of war, invoked the "unpolitical" national culture to represent all of Germany temporarily. That too was a fairy tale, like the marriage of Klaus Heinrich to Imma Spoelmann. But this dream Germany of Eichendorff or Schopenhauer was the most personal wish-fulfillment of Thomas Mann himself. One could read up about the Wilhelminian reality in Heinrich Mann's *Land of Cockaigne*, in his *Man of Straw*, or in Carl Sternheim's comedies dealing with the heroic life of the bourgeoisie. Deep down, Thomas Mann had always known that. In 1922, he said it.

Mann's speech to the student democratic club at the University of Munich on 16 May 1929 also deals with the impending German choice between a state based on justice and the recognition of progressive literature as a necessary constituent of a healthy social development and a sinking into a historical reaction that is to remain regressive, guided as it would be by a regressive society, even though the latter might have, for purposes of camouflage, patched together for itself a fashionable suit of clothes consisting of seemingly highly modern scraps of thought. It is interesting to note that this speech of Thomas Mann appears under the title "Reaction and Progress" in its first published version in August 1929[3] while, a year later, the same speech is presented in one of the essay volumes of the author under the title "The Position of Freud in Modern Intellectual History." The presentation about reaction and progress in contemporary German life is indeed grounded extensively in the psychocultural ideas of Sigmund Freud, but in no way does it coincide with them fully. One feels that the author, in 1930, wanted to direct his thoughts somewhat away from the immediate realm of politics by assigning the new title. For it is decisively a political treatise. The club of democratic students—this was by 1929 a small wilting bourgeois minority at the universities. It had as little backing from the liberal bourgeoisie as did the corresponding political party, the "German Democratic Party," and its leaders in the Reichstag Dr. Theodor Heuss and Dr. Gertrud Bäumer.

For Thomas Mann, in this essay, it is a matter of "justice"; that is, the rescue of the nineteenth century against its fashionable discreditation by the lemures of the various nationalistic currents. The French royalist Leon Daudet has described the era as "the stupid nineteenth century." Thomas Mann wants to demonstrate how even the romantic aspects of this bourgeois epoch secretly point toward the new: "The revolutionary principle—it is the will to the future that Novalis called 'the truly better world' pure and simple. It is that principle of increased consciousness and insight which leads to higher stages of existence."

Even these declarations from the final phases of the Weimar Republic are not without political ambivalence. *On the one hand*, they are meant to be seen as a taking of a stand against the Hitler movement, the German nationalists, the enthusiasm of the national Bolsheviks of the time. Thomas Mann declares his allegiance to the Weimar constitution and, in the party context, primarily in the Reichstag elections of 1930–32, to social democracy. *At the same time*, there is an attempt to show continuity in the renewed invocation of German romanticism (this time less the one of Eichendorff than the one of Hardenberg) for purposes of reconciling the intellectual substance of the "Considerations" with new political positions.

This could not succeed. Nor was it useful to prevent Thomas Mann's exile or his being stripped of his citizenship. Nonetheless, for a period of four years, he again let himself be drawn into ambiguities with his attitude toward the Third Reich. Documents that have become available in the meantime, for example, the memoirs of the publisher Gottfried Bermann-Fischer, throw some light on the possible private motivations. Again, the political ambivalence was probably more important. In the "New Year's letter of 1937" Thomas Mann discusses it. He had wanted to be silent and had believed that "by the sacrifices I had made I had earned a right to be silent that would enable me to maintain something that was sincerely important to me—my contact with the German public."

This too could not be done: only a profoundly unpolitical man could have reasoned thus. From that, Thomas Mann concluded:

> I had never dreamed, it was never sung at my cradle, that I would spend my mature life as an emigrant, disowned and proscribed at home, in an act of vitally necessary political protest. Ever since I entered intellectual life, I have felt secure in a happy agreement with the spiritual predisposition of my nation, and its intellectual tradition. I was sooner born to be a representative than a martyr, much more to bring into the world a

bit of higher gaiety than to nourish struggle and hatred. Severe injustice had to be done to make my life into something so false and unnatural. I tried to prevent it with my weak powers, this horrifyingly false development — and precisely by doing that I paved the way for the destiny that I now must learn to reconcile with my nature, so foreign to that destiny.

From here on, harmony seemed to have been established between Thomas Mann's inner and outer worlds: between the intellectual substance of the storyteller Thomas Mann and the political reality of the war and postwar era. In the "Snow" chapter of *The Magic Mountain* already, Thomas Mann opposes the death-longing of German romanticism and of his own earlier "Considerations" with a declaration of allegiance to that "life" which he had so thoroughly ridiculed as a student in Lubeck, with his brother Heinrich, in the "picture book for nice children." Now it is a matter of a Goethean approach to the pressure of the times; a redesigned myth of enlightened practice and social usefulness is set up in the Joseph novels to counter the Wagner myth of the twilight of the gods. The political writings of the war and postwar time deal with the social transformations of bourgeois democracy, of the cultural and political challenges of a united Europe. It is true that the last essays, influenced by the political postwar developments since 1945, evince a cultural pessimism that appears to hark back to Thomas Buddenbrook's meditations about a renunciation in the face of the will of the world in the vein of Schopenhauer. The secret continuity of these realms of the young Thomas Mann's experience had already manifested itself also in the "Snow" chapter of *The Magic Mountain*.

It is here, however, that the "accompanying" interpretation is not sufficient, in spite of the oversupply of autobiographical commentary with which it is able to work. One cannot answer the question of discontinuity or consistency in Thomas Mann's political development by using texts intended as caesuras. Looked at from the point of view of the respective political situations, Thomas Mann's positions in 1918 and 1938 can to be sure barely be reconciled. Once one refuses to believe in these autobiographical statements, stylized as most of them were, in a naive and immediate way, however, the situation changes. Ever since we have been able to know Thomas Mann better through his letters, we can improve our understanding of the sequence of his pronouncements about society. It can be shown that the development that led to the "Considerations of a Nonpolitical Man" reaches deeply into his intellectual beginnings. There is no possibility of talking about the political derailment of a German patriot.

The monstrous essay of 1918 belongs directly to the world of the *storyteller* Thomas Mann and can be traced back to the first epic sketches and essays on current political issues written by the twenty year old. From this we can conclude that his rejection of the world of those "Considerations" could refer only to the immediate implications of the fundamental stance but not the intellectual ground itself without which the career of Thomas Mann the storyteller is inconceivable.

The usual dualistic approach of those who write on Thomas Mann is deceptive. There is no unified cosmos of the storyteller Thomas Mann, one that could be seen as a unity in technique, motifs, and style: from the early stories to the last chapters of *Felix Krull*. If one maintains — as the author does himself — that the writing style of the first chapters of the confidence man novel had barely changed in all the decades, up to the last period of composition, then it is inconceivable that an obvious political discontinuity is set against such a literary continuity. Mann appears to have viewed himself under these dualistic aspects. The question is whether he was mistaken.

The literary correspondence of the young Thomas Mann is revealing, almost shocking. It has often been remarked that, in contrast to his brother Heinrich, he had barely showed any interest in the powerful literary creativity of his contemporaries. Fundamentally, that never changed. Musil and Döblin, Benn and Brecht, Stefan George and Hans Henny Jahn, expressionists as well as dadaists constantly expressed deep antipathy against Thomas Mann. Mann repaid them by ridicule, irony, or disregard. Before World War I, Heinrich Mann had close connections to Wedekind and Sternheim as well as to various Bohemian elements that were not permitted to enter Thomas Mann's lovely home. The latter liked to see himself instead in social intercourse and correspondence with subordinate and stoutly reactionary literary figures like Kurt Martens. No literary correspondence exists between Thomas Mann and an important contemporary. This is by no means disproved by the exchange with Hermann Hesse for that is a nonliterary correspondence.

This too belongs to the self-representation and self-defense of Thomas Mann. He knows no manner of intellectual and hence political *solidarity*. Since his art strove from the outset simultaneously to glorify and ironize human weakness and solitude, no community is possible for this writer. Hence basically no politics. If, in spite of that, there is political reflection, it is only the reaction of a profoundly unpolitical man. In a letter to Kurt Martens of 28 March 1906 we read:

> Therefore I consider people like Hercules or Siegfried popular figures but not heroes. Heroism for me is an 'In spite of,' weakness overcome, gentleness belongs to it. Klinger's weak little Beethoven, sitting on the great throne of the gods and clenching his fists — that is a hero. Historically, it seems to me that physical suffering is almost a requisite for greatness, and for me that makes psychological sense. I do not believe that Caesar would have become Caesar without his weakness and his epilepsy, and if he had become one, he would have been less of a hero in my eyes without it. After all, is there not a whole lot of heroism in the tenacious role-playing of the exhausted Thomas Buddenbrook?[4]

It is all there already: the antithesis of suffering and greatness, just as it will appear almost thirty years later in the collection of essays entitled *Suffering and Greatness of the Masters*.

In *Death in Venice*, Gustav von Aschenbach is described as follows:

> His ancestors had all been officers, judges, government functionaries, men who had spent their strict, decently austere lives in the service of the king or the state. Inner spirituality had once found itself embodied among them, in the form of a preacher; quicker, more sensuous blood had flowed into the family in the previous generation through the mother of the writer, the daughter of a Bohemian orchestra conductor. From her derived those marks of a foreign stock in his own exterior. The marriage of soberly conscientious officialdom with darker, more fiery impulses made it possible for an artist to come into being, and this particular artist . . . and the bravely moral quality was caused by his being so far removed from having a robust constitution and thus being destined but not actually born for constant exertion.

Two years after *Death in Venice* appeared, however, one could read the following in the equivocal "Thoughts in Wartime" of September 1914:

> Are not art and war connected by metaphorical ties? I for one always felt that it was not the worst artist who recognized himself in the image of the soldier. That victorious military principle of today — organization — is after all the first principle, the essence of art. Contempt for that which is represented as 'security' in the life of the burgher (security is his favorite concept and loudest demand), getting used to an endangered, tense, alert life;[5] lack of consideration for oneself, dedication to the limit, martyrdom, a total risk of all the vital powers of body and soul without which it would seem ludicrous to undertake anything; finally, discipline and honor as shown in the sense for the trim and the splendid — all that is really military and artistic at the same time. There is much justice in calling art a war, a consuming battle.[6]

There is no denying that Thomas Mann's "Considerations" of World War I reach down deep to the impulses of his activity as a creative writer. Admittedly, the text of 1906 comes from Thomas Mann the letter writer, Aschenbach is a fictional character, and an essayist expresses his "Thoughts in Wartime." Still, it would not be amiss to imagine a Gustav von Aschenbach returning to Munich healthy, experiencing the outbreak of the war, and becoming the author of those "Thoughts in Wartime." Whoever rejects the unpolitical critic Thomas Mann of that time, judges in that same act the storyteller Thomas Mann.

This too he knew, as his tendency to self-interpretation and to the autobiographical was always accented by a self-criticism that could almost be called self-torture. With increasing age Thomas Mann became increasingly skeptical toward the course of his own life and its "products," as he referred to them — a characteristic that he had stressed in the case of the old Fontane. The Shakespeare quotation about appearing "in such a questionable shape" is cited or paraphrased several times in later essays and documents—not without a slight savoring of such a self-tormenting intellectual soul baring.

Without the reference to this intellectual evolution and continuing self-examination the arrangement of the main characters in the *Magic Mountain* could hardly be understood. In attending to the quick "ping-pong" of the Settembrini—Naphta debates, one does not usually lose sight of the dominating and charismatic personality of Mynheer Peeperkorn, but that is definitely the case with the upright soldier Joachim Ziemssen. He belongs to his cousin Hans Castorp, as the artist, according to Thomas Mann's early combinations, matches the soldier, as the Prussian king was interpreted in terms of a synthesis of artistic and military modes of existence, and as Aschenbach had been portrayed as such a synthesis. Regarding the two protagonists of *Doctor Faustus*, Thomas Mann stressed later in his notes to the story of the novel, the lack of sharpness of the Leverkühn and Zeitblom characterizations had been intentional. A silent secret hovered over both. The "secret of their identity," as Thomas Mann formulated it ambiguously, was scarcely concealed. Ziemssen and Castorp are allied to each other similarly. Settembrini and Naphta are correlated to each other as dialectical positions. No wonder then that it can—and does—happen that the positions shift, and that one suddenly meets the protagonist in the territory of the antagonist. But the soldier and life's problem child Hans Castorp, Hanseatic citizens as they both are, relegated to Hamburg instead yet again to Lubeck simply for the sake of variety, also share the secret of identity. To be sure, with the reservation that in 1924, at the time of the publication of *The Magic Mountain* Ziemssen's stance could only be portrayed as an anachronism by the author. Joachim's death and his conjuring as "a soldier and an honest man" with the aid of a sonorous baritone singing Gounod is to be taken as a subtle political comment. Also, to be sure, as yet another variation of self-commentary.

Gustav von Aschenbach's death in Venice was already presented as a comprehensive reckoning with oneself. It is no accident that all the writings of the respected author Aschenbach that are enumerated are, as we know today,[7] nothing else than projects Thomas Mann had given up— including Aschenbach's stark tale that is titled "The Wretch" and "demonstrates to a whole grateful generation of youths the possibility of a moral decisiveness beyond the deepest knowledge."

It is evident from Thomas Mann's own notes for a story with that title that what was planned was not merely an epic postlude to the unpleasant and occasionally also undignified polemics between Thomas Mann and Theodor Lessing, but that here was already the nucleus of the debate with Heinrich Mann which could only be published eight years later as *Considerations of a Nonpolitical Man*. When, however, one compares

Death in Venice to Thomas Mann's own political and literary statements at the time of the origin of that famous tale, then one is struck by the considerably greater clarity — in political terms as well — of the novella as against the letters and the essays. Ten years later, during the work on *The Magic Mountain*, this process was to repeat itself. The death of Gustav von Aschenbach and Joachim Ziemssen must be understood as the yielding up of a hopeless ideological position. In both texts the retreat from private political mythologies that are not tenable shows itself as the overcoming of difficult crises in artistic creation.

In later life, Thomas Mann was accustomed to interpret his political-ideological pronouncements from essays, addresses, or newspaper articles as representative. He had again succeeded in becoming a representative figure, after a brief period of comfortable martyrdom.

In the book of memories written down by Heinrich Mann during the war in Californian emigration and finished after the end of the war, in this highly peculiar piece of memoir with the title *An Era is Examined* (*Ein Zeitalter wird besichtigt*), there is a sizable chapter with the title "The Companions." Heinrich Mann begins his analysis with the following words: "When my brother had resettled in the United States, he declared simply and purely: 'German culture is where I am.' These words were spoken in 1939, at the outset of World War II, while the domination of National Socialism appeared stable and stabilized in Germany."[8]

Such an assertion by an individual, be it an ever so important author, could have been considered as hubris, but it was not. One listened to Thomas Mann, and one took him seriously. One agreed with him. It is this that bothers Heinrich Mann in retrospect. He searches for the reasons that, for example, brought the American public to the consensus that "Thomas Mann was to be considered the first author in the world." At the same time, the elder brother remembers that fundamentally the clear-sighted Germans had the same opinion, and that they merely "were variously impeded in expressing it." After this, the memoirist Heinrich Mann continues: "In order for an individual to gain such an undoubted reputation, he must represent more than himself: a country and its culture, even more — a whole tradition, a metanational consciousness. All that up to this time was known as Europe. It was Europe itself."

Undoubtedly, this is all correct. When Heinrich Mann of all people testified to this state of things, then one could not doubt the justification of this thesis. On the other hand, it was precisely Heinrich Mann who, at the climax of the quarrel between the brothers at the beginning of 1918, in a letter that was not sent but preserved in draft form, questioned the suitability of Thomas Mann's character to ever express anything but his own feelings and thoughts. How would political thinking be possible, under such circumstances, a thinking that must be built upon reflection about the fate of other human beings?

A few others besides you experience self-examination and struggle, even if in more modest ways, but then they arrive at regret and new energy as well instead of only an "affirmation" that is not worth all that bother and a "suffering" for its own sake, this raging passion for your own self. You owe this passion a few tight but closed creations. In addition you owe it a total lack of respect for everything that does not suit you, a "contempt" that suits you like nobody else, in short the incapacity ever to conceive the real seriousness of another life. Around you are ranged irrelevant bit players who represent "the people," as in your Song of Songs about the *Royal Highness*. Bit players are supposed to have a fate, an ethos even?[9]

The politically polemical portrait by Heinrich Mann of his brother (1918) culminates in the reproach that, in all of Thomas Mann's life and work "the incapacity ever to take another life seriously" manifested itself. The letter ends with the words: "You though, you have approved of the war, who still approve of it, you who claim my position to be detestable — I put on a piece that gave a pretty good picture of the evil times, and I was the first to give the victims confidence in a better future — you will, God willing, have forty more years in which to test, if not 'assert,' yourself. The time will come, I dare to hope, when you will behold human beings, not shadows, and then you'll see me too."

Was it merely polemics, excitability, insult? As far as one can tell, it cannot be determined whether Thomas Mann ever got a look at the draft letter. Presumably Max Rychner is right when, in his essay about "Thomas Mann and Politics," he insists on interpreting *Considerations of a Nonpolitical Man* as the central pronouncement and considers the many occasional publications documenting a later retreat and self-purification as unimportant. Surely Thomas Mann managed to have political influence later in his political addresses to German listeners. His essays about European unification, functional changes in the democratic system, about a synthesis of planned economy and bourgeois liberalism were widely read and cited. Their effect was hardly more than the production of a misunderstanding that here someone was speaking who took politics seriously. On the contrary, there is much to be said for the opinion that Thomas Mann, in his own opinion too, did indeed let Aschenbach and Ziemssen die, little Naphta also, and Adrian Leverkühn in addition, but that in these writings one cannot find a real as opposed to a merely verbal change in position. I myself can provide some small testimony to that effect. When we were discussing the final volume of the twelve-volume edition of 1955, Thomas Mann demanded explicitly that the word "politics" be omitted in the title of the volume. He reinforced his verbal statement by an insistent telegram. The title was to read: "Essays about Contemporary Events." More than a mere question of formulation was at stake here. Yet again, it was a matter of autobiography and self-criticism. The true political evolution of

Thomas Mann occurred after the death of Aschenbach and Ziemssen — in his tetralogy about the biblical Joseph, his ancestors, and his brothers. It was no secret that this tetralogy was again to be taken autobiographically. It was not so much the connections between Felix Krull and Joseph that are remarkable, with their mythical relationship to Hermes as the god representing commerce and literature — the purest synthesis of Lübeck as a way of life and thought. What was more important was the "taking back" (to evoke the later formulation of Adrian Leverkühn) of the twilight of the gods myth in the *Ring* tetralogy of Wagner. This time, it was to be a restructured myth. A book of beginnings and human ascent instead of the descent of the gods. This was indeed new for Thomas Mann. Max Rychner has interpreted it very precisely:[10]

> In the guise of Joseph Thomas Mann has led a chosen youth into the political arena, has made him grow by it and in it, a flexible yet single-minded tamer of the immediate, the challenging, the real whose excursions into the world of dreams even manage to benefit the general good. And with him the author has done what he had tried to do with Thomas Buddenbrook: he led him through into accomplished maturity, into the ripeness of manhood where the roaming in open individual possibilities ceases and every day puts one to the test. Joseph ascends in alien Egypt, he assimilates and earns a position similar to the one held once by Walter Rathenau in Germany, only under a luckier star; he becomes the "provider," the guardian and multiplier of life and in this capacity the mythical son of the life-giving Father Nile. The mild hand of this adept of Realpolitik is a lucky hand; the innermost needs of men appear to demand it and willingly submit to its gentle rule.

Therefore it is neither in a political speech nor in an article that we find Thomas Mann's last political position as it relates to "contemporary events." If Mann left a political testament, it could be derived from a text of the last period of his life, one that he liked to read aloud, his voice trembling with emotion. It comes from a conversation between Felix Krull and Professor Kuckuck in the dining car between Paris and Lisbon, as the professor lectures (and Thomas Mann with him): "Being, he said, was not well-being; it was pleasure and pain, and all of being in time and space, all matter participated, be it only in the deepest slumber, in this pleasure, this pain, in this sensibility that invited man, the bearer of the most awakened sensibility, to all sympathy."

All sympathy! By no means did Mann conceive of it as of an emotional ecstasy in the manner of the expressionists. Here is what he has to say of them and the likes of them in the speech "My Time": "When I think back, I was never fashionable, have never worn the macabre clown get-up of the fin de siècle, never knew the ambition of being with it in a literary sense or being on top of developments, never belonged to a school or a coterie that just happened to be important at the time, neither the naturalists nor the neo-romanticists, neoclassicists, symbolists, expressionists, or whatever they might be called. For that reason, I never rode the coattails of a school and was only rarely praised by literary figures." Nor did he want "All sympathy" to be taken in the sense of Rilke as an uncritical, undifferentiated "praising of all things."

The Schiller Festival address of 1955, given in Stuttgart and Weimar, closed with the following exhortation: "Let something of his gentle yet forceful will enter us by means of the celebration of his burial and resurrection: his will to the beautiful, the true, and the good, to culture, inner freedom, art, love, peace, to a saving respect of humanity for itself." But the rest of the speech did not share such optimism and humane assurance. The Schiller poem "Lament of Ceres" from which he quoted mourned the progressive decline of interhuman civilization, one that Thomas Mann continued to construe as bourgeois civilization. An old man was speaking here, one who intended to retain faith in the dreams of his youth. Tonio Kröger had already praised "Don Carlos" in front of Hans Hansen. In the Schiller year 1905, the tale "A Weary Hour" proved itself to be an appropriation by the storyteller Thomas Mann of a Schiller who was laboring, hard and despondently, on "Wallenstein." This was the voice of a man who was beholding death and, apparently, was ready to depart without a great deal of regret.

Will we be able to say that the late Thomas Mann who continued *Felix Krull* and planned the Schiller essay took to heart the angry warning of his elder brother who had died in 1950: that one must take other lives seriously? There is still much to disprove that. True enough—the diary says that *Doctor Faustus* was conceived as a report of the demise of a society, that is, the bourgeois society. All of it—the identity of the two main figures, the time spans from the Reformation up to World War II, freaks and enthusiasts from Mann's youth in Lubeck, remembered while writing the book—is used to project the finale of the German bourgeoisie as a satirical-elegiac novel. But, even now, the life of others is only taken seriously when death must be portrayed. Only the boy Nepomuk-Echo is spared the frigid region that surrounds everything else, including the protagonists. For that reason, the child must die—like Aschenbach and Ziemssen.

The work was designed as the novel of an ending, and for Thomas Mann that meant the ending of the novel as a form. Since he fundamentally never perceived reality other than in literary guise, he was bound to interpret the end of an epoch as the end of its characteristic literary form. Since he himself never wanted to be anything but a teller of stories, he interpreted the modern—endangered—state of the novel as a prognosis of death for himself too. He knew only too well that his own art was part of an ending. But he did not see a new or promised literary land near or even afar. The political considerations of Serenus Zeitblom and his author should not mislead us: *Doctor Faustus* too did *not* become a political book. It remained an antithesis of intellect, equated with literature, and political reality. The creator of the earlier "Considerations of a Non-Political Man" remained identical with Zeitblom and Leverkühn, who were in turn identical with each other. The aesthetic realm remained—throughout all of his life and work— Thomas Mann's true sphere. Without having read Kierkegaard with much precision, he unhesitatingly consigned eroticism to the aesthetic realm. Thomas Mann's writing—belles-lettres and essays, political as well as nonpolitical—belong to the erotic-culinary domain in a higher sense, not only by force of the themes. In 1937, he described as the true goal of his efforts the achievement of some "higher serenity," and in 1954 he still praised, with heartfelt approval, precisely this kind of activity on the part of Anton Chekhov.

The later Thomas Mann's thinking about decline—and that of the early one as well, for the world-famous first novel already had the subtitle "The Decline of a Family"—always remained aesthetic. A savoring of decline and collapse. Karl Kraus too was fascinated by thoughts of decline all his life. "The Last Days of Humanity" equate the demise of the Habsburg Empire with the end of the world. But Kraus's interest remains *ethical*, even in politics. Thomas Mann's political considerations, on the other hand, are always a politicizing out of an aesthetic-erotic impulse, as it was with the German romantics whom he never shed.

Søren Kierkegard assigned *irony* to the aesthetic sphere yet described *humor* as the special province of the ethical thinker. Thomas Mann remained aesthetically oriented still in his irony; even his political irony was intended aesthetically. In a "Note on Heine" he admired greatly the episode of Heine's answer to reproaches about the political ineptitude of his book on Ludwig Börne: "But isn't it expressed beautifully?"[11] Heine the eroticist and ironist had already excited the very young Thomas Mann. An article "Heinrich Heine, the Good One" stems from 1893, the contribution of an eighteen year old.[12] In it, the failed high school student and incipient literary man fended off attempts to "rescue" the ethical Heine. The young patrician from Lubeck would not countenance the alienation of Heine from the aesthetic domain, which was his own as well, by ethical manipulation.

All of this only becomes visible when one stops repeating Thomas Mann's many self-interpretations. The judgment of Heinrich Mann remained in force. It was, to be sure, no accident that, ever since 1930, Thomas Mann made essentially the "correct" political prognoses. But nevertheless he did not perceive the claims of other lives. That can be seen through the social classes that are represented in his work, as well as through those that are significantly absent from it. Still, Heinrich Mann was also correct in seeing that the strength of Thomas Mann the author lay precisely in this fundamental decision in favor of the aesthetic, the ironic, the erotic—it was the motive for his "productions."

In the unfinished novel about the confidence man and artist Felix

Krull, the true conceptual center is the *game*. Three major reportages of games are not inserted at random but rather carefully integrated as basic themes: operetta, circus, bullfight. Their erotic aspect is easily recognized. Since all desire wants eternity ("Da alle Lust die Ewigkeit will"), as Nietzsche conjectures, we might interpret the theme of play in *Felix Krull* less as all sympathy than as pan eroticism. Perhaps it is for this reason that the novel remained a fragment—with the heartfelt assent of its author (1970).

Notes

1. Edmond Vermeil, *Les Doctrinaires de la Revolution allemande* (Paris, 1938).

2. Thomas Mann, *Gesammelte Werke in zwölf Bänden* (Aufbau-Verlag, Berlin, 1955).

3. *Neue Rundschau*, August 1929.

4. Thomas Mann, *Briefe 1889–1936* (Frankfurt, 1962), p. 63.

5. Adrian Leverkühn, the German composer, is by his name reminiscent of Nietzsche's idea of "perilous life," the "vivere pericolosamente" of the Nietzschean Benito Mussolini.

6. Thomas Mann, "Gedanken im Kriege," in *Friedrich und die grosse Koalition* (Berlin, 1915), pp. 10–11.

7. Hans Wysling, "Ein Elender: Zu einem Novellenplan Thomas Manns," in Paul Scherrer and Hans Wysling, *Quellenkritische Studien zum Werk Thomas Manns* (Bern and Munich, 1967), pp. 106ff.

8. Heinrich Mann, *Ein Zeitalter wird besichtigt* (Berlin, 1947), pp. 222f.

9. Thomas Mann and Heinrich Mann, *Briefwechsel 1900–1949* (Frankfurt, 1968), pp. 117–18.

10. Max Rychner, "Thomas Mann und die Politik," in *Aufsätze zur Literatur* (Zurich, 1966), pp. 297–98.

11. Thomas Mann, *Reden und Ausätze* (Frankfurt, 1965), II, 6, 8–9.

12. Thomas Mann, op. cit., pp. 669ff.

Living in the Metaphor of Fiction

J. P. Stern*

Perchance, too, God will this descry, that I sought out the hard and laboured with might and main, perchance, perchance it will be counted unto my credit and benefit that I diligently applied myself and strenuously wrought all to its completion.

Yet aside from [all my sins] have I busied myself as a labourer does, nor rested nor slept, but toiled and moiled and undertaken all manner

*Reprinted from *Comparative Criticism: A Yearbook* (1979), ed. E. S. Shaffer, by permission of Cambridge University Press. Quotations from Mann in German have been omitted.

of hard things, following the word of the Apostle: "Whoever seeks hard
things, to him it is hard."
(Thomas Mann, *Doktor Faustus* [1947], chapter 47, translation by the
author)

With the appearance of Thomas Mann's *Doktor Faustus* in 1947, a
period in the political, social and literary history of Germany comes to its
conclusion.[1] The famous lines I have just quoted many of you will have
recognized, for they contain the main purport of Adrian Leverkühn's
confession at the end of that book, the summing up of his life as he and his
creator see it. But beyond that (it seems to me) these lines contain a
summing up and motto of a whole epoch, an epoch to which Leverkühn
belongs as much as does Thomas Mann himself, and which for Thomas
Mann is not historical: by which I mean that he does not stand outside it.

I have tried to show in more than one place that the dominant values
of this age—which I see as an age informed by a morality or moral
theology of strenuousness—make their appearance in its politics as well as
in its literature, and how difficult its greatest writers found it to move
beyond them, to a different vision of man and of what is of paramount
value in him. Their attempts to do so have usually ended in bathos and
literary disaster. Stefan George's Maximin, Ernst Jünger's *Der Arbeiter* or
Hofmannsthal's "Kinderkönig"—a sort of glorified head-boy of the Vien-
nese Boys' Choir—are warning examples of what I have in mind.

Thomas Mann made no such awful mistake. Throughout almost his
entire work he identifies himself with the ideology of strenuousness. He
endorses Adrian Leverkühn's appeal to "das Schwere"; he nowhere criti-
cizes *this* aspect of his thinking and his work, nowhere renders its validity
problematic. He cannot step outside the ideology and view it critically—
and yet he, like Rilke at the end of *his* work, is vouchsafed a deliverance of
sorts. But perhaps that is putting it too grandly. Perhaps it is better to say
that at the end of his time, in *Felix Krull*, his last major work, Thomas
Mann is able to cock a snook at the whole business of "das Schwere" and
the value-scheme of the "dear purchase." In doing so he is playing a sort of
in-joke on Friedrich Nietzsche, the church-father of this theology of
strenuousness. But the joke of *this* last joke is that the farewell to the
ideology and temper of an age is enacted in *his*—in Nietzsche's—terms.
These, I know, are dark words, and the rest of this paper is meant to
elucidate them.

It was Nietzsche in whose writings this ideology of strenuousness was
formulated for the first time and with a consistency of which he himself
was perhaps not fully aware. Nietzsche, we know, meditated on and
criticized the Christian commandments and morality, taking it together
with certain Socratic injunctions to be a model of all other moral schemes
and moralizings. Nietzsche's sustained attacks take as their object not
merely this or that rule or law or commandment. He proposes to reject the
whole business of making moral judgements and to "unmask" it as a

compensatory activity which is wholly based on feelings of inferiority and grudging resentment, and desire for revenge. All this to him are aspects of what in *Zarathustra* he calls "der Geist der Schwere," which he identifies with the Second Reich, and with the Germans generally, whom he accuses of eating and drinking too much and of judging the quality of thought by the quantity of sweat it produces. But "das Schwere" in German means not only heaviness and earnestness and gravity, but also a proud strenuousness and difficulty, and the exacting nature of intellectual and moral effort. In criticizing and repudiating this "Geist der Schwere," this spirit of gravity, Nietzsche, and after him Thomas Mann, speak from a life-long experience of and belief *in* this spirit; they speak as men who believe that in the attainment of that spirit lies the moral and spiritual validation of their age. Both deeply believe in commitment to strenuousness as a sign of some sort of salvation or validation of modern man. From his earliest writings — that is, the second of his *Thoughts out of Season* of 1874 — to the last notes reprinted posthumously in *The Will to Power*, this is the cardinal theme of Nietzsche's philosophizing.

Thus, in the second of the *Thoughts out of Season* (1874), he exhorts his contemporaries "to find an exalted and noble *raison d'être* in life: seek out destruction for its own sake! I know of no better purpose in life than to be destroyed by that which is great and impossible!" (II, §9) — as though its impossibility were what makes his "ideal" great. Again, in the Wagner essay two years later, he commends the cultural and pedagogic function of Bayreuth and offers its tragic masterpieces as lessons to those who are "preparing for death in the fight for justice and love" (IV, §4), as though only death could validate their cause. Youthful romantic rhetoric? The self-destructive strenuousness of this strange morality never changes. When Nietzsche writes (to Seydlitz, 11 June 1878) that he wishes his life to reflect "my views about morality and art (the hardest things that my sense of truth has so fàr wrung from me)"; and again a year later (to Gast, 5 October 1879) referring to the conclusion of *Human, All-too-Human*: "[it is] purchased so dearly and with so much hardship that nobody who had the choice would have written it at that price"; when he proclaims, in the 1886 preface to that book, "I now took sides *against* myself and *for* everything that would hurt me and would come hard to me"; when he insists (to Gast, August 1883) that the main achievement of *Zarathustra* should be seen as "a victory over the Spirit of Heaviness, considering *how difficult* it was to represent the problems with which the book is concerned"; when, in the notes to *The Will to Power* (1887–8) he defines "virtue" as "the delight we take in opposition," adding that "I assess the power of [a man's] will by how much resistance, pain and torment it can endure and turn to its advantage" (§382); when again and again he insists on the need to destroy all forms of positive faith and all comforting certitudes, emphasizing the value of scepticism and of despair itself in the battle against the living death of conformity; and when, finally, in

Antichrist (1888) he roundly condemns every idea of a pre-established harmony between truth and happiness (or even plain utility), claiming that "the experience of all rigorous and profoundly disposed minds teaches the opposite. Every inch of truth has to be wrested from oneself. We have to surrender almost everything that our hearts, our love, our trust in life normally cling to. This requires greatness of soul: the service of truth is the hardest service. . . . *Faith makes blessed*: therefore it lies . . ." (§50), we are left in no doubt that "the experimental philosophy which I live," unlike the other moral "experiments," represents Nietzsche's most intimate personal undertaking and purpose, and informs every phase of his creative life. Its fullest expression is to be found in *Thus Spoke Zarathustra*, that disastrous fiction on which he pinned his highest hopes.

This — the ideology of "the hardest thing," of "the dear purchase" — is one aspect of the legacy Nietzsche left to the twentieth century. But there is another aspect of this legacy, which is more specifically literary, and which is at odds with the ideology of strenuousness.

From his first book, *The Birth of Tragedy* of 1872, to the end of his conscious life, Nietzsche is attempting to offer what he calls "an aesthetic justification of the world" (by which, though he shunned the word, he really meant a kind of redemption). Finding life in the world intolerable, he — the great "Yea-sayer" of the Zarathustrian affirmation — now wishes to present the world as a game or a play (the notorious ambiguity of the German word, "Spiel," leaves the question open), as a spectacle for the gods; he hopes to fashion an aesthetic philosophy in which "the World and all being of man" might be presented as free of the curse of moral value-judgements, "moralinfrei," truly beyond good and evil. Here, from the book of that title, is one of the aphorisms in which this aesthetic "redemption" is described: "Around the hero everything turns into tragedy, around the demi-god everything turns into satyric drama; and around God everything turns into — what? Maybe the 'world'?" *(Jenseits von Gut und Böse [Beyond Good and Evil]* §150). To grasp the full poignancy of this Nietzschean idea of the aesthetic we must bear in mind that it comes from a philosopher who is temperamentally incapable of making any statement, significant or otherwise, without subsuming it by a moral value-judgement of some kind — a philosopher whose countless attacks on Christianity and occasional admiration of Christ derive from the conviction that the religion and its church betrayed its founder, who lived and exemplified a life without judging. The further irony here is that Nietzsche's idea of the aesthetic by definition excludes Nietzsche the thinker and inveterate moralist. And the poignant irony is that he knows it. In what must be one of his most deeply self-revealing reflections he writes: "How could it be other than obvious that this is the ideal of a heavy, a hundredweight spirit — a spirit of gravity!" *(Der Wille zur Macht [The Will to Power]* §1039). Could he not encompass all life in a fiction? Indeed he could. Indeed, he could be bounded in a nutshell and count himself a king of infinite space, were it not that he has bad dreams, dreams of the death of God.

"Only as an aesthetic phenomenon is the world and the being of man eternally justified"—the sentence occurs three times in *The Birth of Tragedy* and he comes back to variations of it in almost every one of his later books. This search for an aesthetic theodicy accompanies the sixteen brief years of Nietzsche's thinking; and just so does the search for the liberation through the genuinely funny fiction accompany the almost sixty very long years of Thomas Mann's métier as a novelist. And an aesthetic redemption—aesthetic in the widest sense of the word—is what, at the end of Thomas Mann's life, Felix Krull is vouchsafed.

But what does "aesthetic in the widest sense" mean? A very short essay of Nietzsche's of 1873, entitled "On Truth and Falsehood in an Extra-Moral Sense" (it is the first of his purely philosophical writings) gives us an idea of what Nietzsche means by "the aesthetic." Men, he says there, are constitutionally incapable of a true knowledge of the world around them. All their so-called truths about this world or any other are pure tautologies. ("If someone hides a thing behind a bush, looks for it there and finds it, then this seeking and finding isn't much to write home about; but that"—Nietzsche goes on—"that is what all seeking and finding inside the realm of reason amounts to.")

Well, we may ask, if man is entirely incapable of finding out the truth about the world, how then is it that he survives in this bleak unknown world of alien forms and shapes, to which he remains forever a stranger? To ask this question is to assume what Nietzsche is unwilling to assume, namely that the truth about the world is necessary for our survival in it. Nietzsche says the opposite: what makes life possible is the fact that the true nature of the world is hidden from us, that we are not able to fictionalize the world as it really is. We create art in order not to perish of the truth (he will write fifteen years later); the conviction that we create the metaphors of myth in order to be able to bear the reality of the world is the foundation on which his entire theory of tragedy rests; and so the artistic activity becomes the creative, life-giving and life-protecting activity par excellence. Or, to put it in the terminology of that early essay, the way that man manages to negotiate and survive in the world is by forming metaphors about the world, and fictions are the most sustained of the metaphors he creates. Human language especially (Nietzsche continues) is totally incapable of saying anything about the real world (to which, he argues, language does not belong), but the relationship of language with that world is entirely imprecise, approximate, haphazard, almost random—indeed, its relationship is merely metaphysical: "What then is truth? A mobile army of metaphors, metonymies, anthropomorphisms—in short, a sum of human relations which, poetically and rhetorically intensified, became transposed and adorned, and which after long usage by a people seemed fixed, canonical and binding on them. Truths are illusions which one has forgotten *are* illusions" ("Über Wahrheit und Lüge im aussermoralischen Sinn").

I don't propose to inquire whether this is a correct view of language (or, indeed, how a correct or true view of language could possibly be formulated if language is seen as such an arbitrary, shifting structure). But there is no doubt that this view represents consistently Nietzsche's own understanding of language throughout his life as a writer, and that this view says a good deal about his particular use of it—that is, about his predominantly and powerfully metaphorical style. The theoretical structure behind his style goes something like this:

Language is related to reality by nothing more precise than metaphor.

Metaphors are the only access we have to reality.

Metaphors are the creation of artists.

Therefore artists are the least misleading, least imprecise users of language; artistic activity is the paradigm or symbol of all positive human activity.

Art, in this argument of Nietzsche's, is not oblivion or even ecstasy (as it is in *The Birth of Tragedy*), but it is involved in the creation of that spiderweb of metaphors which alone makes life in the world possible: art is a creation, however, which is accompanied by at least an intermittent knowledge which those who merely *use* the metaphorical structure without creating it do not possess—the knowledge that the metaphors are not the real thing, that they are indeed only metaphors. Language, Nietzsche claims, cannot designate true causality. The world contains no truth and no undeflected communication; and there is of course no *real* freedom in the world either. Our only freedom is in the realm of "as if": it is a metaphorical or aesthetic freedom—aesthetic in that wider sense that I have now described.

Thomas Mann is the principal heir of Nietzsche's bequest to our age: of *both* aspects of that bequest. Not only do the major figures of his fiction—from Thomas Buddenbrook through Tonio Kröger, Gustav von Aschenbach, Prinz Klaus Heinrich, Hans Castorp, the magician Cipolla, to Jacob and Joseph, the old Goethe and Adrian Leverkühn—embody that ideology of strenuousness which I have described; but all his life too, though intermittently, Thomas Mann hoped for a deliverance from that ideology, searching for a way out of this world of existential strain. Throughout his long career he hoped to write, not merely an ironical novel (he had done enough, and we might even think more than enough, of that: irony clearly offered no escape), not even a humorous novel but, speaking up on more than one occasion for the joys of slapstick, what he hoped to write was a funny novel. A novel which would suspend (I am desperately trying to avoid the villainous Hegelian pun: I mean *aufheben*) the weightiness of the spirit of gravity. And in finally achieving *Felix Krull* he had his life-long wish.

Now this is the point where a good many things might be said to characterize Thomas Mann's undertaking in the novel. There is, first and most obviously, its very rich autobiographical background—he began working on it in 1910 and the first volume, which is all we have, was not concluded until 1954. There is Thomas Mann's parodistic exploration of the *Bildungsroman*, its modification by the picaresque tradition, his treatment of that "art *versus* life" theme to which he had devoted so many earlier works and which has been the standby of every modern language teacher ever since. All these topics have been discussed at length and there is no need to go over them again. Instead, I want to turn to another topic: the strongly anti-mimetic aspect of the work.

Whereas Nietzsche's idea of an aesthetic validation of the world remains a speculative proposal—a proposal to de-pragmatize, aestheticize or fictionalize the world—Thomas Mann turns the proposal into a reality, that is, into an elaborate fiction. Michael Beddow in a recent closely argued essay makes the point: "The narrative pattern reveals a metaphoric determination of such sustained intensity that the text's ostensible claim to be the autobiography of an adventurer is undercut": or rather, that its credibility is seriously, and deliberately, impaired. Similarly, there is no satirical intention worth mentioning behind the work, and any attempt to see it as a socially conscious critique of Edwardian materialistic morality only shows what extraordinarily modest ideas of satire are entertained by some of our socially conscious friends and colleagues.

I think there is no point in beating about the bush. The hero whom Thomas Mann has created and whose device in life is a delightful ease, a lightness of touch, a charming grace and an easy, all-too-easy con-science—that hero is a con man and good-for-nothing who will never pass the Leavisite test of mature adult responsible behaviour. And the novel in which he has his being is what Nietzsche said all life was: a highly immoral or, if you prefer it, *a*moral affair. I do not merely mean that trickery, lechery, mendacity, theft and deceit are rewarded by worldly goods and pleasure *and* an easy conscience, but that all these vices and villainies are metaphorized: presented to us under names and in forms which are designed to cancel out their viciousness. In other words, *Felix Krull* is a novel without any sustained or consistently held moral judge-ments, a story enacted in Nietzsche's "moralinfreie Welt." This is one of the sources and conditions of its humour: this cancelling-out of the grounds of moral judgements, the deliberate and consistent disappointment of our expectations is one of the major sources of fun in the book.

Similarly, the dominant tendency of the *Bildungsroman* to see the world in terms of a hero wholly concerned with *using* it, using it for the sole purpose of enriching his experience at the world's expense—this tendency is not criticized or discredited but guyed and carried to its logical conclusion by turning the hero into a confidence trickster and a thief. Felix Krull, with his magnificent egotism, becomes all the world's benefactor, for in the very act of exploiting and swindling and stealing from others he cannot fail to give them the benefit, the blessing almost, of his charming, easy, generous, uncalculating personality. He is indeed an artist and a virtuoso, but his instrument is life itself. And the women he plays along— from servant-maid to prostitute, to a fashionable lady novelist to, finally, a double affair with the wife and the daughter of a Portuguese anthropologist—have no complaint. Do we believe, though he says so himself, that he is a prodigious erotic performer? "Of course, any possibility of comparison is out of the question. But all the same, it is my private conviction, which can neither be demonstrated nor disproved, that with me the enjoyment of love was twice as acute and twice as sweet as with others" (Felix Krull, chapter 8). Does it matter whether we believe him? The erotic here is the pattern of Krull's attitude to the world at large: he gives pleasure by taking it, the giving and the taking are inseparable, even his boasting is not intended to put others out of countenance but to exhibit his own command of fine words. The words matter, not their truth.

The words—Felix Krull's immense irrepressible grandiloquent flow of words—are not merely descriptive of something that happened in the glorious past (Krull the confidence trickster is writing his memoirs from gaol), they are in and by themselves (the Hegelian manner is catching) a consolation from that past and a continuation of it into the melancholy and grim present. The emphasis, throughout the novel, on Krull's gift of the gab is wholly Wittgensteinian—I mean that it is intended to narrow the traditional distinction between words and world, to show words as active in, and a part of, the world.

The most brilliant example of this process of de-pragmatizing the world by converting it into words, and more specifically into metaphors which stand for other words, and thus for life itself is, of course, the farcical medical examination in the course of which Felix Krull feigns an epileptic attack and is turned down by an army medical board. The scene was written ten years before Jaroslav Hašek in The Good Soldier Schweik and forty years before Joseph Heller in Catch-22 used a similar ploy—the ploy of showing a hero battling against a hostile army bureaucracy and winning the battle by vigorously identifying his own aim with the aim of the enemy. It is by using his own fabulous descriptive powers in order to arouse the army doctor's contradictions that Krull makes him compliant with his desire to be declared unfit for military service, and it is by his constant indignant assurances that he is perfectly well and desperately anxious to become a soldier that Felix Krull eventually works himself into an epileptic fit which is genuine in every sense except the strictly medical one. His fit is the image, the metaphor, of a fit.

Indeed, so perfect is his imitation of it that the category of the 'strictly medical' becomes strictly irrelevant, and so does the idea of dissimulation. The real thing and the pretence or metaphor of the real thing become as one. And this, we now recall, leaving aside the question of intention, happens in several other important scenes in Thomas Mann's novels. How ill is Hans Castorp, the hero of *The Magic Mountain*? How desolate and abandoned by all the world is Joseph when his brothers cast him in the well? How ill is Adrian Leverkühn, and what exactly is the origin and the nature of his disease; how much responsibility does he really bear for the death of his nephew, the little Johann Nepomuk?

All these questions are raised by Thomas Mann and left deliberately open, as though the figurative statement — the intimation of a refusal to answer the question raised — were all that can be said; as though that aspect of language which provides us with firm distinctions between medical and psychic causes, between illness and health, between pretence and truth (an aspect of language not really provided for by Nietzsche's scheme) could not be trusted to convey the full meaning of these scenes; and one had to resort to another kind of language altogether, which contents itself with presenting events and explanations as mere images or metaphors of some ineffable and unworded state of being.

And so it is with Felix Krull's epileptic fit which, as I have said, is perfectly genuine in every sense except the medical one — genuine enough, certainly, to take in the medical commission. It is the very image and metaphor of a fit. When Krull leaves the hall in which he has been examined and scored his triumphant victory (and, incidentally, even here Thomas Mann cannot let go without emphasizing the tremendous cost, in physical and emotional terms, of Krull's victorious deception), a sergeant whose attention he had attracted earlier says to him, "Too bad about you, Krull, or however you spell your name! You're certainly a promising fellow, you might have got somewhere in the army — anyone can see that at a glance!" To this the memoirist himself adds:

> More mature consideration, however, compelled me to realize that to have entered that world [of the Army] would have been a gross mistake and error. I had not, after all, been born under the sign of Mars — at least not in the specific, real sense! For although martial severity, self-discipline and danger have been the conspicuous characteristics of my strange life, its primary pre-condition and basis has been freedom — a condition wholly irreconcilable with any kind of commitment to a grossly factual situation. Accordingly if I lived *like* a soldier but not *as* a soldier, it would have been a silly misapprehension to believe that I must therefore live *as* a soldier. Indeed, if one were to define the value of an emotion as precious as freedom, and make that value available to reason, one might say that to live *like* a soldier, figuratively but not literally, in short to be allowed to live in the symbol, is the meaning of true freedom. (*Felix Krull*, chapter 5)

And here the story I have to tell comes full circle. "How really to live in freedom?" asks Krull, "Where is liberation to be found?" And the answer is, "To live metaphorically, in the 'as if' world of art and of the imagination," and this of course is the answer, too, of Nietzsche's aesthetic theodicy (in the essay of 1873): "Perhaps to live in art—for instance in the art of language, that mobile, unstable army of metaphors, is the only way."

Nietzsche, as we know, was not greatly interested in the novel as a form of fiction (though he has a good deal to say about a few contemporary French novels as forms of psychological disclosure). What he is concerned with, from *The Birth of Tragedy* onwards, is tragic myth, and the idea of myth as extended metaphor is another aspect of that legacy which was taken up by Thomas Mann's generation.

Nietzsche tells us—in that book for the first time, and repeatedly throughout the entire work—that a healthy national culture needs its life-giving and life-protecting myths, and his early enthusiasm for Richard Wagner derives from his belief—in which he later finds himself to have been mistaken—that Wagner will give Germany those life-enhancing myths which she needs in order to achieve cultural greatness and national health (in the same way as did Aeschylus, Sophocles for Athens). But myth, for Nietzsche, is *instinctive* metaphor, is the creation of those who "forget themselves as artistically creative subjects." There is a difficulty in this argument which Nietzsche cannot resolve—or may not even be conscious of: how do you make up a myth? How do you deliberately and purposefully create a cultural situation in which instinctive, non-deliberate, purely inspirational myth-makers will arise and instinctively appeal to the soul of the people? When Bayreuth was created, Valhalla did not become a reality, but a limited company was formed and its shares were traded on the Berlin stock exchange. At this point Nietzsche began to have some doubt about the chthonic and genuinely popular nature of it all. Yet although he then turned his back on Wagner, he still believed that an instinctive inspirational myth is what his world needed, and the complex edifice of *Zarathustra* and of the Superman—a compound of art nouveau emblematic beasts, the syntax and verily-verily tone of the Luther Bible—are the result.

Coming less than half a century later, Thomas Mann wrote no *Zarathustra*. From the late 1920s onwards—from the inception of the biblical Joseph stories—he is drawn toward the idea of building his fiction from the elements of accepted myths, but he is not prepared to sacrifice the articulation of his narrative consciousness or to pretend to a naivety he does not possess. Thus there is nothing in the least naive about the aesthetic validation of the world—the validation through symbol and metaphor—which Krull is describing: the fact *that* he is describing it makes it the opposite of naive, allows him to be conscious of its own artificiality. When the handsome young Felix Krull is in bed with the ageing lady-novelist, Diane Houpflé, her heated poetico-erotic imagination makes him enact the role of the god Hermes, god of thieves, as she invites him to steal her jewelry. He is only too ready to oblige (again: he gives pleasure by taking pleasure). And at this point she discovers that he has never heard of the god—yet of course it is Krull himself, twenty years after, who reports the scene, a scene utterly permeated by self-consciousness and conscious, farcical imitation and re-enactment. Thomas Mann is not only writing a fiction and drawing on a myth, he is also showing the fictionality of the fiction by letting the hero in on the secret, by making him share the author's consciousness of his main narrative devices—by explicitly repudiating the fiction of realism (the single pretence) in favour of the fiction of self-conscious myth (the double pretence). And because the self-consciousness is exploited, is not inadvertent, this Sterneian device comes off.

The difference which arises here between Nietzsche and Thomas Mann is indicative of the generation difference between them. Mann had certainly abundant occasion to experience what Nietzsche did not see— the modern, twentieth-century political uses of the mythopoeic imagination and its products. His consciousness, and indeed his literary self-consciousness, is unabating, and it is his glory. He *says* he is creating myth—both in *Felix Krull* and in the correspondence with Karl Kerényi about the writing of the novel we hear a great deal about Hermes, the god of messengers and travellers and thieves, and about the way Mann hopes to relate certain episodes in his story to the myth. A little irreverently, reading this correspondence, one cannot help being reminded of two giant ants, lugging a huge, mysterious shape along their path with the inscription MYTH on it—they neither wish to abandon it nor do they quite know what to do with it. But one of them, Kerényi, is a good deal more in earnest about it than the other. For in the very act of drawing attention to Hermes and his own mythopoeic undertaking, he—Thomas Mann—is suspending the distinction between consciousness and the mythopoeic imagination and breaking down the phoney isolation of a supposedly unconscious creativeness.

The idea of the aesthetic as we glean it from the works of Thomas Mann's last period is largely what, as far as explicit statement goes, it had been for Nietzsche at the time of *The Birth of Tragedy*: a dream filled with the consciousness of its status as dream, a metaphorical and symbolical freedom which, by being aware of its metaphorical nature, also articulates an awareness of its relative, limited, conditional being—for that, after all, is what all our freedom is: relative, limited, conditional. In the end, the philosophy of Thomas Mann's con man is a thing more modest than the grand aesthetic justification of the world and being which Nietzsche had envisaged. It is, and it is acknowledged to be, an artifact, part of a larger, non-aesthetic world.

I have shown how far Nietzsche's explicit statement goes. But it seems to me that the observations on the metaphorical nature of language in that early essay of Nietzsche's from which I quoted contain an implicit set of stylistic precepts which he was to follow throughout the sixteen brief years of his conscious life: precepts for his remarkable philosophy in a new, metaphorical style, which reveals Nietzsche's unchanging determination not to oppose or critically dissolve the metaphoricity of language, but to develop and exploit it. To put it the other way round: what makes him the dominant influence on German literature in the twentieth century — and a major influence on the English and Scandinavian literature *entre deux guerres* — is of course his incomparably lucid and concrete style, dominated by metaphors and cast precisely in that "middle mode" (which in that essay he calls "jene Mittelsphäre und Mittelkraft") halfway between the traditional language of idealist philosophy and figurative narrative prose.

Where does this style find its vocabulary, how is it assembled? The essay of 1873 ends with a description of the creative intellect that has freed itself from all practical considerations and tasks and sets out, disinterestedly, to re-enact the world in images and concepts. So far the young Nietzsche's argument is pure Schopenhauer. But when Nietzsche goes on to show how this creative mind in its freedom takes up the vocabulary of common discourse and the scaffolding of concepts "in order to dismantle them, break up their order and reconstitute them ironically, bringing together things farthest apart and separating those closest together," for no other purpose than to play with them; and when he concludes that "no regular way leads from such intuitions to the land of ghostly abstractions, it is not for them that the word was created; seeing them, man falls silent or speaks in forbidden metaphors and extravagant combinations of concepts, so that by demolishing and by mocking the old conceptual boundaries (if in no other way) he may show himself equal to the impression with which the mighty intuition seized him." Nietzsche is giving the most accurate description we have of his own future philosophical and literary procedure.

There is a sense in which every forceful, original metaphor is a "forbidden metaphor." The very use of metaphor is a challenge — in some languages perhaps the most radical challenge there is — to the conventionality or, as Nietzsche would say, the disheartening commonness of language. The forbidden metaphors work only when they are used sparingly, tactically, when they are allowed to form patterns of contrast with usages which do not challenge the convention, and this of course is how Nietzsche writes at his best. This is not a very surprising conclusion, yet it does not mean that he writes like everybody else. What that image of the artist at work among forbidden metaphors and untoward combinations of concepts suggests is the act of writing as demolition and de-construction: the breaking up of accepted order is manifest in the pointed brevity of each utterance. And with this goes Nietzsche's discovery that his discrete reflections have value and make sense, that discontinuity can be significant, that "notes for" a philosophy are a philosophy (Bertolt Brecht, Anton von Webern and Jorge Luis Borges made similar discoveries in *their* media). In just this way Nietzsche will "bring together and separate" the elements of those cardinal metaphors for which his writings are famous: "amor fati," invoking choice motivated by love where blind fate is sovereign; "the aesthetic justification," where there is to be no justifying or judging; "the lie in a supra-moral sense"; "the eternal recurrence," where "eternity" is to be merely hideous endlessness; "the death of God," which does not tell us whether he was ever alive; "the will to power," which is forever destroying its products and itself — all examples of a metaphysic of which the least confusing thing to say is that it consistently avoids the dangers of dogma and petrifaction at the price of being consistently paradoxical. Here, finally, is the middle ground on which the literary philosopher and the philosophical novelist meet.

For a philosopher, we may say — for a German philosopher at that — Nietzsche is amazingly readable. And for a novelist (we surely feel this again and again) Mann's prose is remarkably (I won't say: unreadable, but) reflective, philosophical, dominated by concepts and the parody of concepts (which Nietzsche had described as ossified metaphors). From opposite sides they both challenge the genre theories and tacit assumptions on which French and English kinds of discourse are founded — each is forever being accused of writing "neither one thing nor t'other," Nietzsche being attacked for his excessive reliance on metaphor, Thomas Mann for excessive abstractness and reliance on conceptual language. Yet both are concerned with diminishing the difference between the two styles and the two ways of coming to terms with the world. And here, finally, they meet: the one presenting life in the discontinuous metaphors of philosophy, the other presenting life in the sustained metaphor of fiction.

Notes

1. This paper was given as the opening address to the British Comparative Literature Association Conference, Warwick, December 1977.

Thomas Mann and Tradition:
Some Clarifications
T. J. Reed*

I

"You have taken it wiselier than I meant you should."
The Tempest

"Thomas Mann I meet at most by accident, and then 3,000 years look down upon me". Brecht, who was somewhat sensitive about his height, was not an admirer of Thomas Mann. But coolness may further insight. The sardonic comment in a letter of the forties[1] registers a prominent feature of Mann's public image. Increasingly since *Der Zauberberg* (a *Bildungsroman* in two senses) Mann had come to be thought of as an elevated exponent of culture. After 1933, the circumstances of his exile, his opposition to Nazism as a cultural degradation as well as a political evil, thrust him into the role of an embodiment — for many people, *the* embodiment — of German culture. Even if he never spoke the words "German culture is where I am",[2] they sum up a posture which the times justified. In the same period, the Joseph tetralogy and the Goethe novel caused new stress, in criticism and appreciation, on Mann's learning — history of religion, literary scholarship — and on his philosophy. In large measure he was accepted in America (so he complained) as a "ponderous philosopher" (Br iii. 55).[3] In a country which he found painfully lacking in tradition, his "heritage of culture" (xi. 218) was revered at least as much as his narrative art was enjoyed.

All this might seem only a consistent development in a writer who had always made use of philosophical and literary allusion. Still, the sceptical implications of Brecht's remark are worth following out. Its irony is concrete and direct. By compressing the time-span of Western culture into Thomas Mann's glance at a casual meeting, Brecht hints at the incongruity of identifying an individual with the totality of culture. Perhaps he implies disapproval of Mann the public figure for allowing the identification, when Mann the writer certainly knows what precarious arrangements lie behind the façade of the cultural edifice. Brecht speaks as one member of a guild who finds another member's relations with the

*Reprinted by permission from *The Discontinuous Tradition. Studies in German Literature in Honor of E. L. Stahl*, ed. P. F. Ganz (Oxford: Clarendon Press, 1971), 158–81. Author's note: "This essay, as will be evident, was a ground-clearing operation. The positive view which it could only begin to develop — that what matters in Thomas Mann's relation to tradition is not his culture *per se* but the creative and committed use he made of it — was later argued more fully in my book *Thomas Mann: The Uses of Tradition* (Oxford, 1974)."

outside world part irritating, part contemptible. We need not take his judgement as final, but it will do no harm to take it as a warning. For if truth, in Brecht's favourite phrase, is concrete, then the statements literary historians make will need to be so too if they are to command belief. They must correspond, that is, to a conceivable reality and be plausible descriptions of literature as an individual's activity — especially when they try to relate this to the complex abstractions of "period" or "literary tradition."

In this, Thomas Mann scholarship has sometimes been incautious, even naïve. It is easy to find statements like Brecht's "3,000 years" offered in good earnest. Mann is "a latecomer and heir to the whole of Man's cultural past";[4] the "full rich score of his work resounds with our living past and can be adequately explained only by what would come close to a history of our intellectual world";[5] his works have "a memory that reaches back over centuries, even millenia";[6] and, coming to particulars, we may read of "a line of tradition that leads from St. Paul via Luther to romanticism, and thence to Thomas Mann".[7] Now there may be senses in which statements like these are true, but they need more careful definition than they have yet had. All too often, critics have worked with the tacit assumption that any feature or phase of standard culture, especially German literary and philosophic culture, is axiomatically relevant to Thomas Mann's works of any period and may be taken to lie behind them. The opinions just quoted only make this assumption explicit.

Various kinds of confusion are at work here, and a deal of interplay with the attitudes and dicta of Thomas Mann himself. It is perhaps time to clarify the principles involved, and to mark out some essentials of Thomas Mann's real relations with tradition.

A good point from which to start is Kaufmann's erudite study, which sets out to locate in Western philosophical history those "problems not deliberately invoked, various types of solution, reminiscences from time immemorial" which (we are told) used to 'rise around' Thomas Mann as he wrote (p. 17). This might mean simply that a historian of philosophy can identify old philosophical themes in Mann's fiction (as no doubt in many other places). Such echoes and connections are then in the mind of the historian, and claim no real reference — except on a Hegelian view of the Absolute Spirit's imperturbable progress through history. This is how one would read, for instance, the suggestion that "Thomas Mann challenges the Aristotelian-Scholastic tradition of God's immutability" (p. 19), or that Mann "has to be seen in the wake of the romantic tradition, i.e. the intellectual movement from Böhme through Baader and Schelling to Scheler" (p. 25). But on occasion Kaufmann seems to mean that an actual event has taken place in time: "In Mann it is a very personal *appropriation* of the wisdom of Angelus Silesius" (p. 18); or "Mann's typology *developed originally from* Schiller's classical antithesis between naive and sentimen-tal" (p. 27); after which "Mann *accepts* Schelling's and Nietzsche's dialectical amendments of Schiller" (p. 29, all italics mine). This phrasing colours our view of what is implied elsewhere, and we feel moved to object that the links Kaufmann establishes are either so general that they are relevant "essentially" to many modern writers, or so specific that they can be disproved in the case of Thomas Mann.[8] Mann himself disclaimed some of the fruits of Kaufmann's labours, with a touch of unconscious comedy: "Influence of Leibniz very indirect. Same for Schelling" (Br ii. 296). But his reproof was gentle, his comment on Kaufmann's method of the friendliest. It bore clearly enough, he said, the mark of the "German academic tradition" — but why should that not be as welcome in America as the object of Kaufmann's study had proved?

One obvious reason is the traps that attend such a method. In Kaufmann's book, the fallacy *post hoc ergo propter hoc* has had a field-day. And the confusions of this approach are compounded when a scholar ignores such simple facts as are known. A study of Mann and Romanticism under the banner of *Problemgeschichte* will naturally incline away from the concretely historical to the "essential" patterns of detectable problems. Even so, to say that "it is no accident that at that moment *Schiller* figured in a work of Thomas Mann"[9] is (to say the least) unobservant. Precisely the historical chance of the centenary of Schiller's death in 1905 led to Mann's commission to write a Schiller story for *Simplicissimus* — just as the 1932 Goethe centenary was to intensify his interest in Goethe. Even the Hegelian Spirit sometimes likes Its elbow jogged.

At least with the Romantics, unlike so many of the names pressed into Kaufmann's book, we are among writers with whom Mann did at some stage make contact. Yet problems still remain. What kind of contact? When did it occur? What was its demonstrable effect? The later Mann devoted two essays to Kleist, but is Kleist's essay on the puppet theater to be assumed relevant to the early *Tonio Kröger* and its dance-motif?[10] Internal evidence (rarely a conclusive argument) is all there is to go on, and that (*pace* its proponent) weak. If one must at all costs have a literary source, surely Nietzsche — Mann's most fully documented early influence and repeated source — is the first to be considered?[11] But why not allow a place to simple experience as Mann himself did when he recalled "the brown-braided girl that I partnered in my dance lessons who was to become the recipient of love poems" (xi. 100)? It would of course be wrong to speak of an "intraliterary fallacy," since so much of Mann's work is demonstrably of intra-literary provenance. Even so, a sense of proportion is needed. Had Thomas Mann at twenty-six read Kleist's essay? A banal question. Yet it is a banal truth that all of us — even writers destined themselves to become classics — read the classics one after the other, in the course of time, and are not born ready-equipped with them. (Mann, for instance, read nothing of Stifter till he was forty, and thought he was Swiss.)[12] We must not turn Thomas Mann into a mere pawn in the *Geistesgeschichte* game, a timeless cultural entity operating at all stages with the full range of materials which the literary past potentially constitutes, or with the full range of techniques which he later developed. Any method which does this — assumes, for example, that Mann's first story must necessarily have used Wilhelm Meister's "affair with Marianne" as a source[13] because both concern a young man's love for an actress — can only be called naïve. And certainly, some naïvety is needed to suggest that when Tony Buddenbrook greets her brother Thomas on his return from an Italian honeymoon with the words "Do you know the house: on columns rests its roof" we are being "reminded of Mignon's song of Italy . . . *and hence also* of Goethe's *Lehrjahre*[14] (italics mine). Goethe's novel is in no real sense drawn into this quotation from a poem which is accessible and familiar to many moderately educated Germans who might not dream of reading the *Lehrjahre*.

This last would be a trifling quibble if it did not once more point to a recurrent fallacy — to which scholars are particularly prone — which we may call the fallacy of misplaced completeness. This consists in assuming that, rather as the tip of an iceberg implies the presence of vastly more ice under the surface, any detectable literary allusion implies the hidden presence and functional relevance of the larger whole to which it belongs — and of that whole as known and understood by scholars. The virtuoso application of this fallacy is Erich Heller's discussion of *Buddenbrooks* and Schopenhauer.[15] This is worth examining in some detail.

As early as 1913, Wilhelm Alberts[16] pointed out the congruence of Schopenhauer's main argument and the line of development of *Buddenbrooks*. His cue was the prima-facie evidence of that episode in which Thomas Buddenbrook reads some Schopenhauer. Alberts also, like Heller, pointed to the place where Thomas misunderstands his philosopher and draws a life-affirming — Nietzschean — message from an essentially negating work. Later on, Mann provided accounts of the impact which reading Schopenhauer had had on him personally. But he also made it quite clear that *Buddenbrooks* was far advanced in composition when this occurred. Thus Mann was immediately able to give thanks for his experience by weaving it into his novel, which had reached the point "where it was a matter of conveying Thomas Buddenbrook to his death" (xii. 72). Accepting Mann's confirmation of the impact, but ignoring the unequivocal statement about the chronology, Heller was able to assert that *Buddenbrooks* "derived its intellectual plot from Schopenhauer" and that "the imagination which conceived it bears the imprint of Schopenhauer's thought" (pp. 30, 27). Yet even the choice of words in Mann's second account of the matter makes this impossible: "to weave in my more-than-bourgeois experience" (xi. 111) must mean the adding of a strand to an existing design and cannot be twisted to mean the first forming of that design, even were we to have recourse to some elaborate hypothesis of a late total recasting of the novel.[17]

But for Heller's oversight,[18] we should lack an eloquent reading of *Buddenbrooks*; because of it, we have a highly misleading account of the novel's genesis. Once more, the lapse is important as a symptom, namely of the iceberg assumption. Given the use of a piece of Schopenhauer as material, the idea that the whole of him was a determinant of form had irresistible appeal. So much so that it not only overbore clear contrary evidence: it also suggested to the critic that the Schopenhauer episode in *Buddenbrooks* functions in a way which simply is not plausible. For Heller, it is "an inevitable consummation demanded by the syntax of ideas" in the narrative (p. 57). Yet if we look with attention at the Schopenhauer materials Mann used, they are precisely *not* in harmony with the underlying thesis of *Buddenbrooks*. If we will but leave on one side whatever else we may know about Schopenhauer's ideas, Thomas Buddenbrook's misreading becomes at once comprehensible. His almost ecstatic tone may well echo Nietzsche, in a similar way to other passages in Mann's early works.[19] But given that Thomas Buddenbrook did not read all of *Die Welt als Wille und Vorstellung*, but skipped a good deal to get to what Mann calls "the really important part" (i. 655), no effort was required to extract a consoling mysticism. For the chapter "On Death and Its Relation to the Indestructibility of our Being in itself" *is* consoling, taken in isolation. It states the continuity of life despite the decay of individual phenomena. Now in the total argument of the work this is not meant to be consoling. Individual decay is illusory only because individuality as such is illusory. Nirvana will ultimately be shown preferable to individual existence. But all this is far from evident to the reader of the single chapter. Links with the main argument are perceptible only to the reader who has been following that argument. Thomas Buddenbrook, who has not, is weary of his individuality because it is "a hindrance to being something other and better" (i. 657); he is disappointed in his weakling son Hanno. Understandably he welcomes what Schopenhauer at this point seems be evoking: mystical communion with more successful incarnations of the Will, whom he envies and would have wished to be like. When Schopenhauer writes: "Accordingly, we can at any moment exclaim cheerfully: 'In spite of time, death, and decay we are all still together' ",[20] he could not be easier to misconstrue.

Thus, far from epitomizing the theme of Mann's novel, the content of this episode is at cross-purposes with it — and not even primarily because of any "Nietzschean" reading of Schopenhauer. It must go back to being a finely conceived and executed passage, and none the worse for that. It is there because it corresponds to a vivid experience of Mann's own: the basis of his work, even in this most apparently objective novel, is autobiographical. The episode was taken to be something more than this when a part was wrongly thought to entail the whole; and this in turn depended, surely, on a false mental model of the artist's procedures. Unlike the scholar, he is not out to understand exhaustively, but to make piecemeal use of what attracts him. Moral: in the critic, a lot of knowledge is a dangerous thing.

A postscript will show how, nevertheless, the artist is edged into the position of a cultural pundit by the mere fact of having used "cultural" materials. It is of no significance for a novel if one of the characters in it (or even the author himself) misunderstands a philosopher. But Thomas Mann may have felt a little awkward about his presentation of the "essentials" of Schopenhauer. In the *Lebensabriss* he says: "For me, it was not a matter of . . . the doctrine of salvation by negation of the Will, that Buddhistically ascetic appendage: what affected me in a sensual-suprasensual way was the element of mystical erotic unity in this philosophy" (xi. 111). Of Schopenhauer as the great negator he is now aware. He suggests that he knew this aspect, but rejected it in favour of another. Yet to relegate the negation of the Will in Schopenhauer to a mere appendage is idiosyncratic to the point of the absurd, barely possible but for the need to defend an earlier misreading. Subsequently, when Mann comes to write his essay on Schopenhauer (1938), at least he feels able to refer to the "naive misuse of a philosophy" of which artists like Wagner and himself are capable. But still he sticks to his contradictory idea of Schopenhauer's "erotic sweetness".[21] And an earlier draft of the passage "That is how artists deal with a philosophy — they 'understand' it in their own way, an emotional way" (ix. 562) was less conciliatory, and read "and, what is more, 'understand' it better, fundamentally, than do the moralists".[22]

When we come to Mann's major claimed affinity, that with Goethe, the confusions already located recur, now worse confounded by a typological-mythical-mystical supposition to which Mann's talk of a "unio mystica" (Br ii. 72) gave rise. We read of how, despite a "natural shyness," a 'long and painful process of self-examination qualified Mann at last to identify himself with Goethe. They became truly one."[23] In so far as such a statement has any meaning at all, it is hardly a critic's statement. It takes what was subjectively true for the writer and repeats it parrot-fashion. Not that critics have an absolute duty to debunk what an author says. But they must look beyond its immediate meaning to its significance.[24] Whatever effects Mann's sense of "unio mystica" had on him, the effects of his hint on criticism have been wholly unfortunate. Goethe becomes the first line of inquiry for source and influence at any stage. Hence the sledge-hammer of *Wilhelm Meister* to crack the nut of *Gefallen*. Later proves earlier, part entails whole, the critic has a *carte blanche*.

Der Zauberberg furnishes an example of what may result. The work certainly uses some (in themselves hardly recondite) Goethe materials — the parallel of Joachim Ziemssen and Valentin, the Walpurgisnacht re-enactment. Why not conjecture a Goethean source for the chapter "Snow"? That Castorp's vision is mildly reminiscent of classical landscapes might not itself justify the conclusion that the *Italienische Reise*[25] was a source; but the Goethean *carte blanche* will bridge any gaps of doubt. Moreover, birds are singing in Castorp's vision — not named birds, but the description of their song suggests they could be nightingales — and did not Goethe hear nightingales in Sicily? "Of course one cannot prove a connection between the nightingales that Goethe heard and those in Hans Castorp's dream" (p. 14). But never mind.

Some alternative suggestions are less "traditional" but somewhat more convincing. Derivative the vision certainly is, but not from so canonical a source. The text of the section "Of Beauty" in Mahler's *Lied von der Erde*[26] and, especially, some *Jugendstil* paintings by Ludwig von Hofmann,[27] one of which Mann possessed, yielded exact details of the scenery and the disposition of figures in "Snow".

Again a moral is pointed. The scholarly interpreter, perhaps even without Mann's seductive hints, is likely to engage in a rather high-level selection, a precipitate flight to the peaks of the literary landscape, grown timeless through scholarship and syllabus. But were these peaks the sole abode of the writer? To suppose so is to ignore what actually went on in the obscurer unmapped valleys, among cultural undergrowth now long since faded, but which was very alive to contemporaries. (*Jugendstil* provides the perfect example of a rich period source of literary style and motif which has more recently been rediscovered.)[28] If we jump too readily to "Goethean" conclusions, we block off all view of the more characteristic period influences. Our account gains in neatness and unity, but is false. The modern writer is assimilated into a view of literature as a self-perpetuating classicity. He is canonized, but unhistoried.

Here yet another confusion is at work, this time between literary history and criticism. The evaluating critic feels impelled to link in some way those writers he esteems: since they show the art at its highest, it is in comparing them that its technical and moral possibilities can best be appreciated. He may even speak of his favourites as a "tradition." Yet this word really denotes a historical process, not just a sequence.[29] The comparative evaluation may thus slide into suggestions of historical connectedness, but without offering evidence. The *locus classicus* of this is F. R. Leavis's *The Great Tradition* (which, it has been suggested, could well have been called "Novels I've Liked").[30] Leavis's opening chapter teems with statements which straddle the border between history and criticism. What stands in for the missing proof of contacts and fruitful study is the always obliging but always question-begging "internal evidence." Henry James's admiration for Jane Austen is called "that obvious aspect of influence which can be brought out by quotation.")[31] Perhaps it is too late for us to rescue the term "tradition" for the role its etymology claims, but at least we do well to recognize the multitudinous sins looser usage covers.

Yet surely, it will be objected, Thomas Mann's hints justify some attention to Goethe for that phase when his influence is documented?

Indeed. But even here we must distinguish between some generalized, neutral, scholars' Goethe and the specific, angled, limited Goethe Mann knew and used. It is these uses we must look at; we may not extrapolate from them in any direction we please. As Hume wrote, on a subject similarly conducive to unfounded assumption: "When we infer any particular cause from an effect, we must proportion the one to the other and can never be allowed to ascribe to the cause any qualities but what are exactly sufficient to produce the effect."[32] In our case, from observed effects (Mann's use of particular Goethe materials) we may not infer causes (a global knowledge of and interest in Goethe) which are then taken as sufficient to produce further effects (Goethe at every turn).

Yet surely, our objector will persist, there are signs that Mann *did* have just such a global knowledge of Goethe. If two motifs from *Faust I* do not add up to a sovereign manipulation of the Goethe corpus, and if the Goethe essays are admittedly made up largely of biographical anecdote and a small range of often repeated quotations, what of *Lotte in Weimar*, a rich weave of fact, quotation, and allusion? Did that not demand (as Ernst Cassirer felt)[33] a constant retention of Goethe's works, conversations, and letters in Thomas Mann's memory?

Such certainly is the immediate impression. Yet such was the impression left by other works which rested on a highly economical montage technique about which we now know a good deal:[34] a purposeful reading of limited sources and a reverbalization of derived verbal materials. We know how superficial the appropriation of substance could be while still giving a sense of depth and solidity — a *Schein* "illusion" at two or three removes from reality and quite unlike that of Weimar aesthetic theory.[35] The early *Schwere Stunde* was a similar weave of specifically literary allusion: the idea occurred to nobody that it might rest on anything other than total command of the primary sources. The short cuts possible in an Alexandrian age were left out of account — the preselection of materials in secondary works and the stimulus value of the coherent, ready-made picture a critical account can provide.[36]

True, Mann reconstructing Goethe in 1936 is (on our own principle) not necessarily the same as Mann reconstructing Schiller in 1905. To some extent he has certainly experienced what Sartre put in the words: "La Comédie de la culture, à la longue, me cultivait."[37] But in fact Mann's technique of montage — present in *Schwere Stunde*, confessed in the transparent allegory of *Königliche Hoheit* (chapter "The High Calling") and confirmed in a passage of the *Betrachtungen* (xii. 301 f.) — proves to have been the same in *Lotte in Weimar*. The central incident once chosen, intense concentration ensued: on the relevant parts of Bielschowsky's biography, on the areas of Goethe's works and his *Annalen* leading up to 1816, on works which give access to the characters to be evoked — Riemer's *Mitteilungen* (an old source for the more jaundiced parts of the essays) and Wilhelm Bode's book on Goethe's son, August. Also used were other works

Mann chanced to have to hand, not necessarily authoritative, but suggestive: a book on Schiller's role in the composition of *Faust*[38] becomes the sole interpretative basis for a view of Goethe's and Schiller's relationship, which Mann's rendering will make authoritative and popular. Chance also turns up useful newspaper articles — on Goethe's use of spas, on a public lecture devoted to Goethe's vocabulary.[39] The material accumulates — *Lotte* is a longer work than *Schwere Stunde*. It is copied and recopied, notes are followed by abbreviated notes on the notes, until finally dovetailing begins, and details of Goethe's spa visits are at last built into speech: After all, father always used to go to Bohemia for a summer cure — to Karlsbad, Franzensdorf, Töplitz, since 1784, but then to Italy too (1794). Then in 1806 in Franzensbad (Egerwasser) and 1808, 10, 11, 12. Anno 12 he goes off Karlsbad because he has a bad attack of kidney stones there. Then he still went to Töplitz in 1813, spent the whole summer there and took the cure 158 times. But then, in the last 3 years, Berka, Wiesbaden, Tennstädt. — *Two years ago, in summer '14*, he went to the Rhine and Main area: Erfurt, Hünfeld, *Frankfurt* (for the first time in 17 years). Then *Wiesbaden* with Zelter and Oberbergrat Cramer, the mineralogist. Saint Rochus Chapel (the altar painting). *September 14 at the Brentanos' in Winkel on the Rhine.* Wiesbaden. *Frankfurt again (Interjection:* Oberpostamtszeitung).

Stays with Fritz Schlosser. *[Deleted: October] September 14 [Deleted: Acquaintance] with Willemer, old acquaintance. Marianne (age 16) country estate on the Obermain, "Gerbermühle." (Interjection) — Heidelberg. October 14 he finds her married. 18 October bonfires on heights.*[40]

Urzidil's article and Bielschowsky, chapters 13 and 14[41] of volume 2, between them account for these details. The passage is a specimen — rare in Thomas Mann's preserved papers — of a transition from "sources" to "text." It begins resolutely conversational (August is the speaker), but gets burdened increasingly with references to acquired facts. It reverts to the historical present tense or the verblessness of the preparatory notes. Factual corrections are still being made, archaizing touches are in progress — "Teplitz" is already "Toplitz," though "Kur" is not yet "Cur." Already the points where Lotte must interpose something to break the flow of factual matter are indicated by "Interjection." Much thinning out and rearranging is still to do, as the final text shows (ii. 578 ff.). But the procedures are clear.

We should note in passing that the novel's structure is also affected by them. The way it creates anticipation through the successive portraits Goethe's intimates paint of him, before we eavesdrop on his reflections in the seventh chapter, has often been admired, and it is admirable in effect. But the quasi–monologues also allowed a not too complicated block-use of each area of source material: the *Mitteilungen* for Riemer, Bode's book on August for August. *Lotte in Weimar* is more complex than *Schwere Stunde* as well as longer; but complexity has been kept manageable by making a structural virtue out of a genetic necessity. (Imagine the problems of making the various speakers interact plausibly for the whole novel.)

Not the erudition of the scholar, then, but the economy of the constructivist accounts for the *basis* (to be carefully distinguished from the meaning expressed through it) of Mann's novel. There may be some reluctance to give up the image of Thomas Mann as a repository of learning. But why keep an inaccurate picture of his methods? Indeed — and this is the crucial question — why are knowledge and learning thought important in themselves? Are they any enhancement, let alone criteria, of artistic value? As Lessing pointed out in the thirty-fourth part of the *Hamburgische Dramaturgie*, the creative writer is allowed not to know a thousand things that any schoolboy knows. It is not for what his memory holds that we appreciate him. And if we overrate the importance of "tradition" in the sense of mere quantities of learning, we risk a corresponding and equally irrelevant deflation of the writer's reputation if his learning is queried. T. S. Eliot, whose situation was analogous in some ways, wrote: "In my earlier years I obtained, partly by subtlety, partly by effrontery, and partly by accident, a reputation among the credulous for learning and scholarship, of which (having no further use for it) I have since tried to disembarrass myself. Better to confess one's weaknesses, when they are certain to be revealed sooner or later, than to leave them to be exposed to posterity: though it is, I have discovered, easier in our times to acquire an undeserved reputation for learning than to get rid of it."[42]

Knowledge as such — what his correspondent Karl Kerényi well called "static culture"[43] — is indeed, on an objective view, less important in Mann's relations with the culture of the past than its *use*:[44] and both are preceded and guided by *need* — the demands of the writer's impulse to analyse or express himself, or the exigencies of the times, the "Forderung des Tages." Since our rejection of such earnestly held views of Thomas Mann obliges us to make some positive suggestions, to these needs and uses we now turn.

II

And my spirit roams searching, all about me
And, wavering, I grasp any strong hand.
Thomas Mann, "Monolog" (1899)

Space allows us only to sketch an approach, but Mann's relationship to Nietzsche and to Goethe will yield essentials and provide a contrast: the one a formative influence, the other a chosen "affinity."

Nietzsche was virtually the only begetter of Mann's fundamental ideas — on art, disease, genius, vitality, human typology; and of his basic attitudes — critical, analytic, ironical, self-querying. Acknowledgement is not lacking, and Mann's reservation in the 1930 *Sketch of my Life* — "I took nothing of his literally, I *believed* almost nothing" (xi. 110) — is inaccurate, a product of its time, when repudiation of Nietzsche's more hysterical doctrines was a necessary political act. In fact, Mann read and re-read Nietzsche,[45] he experienced through the categories of his thought and re-enacted its conflicts. Thus, having long taken Nietzsche as the patron of a critical intellectualism (even while for most contemporaries he was the inspiration of an anti-rational vitalist current of thought), Mann achieved a volte-face in 1914, abjured the ideals the intellectual Nietzsche had inspired — psychology, critical distance, "literature," and other super-ficialities — to support the vital interests of Germany's organic, allegedly non-political culture. This is debased Nietzsche, paralleling the contradic-tion which runs through all his thought, and Mann realized it. Reading his friend Ernst Bertram's book on Nietzsche,[46] which had grown up side by side with his own *Betrachtungen eines Unpolitischen*, he saw the affinity and asked whether Bertram could ever have understood Nietzsche and his "whole antithetical vital intensity" so well "if you had not, to some extent, experienced the great subject again, in some measure, on a small scale". The book gave Mann "an overview of my own life, insight into its necessity, an understanding of myself . . . a new desire to complete myself".[47]

To take self-comprehension to the lengths of identifying with an-other's life may seem strange, but had in this case some justification. What Mann had absorbed of Nietzsche helped to make him what he was, his uncertain allegiances repeated Nietzsche's, and Nietzsche was thus a proper medium through which to understand himself. Moreover, his actual knowledge of Nietzsche made a judicious comparison possible in retrospect. Yet neither of these things are essential before identification could take place. The prime factor was emotional, the product of Mann's early self-doubt and a sense of isolation. He needed support, confirmation, community — so acutely that he could go more than half-way to meet any potential provider of them.

Thus the impassioned entering into Schiller's situation in *Schwere Stunde* grew from the discovery in a centenary article that Schiller's difficulties, aims, limitations were akin to his own. The material sources of the story are slender.[48] But broad knowledge was not at issue, only an intensely felt sense of familiarity inspired by certain common experiences. In Joseph's words: "Was he known to you or not? He felt intimately familiar. That is more than 'known' " (v. 1429).

But it is also undeniably less, when so produced. Identification — quite unlike that with Nietzsche — becomes a narrowly focused self-recognition, an inspired jumping to conclusions. And this is essentially what it remains. "It is always a blessing to get away from one's individual-ity", Mann wrote in 1929, at the height of his interest in myth (xi. 409). But we must ask how far he ever did get outside himself and the pattern of his own preoccupations. Was his Goethe-image ever composed of elements other than those which self-concern (albeit sometimes a critical self-

concern) made sympathetically accessible? If it was not, then identification was identification with himself, self-reaffirmation through the
selected fragments of another's existence, as is hinted in Mann's observation "that everybody finds only himself in books".[49] As a generalization this
is overstated, as a confession it is significant. The tautology it implies
became the basis for Mann's essay-writing method. In 1932, asked to write
a book on Goethe, he wrote to Bertram "that I am as well or better versed
in this life than Emil Ludwig, and that my way of expressing it might well
have its justification, its legitimacy". Not because of knowledge, which
Mann disclaims (he has not actually read Emil Ludwig's book, and is
requesting Bertram's suggestions of what to read), but because he can
"speak from *experience* — about Goethe from experience: a mythical
confidence trick that might perhaps bridge the gap from 'Joseph' to
'Goethe' ".[50]

The problem is obvious: how does one know that one's experience is
relevant? The claim to empathy is the perfect circular argument. It is
inspired (or justified) by a favourite quotation from Nietzsche. In 1915
Mann wrote apropos *Der Tod in Venedig:*

> How naive most people are in the matter of confession! When I portray
> an artist, even a master artist, I do not mean 'myself'; I do not maintain
> that I am a master or even an artist — only that I *know* something about
> artistry and mastery. Nietzsche says somewhere: "If one wants to get an
> idea of art, let him make a few works of art." And he calls living artists
> heat-conducting media whose activity serves the purpose of "achieving
> the consciousness of the great masters." When I examine myself thor-
> oughly, I see that this and nothing else was always the goal of my
> creative work: to achieve the consciousness of the masters. . . . In
> working artistically, I gained access through knowledge to the existence
> of the artist, even the great artist, and I can say something about it[51]

This only restates the difficulty: will not the "great masters" be given
Thomas Mann's "consciousness" instead of the reverse? The passage does
not refer to Mann's essays, but it is demonstrably relevant to his method in
them, for it recurs in the manuscript notes for the Goethe essays of 1932:
"Nietzsche: 'If one wants to get an idea of art, let him make a few works of
art.' We are conductors of heat between greatness and today's world. Our
experience of it differs from that of the scholars because we relive the
experiences of the great. This is what 'friendship' with the great means".[52]
The only hint that Mann sensed the dubious nature of the assumption, its
possible arbitrary results, comes in the words from Degas which are at the
head of his notes: "A painting must be executed with the same feeling with
which a criminal performs his deed".[53]

Besides the logical limitation on Mann's approach, there is a material
one — his concentration on the biographical. In the letters just quoted, he
claimed understanding of "this *life*" and of "the *existence* of the great
artist". Mann's main quarry for the materials of his essays on Goethe was

Biedermann's great collection[54] of Goethe's conversations and the accounts left by contemporaries of meetings with Goethe. As in Mann's essays on other writers, what most differentiates them — their works — are relatively neglected here. The *Sprüche* (*Aphorisms*) are what he most often quotes — a type of work nearest to the writer's everyday life and his immediate human reactions. Without Mann's Princeton duties, it seems unlikely there would ever have been essays on *Werther* and *Faust*.

Such a predominantly biographical interest is common in writers, but does not normally lead to assertions of identity. In Mann, it bypasses essentials and blurs distinctions. Identification is facilitated — made easier, made more facile. The important differences between Mann and Goethe — in their relationship to nature, the status of their language as a response to experience, the originality of their thought — are either excluded, or minimized by drawing a Goethean phenomenon into the sphere of Mann's outlook. For example, the *Westöstlicher Divan* is regarded as parody; Goethe's connection with the learning of his time is turned into nothing but an exploitation of others' expertise akin to Mann's; Goethe's insight into recurrent experience is assimilated to Mann's ideas on myth.

How should we view Mann's accounts of Goethe, if not as objective illumination? Not as inadequate essays, nor as acts of presumption — querying the "identity" myth need not mean arguing Mann's inferiority to a shibboleth Goethe. A more positive view is possible. If, by the logic of empathy, it would take a great artist to know fully what the mind of a great artist is like, it is equally true that a great artist is the last person likely to achieve unclouded insight into the mind of his predecessors. His own themes and commitments will come between him and the object: he will use this for his own ends. Hence Mann's approach to Goethe via the concepts "the burgher way of life" and "the life of the litterateur" in 1932 — what better clues to the Mann-centredness of those essays! Hence too the "socialist" Nietzsche and the "democratic" Goethe of the thirties and forties.

I propose we take Mann's use of the past as a perfect case of what Nietzsche called "monumental history". It is often overlooked that Nietzsche saw uses as well as drawbacks in the historical consciousness. He set use against mere accumulation of knowledge, against the teams of fact-collectors ("les historiens de M. Thiers"), against the ideal of impersonal objectivity. The past could serve as an ally: "History belongs preeminently to the active and the powerful, to the man who fights a great battle, who needs examples, teachers, consolers, and who . . . cannot find them in the present". But Nietzsche is clear that such use demands simplifications: "How much variety must be overlooked so it may have this strengthening effect, how forcibly the individuality of the past must be constrained into a general form and broken at all the sharp corners and lines for the sake of conformity!". For nothing repeats itself exactly in history (short of a theory of eternal recurrence, which at this stage Nietzsche does no more than glance at). So the seeker for allies must dispense with "full iconic truthfulness", and may even come close to "free invention". There are periods, in fact, "that cannot distinguish in any way between a monumental past and a mythical fiction". At such times, the sources of history flow "like a grey uninterrupted stream, and only individual decorated facts stand out like islands". The epitome of Nietzsche's argument is: "Monumental history deceives through analogy". This is also an epitome of Mann's method.

This surely brings us nearer the truth about the nature of tradition than (for example) T. S. Eliot's insistence on the impersonality of writers' relations with the past.[56] For what we repeatedly observe as historians of literature is the way new personal imperatives wrench tradition from its course, impose new meanings on its components, and use these — reinterpreted, misinterpreted, turned into a symbol, an idol, an Aunt Sally — for present purposes.

It thus becomes pointless to test Mann's texts for their strict accuracy. We must simply understand them as uses of the past for self-expression, self-assertion, self-defence. On this principle what — aside from Mann's delight in intimate personal parallels — do we discover? In *Goethe's Career as Writer* we find a riposte to current anti-intellectualism, now become decidedly political, in the form of a claim that the most sacrosanct "poetic creator" was one of the accursed race of "professional writers". (The distinction, long resented and long combated by Thomas Mann, had long been a blunt instrument used against him in place of more subtle modes of criticism.) Mann's original title was even more provocative: "Goethe the writer".[57] The essay *Goethe as a Representative of the Bourgeois Age* was similarly political in over-all import, warning bourgeois society, from a Marxian historical viewpoint, that now was perhaps its last chance. How deeply this piece is rooted in political concern is clear from the way consecutive passages from the early drafts (which make up a single argument, obviously written *currente calamo*) went into the Goethe essay and the *Speech to an Audience of Workers* given in Vienna in the same year.[58] It is here that the socialist Nietzsche joins hands with the "future-oriented" Goethe as Mann's political allies. ("future/past" is the notation in this period for rational clarity and socialism on the one hand, reactionary irrationalism, fascism, obscurantism on the other.)

"Nietzsche the socialist" ideally illustrates Nietzsche's concept of monumental history. A great struggle was indeed in progress, with Nietzsche himself, the vitalist and critic of "devitalizing" intellect, as an authority claimed by Mann's antagonists. Why not turn the enemy's guns round on him (as Mann said of his use of myth in *Joseph*) and answer the jibes against socialist materialism with Nietzsche's "I entreat you, my brothers, remain faithful to the earth" (xi. 898)? History was not an anodyne seminar where rights and wrongs of interpretation could be analysed at leisure: allies were needed whose sheer authority would count.

Myth had to be opposed by myth, one historical hero by another (or by the same one viewed another way). Hindenburg had been put out as a latter-day "trusty Eckehart" (xii. 749); Stefan Zweig veiled his feelings behind the presentation of his *Erasmus*, which Mann regretted, because it implied the equation of Hitler with Luther (xii. 746). It is the "German desire for legend" (xii. 748) that both sides try to exploit, with historical analogizing sunk to an all-time low: against Nietzsche's words "who is most needed by all? He who commands great things" Mann notes bitterly "how tempting it must be for idiots to 'recognize' all that in the Hitler madness".[59]

This makes it quite clear that Mann understood the workings of "monumental history". But did he also grasp the fact that his own essay technique and beloved identifications were not different in kind? The word "recognize" might suggest he did. Yet in the post-war essay on Nietzsche (where incidentally he is still in places arguing with the pro-Nazi Nietzsche of Alfred Bäumler)[60] he calls the title of *On the Use and Abuse of History* "incorrect insofar as there is barely . . . any discussion of the uses of history—and all the more uses of its disadvantages" (ix. 688). True, it is the negative part of Nietzsche's account of history that gives Mann's essay its central theme; still, history's use is strangely ignored by one who had so effectively used it. A key to self-understanding is missed. Missed or suppressed? Mann's papers for the essay include some skeleton notes on *Vom Nutzen und Nachteil*, and among the sparse quotations one stands out: "Monumental past and mythical fiction cannot be distinguished at all".[61]

III

> Wer nicht von dreitausend Jahren
> Sich weiss Rechenschaft zu geben,
> Bleib im Dunkeln unerfahren,
> Mag von Tag zu Tage leben.

He who cannot account to himself for three thousand years—let him remain inexperienced in the dark; may he live from day to day.
>   Goethe, *Westöstlicher Divan.*

But can a writer ever fully understand himself? Perhaps not while there is an ounce of literary life left in him, since "understanding" automatically becomes a new creative act of some kind, and demands a new appraisal. Nevertheless, from early on Thomas Mann strove for the form of understanding usually left to critics and historians—trying to "place" himself, musing not so much about particular influences and traceable historical processes as about patterns of similarity which he had been unaware of while writing. "One does not know what one is doing", he wrote in 1954 to Max Rychner "but one is glad to find out, especially when one values it as highly as I do to be assured of standing within a firm tradition that reaches as far back as possible".[62] "Tradition" here means the perspective in which *Zauberberg* is seen to be "really" a quester-novel;[63] in which Mann can see the great medieval poets — parodists in an age which cared little for originality — as his essential predecessors;[64] in which it is significant that his works reproduce (deepest of satisfactions) the authentic patterns of myth.[65]

But Mann's pleasure in these things, and in the mirror of *Geistesgeschichte* which Fritz Kaufmann held up to his Narcissus-gaze (the term is Mann's own)[66] must not be confused with assertions about his creative process or the cultural range of his works as a part of their conscious communication. Of course, with sufficient goodwill connections and parallels and echoes can be found with almost anything; but perhaps for clarity's sake, as Hans Eichner suggested, "a helping of bad will"[67] is what we need. This may help us to watch Mann the artist at work — with a large enough volume of materials and a subtle enough range of means, in all conscience — but delighting in the effects rather than gaping at the erudition, drawing no undue inferences about the "cultural representative," whose role was dictated by factors outside his work.

We shall then be able also to allow him his "interestedness in intellectual history"[68] (the word bears two meanings) without necessarily taking over his conclusions: mindful of Robert Faesi's comment on *The Genesis of Doctor Faustus*, that Thomas Mann "is his own literary historian and relieves us of the bother — or doubles it".[69]

Notes

1. Quoted by Wolfdietrich Rasch, "Bertolt Brechts marxistischer Lehrer," in Rasch, *Zur deutschen Literatur seit der Jahrhundertwende*, Stuttgart 1967, p. 250.

2. Heinrich Mann, *Ein Zeitalter wird besichtigt*, Stockholm 1946, p. 231.

3. References in the text are to Thomas Mann, *Gesammelte Werke*, in 12 vols., Frankfurt 1960; and to *Briefe*, 3 vols., Frankfurt 1961-5.

4. R. A. Nicholls, *Nietzsche in the Early Works of Thomas Mann*, Berkeley 1955, p. 6.

5. Fritz Kaufmann, *Thomas Mann. The World as Will and Representation*, Boston 1957, p. xii.

6. Reinhard Baumgart, "Beim Wiederlesen Thomas Manns," in *Sinn und Form*, Sonderheft Thomas Mann, Berlin 1965, p. 178.

7. Herbert Lehnert, *Thomas Mann. Fiktion, Mythos, Religion*, Stuttgart 1965, p. 190.

8. For example, Mann seems to have made his first contact with Schiller's typology in his sources for *Schwere Stunde* (1905). The foundations of a typological outlook had been laid well before this under the influence of Nietzsche and of Merezhkovsky, whose *Tolstoi und Dostojewskij* Mann read about 1903. (His copy with annotations and date 1903 in Thomas-Mann-Archiv, Zürich, referred to henceforth as TMA.) As for Angelus Silesius, there is, for example, a quotation from him at a key point in the essay on Schopenhauer (ix. 556), but it is one taken from the pages of Schopenhauer Mann worked on for the essay (*Welt als Wille und Vorstellung*, 4. Buch, § 68, with annotations in Mann's copy).

9. Käte Hamburger, *Thomas Mann und die Romantik*, Berlin, 1932, p. 82.

10. Paul Weigand, "Thomas Mann's *Tonio Kröger* and Kleist's *Über das Marionetten-theater*," *Symposium*, 12 (1958).

11. e.g. *Also sprach Zarathustra*, erster Teil, "Vom Lesen und Schreiben"; vierter Teil, "Vom höheren Menschen" 19.

12. Ernst Bertram to Ernst Glöckner in *Thomas Mann an Ernst Bertram*, Pfullingen 1960, p. 214.

13. Jürgen Scharfschwerdt, *Thomas Mann und der deutsche Bildungsroman*, Stuttgart 1967, p. 30. The section is headed "Die erste Erzählung und ihr Traditionsbewusstsein" — surely almost a contradiction in terms.

14. Scharfschwerdt, op. cit., p. 15.

15. In *The Ironic German*, London 1957.

16. *Thomas Mann und sein Beruf*, Leipzig 1913, ch. 3.

17. It is evident from Mann's earliest notebook sketches for the novel that the pattern of decline through four generations was his immediate reaction to the problem of how to expand his original idea for a "Knabennovelle" about Hanno. See Paul Scherrer, "Bruchstücke der Buddenbrooks-Handschrift und Zeugnisse zu ihrer Entstehung 1897–1901," *Neue Rundschau*, 69 (1958).

18. It has been pointed out before, by Eberhard Lämmert in *Der deutsche Roman*, ed. B. von Wiese, Düsseldorf 1965, ii. 438, but without any probing of the assumptions which may have led to it.

19. Cf. the passage in *Der Bajazzo* (viii. 125) beginning: "Es gibt eine Art von Menschen, Lieblingskinder Gottes. . . ."

20. *Sämtliche Werke*, ed. Arthur Hübscher, Wiesbaden 1961, iii. 548.

21. Aside from the possible perverting influence of Wagner's *Tristan*, the whole idea may stem from two remarks of Nietzsche's on Schopenhauer and the importance of the age at which a philosophy is conceived (*Menschliches, Allzumenschliches*, ii. 271 and *Genealogie der Moral*, iii. 6). Mann refers to them in his later essay on Nietzsche (ix. 560). But conceiving a philosophy at an age when the erotic dominates is not at all the same as conceiving an erotic philosophy.

22. TMA Mp ix. 190, sheet 4. I wish to express my thanks to Frau Katja Mann for permission to publish passages from Thomas Mann's papers.

23. B. Biermann, "Thomas Mann and Goethe," in *The Stature of Thomas Mann*, New York, 1947, pp. 249, 251.

24. One cannot accept — for any writer, and certainly not for Thomas Mann — the equation "der beste Interpret, der Dichter selbst" proposed by E. Wirtz, "Zitat und Leitmotiv bei Thomas Mann," *GLL* 7 (1953), p. 128.

25. Herbert Lehnert, "Hans Castorps Vision," *Rice Institute Pamphlet* 47 (1960). Henceforth RIP.

26. Michael Mann, "Eine unbekannte 'Quelle' zu Thomas Manns *Zauberberg*," *GRM* 46 (1965).

27. Heinz Saueressig, *Die Bildwelt von Hans Castorps Frosttraum*, Biberach an der Riss 1967.

28. See especially Wolfdietrich Rasch, "Thomas Manns Erzählung 'Tristan,' " in Rasch, op. cit., with references (p. 306) to related work.

29. I.e. it is not enough to see (as Northrop Frye puts it) "the miscellaneous pile strung out along a chronological line" in such a way that "some coherence is given it by sheer sequence" (*Anatomy of Criticism*, Princeton 1957, p. 16).

30. Harry Levin, "The Tradition of Tradition," in *Contexts of Criticism*, Harvard University Press 1957, p. 63.

31. *The Great Tradition*, London 1948, repr. 1962, p. 19.

32. "Of a Providence and Future State," in *Essays Moral, Political, and Literary*, ed. Grose and Green, London 1882, ii. 112.

33. "Thomas Manns Goethe-Bild," *GR* 20 (1945), p. 181.

34. From Gunilla Bergsten, *Thomas Manns Doktor Faustus. Untersuchungen zu den Quellen und zur Struktur des Romans*, Uppsala 1963; Hans-Joachim Sandberg, *Thomas Manns Schiller-Studien*, Oslo 1965; and Hans Wysling, *Quellenkritische Studien zum Werk Thomas Manns* (Thomas-Mann-Studien, Band I), Berne 1967, esp. pp. 258-325.

35. A connection suggested by E. M. Wilkinson, "Aesthetic Excursus on Thomas Mann's *Akribie*," *GR* 31 (1956).

36. Mann told Stefan Zweig in 1920 that great criticism—he had Merezhkovsky in mind—could be more stimulating to him than primary literature. Criticism generally seems to have had this effect, even making direct inspection of the object superfluous, like the hearsay which could stimulate medieval courtships. The extreme case is James Joyce, who fascinated Mann as a phenomenon in the forties although he never read a word of his works. See Lilian R. Furst, "Thomas Mann's Interest in James Joyce," *MLR* 64 (1969).

37. *Les Mots*, Paris 1964, p. 57. "The playing at culture cultivated me in the long run" (Bernard Frechtman, trans., *The Words* New York: George Braziller, 1964, 72).

38. K. A. Meissinger, *Helena. Schillers Anteil am Faust*, Frankfurt 1935. TMA, with annotations.

39. Johannes Urzidil, "Patient und Kurgast Goethe," *Basler National-Zeitung*, 24. Mai 1936; unidentified cutting "Goethe als Wortschöpfer," reporting a public lecture by Professor Otto Pniower. The examples quoted in the report go into Mann's notes. Both items in TMA Mat. 5 (Materialien zu 'Lotte in Weimar'), nos. 5 and 33.

40. TMA Mp xi. 14, sheet 38.

41. Mann's copy, with a dedication dated 1905 and annotations, in TMA.

42. Opening paragraph of "The Classics and the Man of Letters."

43. Thomas Mann—Karl Kerényi, *Gespräch in Briefen*, Zurich 1960, p. 200. Kerényi's comments are relevant to our further discussion: "The old static concept of 'education' in terms of subject matter has long been outdated; it has also become morally unacceptable because it did not and still does not put up the slightest resistance against totalitarian attacks from the uneducated or the pseudo-educated".

44. Although Herman Meyer's chapter on Mann in *Das Zitat in der Erzählkunst*, Stuttgart 1967, studies use, it still makes rather much of the *poeta doctus*—despite reservations implicit in earlier chapters (e.g. on Rabelais, p. 52 and note).

45. Abundant internal evidence is supported by Mann's many discussions of Nietzsche's role and by his preserved Nietzsche collection, which shows a lifelong preoccupation with Nietzsche's thought. Especially the Naumann Grossoktavausgabe, which Mann acquired as it came out from 1895 on, shows intensive use in almost all volumes, with layers of annotation in the handwriting of different periods.

46. *Nietzsche, Versuch einer Mythologie*, Berlin 1918.

47. Ed. cit., p. 76.

48. See Sandberg, op. cit., ch. 3.

49. Note 3 for "Geist und Kunst," in Wysling, op. cit., p. 151.

50. Ed. cit., p. 172.

51. *Briefe an Paul Amann*, Lübeck 1959, p. 32.

52. TMA Mp. ix. 173, sheet 24. Mann's earliest use of the quotation also related to Goethe, though not yet to himself. In note 22 for 'Geist und Kunst' (Wysling, op. cit., p. 165) he wrote: "Hofmannsthal without much ado considers himself a sort of Goethe. We have 'achieved the consciousness of the great masters' (Nietzsche). Something likable in that. A wider sense of responsibility. A higher, more serious life".

53. TMA Mp ix. 173, sheet I.

54. Annotated copy in TMA. The pagination does not correspond to the page references in the MS. notes of 1932. It is clear Mann worked through these materials exhaustively over again in a replacement copy after the loss of most of his library in 1933.

55. This and following quotations from section 2 of *Vom Nutzen und Nachteil der Historie für das Leben*.

56. In the essay "Tradition and the Individual Talent."

57. TMA Mp ix. 180, sheet I.

58. TMA Mp ix. 173, sheets 47 ff.

59. In his copy of Josef Sommer, *Dionysos. Friedrich Nietzsches Vermächtnis*, Leipzig n.d., p. 71.

60. Much of Mann's preparatory work for the essay was done on vol. 4 of a 1931 Reclam edition. It contains Bäumler's selection from Nietzsche's works and introductory essays headed "Der Philosoph" and "Der Politiker." The pro-Nazi bias evident in these, especially the second, also affected the selection. Hence Mann was meeting the opposition on its own ground, and a comparison of his essay with Bäumler's text (e.g. ix. 695 and p. 57) shows how far Mann was arguing simultaneously with Nietzsche and with his intellectual progeny.

61. TMA Mp ix. 199, sheet I.

62. *Blätter der Thomas-Mann-Gesellschaft*, 7 (1967), p. 24.

63. Taking up a suggestion made in a university dissertation. See "Einführung in den 'Zauberberg,' " xi. 615.

64. In the source-material for *Der Erwählte*. See Wysling, op. cit., p. 290.

65. As Karl Kerényi several times assured him. See Mann-Kerényi, op. cit., e.g. p. 202.

66. See Br ii. 295: the "pleasure with which I looked at it was too meditative to call it vain — though, to be sure, a certain narcissism is probably inseparable from a life lived with consciousness and cultivation".

67. "Thomas Mann und die Romantik," in *Das Nachleben der Romantik in der modernen deutschen Literatur*, Heidelberg 1969, p. 156. Eichner shows very precisely how much Thomas Mann's thought, attitudes, and work differ from those of the Romantics: how much his use of Novalis in the essays of the twenties bends or even contradicts Novalis's meaning (monumental history again); and that what Mann understood by Romanticism had more to do with Wagner and Nietzsche than with any earlier phase of literary history.

68. The phrase occurs in a letter thanking Käte Hamburger for her book *Thomas Mann und die Romantik* (Br i. 323): at this point there also occurs the first semi-public (because to a critic) suggestion of Mann's "feeling of being of the same stamp" as Goethe.

69. Thomas Mann-Robert Faesi, *Briefwechsel*, Zürich 1962, p. 89.

The Decline of the West and the Ascent of the East: Thomas Mann, the Joseph Novels, and Spengler.

Helmut Koopmann*

To ask what persuaded Thomas Mann to write the Joseph novels is to ask anything but a positivistic question addressed to the chronology of a work. For in this case the question leads deeply into a relationship and a discussion, one to be sure that did not have many external repercussions. Regarding Thomas Mann's relationship to Oswald Spengler, as a rule only his essay "About the Doctrine of Spengler"[1] is known, along with a few marginal statements. On Spengler's side, no direct public reactions to Thomas Mann exist. Thus, it could appear as though the relationship of Mann to Spengler had been one-sided, clearly not uncritical, burdened with some resentment, but, as far as Mann was concerned, still an acquaintance of a peripheral nature, a product of the times, since Thomas Mann wrote about everything and everyone who could claim public interest in some fashion. On the other hand, there could barely be any mention of a relationship of Spengler to Thomas Mann, since there is, on the side of Spengler, almost nothing that could justify such a description, even if one were to conceive of it negatively, apart from a few private remarks. That Thomas Mann wrote about Spengler nonetheless, was, one might surmise then, the expression of a public, impersonal interest, one that appeared to be extinguished soon after. After publication of the first volume of *The Decline of the West*, Spengler was of course the talk of the town — that can be seen from the lively discussion, almost always critical, mostly carried on by philosophers and historians with an outsider,[2] one to be sure who, even though he had had some predecessors in the nineteenth century,[3] had stirred up the literary world to a degree that could not have been achieved by the latter or by the duly ordained representatives of the academic disciplines. And Thomas Mann, with his essay about Spengler's teaching, appears simply to have joined the debate as one almost expected of him by now — it would have been surprising had he not asked to be recognized in the face of the intensive discussion surrounding Spengler's work. He did, half from a self-imposed authorial duty, half presumably out of interest in the philosopher of decline.

Yet the surface appearance deceives, as so often with Thomas Mann, and one is well advised not to be satisfied with his public pronouncements about Spengler. There are two reasons to suspect that he was more deeply touched and affected by Spengler than was apparent to the outside world

*Translated by the editor from "Der Untergang des Abendlandes und der Aufgang des Morgenlandes," *Jahrbuch der deutschen Schillergesellschaft* 24 (1980):300–331. Reprinted by permission.

from the number of publications and statements. For one, there is the extraordinary assessment that he conceded to Spengler's book as a literary-philosophical achievement. For him, *The Decline of the West* is one of the great "intellectual novels," comparable to Ernst Bertram's Nietzsche book or Gundolf's biography of Goethe, and since we know how highly Thomas Mann valued Bertram at the time, this association does indicate considerable importance. Also, it is striking with what touchiness and irritation Thomas Mann reacted to the appearance and presentation of Spengler. That, according to Mann, he belongs to those modern figures who admittedly teach what is not their business can still pass, but that he appears as a "snob" and "nasty," as an "iron scholar," as "Herr Spengler," that his teaching is, for Thomas Mann, totally "*vieux jeu, bourgeois* through and through," permeated by a domineeringly apodictic loveless-ness, compared to which the doctrine "of a Marx [is] mere blue-sky idealism" — all of this shows that Mann was personally affected in a way that is unusual with a man who usually would much prefer to say something friendly than something hostile.

Thus, if one wants to explore this situation thoroughly, it is a good idea also to search through the periphery of the Spengler essay — and that means the Joseph novels. Whoever occupies himself with them soon asks himself what it really was that brought Thomas Mann to the material and the lengthy working out that he was to give it. And since we know that the novels frequently have essayistic companions in Mann's work, we may well suspect that the Joseph novels might possibly have something to do with the Spengler essay, or vice versa: it is precisely for the period of World War I and the twenties that this "rule" of the essayistic accompaniment to the great novels holds. Hence, if only for that reason, it is wise not to push the Joseph novels aside without further ado in a consideration of Thomas Mann and Spengler, though the chronology of the novel at first reveals nothing of relationships of this sort. Thomas Mann's preparations for the tetralogy, as we have known for quite some time, began in the winter of 1923 from a totally different impetus, when he more or less accidentally saw a portfolio of pictures illustrating the Joseph story. The Munich painter who had visited Thomas Mann at the time asked him for an introduction to his collection of paintings, and Thomas Mann himself testifies in the *Sketch of My Life* that he had checked back into the old family bible and was thoroughly amenable to fulfilling the wish of the painter.[4] He wrote the latter that these paintings preserved the "charming tale" only too well and that they conveyed much of its "amiability." In any case, there was nothing then to indicate that Thomas Mann might have had any further plans for the Joseph story. All his life, he was approached for prefaces and introductions, and we are familiar with his willingness and his friendly but, in the final analysis, noncommittal compliance when faced with things of the sort. In this case, Thomas Mann's epithets already argue for such an initial indifference, for an inner lack of interest in this material. Is the tale of Joseph, with its incredible history of premeditated fratricide, descent into the pit, and last minute rescue, the Egyptian episode that knows not only the heights, really only a "charming tale"? Is it, touching as it may be but surely also cruel and in any case unique, actually "amiable"? It is true that Thomas Mann could refer to Goethe who also had pronounced the Joseph story "most charming." But that involves downgrading the story again to a mere good-naturedly harmless legend that happened to be interesting because there was something humane and kind about it. And it is only too characteristic how Thomas Mann saw the pictures of the painter that illustrated that story: "a nice graphic display." What he had to say to the Joseph story and its artistic presentation then was clearly easy praise, and confirms the impression that Thomas Mann took up the Joseph story once more for the sake of his acquaintance with the painter and by no means on its own account. But then, a remarkable coincidence produced an invitation to a Mediterranean voyage, and we have a confession of Thomas Mann from February 1925 that makes it clear that it was after all not to be just a matter of the preface to the charming Joseph story. On this occasion he notes that it was mostly Egypt that interested him:[5] "I am going to take a look at the desert, the pyramids, the Sphinx; I accepted the invitation for that reason because it might be useful for certain, as yet somewhat shadowy, plans that I secretly cherish." We know that this is the actual beginning of the Joseph novels, or rather the Joseph novella — because originally that was all it was to be, and Thomas Mann immediately added, downright defensively, that in the meantime he still had a lot to do — and plans for all sort of things followed. But not much later, it was the novel after all that he was working at, and on 1 August 1926 he could already report: "I am deep in the preparations for a small, difficult, but thoroughly enticing novel *Joseph in Egypt*. I am going to retell, realistically and humorously, the biblical story itself."[6] Further explanations about the theme follow.

At that time, to be sure, Thomas Mann did not get beyond shadowy sketches, and it is difficult at this point to discern consistent fundamental structures. Occasionally, there is talk of merely constructing "histories," and here Joseph appears next to "Erasmus" and "Philip."[7] But there is something that strikes one from the outset and that has to do with the repeated comments regarding the humorous foundation of the novel. "A sort of essayistic or humorously pseudoscientific laying of foundations," it is called in December 1926, and Thomas Mann emphasized that he was "having fun," "more than with anything else ever," that he was entertaining himself thoroughly with it. And shortly thereafter, we hear again that everything had to be done "in a light, humorously intellectual way."[9] By 1928, there were more explicit comments. "It is a novel with essayistic retardations, a juxtaposition and intertwining of epic and research, of the scenic and the playfully scientific that I find highly entertaining. . . . The subject of the book is the incarnation of myth; . . . its project: to prove that one can be mythical in a humorous manner."[10] Claims that the whole is a highly cheerful tale continue through the following months and years. Thus, in the introduction to a reading from *Joseph* in Vienna still in 1928, we read: "The rather amusing difficulty is that I tell of people who do not know quite clearly who they are, that is, whose sense of self is founded much less on a clear distinction between past and future in their moment of existence, but rather on their identity with their mythical type. . . ."[11] The red thread of statements that the novel is extremely humorous can be followed far. Twenty years afterward, there is mention yet again of "the humorous song of humanity."[12] And, in the same place: "It is true that my way of dealing with myth was fundamentally more closely related to Goethe's "Classic Walpurgis Night" than to Wagner's pathos."[13] And, going even beyond this remark about the humorous atmosphere, Mann writes about the fourth volume of the tetralogy that it was "the brightest and merriest of them all."[14] Two years before his death Thomas Mann still declares that around the figure of Joseph "there doubtless hovered a peculiar humor perceptible by the feelings of every reader."[15] Thomas Mann, to be sure, often spoke in principle of himself as a humorist and gave examples from other of his novels. But, after all, it should astound everyone that the Joseph novel was for Thomas Mann a humorous novel, whatever one might understand under the concept of humor. Surely it could not have been merely the happy ending, for there are enough tragic or nearly tragic moments. After all, Thomas Mann himself stated in his late utterance about humor and irony that Jacob was "a highly pathetic figure." He was only too conscious of the somber constellations in the life of his Jacob—but he coated them all with humor, even the scene "which by the nature of things should absolutely be tragic," that is, that description of Jacob's lament for the supposedly dismembered favorite son.

But no matter how much Thomas Mann said about the humorous mood of the Joseph novel, the question remains—how did he arrive at it? Does it all amount to a humorous Bible critique or just "a droll exactitude" after all, as Thomas Mann himself referred to it in the introduction to his Vienna reading? There have always been humorous aspects to his work, in *Buddenbrooks* as well as in *The Magic Mountain*, and every reader is aware of that, though some of these humorous interpolations, such as the description of a schoolday from the life of little Hanno, are anything but humorous—in this case proving to be the sharpest criticism of the period, culture, and politics of the Wilhelminian era. There is not too much to be gained from Thomas Mann's own pronouncements. He did occasionally speak of the epic spirit of art as of a "spirit of irony,"[16] but then he also said quite clearly that he judged the humorous effects of his art even more highly than the intellectual smile of irony. All that is not very stringent and does not fundamentally help to explain why the Joseph novel turned into a humorous one for him from the outset, or was in any case conceived as such. Surely there are humorous scenes in every novel by Thomas Mann.

But they certainly do not constitute the truly humorous content of a work. And thus the question arises precisely with the Joseph novel as to the source of the humorous structure and mood. *Buddenbrooks*, to be sure a work of "pessimistic humor,"[17] deals with decline, death, and fall, and in *The Magic Mountain*, in spite of humorous situations, the themes of conflict and death are carried to extremes. Against all his claims, it is only with great reservations that one can characterize Thomas Mann as a natural humorist.

I would like to delay a little the question as to what could have played a role in determining or causing the humorous key of the Joseph novel and look for other striking elements of the genesis, for Mann's points of orientation. Of course, one cannot accept the accidental meeting with the Munich painter of the Joseph story as the full explanation for the inner direction of the novels, much less the no less accidental sea voyage through the Mediterranean and up the Nile. Surely it was not creative boredom that brought him to *Joseph* — Mann actually never knew that state, and the years from 1924 on are tightly packed with public appearances. One of Mann's early essay volumes was entitled *The Order of the Day*, and in those years he met such demands only too willingly and too often. From there, no bridges lead to the Joseph material, in either direction. But there are a few statements from these years that do bring us closer to an answer to the question of why Thomas Mann really wrote the Joseph novels. Perhaps the clearest briefing about Mann's intentions and inclinations was the one he gave to this Vienna audience of 1928 to which he read from *Joseph*, and those were in any case far removed from any order of the day. There he confessed that, with his novels, he had not been guided by great examples but rather by contrasts, antitypes. He said to his Vienna listeners: "Before I started to write, I reread *Salammbô* to see how it cannot be done any more today. Give me no archaeological brocade! Nothing learned and consciously artistic and no forced antibourgeois cult of crass exoticism! The archaeological is one attraction among others — decidedly one of the least effective, least decisive ones. The old East attracts me, I have been especially drawn to Egypt and its culture since boyhood. Really, I know more than a little about it, I made myself an Orientalist the way I was a medical man at the time of *The Magic Mountain*."[18] That sounds like a very personal involvement, and at first sight it would seem that a childhood interest in the East brought him to the Joseph material. But he who would be satisfied with this answer would have solved the question about the genesis of the Joseph novels quickly but very insufficiently. For, in spite of this confession, one cannot really say that Thomas Mann was an Orientalist from the outset. Actually, what he tells us is nothing positive but something negative: he is not really telling us what has brought him back to the Egyptians, but he does tell us very well what he did *not* want — Flaubert was not a pattern to be followed but rather a negative, warning example, and the rejection of an academically oriented archaeology was more important than the positive commitment to Egypt. To be sure, Flaubert too had in 1858 gone to the scene of his story like Thomas Mann to Egypt, but *Salammbô* drew other conclusions. Flaubert's novel reveals the senselessness and destructiveness of history; Thomas Mann, however, yet again counters that negative novel with something diametrically opposed — an optimistic novel, serene and humane: history manifests itself as its own fulfillment, not as a destructive power.

Flaubert and his novel do not really have much to do with it, and Thomas Mann did not discuss it any further. Still, these pointers are extraordinarily important because they indicate that Thomas Mann, from the very outset, wrote the Joseph novels out of a motivation that was wholly new for him: he did not see himself as following a tradition but conceived the novel in protest. We have before us a different, changed process of genesis. One could hardly say of the *Buddenbrooks* that it was written in opposition to an existing novel. Later, in his speech about Lubeck as a way of life and thought, Thomas Mann made it quite clear to all his public to what extent he had then been dependent on positive rather than negative models: the art of the Goncourts, he said, had got him going in the first place, and "Scandinavian family novels were available as further models, appropriate because it was after all a family history, and one in a commercial town yet, close to the Scandinavian sphere, that I had in mind."[19] And what he composed was indeed written in the manner of the novels of Alexander Kielland and Jonas Lie. This was a productive, positive dependence; Thomas Mann's self-understanding developed from a sense of direct succession. For *Death in Venice*, the case is similar: it is true that, apart from Plato, we do not know of any literary models, but we are familiar with the factual fidelity of the novella and Mann's dependence on reality itself, not the least on his own biography. In any case, the story is in no way an antistory, just as *Tonio Kröger* was not written against anything. All of it, Thomas Mann has said, had been "simply taken from reality." For *The Magic Mountain* that is still to some degree true, as the novel lacks an antinomial reference, and is clearly located in definite traditions: Mann himself pointed out to what extent his novel, consciously or unconsciously, was indebted to the Grail motif, and he determined with a certain pride that the problems of the novel had been identical with those of the educated public of the time. Whether we read the work as a novel of education or as a parody of one,[20] *The Magic Mountain* still remains in the realm of a tradition that by its very nature invited a considerable breadth of variation in its application. Now, however, there appears to be a radical change. The conception of the Joseph novels is unthinkable without a stance of opposition, and this is not a matter of externals. Nor is the antinomial structure by any means exhausted by the reversal of the *Salammbô* orientation. Rather, the concept of a historical novel told antihistorically belongs to the origin of *Joseph*, and this was in reaction not only to Flaubert but to any tendency toward historicization at all, thus against treating history as history. That the latter made you sick and incapable of life was of course no news: Nietzsche had already said it in his *Thoughts out of Season* in the reflections about "The Uses and Abuses of History." But at this time Nietzsche's influence on Thomas Mann is not to be assessed too highly. The background to Thomas Mann's dehistoricization of history lies rather in the contemporary protest against historical perspectives and beyond that against the historical novel in general. "I would like to tell these pious histories," he writes, "tell them as they *really* happened, or as they might have happened if . . ."[21] In the conclusion, there is the poetological justification of his enterprise and at the same time an indication of that which, in spite of any claim to exactitude, separates the novel from a purely historical narrative: the realism is merely a fictitious one, and it is clearly distinct from the realism of the historiographers. It was precisely this, however, that made the optimistic stance possible in the first place for, in the retelling of the biblical myth of Joseph and his life, Thomas Mann leaped the barriers of the biblical tradition and hence of historiography precisely at the points where the tale he was telling in such detail demanded exegesis. And this exegesis was life-oriented and optimistic about the future. What was told here was, for the first time in Thomas Mann's work, no story of decline and fall, like the *Buddenbrooks, Death in Venice, The Magic Mountain, Tonio Kröger,* and many of the early novellas, but rather the surprising opposite: the story became a promise and a euphoric revelation. The matter of religious history, as Thomas Mann reported while he was still at work on the Joseph novels, was one of the main attractions of the material for him, and he was hoping that Joseph, "the young hopeful of the young Hebraic monotheism," would be good company for *his* pharoah, "this Echnaton who was so boldly gifted in religion."[22] And so Thomas Mann went on relating optimistically — from polytheism as a historically older, not very humanistic and actually contemptible phase in human history, to monotheism as the religion of the future.

This process went far beyond Flaubert — so far that we can hardly consider *Salammbφ* as a *punctum saliens* in the genesis of *Joseph. Joseph and his Brothers* is not an answer to Flaubert, and thus the question remains — what might have persuaded Thomas Mann to create this ahistorical historical novel. One explanation that is often given and that could rely on Mann's own pronouncements is that here he took myth out of the hands of the fascistic obscurantists and restructured it in order to counter Alfred Rosenberg's threatening *Myth of the Twentieth Century* with a newer, better, more humanistic concept of myth. This surely applies to the later phase of the Joseph novels, especially for the Egyptian parts, but it does not concern the original conception and the first part, especially since Rosenberg's book only appeared in 1930.

It is of course always possible to argue from the personal aspect to explain the optimistic, de-historicizing character of the Joseph novels: it is too obvious a possibility to be overlooked that Thomas Mann depicted himself in his hero Joseph in some fashion. The possibility that he had overcome the personal crisis to which the Aschenbach story so clearly testified and was again able to produce an idealized hidden self-portrait cannot be dismissed, though it cannot be proved unambiguously in the text. The autobiographical optimism, veiled in various ways in the text, is new and evidently connected with Mann's changed postwar self-perception, his socialization as an author, his anchor in the present. Still, that does not explain much. It would finally be conceivable that the psychoanalytic optimism of the years following the turn of the century makes itself heard again in literature and has appropriated history. There are some indications of the latter. Already in 1930 we read in Thomas Mann's *Sketch of My Life*: "Advances in knowledge, be it into the darkness of prehistory or into the night of the unconscious, explorations that touch each other at a certain point and coincide, have mightily extended anthropological understanding into the depths of time or, which is actually the same, down into the depths of the soul, and the curiosity for the earliest and oldest contacts with humanity, the prerational, mythical, the history of faith has been awakened in all of us."[23] This is the perspective of an enlightened psychoanalysis that still believed that the soul really could be fully explored — here we see a late phase of Freud's influence as well as an enlightened attitude to history that fundamentally still derives from historicism; Freudianism and a psychologized understanding of history have here formed a peculiar symbiosis, one that is nonetheless very characteristic of the twenties, and that in spite of Thomas Mann's rejection of all learned fussing with history.

All of this, however, is not quite enough to motivate this remarkable faith in history in its productive and humanizing force. For it all neither managed to influence Thomas Mann seriously nor provoked him to a defense. What was it, then, that provided the actual impetus for the writing of the novel, what was the cause of the insistence on humanitarian optimism, the faith in the progress of humanity and the apparently indestructible hope for the moral and religious advancement of humanity, regardless of Flaubert? For *that* the picture portfolio probably inspired Thomas Mann as little as the voyage to Egypt: presumably both had such a strong effect only because there was already a predisposition toward a Joseph story to be read optimistically. And since we know how much Thomas Mann always saw himself as part of a tradition, here to be sure more in resistance to a position, it is probably there that the key is to be found for the understanding of the original conception and the answer to the seemingly simple question of what brought him to the Joseph novel in the first place. It is no different in the later work to follow. Thomas Mann's Goethe novel is the reversal of the legend of Lotte and at the same time the expression of his effort to reintroduce a truer tradition; the *Faustus* novel is, beyond the Nietzsche model, an attempt to counter current ideas of the Faust legend and to see Faustus not as the alien magician but as one's own inner fate. Would it not be reasonable to suspect that something similar already lurks behind the Joseph novel?

With that, we have come to the *nervus rerum*. "Just nothing self-consciously artistic and learned," Thomas Mann had written, nothing historically negative and merely historical, nothing just antiquarian and, especially no stories of decline, projections in the history of religion, and nothing backward-looking—this demand and authorial maxim stands only too clearly behind the first part of the Joseph novel and behind Thomas Mann's proclamations about it. "One has to know how to read the negative positively," Thomas Mann once said in another connection,[24] and we are approaching this requirement quite closely after the survey of the possibilities and impossibilities in the genesis of the Joseph novels. A key to an essential influence on the Joseph novels has not been named yet, but it emerges distinctly from the working schedule of 1924. It was in the winter of 1923–24 that Thomas Mann's attention was first directed to a new interest in the Joseph material; on 9 March 1924 his essay about Spengler appeared in the Munich *Allgemeine Zeitung*; in November, *The Magic Mountain* was published, in March that voyage to Egypt took place that was to have an important mediating function for the Joseph novels.

Of course the dates in themselves carry no conviction, and surely one will not be able to deduce a relationship of dependence of the Joseph novels on Spengler and his great works from them alone. But the familiarity and the debate with Spengler was of longer standing, and it is worthwhile to trace it some in order to see what Spengler really has to do with Thomas Mann and his Joseph stories. The first indication dates from 12 May 1919, and it so happens that the Joseph story and Spengler appear side by side in a letter to the German philologist Philipp Witkop in which Thomas Mann thanks him for a pointer: "*Jaäkob* made a great impression on me too. I do not know Spengler as yet, but have made a note of him."[25] Shortly thereafter Mann did read Spengler's *Decline of the West*. There is a reminder of that reading in a letter to Gustav Blume of 5 July 1919; it demonstrates the extent to which Mann occupied himself with Spengler and shows that he drew conclusions relevant to his own time: "One has to get into a contemplative mood, and a fatalistically serene one, to read Spengler and to understand that the Anglo-American victory seals and delivers the destiny of Western civilizing, rationalizing, utilitarianizing, which is the fate of every aging culture.' "[26] This is said quite in the sense of Spengler and characterizes Thomas Mann's apocalyptic mood after World War I — but it is certainly also a very first attempt to moderate the fatalism through serenity, even though it was more a verbal declaration of intention than an expression of a serious critique. By 1922, however, Thomas Mann's rejection of Spengler has been fixed. Presumably Mann at the time had access to the second, revised edition of *The Decline of the West*. For him,

Spengler is now no more than "the clever ape" of Nietzsche[27] — and he is to remain that for ten years. After 1932, there is mention of "the detestable Nietzsche-parodist Spengler."[28] It is only in 1922 that the public pronouncements of Thomas Mann about Spengler set in, and here we can see something of the negative dependence that apparently characterized Thomas Mann's relationship to Spengler. The speech "The German Republic" of this year also reveals the story of Thomas Mann's attraction to Spengler which then was to become enmity, as well as the reasons for Mann's extreme rejection of Spengler. They are of the same kind as those of the teller of the Joseph novels: the unbounded pessimism of Spengler's doctrine against which Thomas Mann revolted. He speaks admiringly of Novalis: "What a bold contrast to that other teaching about nature and history that is so full of a spurious inexorability with which a clever head recently shocked us and according to which "humanity" is once again an empty word and a nonthought, and history is nothing but the life process of biological entities called cultures that is predetermined by inhuman forces and proceeds according to iron laws."[29] This already contains the whole contradiction: Mann must have interpreted Spengler's works as an antihumanistic polemic, and it is clear that it was most of all Spengler's pessimism that bothered him. All that is confirmed by what follows. Mann's appraisal "in itself" is only too laudatory: an "intellectual novel, reminiscent of Schopenhauer's *World as Will and Idea* in its musical construction." But he had had a revelation that Spengler's cultural prophecies were not a polemical means of preventing certain cultural developments but that Spengler had meant it all literally and seriously, and it was this that necessitated for Mann a break with a cultural philosophy that he perceived as strictly inhumane. He wrote: "In truth one can prophesy a thing like 'civilization,' according to Spengler the biologically inevitable final stage of every culture, and now of the 'Western' one — not in order that it should come but rather in order that it should *not* come, thus preventively, in the sense of an intellectual exorcism; and I had thought that that was the case here. But when I found out that this man wanted to have his prophecy of calcification in dead earnest and straight and that he was instructing young people in this sense . . . — then I turned away from all this animosity and put his book away from my eyes in order not to have to admire that which is noxious and deadly."[30]

What follows is merely a working out of this position: it can be found in the first of the "Letters from Germany" in *Dial*, an almost verbatim repetition of that which had first and foremost awakened Thomas Mann's fear and disgust. The fact that Spengler's book is mentioned first when Mann "would like to report, off and on, about the cultural life" of his country is significant in itself and clearly signals his passionate interest in Spengler's book, even though it was couched externally in disinterest and an anxious defense against Spengler's ideas. The effect of Spengler, writes Thomas Mann, had been "by far the most sensational"[31] — not only in and of itself but apparently in terms of Mann's reaction. His embarrassment is also evident in the absence of a real discussion of Spengler's thoughts, or even—his usual practice—of a simple reporting. Instead, Thomas Mann polemicizes against Spengler, speaks of the fatal Spengler, of "defeatists of humanity"[32] and of the latter's peculiarly disturbing appearance,[33] of the "snob" and of his ridicule of the intellect,[34] and still he cannot deny to what extent he has conducted the debate with Spengler in terms of a personal self-defense. This he freely admits, as he writes at the end: "It is a revelation of the force of a book in which I do not believe that it seduced me into exceeding, in its discussion, the space offered me in such friendly fashion." This is no harmless *captatio benevolentiae* but dead earnest; Thomas Mann must have perceived Spengler's ideas as a downright mortal threat to his own. In 1924, followed the essay for German readers "On the Teaching of Spengler"—which was in many places taken over from the American *Dial* report, word for word, unchanged in attitude toward Spengler. The concluding pointer to the strangely fascinating powers of the work is absent. But Mann's position is even more rigid—as he names Spengler "among the many modern figures who, in a disagreeable manner, teach what they have no right to teach."[35] And after that there is still that "detestable Nietzsche-parodist Spengler" of 1932—an interim closing pronouncement, perhaps even more crushing than Thomas Mann's comments a decade before. The Joseph novels represent the more extensive closing remark, one that tried to counter everything that Mann felt obligated to consider inimical to culture and humanity in Spengler. This has not been recognized up to now by the researchers of Thomas Mann; there is no mention of Spengler in Herbert Lehnert's extensive essays about Mann's preparations for the Joseph novels.[36]

At that time, Thomas Mann probably was not interested in specific aspects of the Spengler work. The overall perspective seemed all the more problematic. Spengler considered the metaphysical ground of the West as exhausted and civilization as the "inescapable *fate* of a culture":[37] "Civilizations are *the most extreme* and *the most artificial* conditions of which a higher kind of man is capable. They are an ending; they follow becoming as that which has been, they follow life as death, development as rigidity." Propositions like these must have concerned Mann as much as Spengler's statement finding that this final phase of a culture was inevitable. Actually, such thoughts were not unfamiliar to him. For he knew pretty much all of this from Nietzsche's *Use and Abuse of History*. But what appeared there as a possibility and a challenge, that is, a pagan life not grounded in history, was negated in Spengler, and what was seen by Nietzsche as a possibility for life thus became an impossibility. Thomas Mann wrote his *Joseph* against all of that; and the structure of the novel makes it thoroughly clear to what extent the Joseph story is directed against Spengler. It is not just that Mann, like Spengler, traveled into the early times of human culture; Mann's central concept of *blessing* became a reversal of Spengler's death sentence on culture. *Blessing*, the promise pregnant with the future, in the course of the novel became nothing less than the opposition to Spengler's idea of *fate*. History, which for Spengler under the influence of nineteenth-century ideas such as those of Ernst von Lasaulx was a dismal cycle, in the Joseph novels becomes progress and fulfillment; the self is not dissolved, as with Spengler, but represents the promise of a future in the phase of nomadic and shepherd life; and against Spengler's linear meaning of "once upon a time" Thomas Mann set up a double sense of a "mixture of legend and annunciation."[38] If myth was, for Spengler, something past stemming from the early stage of culture, then for Mann it was also possible in the present. Behind it all, one can discern that it was also a matter of defending Nietzsche against his clever ape; Thomas Mann protects Nietzsche against his recalcitrant disciple.

To be sure, this does not mean that Mann has not taken over any insights from Spengler. Perhaps the clearest case is the concept of *care*. Spengler had characterized the high culture of Egypt as an incarnation of caring for the future[39] and had even spoken of "careful state formations"; what was Egyptian for Spengler was the "embracing care for lasting economic connections"[40] and hence also the overcoming of a lighthearted individualism. In the Egyptian parts of Mann's novel, we find similar themes in the care for the afterlife of the dead as well as in providing for the economy. Joseph appears in the novel as "a man of provision and distribution," as "master of the long view,"[41] and his inauguration as the supreme economic administrator has the tone of Spengler's description of the providing care. But here already, Mann has restructured Spengler's determinations, insofar as they influenced him at all. Jacob appears as the caring and forward looking one, and it is Joseph who plans the new economic order, not an Egyptian; here too Thomas Mann has transferred that which according to Spengler is characteristic of Egyptians into that which is more deeply true for him in human history, thus changing the mere worry about the future after Joseph's successes into something like the fulfillment of blessing, and, finally, he is not guided by the characterizations of Spengler but by the Bible as a book about humanity. It is part and parcel of the paradoxical nature of this relationship that Spengler had prepared this view in featuring care as a shared "feature of Egypt and the West" and thus not a characteristic of Egyptian culture alone. Doubtless this made it easier for Mann to transfer the caring attitude of the Egyptians onto the Israelites, although in the final analysis Spengler's conclusions were turned into their opposites as a result, since the Egyptians of the novel were incapable of precisely that which Spengler had attributed to them.

We can only guess at what set Mann so violently against Spengler as he increasingly saw himself as the opposite pole and as he, in his Joseph novel, wrote a sort of rise of the East against Spengler's *Decline of the*

West. It would appear that in itself the mood of decline and fall would have been welcome and familiar to him; after all, in his early novellas and novels he had written nothing less than stories of decline and had told of civilized matters in the manner of Spengler. What connected him to the latter beyond that was the common critical attitude toward the "merely civilizing." Most of all, however, they shared the autobiographical approach in writing and presentation. In the foreword to the 1922 edition, Spengler said it clearly enough when he wrote about the "thinker" and thus about himself: "He has no choice. He thinks as he must think, and for him the truth is finally that image of his world with which he was born. It is something that he does not invent but discovers in himself. It is himself once more, his being put into words, the meaning of his personality formed into a doctrine, unchangeable for life because it is *identical* with his life."[42] Thomas Mann too could have said it of himself, and has said, thus or similarly. There are secret identities between Spengler and Thomas Mann, and it might have been this kinship that Thomas Mann recognized and feared in 1924. We will see that this kinship goes deeper. As Thomas Mann saw his works and especially *The Magic Mountain* on which he was still working, Spengler also conceived of his work in 1917 as "a great commentary to a great epoch under whose sign the leading ideas were formed."[43] And the conclusion of Spengler's foreword to the 1922 edition where he writes about his main idea could just as well have been written by Thomas Mann, at least in its content: "It belongs to the whole era; unconsciously, it acts on the thinking of all, and it is only the accidental private version with its weaknesses and advantages without which philosophy is impossible that constitutes the fate—and the happiness—of an individual."[44] When around this time Thomas Mann said that he only needed to speak of himself in order to give expression to the era in general, then it is precisely the same authorial experience that Spengler formulated as demand and description. Beyond that, both share several intellectual ancestors. Spengler did not hide this ancestry and confessed to two clearly in the foreword: "Finally, I feel compelled to mention the names of those to whom I owe almost everything: Goethe and Nietzsche. I get my method from Goethe, my approach to problems from Nietzsche, and if I am to sum up my relationship to the latter, then I would say: from his view, I have made an overview."[45] Goethe and Nietzsche were fixed stars in Thomas Mann's sky as well, and he saw that clearly, guarding himself yet again, as late as 1936, against the unpleasant association with Spengler, even though only privately: "What made him so repugnant to me (after the initial impact of his chief work) was precisely a certain similarity of origin and intellectual interest between us: he too had taken over from Nietzsche primarily the sense for 'decline'—he was mainly interested in the decline of his cultural growths—and I remember well that occasional comparisons were made between *The Decline of the West* and *Buddenbrooks* upon the publication of the former."[46] In spite of his aversion to

Brother Spengler, Thomas Mann could not very well go against his own roots, but later he did manage to differentiate very distinctly his Nietzsche-reception against that of his annoying rival in the portrayal of decadence. What particularly disturbed him in Spengler was the latter's "mistaken contempt of human freedom." As early as 1924 in the Spengler essay Thomas Mann had expressed this, in voicing strong protest against the lovelessness of the Spenglerian presentation and the "lack of respect for the human." But the peculiar kinship still remained despite all these protests, and it was visible, at least for Mann himself. It is this that may explain not only the long persistence of the debate with this philosophy of history *sub specie mortis*, but also the irritability and acrimony with which it was carried on — like the later one with another "Brother," that is "Brother Hitler." This identity extends still one step further, to answering the question about the meaning of one's own activity. Thomas Mann had conceived of his *Considerations of a Nonpolitical Man* as community service; Spengler closes his foreword with the sentence: "I only have one wish to add — that this book may be too unworthy when set beside the military achievements of Germany."[47] It was in the same year, 1917, that the *Considerations of a Nonpolitical Man* were essentially completed. On the one hand, civilization, in the wake of Nietzsche, is seen as the final destination of culture by Spengler; on the other, Thomas Mann's attacks on the "littérateur." The differences are of degree, not of principle.

Seen from such a perspective, it is downright incomprehensible, at least at first glance, what it was that separated Thomas Mann so dramatically from Spengler. The explanation can be found in Mann himself and is easily discernible from the vantage point of his change as described in *Considerations of a Nonpolitical Man*. It is a change toward social awareness, to the representative role of the author, and away from the merely artistic; this change was complete by 1922, and this makes it clear what else Mann was fighting when he was fighting Spengler: a point of view of his own, since surmounted. With *The Magic Mountain* too Thomas Mann had thought of himself as a writer of his time, and the end of the novel at least indicates the possibility of overcoming the longing for death and the mood of decline. In 1922, in his speech "The German Republic," he interpreted his own novel, in only slightly veiled terms, when he wrote: "It could be the object of a novel of education to show that, finally, the experience of death is an experience of life, that it leads to *the human*."[48] This novel appeared two years later, and even then, in the summer of 1922, the course of *The Magic Mountain* had been set; Thomas Mann had got as far as the next to last chapter of the novel, and in 1922 it was clear to him that he had gone through a metamorphosis of the spirit "starting with a sympathy with death and ending with the decision to serve life."[49] That, for him, was the breakthrough to the "positive," to humanity, to politics, to the actual juridical reform of the republic, to a new meaning for political and national life, the opposite of an "undignified decline of the individual within the general." From this vantage point, the message of Spengler must have sounded very disturbing and must have once again presented Mann with the whole decline business of a phase left behind. For a writer who had stated, "I believe that I need only tell of myself in order to loose the tongue of the general public, and without this belief I could just as well forget about writing,"[50] it must have been very unpleasant to read in Spengler: "Generalization from oneself to others is always a mistaken conclusion." This applied to decisive matters in Thomas Mann's new, or at least newly and visibly formulated, self-understanding, and in view of this the almost hostile debate with Spengler is only too understandable.

Thus it is at least in part an earlier stance of his own that Mann attacks in Spengler, with all the vehemence of one who has changed. For Thomas Mann in 1922, Spengler was in many ways an ego *redivivus* (something that Grützmacher saw as early as 1926),[51] and that extended his threat beyond his suspicious cultural philosophy into the personal realm. For Thomas Mann's new self-interpretation as a writer a certain embattled enlightened optimism was essential, one that led to the overcoming of the old decline and fall mood. In this too Spengler's work was an annoyance, since it held up a mirror of earlier days when he himself had paid extensive homage to a muddled philosophy of decline, starting with the early stories and at least up to *Death in Venice*. Some later statements of Thomas Mann also show a peculiar irascibility toward his intellectual opponent. But it was not only personal reasons that compelled Mann to distance himself from Spengler; the objective ones are incomparably more important.

Spengler was a bitter enemy of the Weimar Republic; to be sure, Thomas Mann could not know in 1922 that Spengler in his *Years of Decision*[52] saw the Republic as "a betrayal by the inferior part of our nation of the strong, fresh part that had revolted in 1914" and that he wrote that: "Each line should contribute to its downfall,"[53] for Spengler only published this in 1933. But Mann had probably perceived the peculiarly unrepublican sentiments of Spengler from *The Decline of the West*. He was, moreover, as much of an embattled defender of the Weimar Republic as Spengler was a critic, and doubtless he was even something like one of its intellectual ambassadors, especially in relation to France. It is not an accident that his first clear attack on Spengler appears in the speech "The German Republic" of 1922. To that was added Spengler's morphological approach to culture, which must have appeared to Mann to be directed against humanism and enlightenment, and there was nothing that Thomas Mann had defended more heatedly in the twenties up to the Lessing speech than precisely the enlightenment that he evoked against the chthonic riff-raff of the Nazis.[54] This was not an issue yet around 1924 — but in 1929, in his Spengler essay, Mann did foresee the reappearance of caesarism stirred up by Spengler's prophesies behind the maliciously apodictic nature of the decline doctrine and its antiscientific inexorability. "A Caesar can and will come again, a Goethe never," Thomas Mann wrote then,[55] and in this essay he blamed Spengler at least indirectly for knowing it and not being willing to undertake anything against it. Knowing that, it is only too understandable that soon thereafter he was to see in Spengler predominantly the intellectually militant prophet of the fascist master race. From the Teutomania of Fichte and Jahn, the father of gymnastics, he wrote later,[56] the way lead, in increasing primitivism to "Oswald Spengler, the clever ape of Nietzsche, to Carl Schmidt, the theoretician of German fascism and to Rosenberg's *Myth of the Twentieth Century*." The epithet of the clever ape was still there, but the fatal effects of Spengler are Mann's logical afterthought. The later reckoning of 1947 is sharper still. In the essay of that year "Nietzsche's Philosophy in the Light of Contemporary Events," Spengler is not so much the clever as predominantly the malignant ape of Nietzsche: "With Spengler, his clever ape, the superman of his dream has become a modern *man of fact in great style*; a robber and profiteer who steps over dead bodies, a capitalist magnate, a munitions industrialist, a German general director who finances fascism – in short, in an act of simplistic stupidity, Nietzsche for him becomes a patron of imperialism – which he really did not understand at all. Why else would he have at every opportunity showed his contempt for the merchant and shopkeeper spirit that he considered to be pacifist and instead extolled the heroic spirit of the military? His 'aristocratic radicalism' never contemplated the alliance of industrialism and militarism, their political unity that constitutes imperialism, and the understanding that it is the profit motive that makes wars."[57] Here we see that the antagonism to Spengler was not limited to the beginnings of the Joseph novels. Thomas Mann's statement that, with his novels, he had intended to wrest myth from the hands of the fascist obscurantists does not refer to Rosenberg alone but doubtless also to Spengler as Rosenberg's intellectual ancestor – and thus the rejection of the contemporary who had become so uncomfortable is sharpened even more. Mann always thought in terms of linear history, clear dependencies, and direct succession, and he was firmly convinced of where Spengler belonged. That he saw Spengler as more than just a political failure is evident from Thomas Mann's speech on "The Position of Freud in Modern Intellectual History" of 1929, the same year in which he attacked fascism most sharply in public. There he blames Spengler's pessimistic view of history for "current moods and ways of thought" and for the "peculiar psychological coincidence of disregard for the intellect and hatred of it."[58] Finally, after Spengler's death, Thomas Mann, in a diary entry, calls him a "hyena of history" – "truly his animal-intellect has more in common with a hyena than with a lion. The reverse . . . romanticism of his predator-anthropology."[59] This was precisely what Mann was fighting against in the Nazis as well, and in 1936 he still saw in Spengler and his disciples a fundamental attack on his own spiritual being.

Thus he concentrated on continuing the story of the ascent of the East against the decline of the West for which Spengler had set the stage and that was beginning in 1936.

If one ignores the remark about Spengler in the Nietzsche essay of 1947, then it would seem that Thomas Mann's debate with Spengler had already been completed by 1930. But there is, beyond that, a more subtle and yet sharper, more radical and destructive coming to terms with Spengler's spirit that had become, for Thomas Mann, an antispirit, and this happens in the novel that deals with the Nietzsche tradition, *Doctor Faustus*; this is a final summation of the negative relationship with Spengler that appeared to the outside world closed with the great Spengler essay but which was being carried on under the skin. Of course, we are not speaking of the painter Baptist Spengler in the novel who had played a modest role in Munich society. The real name of the painter who had been part of the social circle of Thomas Mann's mother and who returns in the novel as Baptist Spengler, was Baptist Scherer. In a note from the preparatory stage of the novel, Baptist Spengler is an independent exist-ence — but there he is represented only by his name, and there is no indication of any particular significance, especially since he is a figure from a Munich salon and hence, in the final analysis, a piece of anthropomorphic filler, no more. In the novel itself, Spengler remains inconspicuous if not innocuous, in spite of a "general sympathy for the unusual, even the odd" that speaks for him.[60] Spengler the painter has also read Nietzsche, and he knows, if perhaps not always firsthand, the contradiction between life and disease, of strong and weak natures, and he can express himself pointedly about an aestheticizing art history professor by relegating him to that type who "is constantly yelling: 'How strong and beautiful life is!' while consumption burns on his cheeks."[61] But that is a rather innocuous reminder of Nietzsche, a salon witticism, and has nothing to do with the other, real Spengler.

But he, Oswald Spengler, is nonetheless in this novel, though under a false name. It is the scholar Dr. Chaim Breisacher whom we meet in the same salon as the other, harmless Spengler, but Breisacher is anything but harmless, and we soon find out why. He is of a

> highly bred and intellectually progressive, even dauntless type of a fascinating ugliness and here plays the part of the outside catalyst with a sort of malicious enjoyment. The hostess treasured his conversational eloquence which by the way had a strong flavor of Pfalz dialect, and his tendency to the paradox that lead the ladies to clap their hands in something of a prudish exaltation. As far as he was concerned, it was probably snobbery that let him enjoy this circle as well as the need to astound this elegant simple-mindedness with ideas that most likely would have been less of a sensation at a literary café. I myself [is this Zeitblom or Thomas Mann?] did not take to him at all but always saw

him as an intellectual obstructionist and held to the conviction that he was also repugnant to Adrian, though, for reasons never quite clear to me, we never had any intimate conversation about Breisacher. But his scent for the intellectual directions of the era, his nose for its most recent opinions I have never denied, and I encountered much of that for the very first time in him and his salon conversation.[62]

There is not the slightest doubt about this identity, even if snobbery had not been mentioned; it is no less clear what Zeitblom thinks of him. Thomas Mann's opinion of him is no better than that of this narrating and narrative antitype of himself that is actually an outdated prototype. That we know from his notes in which the dangerous Spengler appears next to the good-natured nonentity Baptist Spengler, and not merely as the snob: "The Jewish scholar Dr. Chaim Breisacher [originally Schalom Mainzer] or Rüdesheimer or Mondstein, Karfunkelstein. *Mystic and fascist.*"[63] It would hardly have been possible for Thomas Mann to apostrophize the clever ape of Nietzsche more recognizably. At the time everyone knew that he was a private scholar; one knew of his reserved stance, of his ugliness. The absence of any exchange between Zeitblom and Leverkühn about Breisacher corresponds perfectly to the nonexisting communication between Thomas Mann and Spengler.

But it gets even closer in the novel, and Thomas Mann does not hesitate to denounce not only the personality but also the work of Breisacher. Further on we read: "He was a polyhistor who felt himself qualified to talk about anything and everything, a cultural philosopher who was, however, set against culture insofar as he pretended to see nothing but a process of decline in its entire course. In his mouth, the most contemptuous sound was 'progress'; he had an annihilating way of pronouncing the word, and one was well aware that he considered the conservative ridicule that he vented upon progress his true ticket to this group, the mark of his social presentability. He did have intellect, but not a very appealing one . . ."[64] Long conversations follow in the novel to document Zeitblom's and Thomas Mann's opinion of Breisacher. The chapter closes with the following sentence: "In any case, it was just this Breisacher who for the first time introduced me to the new world of antihumanism of which my good nature knew nothing at all."

Is the Breisacher of these conversations merely an adherent of this fatal cultural, or rather anticultural, philosophy who resembles Spengler in a confounding way, or is it Spengler himself? The question is not to be finally resolved, of course, but it is actually not that consequential. What is vital here is the spirit, or the antispirit of Spengler. What Thomas Mann really thought of it he expressed in his note about the cast of characters of the novel, and the enlightener Thomas Mann who had defended Lessing against oncoming barbarism, pronounced the sharpest judgment on the obscurantism and chthonic rabble that had dared venture into the daylight, when he wrote: "Mystic and fascist."

Thus there can be no doubt about the judgment of Thomas Mann. Yet this characterization of the cultural philosopher, barbaric as he was, is, in the last analysis, not enough. Since Thomas Mann knew that Nietzsche had been the ancestor of the clever ape-philosopher and also that the learned "Renaissance man" in his work was the living embodiment of the decline of the West — would it not then seem natural to see in the collapse of Germany the fulfillment of what Spengler had described in his book? *Doctor Faustus* is nothing if not the description of the decline of the West. In the chronology of the novel, World War I erupts soon after the appearance of Breisacher — it is not important that the inner chronology is not identical with the outer one since Spengler only prophesied the *Decline of the West* after World War I, or rather, it is important only insofar as the war began the "decline of the West" before the corresponding philosophy of decadence had been written. But we already know that the inner chronology of the novel runs counter to the actual one, or rather that the inner chronology is "right" from a higher viewpoint, even when it contradicts the external one. The mental collapse of Leverkühn takes place in 1930, that of Germany in 1945 — or perhaps the chronology of the novel is, in the final analysis, more correct here too because, for Thomas Mann, it was unalterably clear by 1930 that National Socialism was infernal and that it could not be contained any longer? This argument gains credibility when one realizes that Nietzsche was Spengler's spiritual mentor. As the collapse of Germany is demonstrated with the example of Nietzsche, it would seem logical to extrapolate backward beyond Spengler, and that would mean: if Spengler seems to be a radicalizer of Nietzsche's ideas, then Nietzsche himself too belongs to the forerunners of fascism. Of course, Nietzsche certainly did not want that — but within the chain of historical sequences, seen a posteriori, Nietzsche did prophesy what was to become Germany's doom. Thus, he still somehow stands in the background of this national and European story of decline, and that he makes his final mark in the novel around 1930 is again "right" in a higher sense.

There can also be no doubt that the emergence of fascism impelled Thomas Mann once again to an intensive preoccupation with Spengler, even though the letters and diaries after 1933 contain little about him. It is part of the paradoxical nature of the situation that Spengler himself was anything but enthusiastic about the rise of the Nazis; he was repelled by the "mob character" of the "national upheaval"[65] and he wrote: "Elements came to power that consider the enjoyment of power as an end in itself and who would like to perpetuate a condition that is supportable only for the moment. Correct ideas are being exaggerated by these fanatics to the point of self-destruction. What promised greatness ends up in tragedy or comedy." And, even more distinctly, he called the National Socialist party "the mobilization of the unemployed by the lazy."[66]

Thomas Mann probably was not aware of all that; in any case, he did not react to it. His image of Spengler was finished. A note dated 30

December 1934, however, is particularly revealing. There, Thomas Mann speaks of the "bungling of once genuine phenomena of intellect and history, such as is demonstrated in the relationship of Spengler to Nietzsche and Schopenhauer, of National Socialism to the Reformation. It does not appear to be a question of true history any more but rather of sequels and imitations full of humbug and perversity, a fraud history. That which has not been there before and is not an imitation, as I see it, is the conscious jettisoning of human achievements and a regression to earlier conditions, the moral anachronism that comes from a hatred of reason and progress (particularly well rooted in Germany)."[67] Thus it seems that Thomas Mann saw the *Decline of the West* actualized in the emergence of Spengler after Nietzsche and that of the Nazis after the Reformation. His inclusion of Spengler personally in the story of Western European decline does not demonstrate any particular malice of Thomas Mann toward his opponent. It is rather an attempt to understand the phenomenon of Spengler historically in order to contradict precisely this historical swindle. Yet more important than his attempt to integrate Spengler's view of history into his own, more comprehensive one is the peculiar configuration of these names. Nietzsche and Spengler, the Reformation and the Nazis — this is the force field of *Doctor Faustus*, clearly visible for the first time according to the original plan of 1905, and in the precise terms in which it will be realized almost a decade later. Here too, then, a connection is established between the Joseph novels and *Doctor Faustus*, via Spengler.

It may be that, knowingly or not, Thomas Mann even borrowed some things directly. There is a chapter in Spengler called "Apollinian, Faustian, Magical Soul" — a crucial distinction in *The Decline of the West*. *Faustian*, as explained there, is "a life that is carried on with the highest consciousness, one that watches itself, a decisively personal culture of memoirs, reflections, of looking back and forward, and of conscience."[68] Is this not how Adrian Leverkühn lives? It is *"an unbounded loneliness"*[69] that characterizes the "homeland of the Faustian soul" for Spengler, and there is repeated mention of this isolation of the Faustian soul. The similarity of Zeitblom's characterization of Leverkühn in the first chapter of *Doctor Faustus* is striking: "I would like to compare his loneliness to an abyss in which feelings offered to him sank without sound or trace."[70] But the most striking in this connection is perhaps Spengler's remark that Faustian music dominated all the other arts.[71] This is worked out in detail, as Spengler writes: "This tone language originates in the finally realized possibilities of strings, that deepest and most inward of our music, and as surely as the violin is the noblest of instruments invented and perfected by the Faustian soul in order to be able to speak of its last secrets, its most transcendent and sacred moments of total transfiguration certainly lie in the string quartet and the violin sonata."[72] Adrian Leverkühn composes string quartets,[73] and he writes a violin concerto for his friend Rudi Schwerdtfeger.[74] When Kretzschmar teaches Leverkühn to recognize disintegration and an "excess of musing and speculation, an overabundance of precision and musical science," it is apropos of Beethoven's sonata opus 111 (to be sure, a piano sonata).[75] But, whatever the detailed working out, the fact that Faustus is a musician seems also to point toward Spengler's influence. Finally, Spengler and Thomas Mann share their Wagner enthusiasm, and Mann must have read attentively when Spengler wrote: "With Tristan dies the last of the Faustian arts. This work is the giant keystone of Western music."[76] With Thomas Mann it is "The Lament of Dr. Faustus," a no less giant keystone in the structure of the novel. Thus, in *Doctor Faustus* we do after all have the story of the "decline of the West," written after the story of the ascent of the East.

This, however, forces us to face a final question: does *Doctor Faustus* contradict the novel about *Joseph and his Brothers*, is the Leverkühn story a taking back of the Enlightenment faith and the cultural optimism of the Joseph novels? Thomas Mann has said nothing about this. But we may surmise that he did not yield to his opponent at the end, even though the novel showed such an uncanny fulfillment of Spengler's prophecy of a quarter century before. The Spengler-Breisacher identity revealed in Mann's notes for the end of the novel is itself an indication of Mann's opinion of his cultural-political opponent. For him, Spengler had become a revelation of the exact opposite of himself, and indeed it is difficult to imagine a more powerful distancing of Thomas Mann from Spengler than the one demonstrated in *Doctor Faustus*. And surely it is no coincidence that, in the conversation with the Devil, the latter represents Spengler's ideas when he says: "Since culture has discarded cult and made itself into one, it is nothing more than a discard."[77] But Thomas Mann made another attempt to disprove Spengler in the total configuration of the novel. In writing the story of the decline of the West, he did not credit Spengler. Rather, he made the latter's philosophy of decline part of the process of the story, or, to put it more clearly: in giving narrative fulfillment to Spengler's prophecy, he made the philosopher into an intellectual prede-cessor of that very decline which for him meant the end of German and European civilization, and thus gave him a part in that process. We know how essential the clarification of the early history of National Socialism was for Thomas Mann in these years. To be sure, the "decline of the West" was accomplished more quickly than Spengler had dreamed it in his way, but, according to a higher logic of history, he was, for Mann, the intellectual preparer of the way for National Socialism, at least de facto, since he had predicted as inevitable that which was to be accomplished so quickly and horribly through the Nazis. What, according to Spengler, had to come, had come, and, according to Thomas Mann's view, Spengler had done nothing to prevent the end. Hence he had not only predicted the downfall but also helped it along. Thus the process of history itself, one that had become a history of decline, had pronounced judgment on Spengler.

At the same time that Thomas Mann wrote Spengler's philosophy of decline into the story of *Doctor Faustus*, he attempted to repudiate it with his last word to that novel. The ending of *Doctor Faustus* appears to be an answer to the ending of the first volume of Spengler's *Decline of the West*. There we read: "The Faust of the second part of the tragedy dies because he has *attained* his goal. *The end of the world as the fulfillment of an inwardly necessary development* — that is the twilight of the gods. . . ."[78] Thomas Mann's novel portrays the end of a world too. But the last sentences of *Faustus* have nothing to do with the end of the world. Instead, they read as follows: "When, out of ultimate hopelessness, will the light of hope dawn, the miracle that surpasses faith? A lonely man folds his hands and speaks: God have mercy on your poor soul, my friend, my fatherland." Since *The Magic Mountain*, there are no straightforward conclusions to Thomas Mann's novels, but is it not a question here of expressing, as possibility and expectation, what Spengler had portrayed as downfall, and is the end of the world here, with friend and fatherland once more so explicitly identified, not described as inevitable but rather pitiful? In this, too, the novel appears not to nullify the Joseph story but, yet again, Spengler's philosophy of decline. Or, to put it more precisely: the history of downfall Mann tells in *Doctor Faustus* is still embraced by the "light of hope" at the close of the novel, though cautiously — and this light is still, as it was already in the Joseph stories, that of enlightenment, progress, and humanism.

Thus, Thomas Mann's *Doctor Faustus* does not refute the Joseph story but in effect continues it, this time not in opposition to Spengler's *Decline of the West* but rather by incorporating it. And, in this richly paradoxical relationship between Mann and Spengler, it is paradoxically a late answer to expectations that Spengler had of the novel genre as early as World War I, when he wrote:

> When I consider the literary possibilities which the very unartistic future of Germany still holds for us, I expect little from the lyric and still less from drama. But a novel in the grand style, such as Paris possessed 1750–1850, might emerge from the new appalling conditions *after* this war, assuming that there will be brains capable of an overview of the whole late world of the maturing twentieth century that will be reminiscent of the Roman Empire, with its wealth of new problems, new people, new forms of cosmopolitan civilization. Up to now, we have *only* the novels of Goethe; the rest is trash. A novel ought to explore the *totality* of the existence of an *epoch* (Goethe shaped the era of the Enlightenment from 1749 to the demise of Napoleon). A drama cannot do that. It has too much of the mathematics of form that excludes the richness of the historically unique. A novel can only achieve substance through such *richness*, and for eighty years we have had no inwardly rich human being in our literature. Today, I believe, this is *possible*. Such a novel . . . should begin with the vanishing *visionary* Germany, last reminiscences of the time of Ludwig II, Nietzsche, Leibl, Böcklin; it

should also use contemporary Munich, for Munich is Germany's *old-fashioned* city par excellence which, as compared to Berlin, still subsists on the remnants of its artistic Boheme, and hence is not productive.[79]

Is *Doctor Faustus* not exactly that? It is true that Spengler at the time set himself off from Thomas Mann whom he had always considered a mere mannerist[80] and a disingenuous sentimentalist[81] dealing in "supposedly modern topics, but with a totally outdated substance (philistine sentimentalism or a projection of Heine into cosmopolitan homosexuality)," and that he later added to that: "No images or descriptions à la Thomas Mann."[82] But here Thomas Mann did not oblige him any more.

The story of Thomas Mann's relationship to Spengler has an ending of sorts, a small satiric drama. Thomas Mann himself said very much later that he had the sense of having written the last great novels when he wrote *The Holy Sinner* and the Joseph novels; there did not appear to be much coming after that. He formulated it a bit more cautiously, but in substance he let on clearly enough that after him, as after little Hanno in *Buddenbrooks*, no more was possible: "I have little objection against being a latecomer, a last and concluding one, and I do not believe that this story and the Joseph stories will be told again after me. When I was quite young, I had little Hanno Buddenbrook draw a long line under the genealogy of his family, and, as he was scolded for it, I had him stammer: 'I thought — I thought — there would be no more.' It seems to me there will be no more. Our contemporary literature, the best and finest of it, often strikes me as a leavetaking, a quick recollection, a last summoning and recapitulation of the Western myth — before night falls, perhaps a long night and a deep forgetting."[83] Precisely here, however, he very belatedly matches a sentence of Spengler that the latter had written to describe the civilization stage of culture in *Decline of the West:* "Western European self-confidence appears to need the enactment of a final balance with its own existence."[84] But by then Thomas Mann had come so far from Spengler and his book that he surely did not recognize this reminiscence, this possibly conscious taunt of Spengler. And it most certainly did not bother him at all any more.

Notes

Presented in shorter form as a lecture at the University of Bristol, various American universities (Columbia, University of Kansas), and in Vienna and Würzburg.

1. Thomas Mann's essay first appeared in 1924. Still, he thought enough of it to include it in "Altes und Neues" [Old and new], the collection that, according to Mann himself, lined up "what good friends might welcome as something of a substitute for an autobiography, an accumulation of what grew between the books over the decades."

2. There is sufficient testimony to the effect. To cite only one: Hans Freyer has reported in retrospect that "in the year 1919" everyone read and discussed Spengler: "the educated in

the broadest sense, the young people returned from the war, and the specialists, these too in the broadest sense—for what specialty had not been involved?" (Cf. Hans Erich Stier, *Zur geschichtlichen Wesensbestimmung Europas*, among the Spengler studies cited later.) The technical debate was to come a little later, especially in 1921 and 1922; more extensive discussions or repudiations were rare; most of the pronouncements were in the form of short essays. To mention only a few out of the great flood of contemporary publications: A short piece by Heinrich Scholz, "Zum Untergang des Abendlandes" [About *The Decline of the West*, a discussion of Oswald Spengler], appeared in 1920 in the first and in 1922 in the second printing (Berlin 1920–21); Otto Selz wrote about "Oswald Spengler und die intuitive Methode in der Geschichtsforschung" [Oswald Spengler and the intuitive historical method], also a short essay based on a lecture (Bonn 1922); significantly, the lecture had been held as part of a series "Lectures on Current Public Questions." There were a few more specific contributions: a small essay by Th. Schulz on "Der Sinn der Antike und Spenglers neue Lehre" [the meaning of classical antiquity and Spengler's new doctrine] (Gotha, 1921), that had started as an inauguration lecture at the University of Leipzig; Karl Heym and Richard H. Grützmacher wrote two "critical essays" about "Oswald Spengler and Christianity" (Munich, 1921); Goetz Briefs also expressed himself in a piece of modest size about the "Untergang des Abendlandes: Christentum und Sozialismus. Eine Auseinandersetzung mit Oswald Spengler" [*The Decline of the West*: Christianity and socialism, a discussion of Oswald Spengler] (Freiberg im Breisgau, 1921). Karl Schück contributed a "critique": "Spenglers Geschichts-Philosophie. Eine Kritik" (Karlsruhe, 1921). More extensive explanations and discussions were not as frequent: thus Theodor L. Haering published a larger work "Die Struktur der Weltgeschichte" with the subtitle "Philosophische Grundlegung zu einer jeden Geschichtsphilosophie in Form einer Kritik Oswald Spenglers" [The structure of world history: Philosophical foundations for every philosophy of history in the form of a critique of Oswald Spengler] (Tübingen, 1921). Haering mentions that the Württemberg Association for the Promotion of Popular Education had asked him to give "lectures about questions of history of philosophy, in connection with Spengler's book that almost everyone has"—here, too, the novelty effect is still there. In the *Historische Vierteljahrschrift* an essay by Erich Brandenburg appeared about "Spenglers 'Untergang des Abendlandes' " (Dresden, 1922), and in "Hochland" there was a comparative work with the title "Die ewige Wiederkehr: Ibn Chaldun and Oswald Spengler" [Eternal return: Ibn Chaldun and Oswald Spengler] (Kempten, 1922–23). Most of the discussion occurred before the appearance of the second revised edition of the first part; but by then six unrevised printings of the first part had appeared, and the immense echo of Spengler's theses testifies to the peculiar receptivity and sensitivity of the times for them. The public interest in Spengler's work answered Friedrich Meinecke's question: "Bedeutet Oswald Spengler ein Ereignis oder eine blosse Sensation in unserem Geistesleben?" [Is Oswald Spengler an event or a mere sensation in our intellectual life?], in *Wissen und Leben*, 16 (1923): 549–61, unanimously in favor of the "event." However, the Spengler debate had pretty much run its course before the appearance of the second volume; besides Dempf's critique and Meinecke's appreciation and a speech by Eduard Meyer about "Spenglers Untergang des Abendlandes" at the historians' conference in 1924 (Berlin, 1925) not much appeared thereafter; cf. also Anton Mirko Koktanek, "Oswald Spengler in seiner Zeit" [Oswald Spengler and his times] (Munich, 1968), 270. Among more recent appreciation and discussions, besides Koktanek's book and that by Manfred Schröter, "Metaphysik des Untergangs" (The metaphysics of decline) (Munich, 1949), let us name the following: *Spengler-Studien: Festgabe für Manfred Schröter zum 85. Geburtstag [Spengler studies: dedicated to Manfred Schröter for his 85th Birthday]* (Munich, 1965) (including the important essay by Georgi Schischkoff, "Spengler und Toynbee," 59–75); Gert Müller, "Oswald Spenglers Bedeutung für die Geschichtswissenschaft" [The importance of Oswald Spengler for historiography], *Zeitschrift f. philosophische Forschung* 17, no. 3, 483–98; Joachim Günther, "Neubesinnung über Oswald Spengler" [Reconsiderations about Oswald Spengler], in *Neue Deutsche Hefte* 10 (1963): 97–107, as well as Northrup Frye's essay " 'The Decline of the West' by Oswald Spengler," in *Daedalus*, 1974, 1–13.

3. Spengler's ancestry stretches back far into the nineteenth century; there were doctrines of eternal cycles in history as early as the 1830s, and there is a brief discussion about the topic, comparing other competing philosophies of history, in a small essay by Heine, with the title (provided later, by others) "Verschiedenartige Geschichtsauffassung" (Various conceptions of history), probably from the early 1830s, possibly in the wake of the July Revolution and the discussion about the proper understanding of history that followed it. Hans Joachim Schoeps has pointed out other antecedents, Nikolaj Danilevkj and especially Karl Vollgraff and Ernst von Lasaulx, in his informative piece "Vorläufer Spenglers. Studien zum Geschichtspessimismus im 19. Jahrhundert" [Spengler's forerunners. Studies in historical pessimism in the nineteenth century] (Leiden, 1953). Schoeps points out that Vollgraff's monstrous work with the no less monstrous title "Erster Versuch einer wissenschaftlichen Begründung sowohl der allgemeinen Ethnologie durch die Anthropologie wie auch der Staats- und Rechtsphilosophie durch die Ethnologie der Nationalität der Völker in drei Teilen" [A first attempt at explaining general ethnology by anthropology as well as political and juridical philosophy by the ethnology of the nationality of peoples in three parts], actually described exactly the same thing that Spengler portrays: the decline of the West.

4. *Reden und Aufsätze*, vol. I (Frankfurt a.M. 1965), 558.

5. Letter to Ernst Bertram, 4 February 1925, in *Thomas Mann an Ernst Bertram. Briefe aus den Jahren 1910–1955*, ed. Inge Jens (Pfullingen, 1960), 136.

6. Letter to Felix Bertaux, 1 August 1926, unpublished, Thomas Mann Archive, Zurich.

7. Letter to Ernst Bertram, 14 June 1925.

8. Letter to Erika Mann, 23 December 1926, in *Briefe 1889–1936*, ed. Erika Mann (Frankfurt a.M. 1962), 261.

9. Letter to Ernst Bertram, 28 December 1926; see note 5, p. 155.

10. *Reden und Aufsätze*, I: 766.

11. Ibid., 768.

12. *Altes und Neues* (Frankfurt a.M., 1961), 636.

13. Ibid., 643.

14. Ibid., 645.

15. *Nachlese: Prosa 1951–1955* (Frankfurt a.M., 1956), 167.

16. Ibid., 166.

17. Ibid., 167.

18. *Reden und Aufsätze*, I: 767.

19. Ibid., 277.

20. There is evidence for both interpretations in the Thomas Mann literature; however, there was doubt early on about whether Thomas Mann's novel could be integrated in the straight line development of the novel of education. Wolfgang von Einsiedel wrote an essay questioning that ("Thomas Manns 'Zauberberg' — ein Bildungsroman?," in *Zeitschr. für Deutschkunde* 42 [1928]:241–53), and Jürgen Scharfschwerdt has discussed the novel as a parody of the novel of education in his book on Thomas Mann and the German "Bildungsroman" (*Thomas Mann und der deutsche Bildungsroman: Eine Untersuchung zu den Problemen einer literarischen Tradition* [Thomas Mann and the German novel of education: an investigation into a problem of a literary tradition] (Stuttgart, 1967).

21. *Reden und Aufsätze*, I:768.

22. Ibid., 769.

23. Ibid., 559.

24. *Altes und Neues*, 373.

25. *Briefe 1889–1936*, 161.

26. Ibid., 165.

27. Ibid., 202.

28. Ibid., 321.

29. *Reden und Aufsätze*, vol. 2 (Frankfurt a.m., 1965), 40.

30. Ibid., 41f. Occasionally one finds indications in the Mann literature that Spengler had already exercised influence on *The Magic Mountain*. Thus Johannes Krey ("Die gesellschaftliche Bedeutung der Musik im Werk vonThomas Mann" [The social significance of music in the work of Thomas Mann], in *Wissenschaftliche Zeitschrift der Friedrich-Schiller – Universität Jena, 3 [1953*–4], Gesellschafts-und Sprachwissenschaftl. Reihe, Heft 2/3, 312), notes that several theses of Spengler return in the guise of Naphta. Ernst Keller (*Der unpolitische Deutsche: Eine Studie zu den 'Betrachtungen eines Unpolitischen' von Thomas Mann* (Bern, 1965), see esp. 108–11). Gunilla Bergsten also indicates that the "Considerations of a Nonpolitical Man" and the Spengler work did not appear in the same year by accident (*Thomas Manns Doktor Faustus: Untersuchungen zu den Quellen und zur Struktur des Romans* [Tübingen, 1974] 135, 198). All these statements about the influence of Spengler on the "Considerations" and *The Magic Mountain* can refer back to a remark in a letter by Thomas Mann of 1919 to Joseph Ponten: "I am continuing to work on the *Magic Mountain* novel whose fundamental theme (romanticism and enlightenment, death and virtue: the theme of *Death in Venice* yet again, and also that of the 'Considerations') has entranced me anew. But occupying oneself with art today when the end of all of Western culture seems to be near is very problematical" (*Briefe 1889–1936*, 163). Yet Spengler does not appear to have left more than very general traces in *The Magic Mountain* and the "Considerations." The increasing acrimony of Thomas Mann's debate with Spengler only occurred when it became clear to Mann that Spengler was not only the prophet of the end but also its preparer.

31. Thomas Mann, *Gesammelte Werke* (Frankfurt a.M., 1974), 13:265f.

32. Ibid., 266.

33. Ibid., 270.

34. Ibid., 271.

35. *Altes und Neues*, 142.

36. Thomas Manns Vorstudien zur Josephstetralogie," in *Jahrb. d. Dt. Schillerge-sellsch.* 7 (1963): 458–520, and "Thomas Manns Josephstudien 1927–1939," in *Jahrb. d. Dt. Schillergesellsch.* 10 (1966): 378–406. Of course, Spengler's *Decline of the West* is not a "source" in the sense in which Lehnert defines it. But, in considering the psychoanalytical influences, the biblical research consulted by Thomas Mann, the mythological materials, and the Egyptian studies, one should not forget the contemporary context, or one risks overemphasizing the antiquarian escapist perspective of the Joseph novels.

37. Oswald Spengler, *Der Untergang des Abendlandes*, vol. I (Munich, 1923), 42.

38. *Joseph und seine Brüder* (Frankfurt a.M., 1959), 34.

39. Cf. Otto Selz, *Oswald Spengler und die intuitive Methode in der Geschichtsfors-chung* [Oswald Spengler and the intuitive method of historiography] (Bonn, 1922), esp. 20.

40. *Der Untergang des Abendlandes*, I:181.

41. *Joseph und seine Brüder*, 1476.

42. *Der Untergang des Abendlandes*, I:vii.

43. Ibid., x.

44. Ibid.

45. Ibid., ix.

46. *Tagebücher 1935–1936*, ed. Peter de Mendelssohn (Frankfurt a.M., 1978), 343.

47. *Der Untergang des Abendlandes*, I: xi.

48. *Reden und Aufsätze*, 2:51.

49. Ibid.

50. *Reden und Aufsätze*, I: 734 f.

51. R. H. Grützmacher, "Spengler, Keyserlingk und Thomas Mann," in *Welt und Werk, Sonntagsbeil, d. Dt. Allg. Z.*, no. 264 (1925). Georg Besselt wrote about the relationship between "Nietzsche, Spengler, Thomas Mann" as early as 1922 (*Weser-Zeitung* 79, no. 664 [1922]:10, 25).

52. *Jahre der Entscheidung*, pt. 1, *Deutschland und die weltgeschichtliche Entwicklung* (Munich, 1933). Nowhere else is the fascistic quality of Spengler's thought as evident as in this work, but nowhere is his prophetic gift as clear as it is here when he wrote: "We may well be very close to the second world war, with its unknown distribution of powers and unforseeable military, economic, and revolutionary means and ends" (xi).

53. *Jahre der Entscheidung*, I. Cf. Richard Samuel, "Oswald Spengler redivivus?," in *Deutsche Rundschau* 89, no. 1 (1963):20–28. Samuel rightly emphasizes the "pre-National Socialist style" of Spengler's perspective.

54. We can see how unenlightened Spengler's conception was in his substituting his thesis of botanical flowering and wilting that goes along with his doctrine of "cultural organisms" or "cultural entities" for the old Enlightenment teaching of the continuous progress of mankind to which Thomas Mann—still or again—paid allegiance; a circular conception, thus, that belongs more to the twentieth century but in any case contradicts Enlightenment optimism. Accordingly, there is no meaning in history according to Spengler; he does not even inquire into it. Thomas Mann attempted to find the answer more and more clearly. Regarding Spengler's attitude, cf. Schischkoff, *Spengler und Toynbee*, 59, 62f.

55. *Altes and Neues*, 139.

56. *Reden un Ausätze*, 2:602.

57. *Neue Studien* (Frankfurt a.M., 1948), 145f.

58. *Altes und Neues*, 162.

59. *Tagebücher 1935-1936*, 343.

60. *Doktor Faustus* (Frankfurt a.M., 1956), 367.

61. Ibid., 382.

62. Ibid., 370f.

63. Cited in Lieselotte Voss, *Die Entstehung von Thomas Manns Roman "Doktor Faustus": Dargestellt anhand von unveröffentlichen Vorarbeiten* (The genesis of Thomas Mann's novel *Doctor Faustus*: an interpretation using unpublished materials) (Tübingen, 1975), 89. Later Thomas Mann expressed himself more distinctly about the fascism of the Breisacher standpoint when he wrote about "the 'racial and national hygiene' of killing defective and retarded people" (Voss, 159). Helmut Jendreiek also has some hints about Spengler as Breisacher (*Thomas Mann: Der demokratische Roman* [Düsseldorf, 1977], 429, 468). T. J. Reed in *Thomas Mann: The Uses of Tradition* (Oxford, 1974), 378, is unclear and inexact about it. Johannes Krey speaks of the connection in "Die gesellschaftliche Bedeutung der Musik im Werk von Thomas Mann," *Wissensch. Zeitschr. d. Friedr. Schiller-Univ. Jena* 3 (1954):312. Cf. also the more general work of Michel Vanhelleputte, "Thomas Mann et *Le Declin de l'Occident* (1919-1924)," *Université Libre Revue* (Brussels) 18 (1965–66): 450–65. There are some remarks about Thomas Mann and Spengler in Hans Joachim Maitre's *Thomas Mann: Aspekte der Kulturkritik is seiner Essayistik* (Bonn, 1970), 44–47. Heinz Saueressig represents the viewpoint that the mythologist Oskar Goldberg was the prototype for Chaim Breisacher ("Die Welt des Doktor Faustus. Personen und Landschaften in Thomas Manns Roman" [The world of Doctor Faustus: people and places in Thomas Mann's novel], *Die Lesestunde* 43, no. 1 (1966): 74); supposedly the author had also been thinking about the social critic Theodor Lessing.

64. *Doktor Faustus*, 371.

65. Cf. Richard Samuel, "Oswald Spengler redivivus?" 22.

66. Cf. Joachim Günther, *Neubesinnung über Oswald Spengler* (Reconsideration of O.S.), 101.

67. *Tagebücher 1933–1934*, ed. Peter de Mendelssohn (Frankfurt am Main, 1977) 596 f.

68. *Der Untergang des Abendlandes*, 1:237.

69. Ibid., 241.

70. *Doktor Faustus*, 13.

71. *Der Untergang des Abendlandes*, 1:301.

72. Ibid., 300f.

73. *Doktor Faustus*, 212.

74. Ibid., 272.

75. Ibid., 72.

76. *Der Untergang des Abendlandes* 1:375.

77. *Doktor Faustus*, 325.

78. *Der Untergang des Abendlandes* 1:550.

79. Spengler, *Briefe 1913–1936*, ed. Anton M. Koktanek in cooperation with Manfred Schröter (Munich, 1963), 34f.

80. Ibid., 23.

81. Ibid., 24.

82. Ibid., 46.

83. *Altes und Neues*, 246.

84. *Der Untergang des Abendlandes* 1:26.

INDEX

Aeschylus, 215
Agathon, 100
Alberts, 222
Angelus Silesius, 220
Anti-Christ, 209
Ardinghello, 100
Aristophanes, 190
Aristotle, 121
Arnheim, Rudolf, 51
Austen, Jane, 225

Baader, Franz, 220
Balzac, 25–26, 28, 129
Barnouw, Dagmar, 3–4
Barthes, Roland, 5, 129, 137
Bäumler, Alfred, 233
Beale, Mavis, 177
Bear, The, 53
Beddow, Michael, 212
Benn, Gottfried, 198
Bergsten, Gunilla, 8
Bermann-Fischer, Gottfried, 196
Bernstein, Max, 60
Bertram, Ernst, 229, 230, 239
Beyond Good and Evil, 209
Bielschowsky, Albert, 226
Birth of Tragedy, The, 209–11, 215–16
Blackmur, R. P., 6, 78
Blume, Bernhard, 8
Bode, Wilhelm, 225–26
Boehme, 220
Borges, Jorge Luis, 217
Bouvard and Pecuchet, 54
Brecht, Bertolt, 198, 217, 219–20
Broch, Hermann, 16
Brooke-Rose, Christine, 137
Büchner, Georg, 4, 45, 46

Cabinet des Antiquites, Le, 26
Caesar, Julius, 119

Cassirer, Ernst, 47, 226
Cat on a Hot Tin Roof, 55
Cervantes, Miguel de, 64, 190
Cohn, Dorrit, 6, 124
Coleridge, Samuel Taylor, 53
Compton-Burnett, Ivy, 183
Cox, Harvey, 121–22

D'Annunzio, Gabriele, 194
Dante, Alighieri, 52
Daudet, Leon, 196
Decline of the West, 238–39, 246, 249–50, 252, 256–57, 260
Degas, Edgar, 230
Dichtung und Wahrheit, 72, 96, 116, 192
Doblin, Alfred, 198
Don Quixote, 61, 64
Dostoevski, Fëdor, 92, 146–48, 194
Dürer, Albrecht, 152

Ebert, Friedrich, 193
Effi Briest, 33
Eichendorff, Joseph von, 194, 196
Eichner, Hans, 7, 93, 177, 234
Elective Affinities, 97
Eliot, T. S., 87, 228, 232
Emilia Galotti, 47
Engels, Friedrich, 45
Era is Examined, An, 201
Erasmus, 121, 240

Faesi, Robert, 234
Faulkner, William, 53
Faust, 28, 122, 231
Feuerbach, Ludwig, 46
Flaubert, Gustave, 242–43, 245
Fontane, Theodor, 33, 152, 177
Frederick the Great, 152
Freud, Sigmund, 2, 17, 116, 119, 152, 168, 195, 245
Frost, Robert, 118

Gay, Peter, 122
Genesis, 117
George, Stefan, 198, 207
Gesellschaft, Die, 12
Goethe, Johann Wolfgang von, 2, 4, 8,
    14–20, 22–23, 25, 27–28, 31, 34–35,
    43–44, 48–54, 72, 116, 119, 146–52,
    161, 168, 178, 183, 192, 222, 224,
    226–28, 230–33, 239–41, 250
Good-for-Nothing, 194
Gorky, Maxim, 46
Gray, Ronald, 116
Grigson, Geoffrey, 51–52
Gundolf, Friedrich, 239

Hamburger, Käte, 6, 58, 121, 176
Hamburgische Dramaturgie, 228
Hansen, Max, 60
Hašek, Jaroslav, 213
Hatfield, Henry, 6–7, 115
Hatzfeld, Adolf von, 95
Hauptmann, Gerhart, 13, 193
Hazlitt, William, 180
Hegel, Georg Wilhelm Friedrich, 26, 29,
    34, 46, 65
Heine, Heinrich, 45, 46, 205
Heinse, Wilhelm, 100
Heller, Erich, 7, 8, 176, 192, 222
Heller, Joseph, 213
Hellersberg-Wendriner, Anna, 116, 176
Herbert, George, 78
Hermann und Dorothea, 98
Hermes, 120, 203
Hesse, Hermann, 173
Hitler, Adolf, 41, 119, 196, 233
Hoffmann, E. T. A., 39
Hofmann, Ludwig von, 225
Hofmannsthal, Hugo von, 207
Holz, Arno, 13
Hölderlin, Johann Christian Friedrich,
    45–46, 155, 160
Human all too Human, 208
Høffding, Harald, 61

Ibsen, Henrik, 12, 152
Ikhnaton, 120
In Memoriam, 47
Irrungen Wirrungen, 33

Jahn, Hans Henny, 198
James, Henry, 225
James, William, 85
Joyce, James, 183

Jugendstil, 225
Jünger, Ernst, 192, 207

Kafka, Franz, 118
Kant, Immanuel, 29
Karst, Roman, 192
Kaufmann, Fritz, 221–22, 234
Keller, Gottfried, 25, 28, 39
Kerényi, Karl, 216, 228
Kesting, Hanjo, 3
Kielland, Alexander, 243
Kierkegaard, Søren, 61, 201
Kleist, Heirich von, 38, 221
Koeppen, Wolfgang, 4
Koopmann, Helmut, 7, 238
Kraus, Karl, 205

Land of Cockaigne, 195
Lasaulks, Ernst von, 249
Last Days of Humanity, The, 205
Last Puritan, The, 119
Leavis, F. R., 225
Lehnert, Herbert, 2, 248
Leibnitz, Gottfried Wilhelm, 221
Lemminge, Die, 95, 99, 105, 109
Lenin, V. I., 45
Lessing, Gotthold Ephraim, 14, 46, 152,
    155, 156, 162, 164–67, 228, 255
Lie, Jonas, 243
Ludwig, Emil, 230
Lukács, Georg, 3, 7, 24
Luther, Martin, 121, 220, 233
Lycidas, 47

Mahler, Gustav, 225
Man of Straw, 195
Mann, Heinrich, 195, 198, 200, 201
Mann, Thomas, Works:
    Bajazzo, Der, 11–12, 30
    Bilse and I, 191
    Black Swan, The, 58
    Buddenbrooks, 1, 12, 14, 20, 29, 30,
        32, 33, 64, 76, 115, 144, 158, 169,
        177, 178, 180, 191, 222, 223, 241–44,
        250, 260
    Death in Venice, 6, 20, 31, 32, 33, 64,
        74, 75, 95, 97, 98, 108, 124–43, 153,
        190, 199, 201, 230, 244, 252
    Disorder and Early Sorrow, 40
    Doctor Faustus, 6, 7, 55, 56, 58, 66,
        69, 70, 93–95, 104, 108–12, 118, 140,
        144, 153, 156, 170, 171, 173, 178,
        181, 188, 200, 204, 207, 254, 256–60
    Felix Krull, 6, 7, 20–23, 58, 71–75,

95–97, 104, 108, 110, 111, 116, 124, 158, 176–78, 180, 181, 183, 198, 203, 204, 206, 207, 211–16
Fiorenza, 64
Friedrich und die Grosse Koalition, 14
Gefallen, 224
Genesis of Doctor Faustus, The, 234
German Republic, The, 195, 252
Gesang vom Kindchen, 95, 98, 99
Gesetz, Das, 120
Goethe and Tolstoy 14, 163
Goethe as Representative of the Bourgeois Age, 43, 232
Goethe's Career as a Writer, 232
Herr und Hund, 179
Holy Sinner, The, 58, 66, 67, 69, 70, 116, 156, 176, 178, 184–86, 266
Joseph and His Brothers, 6, 14, 15, 22, 49, 58, 61, 62, 66, 67, 76, 82, 95, 107, 108, 115–23, 136, 144, 163, 164, 169, 171, 203, 219, 230, 232, 238–60
Kleiderschrank, Der, 178
Letters from Germany, 247
Little Herr Friedemann, 64
Lotte in Weimar, 12, 14–18, 22, 43, 75, 76, 108, 112, 169, 178, 179, 188, 226, 227
Magic Mountain, The, 4, 6–8, 14, 15, 17, 34, 38–41, 48, 54, 60, 75, 76, 78–93, 95, 97, 99, 100, 104–7, 115, 125, 144, 153, 176, 178–80, 183, 184, 186–88, 197, 200, 201, 214, 219, 224, 234, 241–44, 246, 250–51
Monolog, 12, 28
Position of Freud in Modern Intellectual History, The, 195, 253
Railway Accident, The, 33, 178
Reflections of a Nonpolitical Man, 8, 34, 59, 64, 65, 71, 145, 154, 156, 161, 192–95, 197, 199, 200, 202, 205, 226, 229, 257
Royal Highness, 33, 39, 60, 76, 158, 178, 180, 189, 190, 194, 226
Schwere Stunde, 13
Sketch of My Life (Lebensabriss), 13, 72, 224, 228, 239, 245
Speech to an Audience of Workers, 232
Suffering and Greatness of the Masters, 199
Suffering for Germany, 193
Thoughts in Wartime, 193, 199
Tonio Kröger, 6, 21, 31, 32, 46, 54, 55, 64, 65, 136, 158, 169, 188, 189, 204, 221, 243–44

Transposed Heads, The, 62–65, 67, 115
Tristan, 64, 65, 187
Way to the Cemetery, The, 64, 65
Weary Hour, A, 44, 226, 227, 229
Marienbad Elegie, 47
Marten, Kurt, 178, 198
Marx, Karl, 45–46, 160
Mayer, Hans, 8, 191
Meistersinger, Die, 194, 195
Mendelssohn, Peter de, 8
Milton, John, 52
Molière, Jean Baptiste, 63, 190
Mörike, Eduard, 45
Moses, 120–21
Munnings, Alfred, 51
Musil, Robert, 198
Myth of the Twentieth Century, 244

Napoleon, 34, 35, 119
Nietzsche, Friedrich, 1, 2, 6–8, 12, 18, 27, 36, 38, 46, 92, 119, 152, 163, 167–68, 194–95, 206–8, 220–21, 223, 228–33, 239, 244, 249–50, 253–54, 257
Nossack, Hans Erich, 4
Novalis, 152, 196

Obenauer, Franz, 193
On Truth and Falsehood in an Extra-Moral Sense, 210
Ovid, 103

Palestrina, 194
Peacock, Ronald, 6, 60, 175
Pfitzner, Hans, 194
Phaedrus, 130, 134
Phenomenology of Mind, 34
Platen, August von, 3, 36
Pushkin, Alexander, 46

Rabelais, 183, 190
Rathenau, Walter, 33, 192
Reaction and Progress, 195
Reed, T. J., 7, 138, 139, 219
Republic, 134
Reuter, Fritz, 177
Riemer, Friedrich Wilhelm, 226–27
Rilke, Rainer Maria, 13
Robertson, J. G., 175–76
Robespierre, Maximilien, 45
Rodin, René Auguste, 13
Rosenberg, Alfred, 41, 244, 253
Rostand, Edmond, 63
Rousseau, J. J., 151
Rychner, Max, 202, 203, 233

Saint Paul, 220
Salammbo, 242–43
Santayana, George, 119, 154, 166
Schach von Wuthenow, 33
Scheler, Max, 220
Schelling, Friedrich Wilhelm von, 26, 220
Schiller, Friedrich, 4, 13, 28–29, 35, 44,
    51–53, 146, 151, 172, 178, 204, 220–21,
    226–27, 229
Schlegel, Friedrich, 100
Schmidt, Carl, 253
Schopenhauer, Arthur, 1, 2, 8, 15, 27, 38,
    46, 152, 197, 215, 222–24, 247
Schulte, Hans H., 3–4
Seidlin, Oskar, 133
Seneca, 119
Shakespeare, William, 46, 47
Shaw, G. B., 60
Sidney, Sir Philip, 50
Sontheimer, Kurt, 192
Sophocles, 215
Sorrows of Young Werther, The, 15, 17,
    19, 28, 179, 188, 231
Spengler, Oswald, 1, 6, 7, 192, 238–60
Spiegel, Der, 3
Stalin, Joseph, 45
Stanzel, Franz, 125
Stature of Thomas Mann, The, 176
Stern, J. P., 7, 206
Sternheim, Karl, 195, 198
Storm, Theodor, 3, 36
Symposium, 130, 134

Tasso, 28
Theorie des Erzahlens, 125
Thomas Mann: The Uses of Tradition, 138
Thoughts out of Season, 208, 244
Thus Spoke Zarathustra, 208–9, 215

Tod des Vergil, 16
Tolstoy, Leo, 25–26, 28, 146–52
Trial, The, 118
Troilus and Cressida, 47
Truth and Poetry, 72, 96, 116, 192

Urzidil, Johannes, 227
Use and Abuse of History, 234, 244, 248

Vaget, Hans, 2–5
Van den Bruck, Moeller, 192
Van Doren, Mark, 117
Vermeil, Edmund, 192

Wagner, Richard, 1–2, 27, 34–35, 46, 152,
    167–68, 170, 194, 203, 241
Walser, Martin, 4
Weber, Max, 33
Webern, Anton von, 217
Weigand, Hermann, 8, 11, 19
Westöstlicher Divan, 18, 23, 231, 233
Whitman, Walt, 152
Wieland, Christoph Martin, 100
Wilhelm Meister, 25, 28, 72, 100–6,
    108–11, 222, 224
Wilkinson, Elizabeth, 7, 47
Will to Power, The, 208–9
Williams, Tennessee, 55
Wilson, Kenneth, 54
World as Will and Idea, The, 27, 223,
    247
Wysling, Hans, 2

Yacoby, Tamar, 139
Years of Decision, 252

Zola, Emile, 152
Zweig, Stefan, 233